# Disrobing the
# Aboriginal Industry

## The Deception behind Indigenous
## Cultural Preservation

FRANCES WIDDOWSON AND ALBERT HOWARD

McGill-Queen's University Press
Montreal & Kingston • London • Ithaca

© McGill-Queen's University Press 2008

ISBN 978-0-7735-3420-9 (cloth)
ISBN 978-0-7735-3421-6 (paper)
ISBN 978-0-7735-7512-7 (ePDF)
ISBN 978-0-7735-7747-3 (ePUB)

Legal deposit third quarter 2008
Bibliothèque nationale du Québec

Printed in Canada on acid-free paper that is 100% ancient forest free
(100% post-consumer recycled), processed chlorine free
Reprinted 2009, 2012, 2014

McGill-Queen's University Press acknowledges the support of the Canada
Council for the Arts for our publishing program. We also acknowledge the
financial support of the Government of Canada through the Canada Book
Fund for our publishing activities.

Library and Archives Canada Cataloguing in Publication

Widdowson, Frances, 1966–
    Disrobing the aboriginal industry : the deception behind indigenous
cultural preservation / Frances Widdowson and Albert Howard.

Includes bibliographical references and index.
ISBN 978-0-7735-3420-9 (bound)
ISBN 978-0-7735-3421-6 (pbk)
ISBN 978-0-7735-7512-7 (ePDF)
ISBN 978-0-7735-7747-3 (ePUB)

1. Native peoples – Canada. 2. Native peoples – Canada – Social
conditions. 3. Native peoples – Canada – Government relations.
I. Howard, Albert II. Title.

E98.C2W4885 2008     305.897'071     C2008-903029-X

This book was typeset by Jay Tee Graphics Ltd. in 10.5/.13 Sabon

# Contents

# Acknowledgments

There are numerous people to whom we are grateful for seeing us through this challenging project over the years. We would especially like to thank Andrew Hodgkins and Thomas Widdowson for engaging us in many enlightening discussions, reading drafts of the manuscript and offering detailed and helpful comments on a number of chapters. Many others – Greg Albo, Jaypeetee Arnakak, Luciano Azzolini, Colin Alexander, Dennis and Alice Bartels, Elizabeth Behrens, David Boulet, Alan Cairns, Joseph Carroll, Petr Cizek, Suzanne Desfossés, Garrett Fagan, Jack and Kelly Fertile, Tom Flanagan, Robin Fox, Brendan Howley, Olaf and Ellen Janzen, Gary Juniper, Harvey Lemelin, Norman Levitt, Robert McGhee, Neil McLaughlin, Frank Miller, Emerald Murphy, Leo Panitch, Elizabeth Rata, Nancy Rempel, Roger Sandall, Raymond Shirritt-Beaumont, Alan Sokal, Ian Stirling, Katherine Widdowson and a number of journalists working for CBC North (you know who you are) – have offered us assistance in a variety of ways, even if they do not necessarily agree with our views. We would also like to thank Daniel Arseneault, Kate Ashman, Linda Bruce, Sue Butkiewicz, Tiziana Carafa, Leslie and Bubs Coleman, Michael Dartnell, Don Desserud, Jim Duffy, Joanna Everitt, Darrel Furlotte, Larry Gaynor, Margot Gibb- Clark, Tom Graham, John Holman, Doug Johnson, Tim Maki, Stephanie McKenzie, Keith and Heather Nicol, Nick Novakowski, Dennis Pilon, Bal and Mary Russell, Chuck Smith, Donnie Tobobandung, Ann Widdowson, and Tim and Gloria Williams for offering us their encouragement and support. And finally, special gratitude is owed to Philip Cercone, Joan McGilvray, Ligy Alakkat-tussery, and Maureen Garvie at McGill-Queen's University Press.

# A STORY

# Discovering the Emperor's Nudity

One cold and bright day in Yellowknife, we trudged to the Prince of Wales Northern Heritage Centre where we witnessed an event that would dramatically alter our perception of aboriginal policy in Canada. It was 13 February 1996, and the event in question was the Federal Environmental Assessment Review of Broken Hill Properties (BHP) Inc.'s proposed diamond mine in the Northwest Territories, where a panel of four experts was appointed by the Canadian government to probe the implications of the initiative. The review was significant not only because it concerned the first diamond mine development proposal in Canada; it also sparked a great deal of interest by directing BHP to give "full and equal consideration" to aboriginal peoples' "traditional knowledge" in assessing the impacts of the proposed mine.[1]

Traditional knowledge had become a buzzword in aboriginal and environmental policy. The importance of aboriginal peoples' traditional knowledge (also referred to as "TK") was beginning to be recognized in international circles and within the Canadian government. It had become particularly popular in the North, and in 1993 the Government of the Northwest Territories developed an unprecedented "Traditional Knowledge Policy" that directed government employees to incorporate traditional knowledge into all government programs and services. This policy defined traditional knowledge as "knowledge and values which have been acquired through experience, observation, from the land or from spiritual teachings, and handed down from one generation to another." It also declared that traditional knowledge was a "valid and essential source of information," since aboriginal peoples had lived in close contact with their environment for thousands of years.

Despite the expectations that had been raised about the incorporation of traditional knowledge into environmental assessment, and the praise heaped upon the panel for issuing a directive to equally consider it, we were surprised when the technical session on traditional knowledge proved to be nothing more than a compilation of jejune platitudes interspersed with various intellectual dodges. Not only had the panel chosen to avoid establishing criteria and standards to evaluate traditional knowledge research, but no one at the session seemed to be able to identify what traditional knowledge was, let alone how it could be applied. Instead, BHP's anthropological consultants spent a great deal of time explaining that it had been difficult for them to obtain traditional knowledge because it could not be separated from its "cultural context." These anthropologists explained that traditional knowledge meant different things to different aboriginal groups, and it would take many years to document. BHP then made the extraordinary statement that it would pay for traditional knowledge research despite not understanding what it was. Even more perplexing was the company's agreement to respect the demands of aboriginal groups that they retain "proprietary rights" over any traditional knowledge studies commissioned.

The presentations made by aboriginal groups, the Government of the Northwest Territories, and the Department of Indian and Northern Affairs were also unable to shed light on the methodology of traditional knowledge or how it would assess the environmental impacts of a diamond mine. Nevertheless, it was taken for granted that there was a great deal of information that could be acquired and that government and industry should further increase their allocation of funds to collect aboriginal peoples' special knowledge. A spokesman for the Department of Indian and Northern Affairs claimed in his presentation that a "huge database" of traditional knowledge already existed that could be used for future research. And while a great deal of concern was expressed about combining traditional knowledge with scientific studies, since there was potential for destroying the "cultural context" of traditional knowledge and infringing upon the "intellectual property rights" of various aboriginal groups, there was no attempt to elucidate how the different "knowledge systems" or "world views" could be incorporated to more fully understand ecological processes.

As disinterested observers, we were astonished at how the panel, BHP, the government, and aboriginal groups were so confident that traditional knowledge was essential to the environmental assessment process when they didn't even seem to know what it was or how it could be used. After all, no one had recognized the necessity of traditional knowledge until the panel had directed that it be considered. In order to try to understand the nature of traditional knowledge and how it differed from science, we asked a number of questions both publicly and informally at the panel review. It was to form the basis of our understanding of aboriginal policy because it inadvertently uncovered the subterfuge. And the extensive chicanery was only the tip of the iceberg where aboriginal policy was concerned.

An informal question posed to the Indian and Northern Affairs representative revealed that there was no "database" of traditional knowledge available after all. Instead, there were boxes of tapes and handwritten notes documenting unstructured and unverified anecdotes from aboriginal elders. Aboriginal groups giving presentations also were unable to answer questions concerning the methodology of traditional knowledge or how it differed from scientific research. They gave long rambling pontifications about the still unspecified but nevertheless important "cultural context" of traditional knowledge, and stated that its "complexity" made it difficult for them to describe. Bill Erasmus, the grand chief of the Dene Nation, for example, maintained that traditional knowledge should be called "Dene science," but when we asked how its methodology compared with modern research, he gave the following comments:

I call it Dene science because in the literature it is regarded as a science ... For example, we have been trying to explain a number of aspects where you can understand how the mind of the people works. [François Paulette] gave examples: If someone wanted to be a leader in the field of medicine within our communities, there's a scientific way of doing it. If all the standards are not met, then the individual does not reach the level where people will recognize the person as a helper, or people will not recognize the individual as having the capability or the trust necessary to help. When you work in the field of medicine, a big aspect of a person being healed, cured or ridden of the disease is belief and faith in the individual. The scientific process we talk about is very complex. It takes a lot to describe ... Without quoting experts in the field it's hard to describe. It is a science. There's a method to the way people work ... We've managed to survive all of these years. We can give you many examples. This is how society works.[2]

The "examples" that François Paulette, Erasmus's colleague and representative for the Treaty 8 Indians, gave at the session were buried in lengthy musings that eventually asserted that a man was incapable of "holding" traditional knowledge if he was abusing alcohol, using drugs, gambling, or "messing around on his wife," and that manifestations of this "knowledge" included giving offerings to the land, holding potlatches, and thinking in a cyclical fashion. He then went on to make this contribution to Erasmus's attempt to show how traditional knowledge was a science:

> The way we know science, there's physical and spiritual. Physical is if you ask an elder how big the fish was they caught, they would say it was this big. If you were to ask a white man, they would say it was this big. For him there's nothing in here, what is that [sic]. There is nothing tangible you can see it's irrelevant [sic]. In the spirit world, if you ask ... My father taught me many spiritual things. One thing he said was that the rock moves. You have a tough time understanding and believing that. It's another dimension we don't learn every day. There is physical science and spiritual science. It can be as one at times or it can be separate. It takes a lifetime to understand. What I'm sharing with you is just touching the surface. I have witnessed all of the things I've talked about. *Mahsi* [Thank you].[3]

Although the language in both quotations makes it difficult to decipher the exact meaning of the answers provided by Erasmus and Paulette, two underlying assertions can be discerned about the nature of traditional knowledge vis-à-vis science. The first is that the existence of traditional knowledge is dependent upon the undefined qualities of the person who allegedly holds it. All that is explained is that it is impossible for certain people – those who "mess around" on their wives, for example – to have this "knowledge." Secondly, traditional knowledge has a "world view" that is rooted in native spirituality. Unlike physical science, traditional knowledge assumes that all objects in the universe are governed by spiritual forces that cannot be seen by a white man. The elusive cultural context of traditional knowledge, therefore, appears to be the particular spiritual beliefs or animistic world view held by aboriginal peoples and their faith that particular individuals have the power to heal others (i.e., a belief in shamanism or "medicine power"). This makes it incompatible with modern research, since scientific methodology attempts to verify hypotheses by using evidence that is open to evaluation. Scientific understanding does not rely on the alleged "spiritual qualities" of a scientist, or processes that are visible only to people of a certain racial ancestry. Postmodern rhetoric like "cultural context" and "cyclical thinking," however, acts to mystify the true character of traditional knowledge, preventing the implications of its use in public policy from being understood.

The acceptance of this continuous obfuscation in a forum that was devoted to understanding traditional knowledge's importance was not the only surprising circumstance that occurred. After the session was over, a number of people expressed support for our questions that attempted to clarify the difference between traditional knowledge and science. Chief Bill Erasmus remarked that these were "good questions" and that we should discuss these issues further "over coffee" sometime. The fact that he was unable to answer fundamental questions publicly about the subject that he was so ardently promoting didn't seem to faze him. Two BHP representatives also admitted to us confidentially that they were glad these questions were asked, since the company was prevented from raising similar concerns. And finally, one of the panel members approached us and expressed gratitude for the questions, reiterating that there was apprehension about discussing traditional knowledge openly.

The panel's hearing exemplified a well-known pattern of behaviour in the North; publicly, everyone declared unconditionally that traditional knowledge was a valid and essential source of information for environmental assessment and that it could enhance the scientific research that was being undertaken. When questions were asked about what this information was, or how it could be incorporated with scientific methods, however, no clarification was available. And although, as became apparent in our private discussions, many people had concerns about traditional knowledge's usefulness, no one gave voice to them publicly – even in a forum that had been specifically tasked with discussing how to incorporate traditional knowledge into the environmental assessment process currently being undertaken by BHP.

Reflecting on our experience at the panel meeting, we were reminded of Hans Christian Andersen's 1837 tale "The Emperor's New Clothes," in which an emperor, his servants, and the public at large are duped by two con men who sell a suit of clothes that does not really exist. Recall that Andersen's scam-artists use two tactics. First, they construct a powerful taboo that inhibits the clothes' existence from being openly questioned; they claim that the "silk" from which the clothes are woven has the special quality of being invisible to those who are incompetent or stupid. Then, the taboo firmly in place, they set up a workshop in the

emperor's palace with all the implements required for weaving and tai-
loring. Sitting at a loom and making the motions of passing thread back
and forth, then using scissors and needles to cut and sew non-existent
cloth, they pretend to work day and night in creating the emperor's new
suit. Not until a child oblivious to the taboo cries, "But the emperor has
nothing at all on!" is the silence broken and all immediately begin to
state what they perceived all along – that the emperor is, in fact, naked.

Andersen's story was written over 170 years ago, but it retains a powerful message for people today. It refers to a variety of phenomena that
are touted as true even when their veracity is doubted. Andersen's tale
draws attention to the fact that people often perpetuate false information publicly because they fear the consequences of nonconformity.
Social consensus makes dissent difficult because, as Andersen's parable
implies, those who challenge it face ridicule or persecution.

Living in the Northwest Territories and observing initiatives like the
Federal Environmental Assessment Panel Review provided us with
insights into how circumstances like those outlined above were influencing the development of aboriginal policy in Canada. Before living in
the North, we, like most Canadians, had little experience with aboriginal politics. For the most part, aboriginal politics takes place behind
closed doors between bureaucracies and aboriginal organizations, or on
isolated Indian reserves. The Northwest Territories, however, was a
special case, since at the time we lived there the majority of its residents
were native. This made the formulation of aboriginal policy a much
more public endeavour, exposing the fact that various initiatives were
being undertaken that were nothing more than invisible silk. In the case
of traditional knowledge, a yarn of sophistic tactics, taboos, and testimony from designated "experts" was being woven, the end result of
which was to extract large sums of money from the government. Until
seeing for ourselves the ritual absurdity of the traditional knowledge
session, we could not have understood this.

The overwhelming view of those who are concerned about the terrible social conditions in aboriginal communities is that aboriginal peoples should "decide for themselves" how to run their affairs. To this
end, two major initiatives are advocated: land claims and self-government. Land claims supposedly compensate aboriginal peoples for past
wrongs and give them an economic base from which to regain their
self-sufficiency. Self-government is meant to make good the "cultural
loss," low self-esteem, and consequent social problems that government
tutelage has caused. By obtaining self-government, the argument rea-

sons, aboriginal peoples' pride in their culture will be restored, ending their marginalization and social dysfunction.

However, land claims and demands for self-government did not originate within the aboriginal population and are not being formulated and implemented by aboriginal peoples themselves. Rather, they are the result of a long historical process in which an ever-expanding, parasitical Aboriginal Industry – first clergy, then consultants, lawyers, and anthropologists – have used the plight of aboriginal peoples to justify a self-serving agenda. The legal and "culturally sensitive" bureaucratic solutions to aboriginal problems that the Industry proposes would continue to keep natives isolated and dependent, thus perpetuating existing social pathologies and, not incidentally, justifying demands for more funding and programs for the Aboriginal Industry.

The counterpart of the imaginary threads and feigned weaving in land claims and self-government initiatives is the huge infrastructure of policies and programs being created, run, and evaluated by spinners for the Aboriginal Industry's demands for more and more government money. Sinecures and unproductive businesses make it appear that unviable aboriginal communities are "developing," while the adoption of low standards hides the fact that most native people have not developed the skills, knowledge, or values to survive in the modern world. Even worse, a number of "institutes," journals, university departments, and government-funded agencies – all controlled by associates of the Aboriginal Industry – give credence to these initiatives. These entities have compiled whole libraries of "scholarship" that obscures the actual implications of current aboriginal policies.

The result is the squandering of billions of dollars each year while the problems of spousal and sexual assault, child abuse and neglect, suicides, Fetal Alcohol Syndrome (FAS), and addictions fester. Furthermore, the solution touted for aboriginal deprivation – the devolution of control to aboriginal communities themselves – has resulted in a large amount of corruption where powerful families siphon off most of the resources while the majority remain mired in poverty and social dysfunction. Privileged leaders live in luxury and are paid huge salaries, while most aboriginal people rely on social assistance. And yet, despite the obvious policy failure, the aboriginal leadership, governments, and the general public continue to accept the argument that land claims and self-government are the answer to aboriginal problems.

To maintain the gap between perception and reality, the Aboriginal Industry has constructed a taboo that would make even Andersen's scoundrels envious. This taboo is the cry of "racism" that meets any honest analysis of aboriginal problems and circumstances. It is sustained by the presumption that any criticism of aboriginal policy constitutes a denigration of native people themselves. Essentially, whenever a criticism is raised about the current policy of acquiring more and more funding with less accountability, the Aboriginal Industry sets to work attacking the credibility of the critic rather than answering the charges. And since most Canadians understandably want to avoid the label of being insensitive to the aspirations of the most deprived ethnic group in our society, virtually all criticism, let alone honest analysis of aboriginal policy, is effectively silenced.

The time has come to raise the cry "The emperor has no clothes!" Up to this point, the aboriginal leadership has provided a shield for opportunists working behind the scenes. It is important to stress that the native leadership is *not* a component of the Aboriginal Industry, as some have asserted.[4] Torn between the comfort of traditional culture and the attractions of advanced civilization, these "leaders" have become a comprador element created by the real beneficiaries of the huge monetary transfers. As such, they either obtain material incentives of money and power from the Industry in exchange for supporting their agenda, or they are duped, much like the emperor in Andersen's parable, by obsequious "advisors" who appeal to their vanity or cultural pride. The Industry uses these quislings to bring the aboriginal population on side with promises of a share in the "compensation," maintaining their isolation by rationalizing racial segregation instead of human integration. Native people are manipulated to believe that they will receive huge lump-sum payments when land claims are settled, only to become resentful of "white people" when the money is siphoned off by powerful families and the Industry.

The vanity and arrogance of an unprincipled native leadership is supported by the equivalent of the servants in Andersen's parable – the bureaucrats and academics whose careers would be jeopardized by exposing the non-performance of current aboriginal policies. These bureaucrats and academics, like the native leadership, are *not* an element of the Aboriginal Industry; they do not have a vested interest in maintaining aboriginal dependency, and an elimination of the Industry would enable them to devote their energies to developing real solutions to the aboriginal question. These professionals currently administering government programs and analyzing aboriginal affairs often realize that land claims and self-government initiatives are unworkable in the modern context, but they remain publicly mute because of Aboriginal Industry pressure. The racism accusation taboo instigated by the industry has insinuated itself into the bureaucracy and academe, directly affecting opportunities for promotion and advancement. So while grumbling may be heard behind closed doors in universities and government departments, various professional incentives and sanctions effectively block public criticism of the current policy direction.

Due to historical circumstances in Canada – aboriginal tribes' participation in the fur trade and in military alliances during the country's early history, as well as the more recent use of the claims of "First Nations" to thwart Quebec sovereignty – the Aboriginal Industry is particularly concentrated in this area of the world. This, as well as our own experience with the Aboriginal Industry in this country, has led us to focus primarily on Canadian aboriginal issues. However, as a number of policy areas in this book show, the Aboriginal Industry is not just a Canadian phenomenon. The United States, Latin America, Australia, New Zealand, Russia, and many other countries are also implicated. Many consultants and lawyers, buoyed by the success of the Canadian Aboriginal Industry, have developed ties to aboriginal movements in other countries. And nowhere is this more apparent than in the case of traditional knowledge, where research promoting aboriginal peoples' special "world view" is common throughout universities in the western world. A number of international organizations advocating the incorporation of traditional knowledge into government policies, including ones associated with the United Nations, have also sprouted up over the last twenty years, adding even more infrastructure to what has now become a global enterprise.

Quite apart from camouflaging the non-performance of aboriginal policy, the Aboriginal Industry's accusations of racism and its obscurantist "research" perpetrates a greater and more harmful deception. It obscures the unprecedented and special character of the circumstances facing aboriginal peoples. Never has the cultural gap between two sets of peoples at the time of contact been wider. As is explained in more detail throughout this book, at the time of contact aboriginal peoples in what is now Canada were in an earlier stage of cultural development in comparison to Europeans who were making the transition from feudalism to capitalism. In archaeological terms, various aboriginal groups were either in a paleolithic or neolithic stage. Paleolithic societies existed over the longest period of human history, and were those that used chipping and flaking techniques in the making of stone tools.

Those cultures that are classified as "neolithic" in archaeology, on the other hand, added grinding and polishing to the stone tool-making process.[5] Although this was a significant advancement in technology and facilitated the transition to food production, such cultures did not develop metallurgy, and so remained in the Stone Age.

The characterization of cultures in terms of the materials they used for making tools (the Stone, Bronze, and Iron Ages) is complemented in anthropology by the classification of human development in terms of three stages – "savagery," "barbarism," and "civilization." Originally proposed by Edward Tylor and then refined by Lewis Henry Morgan in 1877, this classification links technology with "the enlargement of man's sources of subsistence,"[6] delineating successive stages in economic and social development.[7] The stages of savagery and barbarism refer to hunter-gatherers and horticulturalists respectively, and these types of societies roughly correspond to the paleolithic (in the case of savagery) and neolithic (in the case of barbarism) periods.[8] "Civilization," on the other hand, refers to the stage of human history that invented writing and the alphabet (during the latter part of the Iron Age) – developments that enabled large social groupings to form, necessitating the emergence of complex government institutions and legal systems.

The fact that aboriginal societies in North America had not surpassed the neolithic period (and the stage of barbarism) when they encountered Europeans, who had already experienced thousands of years of civilization, is generally ignored in the literature because it is perceived as being demeaning to native people. But this is what the biologist Jared Diamond has referred to as the tendency to "confuse an explanation of causes with a justification or acceptance of results." As Diamond explains, "what use one makes of a historical explanation is a question separate from the explanation itself."[9] In other words, recognizing the gap in cultural evolution that led to the marginalization of aboriginal peoples does not justify the terrible harm they have endured. Instead, understanding the gap in development between hunting and gathering/horticultural and modern social formations can help to address the circumstances contributing to aboriginal deprivation.

The perception that the term "neolithic" has a negative connotation is also related to the misconception that this must mean that aboriginal peoples are *currently* at this stage of development. This view is shown to be false by the number of aboriginal people who have successfully integrated into modern society. More importantly, it must be recognized that all aboriginal groups have been influenced by modernity, and therefore their cultural development is uneven. Native peoples in Canada have had the ministrations of the church for hundreds of years and have been schooled for generations; they also use modern technology such as computers, pickup trucks, and cell phones. However, much of the aboriginal participation in modern societies is as consumers, not producers. Isolation from economic processes has meant that a number of neolithic cultural features, including undisciplined work habits, tribal forms of political identification, animistic beliefs, and difficulties in developing abstract reasoning, persist despite hundreds of years of contact.

It is the persistence of these obsolete cultural features that has maintained the developmental gap, preventing the integration of many aboriginal peoples into the Canadian social dynamic. As in other countries such as the United States, Australia, and New Zealand, the fast pace of capitalist development has made it difficult to incorporate hunters and gatherers and horticulturalists into modern economic processes. As will be explained in more detail in chapter 2, aboriginal circumstances differed from undeveloped cultures in other parts of the world. While the lives of slaves in the United States, peasants in Europe, and fishers in Asia were undoubtedly miserable, these groups were important producers in the economic system. This was not the case for the aboriginal population, and their isolation from economic processes after the fur trade meant that certain neolithic features from the past were retained. And since European settlers did not have the benefit of the social conscience existing today, aboriginal peoples were warehoused on reserves, and in some cases even exterminated, when their subsistence culture became an impediment to development.

Solving aboriginal problems today requires that the cultural gap existing between the neolithic stage and late capitalism be acknowledged. It is this gap, not the Aboriginal Industry's lamentations about "cultural loss," that is at the root of aboriginal dependency and related social problems in Canada and throughout the industrialized world. However, the Aboriginal Industry's tactics prevent an understanding of this circumstance, so no programs are developed to address it. This, of course, benefits the lawyers, consultants, and aboriginal leaders who profit from keeping native people in a state of segregated dependency.

It is important to state that we do not imply, nor wish it to be inferred, that all participants in what is inarguably a clandestine industry are opportunistic and conscious of the maintenance and exploitation of aboriginal circumstances that are at the core of their employment. We are aware of many dedicated people who honestly and with empathy carry out their professional duties with the interests of native people in mind. Indeed, it is these committed people who often suffer the greatest disillusionment when their efforts seem to accomplish nothing. They too are misled by the hucksters and inadvertently become part of the problem.

The task of "disrobing" the Canadian form of the global Aboriginal Industry divides this book into three parts. The first, "Origins," examines the historical development of the Aboriginal Industry and identifies its major players, as well as their tactics and motivations. It also provides an analysis of what the Aboriginal Industry is hiding – the gap in development between aboriginal culture and the modern world. We examine the problems with these policies in more detail in the second part of the book, "Taboos, Fabrications, and Sophistry," beginning with an overview of the two major focuses of aboriginal organizations – land claims and self-government. This is followed with an analysis of specific self-government initiatives – justice, child welfare, health, education, and environmental management. Each chapter analyzes the involvement of the different components of the Aboriginal Industry in formulating particular policies. We also draw attention to the harmful effects of these policies on the native population, and the means that are used to prevent them from being scrutinized. Part three, "Spheres of Deception," provides an integrated analysis of Aboriginal Industry initiatives. Using the case of traditional knowledge, we trace the regional, national, and international influences of the Aboriginal Industry.

Before beginning, however, a disclaimer is necessary. Because of the Aboriginal Industry's racism accusation taboo, and the mistaken assumption that criticisms of current aboriginal policies are somehow a denigration of aboriginal peoples themselves, the political left has uncritically supported land claims and self-government initiatives, abandoning all analysis to political conservatives. This has meant that some of the material that we have had to rely upon has come from right-wing commentators. While the use of such sources indicates our agreement with the correct observations that the political right has made, it in no way means that we accept its interpretation of aboriginal circumstances. As will be shown in what follows, we strongly oppose conservative proposals for solving aboriginal problems.

Our own political perspective is consistent with the theoretical framework known as historical materialism. Historical materialism assumes that the means used by human beings to produce and reproduce their existence is the foundation for historical development and social progress. Such an understanding maintains that human societies have evolved through technological advancement and a greater division of labour, but that these developments also have increased stratification to the point that private ownership by one group deprives another of access to basic resources. The result is accelerated class antagonisms and the apparently irreconcilable conflicts that plague human societies. Addressing these conflicts requires socializing ownership so that goods and services are produced not to obtain profits but to satisfy human need.

This historical materialist perspective informs the analysis of aboriginal problems found in the following chapters. It is very different from perspectives that are currently claiming to be affiliated with the left, since they have more in common with right-wing romantic philosophies than those that seek substantial equality for all members of society. We argue that a real left-wing analysis of aboriginal policy requires a critical eye rather than a bleeding heart. Addressing the aboriginal question entails understanding its root causes, not glorifying the educational deficiencies, dependency, and dysfunction that currently plague the native population.

# PART ONE

# Origins

# 1

# The Aboriginal Industry: Weavers of Illusory Silk

Several winters ago we encountered our dentist at a ski resort in the lunchtime lineup. While chatting about what a good time we were having, he joked that one of our recent root canals was paying for his weekend. The dentist's ironic sense of humour exemplified an overlooked aspect of the monetary relationship between care-givers and their clients: a patient's detriment is the practitioner's benefit. The obvious business-development strategy would be to encourage sugar consumption and negligent dental hygiene, but of course both personal and professional ethics preclude such outrageous tactics.

Most of us can identify the portion of our work that earned a vacation, a bottle of wine, or a new car, and we feel justified in encouraging the purchase of what we produce; but care-givers face a conflict of interest in that their advice, when followed, diminishes the demand for their services. Practising doctors and dentists make their living by *treating* health problems, not in eradicating their source. The dichotomy is reflected in many areas where services are created to respond to preventable conditions

The charity and poverty industries are examples of the supply of service without addressing the problem. No one suggests that handing out soup and blankets to the homeless will affect the homelessness situation. Charity fundraising depends on whatever disease or disaster is the object of the campaign. Although fundraisers are rarely in a position to actively maintain the conditions that assure the need for their services, whole industries have developed around conditions for which the real remedy is fundamental change.[1]

There is, however, a socially accepted industry that provides a product, the consumption of which actively increases the need for more. It is funded by Canadians through labour exploitation and taxation, and it is highly profitable. The Aboriginal Industry is an amalgamation of lawyers, consultants, anthropologists, linguists, accountants, and other occupations that thrive on aboriginal dependency.[2] The industry's strategy is pushing atavism – reverting to the past for solutions to present problems. Jean Allard, a Métis lawyer and politician, describes the interdependent relationship between service providers and their clients[3] to elaborate upon the motivations of the Aboriginal Industry. According to Allard, "the impoverished Indians living in Third World conditions are essential to the continued existence of the multitude of consultants, program analysts, researchers, administrators and managers who swell the ranks of the bureaucracy. These are largely middle class professionals who have families to support and households to maintain. They are part of the Canadian economy. If Indian Affairs was successful in addressing the needs of its clients, its *raison d'être* would cease. All those people who make up the bureaucracy would find themselves unemployed."[4]

The activities of the Aboriginal Industry, in fact, are cynically referred to in bureaucratic circles as "The Great Game." The nature of this "game" was spelled out succinctly by David Crombie, the minister of Indian and Northern Affairs between 1984 and 1986, who naïvely thought he could transform aboriginal policy during his tenure in the department:

> You get a whole bunch of obfuscation, meeting after meeting, word games, magic shows of all kinds. And that's why so much of Indian Affairs is a convoluted process of negotiation, meeting, consultation ... Because for bureaucrats, 'Oh well, we've got to go out and consult,' well, that meant you didn't have to decide for a very long time. And for the Indian leadership it was just as good, because consultation meant money ... Consultation was the word that allowed the solutions to the problems to be postponed. A whole round of activity that was an industry. There is a consultation industry, and that means work for politicians, lawyers. It means money for Indians. It means everything but getting on with the task at hand.[5]

The magnitude of the Industry's processes can be seen in the number of government agencies among the participants. In addition to the Department of Indian and Northern Affairs, almost every government department now funds an aboriginal division and numerous programs that target the aboriginal population. Such funding enables the Aboriginal Industry to pursue endless negotiations, the main function of which is to pave the way for more meetings.

It is important to point out, however, that the actions of the Aboriginal Industry are not necessarily a case of vulgar opportunism like the hypothetical dentist proffering candy or Andersen's swindling tailors; its motivations are far more subtle and complex. Many members of the Aboriginal Industry are not even aware that they are part of it. There is no conspiracy being perpetrated by the lawyers, consultants, and anthropologists working for aboriginal organizations. What exists is a natural impulse to follow material interests, to veer ultimately toward self-interest. It is understandable that Industry members advocate policies that lead to jobs, contracts, and payments to members of their group. Politics is all about interests, and so it is hardly surprising that political actors turn out to be self-interested.

What is notable about the Aboriginal Industry is its altruistic posture. Its members claim to be trying to "work themselves out of a job," while they pursue initiatives that ensure the continual need for their involvement in aboriginal policy. The atavistic programs and services they advocate as aiding "self-determination" actually maintain native dependency and dysfunction, thereby justifying demands for increases in government funding. And while they may truly believe their intervention is beneficial, their interests tend to prevent them from examining inconvenient facts and theories that would reveal the destructive character of the initiatives they propose and implement. Their arguments supporting current aboriginal policies become a form of mystification, and everyone involved in the industry is inclined to support them because they are all benefiting from keeping the processes going.

It is also important point out that there is a diversity of motivations within the Aboriginal Industry itself.[6] First, there is the idealistic group, emotionally motivated by a sincere desire to help native people. Some uncritically accept that the best future for aboriginals is some level of return to the Rousseauian ideal, where they will live in some kind of mythic pre-contact Eden. Others simply support whatever aboriginal organizations demand because of the belief that this must be what aboriginal peoples "want."

A second group can, for lack of a better term, be considered professionals. They are hired to promote the cause within the capacity of their discipline. Their role is to fill the demand for a pre-determined purpose; they may teach, consult, supply professional services, and so on. Their attitudes range from cynicism to disinterest.

A third group often encompasses the attributes of the first two but is defined by the fact that its members are the initiators of the reactionary policies that maintain native people in the state of dependency that all three groups supply. These are the members that most closely resemble the scoundrel-tailors of the parable. They are the bureaucrats who instigate useless, money-gobbling policy programs, then quit the government and head the program. They are the linguists who promote unilingual native language teaching in elementary grades, then develop course materials and teach them, sentencing the children to a future of low academic achievement and the resulting social dysfunction. They are the anthropologists who encourage a backward spiritualism and mythology in which they themselves do not believe, but which keeps native people in a convenient state of passivity. They are the consultants who dream up studies or research that are neither. And especially, they are the lawyers who collect enormous fees for conflicts they initiated, for agreements that require endless negotiations, for land claims settlements they use as retirement funds.

The development and increasing prominence of the Aboriginal Industry can only be understood by situating it within its wider historical context. When Europeans first arrived in what is now Canada, aboriginal peoples' hunting and gathering skills provided useful services to the fur trade. As the country made the transition to agriculture and industry between the eighteenth and the twentieth centuries,[7] however, these skills became obsolete, and aboriginal peoples were largely excluded from participation in the production of socially necessary goods and services. The subsistence lifestyle before European contact did not provide the cultural prerequisites to engage easily in wage labour and intensive agriculture. Aboriginal peoples had practised only hunting and gathering and horticulture, which (as discussed in chapters 2 and 3), did not require the same degree of forethought, discipline, and cooperative labour necessary in more complex and productive economic systems. Economic marginalization meant that aboriginal peoples were largely denied access to the resources needed to further their development; it was taken for granted that those who did not adapt to the changing world order would just "die out." A frontier mentality assumed that those who were unable to contribute to economic development on the occupied lands Europeans wanted to settle were obstacles to progress, rather than human beings needing support in their struggle to become part of the civilized world. All concerns about the provision of goods and services to the indigent aboriginal population, like the treatment of "the poor" more generally, were left to philan-thropic institutions and not considered a state obligation.

While the relative lack of productivity of subsistence economies and societies made it easy for colonial governments to neglect and ignore the needs of the aboriginal population, it also presented an interesting challenge for British law. Never before had British explorers encoun-tered cultures at such an early stage of economic and social develop-ment, yet legal precedents required that, in lieu of conquest, new territories must be ceded to, or purchased by, the Crown before settle-ment occurred. In order to maintain peaceful relations with aboriginal groups so that development could proceed unencumbered, British authorities originally proposed that native "Nations or Tribes" should remain autonomous and not be "molested or disturbed" on designated "hunting grounds."[8] But the looming obsolescence of aboriginal econo-mies in the modern context soon required the development of new legal designations; "treaties" were signed and various forms of guardianship asserted so that aboriginal practices could be temporarily reconciled with agricultural and industrial development. Although the government intended that the invention of the category "Indian" would gradually disappear as aboriginals developed the skills to become participants in modern society,[9] legal fictions like aboriginal "nationhood" and "sovereignty" persisted because the wording in legal documents remained. And as aboriginal people remained isolated from wider social processes, they became increasingly preoccupied with their "spe-cial relationship" to the Crown, based on the perception that the trea-ties constitute a "sacred covenant,"[10] even though the reason for it no longer existed.[11]

The marginalization of aboriginal peoples has made them particu-larly vulnerable to manipulation. The aboriginal leadership, in fact, is a *creation* of the Aboriginal Industry. Various service providers befriended promising young natives who could become figureheads in newly created, Industry-controlled organizations that took responsibil-ity for services rather than having the government deliver them. The bureaucracy was encouraged to divert funds to these entities, and the industry controlled the spending. The result has been an entrenched comprador element within the aboriginal population. Corruption of leaders, by way of proffering privileges, is a tactic that has served the powerful through history, be they labour leaders or chieftains in oil-rich countries. The wealth and advantage they obtain distances them from the people they purport to represent, and their interests become aligned with the dominant power. In aboriginal communities the status of chief now embraces a coterie of bureaucrats, association executives, board of director appointments, and other sinecures. To protect their own privileges, these "leaders" shield the Aboriginal Industry from scrutiny.

This combination of circumstances has enabled four groups to use aboriginal advocacy to further their own interests – clergy, government consultants, lawyers, and anthropologists. These advocates continue to be the major players in the Aboriginal Industry's "Great Game" and, along with the comprador leadership that they have created, are the major beneficiaries of the legal and bureaucratic initiatives that maintain native dependency and the funding it generates.

### CULTIVATING THE SILKWORMS: CREATING SPIRITUAL DEPENDENCY

In addition to various government agencies, much of the blame for aboriginal circumstances has been directed at the various missionary groups that historically interacted with the native population. Beginning in the nineteenth century, the colonial government gave a number of churches funds to educate, Christianize, and civilize the native population so that they would become productive members of Canadian society. The most significant initiative with respect to this agenda came to be the residential school system; removing aboriginal children from their communities was intended to reduce the impediment of a tribal and subsistence lifestyle on their development. Thus the pace of the civilizing process could be increased and aboriginal peoples more effectively assimilated into the social fabric.

The emerging consensus is that this assimilation strategy was a mistake. A number of different arguments to this effect range from assertions that aboriginal peoples should have been "left alone" to those maintaining that the process was lacking in sufficient "respect" and "cultural sensitivity." Aside from the horrors of physical and sexual abuse, the church is accused of destroying aboriginal culture by forcing aboriginal children to speak English and adopt Christianity, by disrupting community child-rearing practices, and by subjecting aboriginal children to disciplines that were alien to their traditions. These practices, it is argued, deprived aboriginal peoples of their cultural pride and community integrity, resulting in the dependency and social pathologies in existence today.[12]

With the burgeoning number of lawsuits being brought against the churches, these accusations are becoming more and more vehement. While in the past it was accepted that missionary involvement was a necessary (albeit poorly executed) attempt to give aboriginal children the skills, values, and attitudes for participating in modern society, current examinations of the subject conclude that these initiatives were part of a conscious racist strategy to exterminate aboriginal peoples. Roland Chrisjohn and Sherri Young in their book *The Circle Game*, for example, compare the residential school experience to the Holocaust, arguing that the missionaries were part of a conspiracy on par with Hitler's attempts to create an Aryan master race in Europe.[13]

Labelling the missionaries' efforts as "genocide," however, obscures the fact that "obliterating" various traditions is essential to human survival. Conservation of obsolete customs deters development, and cultural evolution is the process that overcomes these obstacles. Many of the activities held as destructive to aboriginal peoples – the teaching of English, the discouraging of animistic superstitions, and encouraging of self-discipline – were positive measures intended to overcome the social isolation and economic dependency that was (and continues to be) so debilitating to the native population. Accusations of genocide are affected to avoid the reality that when cultures at vastly different levels of development come into contact, more components of the relatively simple culture have to be discarded in comparison to those of the more complex. So, oral cultures are "stolen" from pre-literate societies when they learn to write, as are creation myths when they are faced with the scientific theory of evolution. Although the missionaries deserve criticism for the methods they employed in attempting to bring about this transition, the "loss" of many cultural attributes is necessary for humans to thrive as a species in an increasingly interconnected and complex global system.

The spurious logic of retaining atavistic cultural features, coupled with assertions of genocide, suggests a causal effect of the missionaries' failed assimilation attempts on the current conditions in aboriginal communities. In examining this case, we have to consider the question of what aboriginal communities would be like were it *not* for residential schools. Leaving aside the tragedy of incidental sexual abuse, what would have been the result if aboriginal people had not been taught to read and write, to adopt a wider human consciousness, or to develop some degree of contemporary knowledge and disciplines? Hunting and gathering economies are unviable in an era of industrialization, and so were it not for the educational and socialization efforts provided by the residential schools, aboriginal peoples would be even more marginalized and dysfunctional than they are today.

Charges of "genocide" have been able to stick because authors like Chrisjohn and Young adopt the sophistry of using modern values to judge actions of the past. Enlightened attitudes against physically assaulting children did not exist because, well into the twentieth century, corporal punishment was believed to "build character." (The old adage "spare the rod and spoil the child" continues to be practised by a number of religious sects today.) Religious imposition was taken for granted because Christianity was assumed to be a universal truth. The claim that these activities were racially motivated is senseless, since they reflected attitudes that affected all people in Canada; present-day rejection simply demonstrates an ability to learn from past mistakes. Besides, attempting to impose one's own culture on others can hardly be called genocide, regardless of how offensive the process is considered. The argument that all cultural change is genocidal defies both definitive and historical fact and imparts the negativity to education that currently undermines native schooling.

Instead of hysterically equating assimilation with genocide, it would be more constructive to analyze the failure of previous efforts to address aboriginal dependency, to examine the historical relationship between the government, the churches and aboriginal peoples. Why was the responsibility for the servicing of the aboriginal population left to the missionaries in the first place? What did it mean for the assimilation of native tribes into modern society?

Increasing references to the term "genocide" in current aboriginal policy debates is a distraction from the fact that it was generally neglect, not a deeply entrenched racism (although racist attitudes did exist),[14] that characterized the government's relationship with natives until the 1940s.[15] In the nineteenth century the welfare state was still a long way off, and care for the poor and abandoned, which included the aboriginal population, was simply left to the whims of the churches.[16] As a result, aboriginal peoples received inferior health and education services in comparison with other Canadians, and religious indoctrination was much more pronounced in aboriginal communities. In 1920, for example, early Canadian anthropologist Diamond Jenness observed that in elementary mission schools for native children "the standard of teaching was exceedingly low," ensuring that they were "well indoctrinated in the Christian faith, but totally unfitted for life in an Indian community and, of course, not acceptable in any white one."[17]

These lower educational standards were further exacerbated by the lack of any formal education system before contact, and aboriginal parents had no understanding of modern educational disciplines. Today, deficiencies in instruction could be addressed with various remedial programs, but that was not part of the method in the early twentieth century. The scarce resources devoted to aboriginal education meant that the adult population was ignored; a generational division was created within aboriginal groups, and education came to be seen as a destructive force. The entrenchment of such attitudes, along with the promotion of irrational ideology, continues to plague native communities today. It is reflected in the poor educational levels aboriginal children achieve in all subjects, especially science and math. As will be shown in chapter 8, the answer has been to lower standards, perpetuating a domino effect into university levels where "Aboriginal" programs increasingly appear.

The isolating effect of inferior services, along with the diminishing role of religion in Canadian society, set the stage for a transition in the missionaries' role from assimilationists to advocates for segregation. Initially the churches shared the government's interest in aboriginal modernization; the power of the churches in early Canadian history was based on the extraction of tithes from small family farms, so creating aboriginal agricultural communities would increase the wealth of a particular denomination. But as the country became more secularized and the industrial sector grew, the agricultural base of church power eroded. The churches became increasingly oriented toward maintaining aboriginal dependency rather than providing tribes with the necessary skills to integrate with Canadian society. To retain the loyalty of the native population, it became necessary to isolate aboriginal peoples from "corrupt" influences.[18] Isolation ensured that the church, not public institutions, would receive funding for education and health services designated for aboriginal communities.

Their interest in maintaining aboriginal dependency led the churches to become the first lobbyists for land claims. The advocacy role of the missionaries has largely been ignored in current historical accounts, but it was instrumental in the formulation of the legal agenda that now dominates aboriginal policy.[19] The church increased its power by obtaining land, compensation, and special rights for the native population. This led to religious sects encouraging political divisions within native communities in order to set up rival missions and gain control over Crown land and resources.[20]

Control over the aboriginal population was solidified through co-optation of the aboriginal leadership. This was done through the church-controlled education process, where the most capable aboriginal students were groomed to become members of the clergy. Like the "trading captains" or "chiefs" who were given presents for bringing furs to particular forts, those who were loyal to the church were rewarded with paid leadership positions and the perks that came with them. These privileged positions bought their support for the churches' legal agenda since it assured them the lion's share of any compensation obtained.[21]

The native leadership needed the missionaries' knowledge of European law to negotiate with the authorities, while aboriginal involvement gave legitimacy to the missionaries. Although this relationship was to achieve a much more sophisticated form with the involvement of consultants and lawyers, the missionaries' authoritative position in aboriginal communities at this time made them the most significant advisors to aboriginal groups. They wrote petitions and letters, were interpreters at meetings, and organized the conferences and excursions necessary to make effective demands on governments and international authorities. Furthermore, they had access to funds for various legal processes and "nation-to-nation" junkets. It is these resources that made it possible for missionaries and native leaders in British Columbia and Ontario to form a number of "aboriginal delegations" that presented demands for native legal rights to Britain between 1850 and 1930.[22]

Although the missionaries were undoubtedly motivated to some extent by the poor treatment aboriginal peoples were receiving from the British and Canadian governments, the churches were, and continue to be, dubious friends of aboriginal peoples. Their main interest has always been in maintaining the political power and resources of the church, not the concerns of the native population. As the churches have receded in importance, they have increased their advocacy for land claims and self-government initiatives.[23] They now support the retention of aboriginal cultural practices rather than native indoctrination. The Catholic Church and various Protestant sects are even incorporating native spirituality into their teachings in the hopes of maintaining their hold over aboriginal peoples.[24] And though the churches still raise money to support aboriginal causes, their advisory capacity has been taken over by two far more sophisticated, professions – consultants and lawyers. These two groups now dominate all aspects of aboriginal policy in Canada: the legacy of government neglect and the missionaries' exploitation of aboriginal vulnerability.

## PREPARING THE SILK THREAD: LET THE CONSULTATIONS BEGIN

Whether it was the fight against the Indian Act in the 1960s, land claims struggles in the 1970s, or attempts to entrench the "inherent right" to self-government in the 1980s, a common thread runs throughout: the large number of non-aboriginal consultants who are paid to construct legal demands and bureaucratic processes on behalf of aboriginal organizations. The presence of these non-aboriginal advisors was made possible through the provision of government funding to these groups. Ironically, under the auspices of helping aboriginal peoples to run their own affairs, non-aboriginal advisors are paid to fundraise, conduct research, run meetings, write speeches or "political manifestos," lobby governments, and prepare court cases. These initiatives take place behind closed doors, while the native leadership is paraded before the public to make it seem as if these ideas originated within the aboriginal population.

Aboriginal leaders are often candid about their dependence on outside advisors, justifying it with claims that they are no different from other politicians.[25] But the leadership of an oppressed people differs radically from representatives in mainstream politics, and many aboriginal leaders' identification with political opponents is significant of their impotence. Outside advisors are the most immediate example of the Aboriginal Industry in action – telling natives what to do. A scenario of native leaders turning up at meetings and conferences with their non-native handlers, who interpret and "translate" the proceedings, is commonplace. But the more disturbing element of this phenomenon is high-profile leaders whose objectives are personal gain through sinecures and attendance fees. These compradors front for the Aboriginal Industry by gaining public sympathy and government funding as representatives of an oppressed group.

The development of aboriginal organizations differs fundamentally from other political liberation movements because native groups receive their primary funding from government sources, not the people they supposedly represent. The leaders of labour unions, radical movements, and other oppositional groups are under the control of those who fund them, and breaches of trust and the taking of privileges are recognized as corruption. But because the native leadership receives funding from the very entity it pretends to contest, it has been easy for the Aboriginal Industry to shape aboriginal politics in its own interests.

This history has created organizations that are completely unconnected to any grassroots political activity.[26] Concerns of the leadership have become intertwined with maintaining the salaries and prestige of privileged friends and relatives, not with the widespread political mobilization of "their people."[27] The marginalization of the native population actually justifies more funding to the leadership, giving these organizations an interest in maintaining aboriginal dependency. So while movements of blacks, women, and Quebec sovereigntists have historically sprung from the aspirations of the people in struggle, and their leadership emerged from within that group, aboriginal leaders hire non-aboriginal professionals so that they can achieve their primary goal: getting more money from the government. The government, in turn, uses the dispersal of funds in its attempts to manage the discontent of the native population.[28]

Government funding for aboriginal groups first became available in the 1940s with the postwar era's more progressive ideas about human rights. The deplorable circumstances in aboriginal communities were beginning to be publicized, and pressure was brought to bear on the government to "do something" about the problem. Originally the new government approach focused on reforming the Indian Act, the piece of federal legislation that had designated aboriginal peoples as "wards of the state" since 1876. The government initially attempted to revise the act, now deemed to be discriminatory and paternalistic, so that it would be more conducive to aboriginal peoples entering into modern society. However, as noted before, the leadership was politically attached to this legal fiction, historically resisting "enfranchisement" (becoming citizens like other Canadians) because it would mean giving up the privileges associated with their "special relationship" to the Crown. This tension was to weigh on all government efforts to develop aboriginal communities.

Recognizing that assimilation would continue to be resisted, the government began to look at other self-determination movements around the world and to consider the possibility of giving aboriginal communities the "organizational tools" to solve their own problems. Money began to flow into aboriginal organizations to fund their participation in governmental consultations, and a number of "community organizing" programs were initiated whereby idealistic university students and graduates, armed with new theories of social change, were dispersed into aboriginal communities to aid their political development.

While the government intended that the workers would be a temporary presence, many community organizers began to oppose the government, becoming fixtures in aboriginal politics long after these programs had been abandoned. Because of their populist visions of empowerment, many organizers identified with native issues and began to aid the aboriginal leadership in their resistance to governmental authority. Like the missionaries before them, community workers found themselves pulled in two directions. Propelled by their ideological agenda and a rejection of what they perceived to be government paternalism, they began siding with the band councils and chiefs in opposition to the government that employed them.

In an attempt to overcome the resulting conflicts between its integrationist agenda and the political demands of community workers, the Canadian government began to fund aboriginal organizations to run these programs themselves. By 1971, five provincial Indian organizations – the Indian Association of Alberta, the Federation of Saskatchewan Indians, the Manitoba Indian Brotherhood, the Union of Nova Scotia Indians, and the Union of New Brunswick Indians – were receiving service contracts from the Department of Indian Affairs to hire community organizers of their own.[29] The many educated non-aboriginals who continued to live in native communities after finishing their stint as government employees were (along with the leadership) the main beneficiaries of this funding. They had the writing and research skills to lobby the government and became a major force in aboriginal politics.

Besides being influenced by the interests of non-aboriginal community organizers, aboriginal policy has been shaped by consultants hired to study aboriginal problems. At the same time as the community organization efforts were underway, the government embarked on its most ambitious study of aboriginal peoples, known as the Hawthorn Report. In 1963 the federal government appointed anthropologist Harry Hawthorn to investigate the conditions of native communities. The report compiled the work of fifty-two academics, mostly anthropologists, who studied specific reserves in a consultancy capacity.[30]

Hawthorn's survey was a milestone in the development of modern aboriginal policy because it was the first government-funded study to alter the goal of integration by advocating the idea of "citizens plus" for aboriginals. This concept assumed that "in addition to the normal rights and duties of citizenship, Indians possess certain additional rights as charter members of the Canadian community." To support this idea, the report recommended that the government provide additional funds to aboriginal political organizations to encourage their growth.[31] It also maintained that an aboriginal person should not be forced to "acquire those values of the majority society he does not hold or wish to acquire."[32]

This vision, however, came into direct conflict with the liberal ideas of Prime Minister Pierre Elliott Trudeau. Trudeau's fight against Quebec sovereignty had led him to be hostile toward the political claims of cultural groups and to reject the recommendations put forward by the Hawthorn Report. He countered "citizens plus" with the White Paper on Indian Policy in 1969, which proposed the phasing out of special status for aboriginal peoples. It recommended eliminating the Indian Act, privatizing reserves, and transferring the responsibility for aboriginal peoples to the provinces, in an attempt to provide natives with the same opportunities offered to other Canadian citizens. The White Paper also maintained that it was important to help the poorest aboriginal communities first rather than giving blanket privileges on the basis of ancestry – a proposal that was vehemently rejected by the native elite.[33]

Trudeau's White Paper was a turning point in Canadian aboriginal policy. The resistance that it generated caused the pendulum to swing in favour of Hawthorn's recommendations. In 1970 the Indian Association of Alberta even produced a paper entitled "Citizens Plus," which proposed the "retention of status, full preservation of culture, protection of federal jurisdiction, equal economic help to all reserves (rather than the poorest first), the recognition of the spirit and intent of the treaties, and ownership of land, communally and in trust, by Indian people." It also argued that the Indian Act should remain in law, but that it should facilitate aboriginal control over their affairs.[34]

The growing opposition forced the Trudeau government to withdraw its proposals, but two developments in its aftermath would change aboriginal policy dramatically over the next thirty years. First, the funding that was meant to be used to implement the White Paper was instead used by aboriginal groups to pursue their legal struggles against the government. These, according to Jean Chrétien, were the "glory days" of the Department of Indian and Northern Affairs.[35] Secondly, the federal government decided that it would entertain land claims and in 1974 set up an Office of Native Claims. These two developments created both the financial and organizational support for the primary beneficiaries of current aboriginal policies – lawyers.

## THE WEAVING THAT NEVER ENDS – LAWYERS NEVER SETTLE

Anyone who has had experience with the courts – whether an accident claim, custody battle, or divorce settlement – will be familiar with the truism "lawyers never settle." There are endless precedents to be researched, notices and briefs to be prepared, pre-trial hearings, consultations with other lawyers, days of complex and inaccessible arguments, and the inevitable appeals. Although such a process takes up a great deal of time and money, most people grit their teeth and bear it because they hope that the benefits from proceeding with their case will outweigh the costs. But while rewards for clients are often elusive, lawyers always benefit because they are making money off the process, not the results. This gives them a vested interest in drawing out acrimonious proceedings rather than finding a quick, uncomplicated solution to a dispute. And instead of trying to reconcile the conflict, their objective is to obtain "compensation" for its victims. No one expects that the legal process will address the cause of the conflict; the resulting bitterness may even increase its intensity.

The role that they play in an adversarial legal system has led lawyers to be referred to as advocates. Paid to argue a particular point of view regardless of their own conviction, lawyers have earned a reputation as unprincipled hucksters. Michael Mandel, in his scathing critique of the use of the courts to achieve social justice, argues that lawyers are "a variation on the mercenary soldier or the professional mourner" since they take on causes for monetary gain.[36] The arguments of lawyers, therefore, should not be confused with those of philosophers or the leaders of political movements. A lawyer's goal is not to determine the truth or achieve a particular vision of society. Lawyers are paid to obtain a favourable judgment for their client, regardless of ethical viability or social cost.

This makes the involvement of lawyers in aboriginal affairs very different from the initial advocacy role played by missionaries and community organizers who were, at least in the beginning, sympathetic to the plight of aboriginal peoples. For many lawyers, aboriginal marginalization and dependent legal status is a lucrative opportunity.[37] This has made them push much harder than other advocates to expand aboriginal rights on behalf of native tribes. And because the legal profession needs assurance that fees will be paid, compensation and control over government funds have now become the major demands in all negotiation processes. Questions about how increased funding with less accountability will help aboriginal peoples are completely absent from this legal agenda. In addition, scrutiny of billing procedures by government is non-existent because it fears criticism for restricting aboriginal legal rights.

The focus on compensation leads to an endless process in which any real action to solve aboriginal problems is impossible. It takes decades to negotiate land claims and self-government agreements, and even when they are "settled," more lawsuits and negotiations invariably follow to clarify the various rights and responsibilities. An antagonistic process has been created between government lawyers seeking a narrow interpretation of rights so as to limit compensation, and aboriginal organizations' lawyers seeking a broad interpretation to increase it. As a result, billions of dollars have been diverted from the services sorely needed by native people.

Although the involvement of lawyers has been most visible since the government began dispersing large amounts of money into aboriginal communities in the 1970s, the profession has been on the scene since aboriginals were given a special designation in the developing British/Canadian legal system. The most significant initiative for the growth of the Aboriginal Industry was the signing of treaties, since this provided lawyers with a contract that they could use to take the government to court. Their legal fees had originally been obtained from band funds or by taking cases on a contingency basis, enabling a burgeoning industry to form in the late nineteenth century. Between the 1890s and 1920s, nine separate legal actions were being pursued by lawyers hired by aboriginal tribes.[38] These cases involved a number of legal firms making demands for compensation from the Canadian and U.S. governments. One lawyer in particular, A.G. Chisholm, appeared as counsel in five of these cases, and he spent fifty years as an advocate for various tribes in Ontario. A particularly lucrative claim over which Chisholm presided, the Six Nations' dispute concerning the inappropriate investment of band funds in a navigation company, even outlived him since it involved fifty-six years of legal wrangling!

Another lawyer who acted for aboriginal leaders in the case of the British Columbia land question became a missionary, showing the linkages that can develop between two elements of the Aboriginal Industry. Arthur O'Meara's legal background enabled him to push legal initiatives in British Columbia further than ever before. For some time missionaries had recognized that British Columbia was a special case because, unlike other areas in Canada, treaties had not been signed when lands were settled. O'Meara's training enabled him to link this circumstance to documents in British law that stipulated that treaties must be negotiated before the Crown could assert ownership of the land. On the basis of this legal argument O'Meara attempted to make the case that aboriginal groups must be compensated with money, parcels of land, and privileges before Crown ownership could be established over the territories originally used by the native population.

O'Meara's involvement would stretch over a period of twenty years. Numerous lobbying forays to provincial, federal, and British authorities were made, including the preparation of a petition to the Judicial Committee of the Privy Council in London. Here for the first time land claims in British Columbia were publicly linked to the promises made by the Royal Proclamation of 1763. Although these initiatives were largely financed by O'Meara's formation of the Society of Friends, an organization that used the aboriginal land question as a cause to extract donations from parishioners, approximately $100,000 was obtained from band funds in the initial pursuit of the land question.[39]

Originally the Canadian government was ambivalent toward the involvement of lawyers in aboriginal affairs. When lawsuits were being undertaken against the u.s. government on behalf of aboriginals living in Canada (usually because of the non-fulfillment of a treaty), the Canadian government tended to be amiable toward lawyers working for aboriginal groups and even offered financial or research assistance, since awards of compensation would not be the Crown's responsibility. Claims directed against the Crown, on the other hand, were generally met with opposition, but in a few instances the federal government agreed to fund test cases or commissions so that legal questions could be settled. As claims stretched on for decades, however, the government became more and more sceptical of the ability of these lawsuits and bureaucratic processes to settle anything. Common ground between the government and aboriginal groups was almost impossible to find, since lawyers working for aboriginal groups had an interest in keeping the door open for further litigation. The large amounts of legal fees being generated by lawyers working for aboriginal groups led Charles Stewart, the superintendent general of Indian Affairs, to comment in 1927 that "for years the British Columbia Indians have been paying certain persons for their services in connection with claims which it had been represented could be enforced. I think those Indians have claims – at all events for consideration. But from one end of Canada to the other it is becoming a common practice to represent to the Indians that they have certain rights, and those making the representations usually manage to get the Indians to enter into a contract providing substantial remuneration for their advisers. We think it is to the advantage of the Indians that these contracts be scrutinized by the Department in order to protect them from exploitation."[40] The government responded by amending the Indian Act so that money could no longer be raised by lawyers to pursue claims without its approval. This effectively stopped legal initiatives until 1951, when government funding to aboriginal organizations was reinstated.

Since the defeat of the White Paper in 1969, the funding of aboriginal organizations has been the government's way of dealing with native grievances. Beginning with the formation of the Office of Native Claims in 1974, the government has provided native groups with various grants and loans to hire experts to research and present their grievances. Large sums of money have been given directly to aboriginal organizations to participate in the Indian Act and constitutional development consultations. The primary beneficiaries of this money are, once again, lawyers, since only they have the capacity to provide the legal arguments for the compensation and privileges demanded by aboriginal groups. Demands for exclusive benefits on the basis of ancestry would never be accepted if they were made politically, so lawyers must be hired to find a legal rationale for their assertion. Legal rights can then be used as trump cards to override the inevitable political opposition that arises when one group is granted privileges at the expense of another.[41]

In the quest to obtain compensation for past wrongs through the entrenchment of special rights, lawyers have employed two strategies. The first is stealth, where they push to have seemingly innocuous rights acknowledged, and then use these minor legal gains as a basis for cases where much more significant entitlements are demanded. The second is evasiveness. This approach attempts to have a particular, but not clearly defined, principle adopted in Canadian law. Then years are spent attempting to reach an agreement on a definition, usually without success. Both strategies are attractive to the Aboriginal Industry because they avoid the actual implications of legislation becoming known at the time it is adopted, thus making public acceptance more feasible. And when the implications do become known (if they ever get past the legal processes), it will be too late for the public to do anything about it. Often the government initiating the process is no longer in office, and the principle has become entangled with other legal obligations. As a result, various initiatives can be justified by a legal framework already in place, even if newly defined aboriginal rights are contested politically at a later date.

But even though the majority of natives undoubtedly resent the huge expense of legal fees (as is evidenced by periodic demands to purge "white advisors"), these legal processes are perceived as a necessary evil to receive compensation. Lawyers have generated unrealistically high expectations about the benefits from various agreements, implying that aboriginal peoples will be able to live happily ever after on government grants and royalties. And since the funding for these negotiations is received either directly from the government or as a deduction from land claims settlements yet to be finalized, most aboriginal peoples are not even aware of the amounts that are involved. They simply wait to benefit from these settlements just as people dream about winning the lottery. But as with lotteries, only a very few will share in these elusive winnings. The rest will spend their lives hoping, becoming increasingly resentful as the glorified welfare never comes.

Despite the fact that some aboriginal leaders have recognized that "lawyers are like cockroaches who feed off the misery of native people,"[42] and that legal fees are "misery money,"[43] most encourage the hiring of legal professionals.[44] Lawyers, therefore, like all other Aboriginal Industry advocates, have formed a symbiotic relationship with aboriginal leaders. Aboriginal leaders hire lawyers because an understanding of legalese is lacking in aboriginal culture (and in the Canadian population generally), while lawyers require the presence of aboriginal leaders to justify their involvement. The parasitical relationship between aboriginal deprivation and lawyers would be exposed, without the native leadership at their side. And because aboriginal leaders regurgitate arguments formulated by their lawyers, it appears that these demands are being developed by aboriginal peoples themselves.

This symbiotic relationship has been taken one step further in recent years by incorporating the most educated segment of the native population into the legal profession. Much like the missionaries' attempts to bring aboriginal peoples into leadership positions to maintain aboriginal loyalty to the church, the legal profession has made a concerted effort in the last thirty years to increase the numbers of aboriginal

lawyers in Canada. Many law schools now offer "native law" programs, where standards are lowered so that aboriginal students, denied
quality preparatory education, can pass. They then go on to work for
aboriginal organizations or law firms that specialize in "native issues."

While the financial benefits obviously garner support for these initiatives within the aboriginal population, it is harder to understand the
government's encouragement of a process that costs so much, yet
achieves so little. Governments provide funding for these legal processes; they also have assumed that aboriginal rights exist before the
judgments are reached by the courts.[45] This seemingly irrational behaviour can be explained by the fact that the courts have become a useful
tool in managing aboriginal opposition. As Michael Mandel points out,
"as long as you could get the aboriginal peoples to stay in court or at
the constitutional bargaining table nothing radical could possibly happen; and when the long drawn-out legal processes had exhausted themselves you could generally count on being back where you started, with
those who had dared to challenge the status quo a lot worse for
wear."[46] By turning aboriginal policy into a legal question, the government disguises its impotence in dealing with aboriginal problems. And
since these legal processes are likely to stretch far into the future, the
politicians encouraging them will never have to take responsibility for
the inevitable policy failure.

Attempts to diffuse aboriginal discontent through legal action can be
seen in the governmental support of an increasingly activist judiciary in
the area of aboriginal issues. This activism first appeared in the North
where the clash between aboriginal custom and modern justice was the
most pronounced. Since primitive practices like blood feuds and infanti-
cide often brought aboriginals into conflict with the Canadian legal system, the federal government appointed two "culturally sensitive" justices
– first J.H. Sissons and then William G. Morrow – as a "solution" to the
problem.[47] Since both were in favour of using the bench for political
ends, including the preservation of aboriginal culture, they were not
"averse to bending the law a bit here and there to shield Canada's
aboriginals from the law's harshest dictates." This view was especially
prevalent in Morrow's case, since he had been a lawyer defending aboriginal peoples in the North before being appointed as a judge. In his opinion, "Northern ways must be taken into account, and respected, however
unpalatable they might sometimes be to Southerners."[48]

The infiltration of advocacy into the judiciary is now coming in
through the back door in the area of legal scholarship. The University

of British Columbia's Alan Cairns explains how legal scholars like Kent McNeil, Bruce Ryder, Patrick Macklem, and Brian Slattery have influenced court rulings on aboriginal rights, especially groundbreaking Supreme Court decisions. According to Cairns, these legal scholars "write not as judges or mediators reconciling opposing parties, but as advocates." In their attempts to "maximize the autonomy of First Nations" by "devising innovative constitutional doctrine," these scholars "are more akin to an intellectual social movement than participants in a broad-ranging debate with checks and balances."[49]

In order to gain public acceptance for these initiatives, however, advocates cannot simply rely on obscure legal documents. They also must provide evidence that aboriginal land claims and self-government are viable in the modern context. This feat has been achieved through the co-opting of other supposedly scholarly disciplines that study aboriginal groups. By conducting research that is funded by native organizations, and by being concerned about how their findings will impact legal claims for aboriginal rights, a number of social scientists have been seriously compromised by advocacy goals. The discipline that has been most affected is anthropology, because favourable court decisions have required revisionism in one of the discipline's main areas of study: aboriginal culture.

### ADMIRING INVISIBLE CLOTH: THE ENCOURAGEMENT OF ATAVISM

During debates over the health effects of smoking, the tobacco lobby commissioned scientists who presented findings denying the link between cigarettes and lung cancer. This research was immediately criticized for the obvious reason that it was conducted for the purpose of advocacy, not to ascertain the truth. Because tobacco companies support only those research projects consistent with their agenda, scientific conclusions become distorted.

The relationship between interest and tainted scientific research, however, is ignored in studies of aboriginal peoples and in the evaluation of aboriginal programs. Many of the researchers involved in such studies have ties to aboriginal organizations, often receiving funding directly from them. As a result, there is a complete distortion of the understanding of aboriginal–non-aboriginal relations and the causes of aboriginal problems. This "research" has been the primary justification for the increasingly legal character of aboriginal policy.

The most significant perpetrator of distorted research is the discipline of anthropology. Historically, the work of anthropologists has necessitated a close relationship with aboriginal groups. This circumstance often turned into a quid pro quo; in exchange for information about their subjects, anthropologists advised aboriginal peoples in their disputes with the government. Often this advice progressed to the next stage: anthropologists working as lobbyists for aboriginal organizations. In the early land claims struggles of British Columbia, for example, James Teit, Franz Boas's assistant, became involved with aboriginal groups through his fieldwork. According to Teit, "the Inds. almost everywhere would bring up questions of their grievances concerning their title, reserves, hunting and fishing rights, policies of Agents and missionaries, dances, potlatches, education, etc. etc. and although I had nothing to do with these matters they invariably wanted to discuss them with me or get me to help them, and to please them and thus to better facilitate my research work I had to listen and give them some advice or information."[50]

Teit became so well known to the aboriginal groups in British Columbia that he was convinced in 1908 to become a member of the Interior Tribes of British Columbia. Until his death in 1922 he was a central figure in the aboriginal movement in the province, using "his translation skills and his anthropological expertise to assist in a writing campaign aimed at land reparations and other concerns."[51]

Many anthropologists have followed in Teit's footsteps. One of the most significant was Wilson Duff, a curator of anthropology at the British Columbia Provincial Museum (1950–1965) and then a professor of anthropology at the University of British Columbia until his death in 1976. Known as a person who "delved beneath the surface appearance of things to search for the less obvious deeper meanings,"[52] Duff played an important role in the initiation of land claims in British Columbia. He was sought out by the lawyer Thomas Berger in 1963 because his views on "aboriginal title" could be used to support the court cases being pursued on behalf of aboriginals.[53]

Duff's research, however, cannot be considered objective because of his close association with aboriginal groups. As is shown by a book written in his memory, *The World Is as Sharp as a Knife*, his career was as much about advocacy as anthropology. We are told that his death "deprived the native peoples of the Pacific Northwest of one of their true and most actively helpful non-Indian friends" and that he promoted the idea that anthropologists should, if possible, try to help the peoples they study.[54] But the help that anthropologists are supposed to provide is always seen in terms of supporting land claims and self-government; this support is demanded regardless of whether or not these initiatives address the objective needs of native peoples.

It is now expected that anthropologists will advocate on behalf of marginalized groups, not merely study them – a development that has been referred to as "decolonizing the discipline."[55] Such political involvement in aboriginal organizations has disastrous implications for anthropological theory and the social sciences more generally. There is a fine line between assistance and advocacy, and anthropologists who are paid as consultants for aboriginal groups have obliterated this marker. Unlike Teit, who claimed to have been unable to avoid his involvement in aboriginal politics, many anthropologists today eagerly offer their services to aboriginal organizations who pay for "research" that will be used to support their legal demands. This puts anthropologists in a serious conflict of interest, not unlike the scientists for tobacco companies who receive funds to deny the health hazards of tobacco.

Some anthropologists have even admitted to omitting certain details to buttress these legal demands. Noel Dyck, an associate professor of anthropology at Simon Fraser University, acknowledges in his article "Telling It Like It Is: Some Dilemmas of Fourth World Ethnography and Advocacy" that most anthropologists do not speak of the serious problems existing in aboriginal communities. He points out that "appalling and, arguably, worsening social conditions" as well as the "misuse of band funds and other resources" are common problems that go unmentioned in anthropological accounts of native life. These circumstances have evidently prompted Dyck and his colleagues to engage in a great deal of soul searching, because "in not exploring or writing about matters we know to be important ... anthropologists give short shrift to awkward but pressing social and political problems at the reserve or settlement level. This is a situation that most intellectuals would, in principle, be unwilling to tolerate in any other context. Why, then, is it accepted in this one?"[56]

In an attempt to answer this question, Dyck argues that "moral and ethical constraints" are at the roots of the discipline's failings, since anthropologists are reluctant to compromise the political agenda of those whom they study. There is an underlying expectation that "anthropologists should identify personally with the people they study and that they ought to protect their 'subjects' interests." And because anthropologists are "cognizant of the vulnerability of the political gains registered by Native peoples in Canada during the past two decades," they avoid discussing matters that would reduce public support for the demands that aboriginal groups are making.

Dyck's concern is that self-censorship is preventing anthropologists from offering a "sympathetic" reading of these problems, thus leaving the discussion to "those with less tender sensibilities" – presumably, the public. He is also troubled about the integrity of a discipline that chooses to censor certain facts for political reasons. His view is that "however meritorious or convenient the motives which inspire anthropological silence on these issues, we run the risk of producing diminished, analytically atrophied, and thus misleading ethnography and advocacy which in the end will be of little use to Native communities, the Canadian public, or the discipline."[57]

But how can the goal of advocacy be reconciled with social science? Doesn't advocacy require the exact opposite – constructing arguments that support a particular viewpoint rather than objectively analyzing and discarding ideas that are inconsistent with the evidence? The fact that anthropologists like Dyck have systematically neglected discussion of certain features of aboriginal politics underlines this contradiction. Their overriding concern with supporting land claims and self-government means that evidence that would challenge these initiatives is suppressed.

Dyck does not ask or explain why anthropologists have come to see themselves as advocates rather than scientists. While this disciplinary development is related to the postmodern rejection of science that is discussed in the next chapter, it is also rooted in the increasingly legal character of the solutions being proposed for aboriginal peoples. As we explained earlier, advocacy is generally associated with the legal profession because lawyers are expected to select evidence that best supports the case of their client. In legal processes all pieces of evidence are deemed to be "equally contingent," and lawyers on each side have "every incentive to overstate the weakness of the other's case." This is very different from the scientific enterprise, where "facts are established by incremental adjustments and carefully bounded negotiations among communities who share a commitment to closure" because of their common interest in determining an accurate understanding of the world.[58]

This difference between legal and scientific processes becomes very problematic for anthropology when academic disagreements within the discipline are decided in the courtroom. Anthropologist James Clifton described how he experienced this problem personally during his stint as an "expert witness" on behalf of a number of American aboriginal groups:

> In these trials by history (i.e., law office history), watching the highly skilled, forceful attorneys serving the Indian cause at work was a thoroughly eye-opening experience. From them I learned much about the selective use and suppression of historical and anthropological evidence, systematic distortion of facts in support of a preconceived "theory of the case," the dexterous manipulation of judicial and public sentiments, perfectly astounding hyperbole, and the most outrageous fabrications. Watching some "experts" approach the witness stand with hats in hand, and others demur when caustically coached about how and what they should testify to, balking myself when pressed to distort or suppress interpretations and sources, I concluded that in Indian treaty rights cases the standards of evidence and logic are not what they are elsewhere, especially so in scholarly work ... the paramount aim, at last I had explained to me by an unusually impetuous counsel, was not veracity but to win at all costs. These particular attorneys were interested in neither truth nor social consequences, except those of obtaining for their clients the largest short-term benefits attainable – money and power.[59]

Lawyers working for aboriginal organizations, therefore, use academic work only if it supports their demands. At the same time, government attempts to pacify aboriginal groups inhibit Crown lawyers from presenting scientific evidence in opposition. This means that although at any given time a number of different theories may be circulating about aboriginal peoples' position in modern society, the increasing amount of funding being made available for aboriginal rights claims seriously limits the kind of research deemed to be acceptable. And with so much money at stake, aboriginal peoples themselves become intellectually corrupted, refusing to cooperate with any researcher who attempts to "tell it like it is" if that version undermines their own interest.[60]

An increasing preoccupation with the legal gains being made by aboriginal groups has also led to the use of methodologies that result in distorted or subjectively interpreted data. The most flagrant of these is the use of "oral histories" in documenting the features of aboriginal cultures in the past. Oral histories must be regarded with extreme scepticism, not only because memory is often faulty but also because, as McGill anthropologist Bruce Trigger has pointed out, there is a "tendency for lore to be refashioned as circumstances change."[61] The archaeologist Mark Whittow has noted that locals visiting a twelfth century archaeological site in Jordan had "vivid and contradictory accounts of their father or grandfather living in the house the team was excavating," even though the site had not been occupied for hundreds of years. He goes on to point out that "anthropologists have demonstrated how fluid and adaptable oral history can be" and that "the oral history of a tribe was primarily concerned to explain the present" and "would adapt and shape its view of the past, creating stories with supporting details to explain and justify present circumstances." According to Whittow, even during continuous settlement of an area, accurate memory lasts no more two generations and "in times of ... social upheaval change is quicker and more profound."[62]

The "evidence" from "oral histories" is even more problematic when economic interests are involved. Oral histories have been known to change when a claim is necessary to obtain access to valuable resources. For example, the "memories" of elders from the Yellowknives Dene First Nation in the Northwest Territories about the "traditional use" of their territory mysteriously altered when diamonds were discovered outside the area that they had claimed. Since aboriginal peoples did not have writing before contact, it becomes easy for aboriginal organizations to change "oral histories" in support of their claims for compensation and privileges. A further complication is that many of the "oral historians" are unilingual native speakers and require a translator who is in a position to freely interpret the message.

In order to access the substantial funds associated with land claims and self-government, oral testimonies masquerading as history have been used to establish that conceptions of ownership and sovereignty, and their associated "institutions," existed before contact with Europeans. One prominent example of this was the land claim of the Gitksan Wet'suwet'en in British Columbia.[63] Since the recognition of "aboriginal title" depended upon establishing that aboriginal peoples had forms of ownership and governance before contact, the testimony of anthropologists became paramount. In this case, the "expertise" of anthropologists working for aboriginal organizations supported claims on behalf of the tribal leadership. These lobbyists, in their association with Aboriginal Industry lawyers, also were attempting to elevate oral histories from the status of hearsay, inadmissible in a court of law, to a form of evidence held on equal footing with written documents. This giant step backward for the Canadian legal system was supported by labelling requirements for concrete historical documentation as "ethnocentric," "colonialist," and "insensitive" to aboriginal cultural traditions.

With the appeal of the Gitksan Wet'suwet'en case, the views of anthropological advocates were to become much more dominant in Canadian aboriginal policy. The original ruling, which denied the aboriginal claim, was eventually reversed in a unanimous decision by the Supreme Court of Canada on 8 December 1997. Justice Antonio Lamer wrote the decision, with his fellow justices on the highest court in the land concurring. He stated that "notwithstanding the challenges created by the use of oral histories as proof of historical facts, the laws of evidence must be adapted in order that this type of evidence can be accommodated and placed on an equal footing with the types of historical evidence that courts are familiar with, which largely consists of historical documents."

"Placing" these "histories" on "equal footing" with other types of evidence, however, means not subjecting them to the same tests used in evaluating other forms of evidence.[64] As Alexander von Gernet, an anthropologist who has analyzed the use of oral histories in court cases, has noted, such a view "will almost certainly be regarded by some not as merely as an effort to level the field or lower the standard, but as an outright abandonment of the rigorous scrutiny that is essential to any fact-finding process. When taken to its logical conclusion this would seem unworkable in conflict resolution and, as others have noted, it would open the way for a radical reinvention of the law itself."[65] The effects of the Supreme Court's use of this "evidence" will be felt for decades to come. It is already resulting in challenges to the Gitksan Wet'suwet'en decision. Because the memories of elders have no corroborating evidence, they are open to challenge from competing "oral histories." This has already sparked new lawsuits from other aboriginal groups who claim that their historical memories, not those of the Gitksan Wet'suwet'en elders, are the ones that are actually true.[66]

Besides the havoc that anthropological advocacy will bring to the Canadian legal system, it is also undermining any rational basis for current aboriginal policy. As we have seen with Noel Dyck's comments, advocates working for aboriginal organizations avoid discussing the dysfunction and corruption in aboriginal communities so that the public will continue to support existing legal initiatives. More importantly, specious research prevents the fundamental cause of aboriginal problems – the evolutionary gap between aboriginal culture and the modern world – from being understood.

## PARADING THE EMPEROR: THE "ELEVENTH COMMANDMENT"

A highly significant aspect of aboriginal policy is the extent to which open and honest debate is constrained. This circumstance is related to what James Clifton notes is "one of the most stringently observed canons governing the behavior of those who work among Indians" – referred to behind closed doors as the "Eleventh Commandment." This "commandment," according to Clifton, is "Thou Shall Not Say No to an Indian." Anyone who does not abide by its associated "norms and taboos of deferential conduct" is immediately labelled as an enemy of aboriginal peoples. In Canada, "racism," "colonialism," and "insensitivity" are the usual accusations that constrain debate, but Clifton provides a multipage appendix of the verbal sanctions that have been deployed over the years.[67]

The lack of critical analysis inhibits the understanding that the prevailing view of aboriginal peoples is actually racist. This view maintains that because aboriginal peoples' culture is tied to their ancestry or "race" (an idea based on the belief that the native population was put in North America by "the Creator" instead of evolving with other human beings out of an ape-like ancestor in Africa), they must retain all their traditions and remain separated from modern society. This perspective forms the basis of the "two row wampum" approach to aboriginal/non-aboriginal relations, or what Alan Cairns has referred to as "parallelism."[68] The most racially segregationist account of this vision can be found in H. Millar's "Record of the Two Row Wampum Belt," an "oral history" provided approvingly as the opening quotation in an article by the anthropologist Marc G. Stevenson:

The Whiteman said, "... I confirm what you have said ... Now it is understood that we shall never interfere with one another's beliefs or laws for generations to come." The Onkwehonweh replied: "I have a canoe and you have a vessel with sails and this is what we shall do: I will put in my canoe my belief and laws; in your vessel you will put your belief and laws; all of my people in my canoe; your people in your vessel. We shall put these boats in the water and they shall always be parallel. As long as there is Mother Earth, this will be everlasting. The Whiteman said, "What will happen if any of your people may someday want to have one foot in each of the boats we have placed parallel?" The Onkwehonweh replied "If this so happens that my people wish to have their feet in each of the two boats, there will be a high wind and the boats will separate and the person that has his feet in each of the boats shall fall between the boats; and there is not a living soul who will be able to bring him back to the right way given by the Creator, but only one: The Creator Himself."[69]

Due to a generally sympathetic attitude toward the plight of aboriginal peoples, Canadians lean to the romanticization of native culture as a way of righting past wrongs and thus have not challenged these dubious (and racist) assertions. But romanticism does not help the romanticized; it isolates them from rational thought, giving an unrealistic assessment of their abilities and place in the world. As Roger Sandall has pointed out in the Australian context, aboriginal peoples have become "the deluded victims of the extravagances of their admirers."[70] Condescending attitudes have doubly victimized aboriginal people – first by a government that justifies non-intervention, and secondly by consultants and aboriginal leaders who increase their wealth by maintaining the dependency that comes with the retention of aboriginal peoples' undeveloped cultural characteristics.

Aside from keeping aboriginal peoples in a time-warp of isolation and despair, the romanticization of aboriginal culture has harmful consequences for non-natives as well. The creation of a separate legal category for aboriginal peoples under the guise of "preserving their culture" has led to increasing social conflict. Aboriginal peoples, because of their "status," receive privileges and immunities to which others with similar circumstances are not entitled. On the basis of the historical injustice committed by one group's ancestors, economically disadvantaged aboriginals and non-aboriginals have come to view each other as enemies instead of people with common political interests.

What must be understood is that it is not the Aboriginal Industry's interminable quest for compensation but a government strategy for aboriginal cultural development that is currently needed. Aboriginal problems stem from the fact that they are poorly educated and culturally deprived, not because they lack money. Many aboriginal leaders who make hundreds of thousands of dollars each year suffer from the same social dysfunction as those who are impoverished. Even when the most marginalized hit the land claims jackpot (as is the case with oil rich reserves), the problems continue. As occurs with many lottery winners, the money is spent on fancy trucks, gambling, and drugs,[71] not on services that will help aboriginal people to become "self-determining." This circumstance was admitted in a CBC documentary by Tony Merchant, the owner of one of the largest law firms representing aboriginal groups in the residential school dispute.[72]

Now that the cry the "emperor has no clothes" has been sounded, we can examine the developmental gap that the racism accusation taboo is hiding. The historical relationship between aboriginal peoples and Europeans is complicated and has not been understood so far because obfuscation serves the interest of the Aboriginal Industry. The task of this book is to explain the nature of this relationship, so that real solutions, not compensation for continuing marginalization, can be found. As members of the same species with common needs and aspirations, only through eliminating racially based theories of human development can we move toward substantive equality for the whole of humanity. Then the process of allowing aboriginal peoples to become equal participants, rather than justifying their exclusion and cultural deprivation, can begin.

# 2

# Denying the Developmental Gap: Preserving Culture in a Jar

The aboriginal tribes of North America have puzzled European philosophers, missionaries, and adventurers since first contact. Who were they and where did they come from? Were they human beings fundamentally similar to the people encountered in the Old World, or sub-humans with a completely different place in the "natural order" of things? And if they were human beings like any other, why did they behave so differently from Europeans? Why, for example, hadn't they developed cities or institutions like those in the Old World? What prevented them from developing the wheel, manufacturing iron implements, having writing systems, or accumulating material wealth?

Because contact occurred when Christian beliefs were taken as fact, the answers to these questions were inevitably sought within the realm of divine stratagem. Some thought that North America represented an Eden where people lived as children of nature, free from the corrupting vices of civilization. Admirers of European society and its institutions, on the other hand, saw aboriginal peoples as godless, lacking the disciplines, sociability, and beliefs necessary for achieving eternal salvation. Both interpretations were usually attributed to the racial makeup of aboriginal peoples, so North American Indians as a race were believed to be either naturally noble or naturally inferior.

One of the first promoters of the "noble savage" was the French aristocrat Louis Armand Baron de Lahontan, a marine lieutenant who documented his travels to North America in the seventeenth century, becoming famous as one of the first authorities on aboriginal tribes residing there.[1] The main piece of evidence that Lahontan used to support his noble savage view was a collection of personal conversations with a Huron chief referred to as "Adario." In hundreds of pages of dialogue, Lahontan and Adario supposedly compare the manners and customs of Europeans with those of "the savages." During these conversations, Adario claims to be an expert on the subject because of his travels to France, New York, and Quebec, where he evidently "Study'd the Customs and Doctrines of the English and French."[2] He also exhibits a unique but contemplative perception of European culture by comparing the freedom of his own relationship with the Great Spirit to European "slavery and dependence." Adario is shown to be perplexed by Lahontan's refusal to turn Huron and be free from the hierarchical relationships and drudgery he has observed in French society.[3]

A number of sentiments like these were taken to be a true reflection of the "savage mind," influencing European philosophers including Montesquieu, Voltaire, Swift, and most notably, Jean-Jacques Rousseau.[4] In response to the increasing alienation, misery, urban filth, and poverty brought about by the Industrial Revolution and capitalist exploitation, some romantic reactionaries have looked upon the past as a simpler, happier, and more natural existence. Instead of conceptualizing technological advancements and increasing productivity as being a defining characteristic of our species' evolution, they viewed them as a kind of hubris, separating humans from their innate innocence and causing their "fall from grace." These romantic ideas are everywhere in current accounts of aboriginal culture, where tribal societies are interpreted as having instinctively socialistic philosophies, egalitarian political structures, and a widespread ecological consciousness. Robert McGhee, a curator with the Canadian Museum of Civilization, notes that such romantic primitivism is referred to in French as *nostalgie de la boue* (literally "wistfulness for mud").[5]

What Rousseau and those who followed in his philosophical footsteps did not know, however, was that the Baron de Lahontan was a "travel liar."[6] Far from being a scientist attempting to record his observations of the New World objectively in contribution to the progression of historical knowledge, he often exaggerated or completely fabricated people, events, and discoveries to make his books more marketable to European audiences.[7] The most significant of these fabrications was the creation of "Adario." There is no evidence that any Huron chief espoused the ideas Lahontan attributed to his Adario or that such a person had travelled and studied the "doctrines and customs" of the English and French.[8]

The lack of historical evidence to support the existence of an educated and well-travelled Huron chief in this period has led historians to conclude that Adario was a literary device used by Lahontan to give legitimacy to his critique of European civilization.[9] Since opposition to authority at this time could have resulted in charges of treason or blasphemy, attributing his own criticisms of Catholic beliefs and the French monarchy to a tribal chieftain was an ingenious way for Lahontan to protect himself from reprisals. Using an aboriginal person as a foil also made his own ideas far more interesting to his audiences.

Although Lahontan is long dead and buried, the ghost of Adario illuminates many accounts of New World history. The device is so common that James Clifton notes that it is now known as the "Adario motif," characterized by "invented speeches or dialogues presented as if they are verbatim records of words issuing from the mouths of real, historical figures," with usually "a Wise Old Indian Uttering Marvelous Lessons for the Whiteman's Edification."[10] Chief Seattle, Deganawidah, Hiawatha, Jingosaseh, and Don Juan are just a few of these resurrected Adarios. And while they may be either actual persons or total fabrications, the words attributed to them are fictional.

The Adario motif's deep roots in European culture have made it one of the most popular fabrications of the Aboriginal Industry. The motif gives credence to the conception of history that aboriginal problems were caused by the destruction of viable and "sovereign nations" during European conquest, and therefore restoring aboriginal traditions through land claims and self-government must be the answer to native dependency and social dysfunction. This claim requires an extensive revision of history because the small bands of hunters and gatherers and horticulturalists that existed at the time of contact were much less economically and politically developed than European nation states making the transition to industrial capitalism. The various Adarios that have been created are necessary to keep this developmental gap invisible.

How can we get beyond these distortions and develop a more accurate understanding of the history of aboriginal peoples and the roots of their current problems? Essentially, such an endeavour involves evaluating both the credibility of sources and the extent to which information about the past is consistent with current knowledge. The former entails asking questions about the motivations of the people who provide evidence of what the past was like – that is, have they been shown to have a bias or to be prone to sloppy research? The latter involves an analysis of how historical information has been gathered and the various conclusions reached. Does the research rule out the possibility that certain traits attributed to pre-contact aboriginal societies were actually the result of post-contact European influences? Do the inferences made follow logically from the data obtained, or are they based on bootless speculation? And finally, are the findings consistent with the cumulative body of archaeological evidence and historical records?

Lahontan's claims about Adario, for example, do not meet any of these criteria. Lahontan cannot be considered a reliable source, and his assertions are not consistent with our knowledge about aboriginal peoples during this period. Nowhere do other seventeenth century sources mention a Huron chief who studied the "doctrine and customs" of the English and French, or any other aboriginal person who engaged in these pursuits. Adario, like all other aboriginal peoples of the period, was illiterate (he proudly declares this to Lahontan in one of their conversations). This would have precluded him from being engaged in the scholarship that Lahontan recounts, since writing is essential for undertaking a detailed comparative analysis. So, while it is possible that Lahontan befriended a Huron chief, our current understanding of the relationship between literacy and scholarship indicates that Adario and his "natural philosophy" were fabrications.

Although Lahontan's Adario is generally recognized as bogus, other assertions concerning aboriginal peoples, such as the "Great Law of Peace," the Iroquois Confederacy's influence on the American Constitution, a native "conservation ethic," ethnobotany, and the existence of pre-contact wheeled toys and the zero in what is now Latin America are often uncritically accepted. This is because attempts to understand history, unlike the methods used in the physical sciences, lack the rigour required to make claims with certainty. Historians must rely on observations that are hundreds of years old, which could easily be influenced by irrational beliefs or hidden political agendas. Often particular interests – religious, economic, or militaristic – distorted the recording of events for the purpose of legitimating the usurpation of power. Before written records, there is even more uncertainty, as archaeologists try to reconstruct the past from the sporadic artifacts that have been discovered in the garbage dumps and graves of aboriginal peoples. Such uncertainties make it easy for politically distorted views to gain acceptance.

## THE THEORY OF UNEVEN AND COMBINED DEVELOPMENT

It is commonly understood that humanity originated about one million years ago, in what is now Africa, and very slowly began the process of spreading over the globe. It is also recognized that despite our common origins, human beings have lived in vastly different societies across space and time. In attempting to explain why our species has produced such different peoples from a singular genetic ancestry, the philosophical extremes range from the view of the elevated individual determining human life and destiny (as represented by Thomas Carlyle's statement that "the history of the world is but the biography of great men") to the notion of fatalism wherein the individual has no power to control or shape the course of events. Historical and material evidence rejects both extremes; we can observe that there is interplay between subjective and objective elements, with the broad forces of change taking priority over individual effort.

Looking at the archaeological record in its entirety, it becomes obvious that human history is the result of the contribution of all of our ancestors' accomplishments. Our forebears gradually changed the elements of nature to satisfy their needs over a long period of time.[11] This occurred in the past, as it does today, by their adoption of new techniques and forms of social interaction that were favourable to survival – the maximization of a group's subsistence, reproduction, and protection. The development of humanity, therefore, is not arbitrary; it has been determined by the success of various societies in surviving and reproducing themselves from humankind's beginnings to the present.

Lewis Henry Morgan, as the principal founder of anthropology as a science, attempted to develop an objective understanding of these historical factors. He developed a great empathy for the American Indian people, and his study of the social organization of the Iroquois led to the formation of his theory of cultural evolution. In this theory, Morgan made two general hypotheses about the nature of humanity's evolution. First, he maintained that historical progress was rooted in the "enlargement of the sources of subsistence" through increases in efficiency of productive technology.[12] Secondly, he argued that the development of economic efficiency was correlated to the increasing complexity of social and political organization.[13]

Although all aspects of increasing social complexity are related to Morgan's idea of the "enlargement of the sources of subsistence," he also elucidated another important principle in human development: the idea of historical sequence. In Morgan's view, humanity's progress was cumulative and continuous, only moving forward when the necessary prerequisites were in place.[14] This meant that the development of various tools, techniques, ideas, and practices occurred in a chain, with each having a less developed ancestor. If the material requirements for development were lacking, human progress would be arrested until environmental conditions provided the necessary components for further cultural evolution.

From this understanding of historical sequence and increasing productivity Morgan was able to identify where various groups were placed in the developmental trajectory of humankind. He used "primitive" and "advanced" to describe the various cultural features of different social groups, depending upon where these entities fitted in the evolutionary chain. The first cultural features that are documented in the archaeological record are considered to be the most primitive, since they are first in the sequence. This means that stone tools are considered more primitive than bronze tools, which, in turn, are more primitive than those made of iron. At the same time, these tools can also be characterized as primitive or advanced on the basis of the extent to which they "enlarge the sources of subsistence." Bronze enabled more effective axes and knives to be developed in comparison to their stone counterparts, making it possible for certain groups to enhance their survival at the expense of others. This was also the case with the discovery of iron and all the other technological inventions throughout human history.

The same logic can be applied to various social groupings. Those groupings that exhibit characteristics that are closest to those of our earliest ancestors are classified as "primitive." Others that have evolved out of later forms are classified as "advanced." Although these adjectives are often rejected today because it is implied that they are insulting to the groups to which they are applied,[15] using this terminology does not require a value judgment. Recognition of evolutionary principles is not a statement about whether or not evolution is "good" or "bad"; it is merely to make a statement of fact. We do not argue that reptiles are "superior" to amphibians because they appeared later in evolutionary development.[16] Thus to refer to the hunting and gathering mode of production as primitive is not to denigrate the people who practise it. It is merely to recognize that, although the practice continues to exist today, it resembles a mode of production of our ancestors more than that of agricultural or industrial societies (which evolved out of hunting and gathering societies).

On the basis of the evolutionary principles described above, Morgan divided humanity into three distinct epochs. The earliest stage in this cultural evolution was characterized by a hunting and foraging economy with stone tools, the use of fish and fire, and the development of the bow and arrow. This was the stage all of our ancestors had to pass through before learning to domesticate plants and animals. Although Morgan determined the bow and arrow to be the most significant technological achievement of this period, since it enabled humans to dramatically increase their successes in both hunting and combat, he also identified a number of other important inventions that occurred simultaneously – wooden (but not pottery) vessels, utensils, ground ovens, canoes, and baskets – that resulted in an important increase in control over nature and in the amount and variety of food obtained.[17] The productive capacity of social groups at the time was comparatively low, however, and populations were small and there was almost no social differentiation or specialization. Because the production of very small surpluses meant that wealth could not be accumulated by a segment of the group, these societies are described by anthropologist Morton Fried as "egalitarian."[18] This period, because progress occurred at a very slow rate, was the longest in human history, lasting for hundreds of thousands of years.

To mark the end of this stage and the transition to the next, Morgan identified the invention of pottery since it "presupposes village life, and considerable progress in the simple arts."[19] As Brian M. Fagan noted more recently, "the invention of pottery seems to coincide with the beginnings of more permanent settlement," since "clay receptacles have the advantage of being both durable and long-lived."[20] Consequently, pottery appears with other cultural features associated with settlement – the domestication of animals and/or the cultivation of plants by irrigation, the use of stone or brick architecture, and the discovery of iron. These developments exponentially increased the productivity, military prowess, and size of societies and made the development of specialists like priests, craftsmen, chiefs, and military leaders both possible and necessary. The use of stone and adobe bricks also created the structures and fortifications necessary for the development of permanent urban settlements, which were the precursors of the cities of the third stage of cultural evolution, which Morgan called "civilization."

The most significant indicator of civilization was the development of the phonetic alphabet and written records.[21] The existence of a phonetic alphabet is an indication of economic, political, and social advancement, since writing greatly facilitates the exchange of information necessary to maintain a complex society. Before the phonetic alphabet was developed, record-keeping was imprecise and difficult for large numbers of people to learn. The phonetic alphabet also is closely connected to the development of laws, since precise records are needed to specify enforceable dictates. Laws, and the existence of a state apparatus to enforce them, are the essential characteristics of civilization, for in their absence no overarching principles could be accepted so that rival families, clans, and tribes could live under one government.

This insight is related to Morgan's distinction between "social" and "political" forms of organization.[22] "Social" forms of organization (*societas*) are those groups that distribute resources according to "personal" relationships. Such societies are small and held together through ties of blood and marriage, which extend outwards in a web to include all members of the community. As productive capacity increases, however, and groups become larger and more functionally specialized and structurally differentiated, it becomes impossible to know everyone's personal relationship to each other, and the bonds of kinship are no longer sufficient to ensure the orderly functioning of the society. At the same time, increasing productivity escalates social inequalities, to the point that property relations replace the reciprocal network that existed in kinship-based groups. This necessitates the formation of a "political" society (*civitas*), where a coercive state enforces the right to own private property within its geographical boundaries. The result is the transition from members of a tribe or clan organized by customary relations to subjects or citizens who are required to obey the laws and be subject to the judgments of an impersonal entity.

The seeds were sown for this transition to civilization, or "social" forms of organization to "political" ones, according to Morgan, with the discovery of iron. Iron made the development of advanced weaponry and agricultural techniques possible, since it was harder and more abundant than previously discovered metals.[23] One of the most dramatic results was the use of draught animals and iron-tipped ploughs in field agriculture, which greatly increased the productivity, density, and complexity of societies. The great increase in production brought on by the Iron Age required laws to organize the ensuing larger social groups.

These examples show that cultural evolution is a profoundly practical process. Groups do not evolve because one person suddenly has an idea about how to improve technological efficiency or increase cooperation with others. Rather, they gradually progress through trial and error, where cultural features that enhance survival are retained, while less efficient forms of technology and social organization are discarded. This explains why the cultural evolutionary process is so slow at the beginning, and speeds up exponentially. It also explains why culture in general progresses in a particular sequence. Hunting and gathering must precede horticulture because the domestication of plants and animals is gradually learned as the former is practised. Geographical forms of political organization cannot precede kinship-based systems, since kinship relations emerge out of earlier biological ones; it is only when a certain population size is reached that kinship becomes unworkable as an organizing principle, and geographic boundaries are required. This process also occurs in the case of language, where speech is needed before writing can emerge, and pictographs must precede more advanced writing forms such as the alphabet.

But this sequence of cultural evolution *in general* does not mean that all cultures have to go through all components of the sequence.[24] What Morgan argued was that culture *as a whole* had to go through these stages; individual societies, on the other hand, could assimilate stages if they were influenced by a more advanced culture. It is also important to point out that Morgan realized that exceptions could exist within each ethnological period. Certain environmental conditions would enable certain groups to be more productive than this general schema would indicate. The aboriginal groups of the Pacific Northwest provide just such an example. Although the aboriginal groups living in this area were hunters and gatherers, the abundance of fish and shellfish made the existence of denser and more complex forms of social organization possible. This does not refute the main tenet of Morgan's theory – the linkage between technology and social complexity; it only demonstrates that exceptional environmental circumstances can offset technological deficits.

The theory of cultural evolution is also significant because it has influenced the perspective known as historical materialism. Morgan's ideas, because of their focus on productive processes, were used extensively by Karl Marx and Frederick Engels in their attempts to understand the economic, political, and social processes that led to the development of capitalism. Marx's analysis of Morgan's *Ancient Society* became the basis of Engels's classic work in anthropology, *The Origin of the Family, Private Property and the State*. Morgan's ideas about cultural evolution were then synthesized and linked to more recent economic and political developments by Leon Trotsky, one of the central figures in the Russian Revolution. In what he called "the law of uneven and combined development," Trotsky stressed the role of different rates of independent cultural development (unevenness) and cultural diffusion (combination) in the progression of humanity. The Marxist scholar George Novack explains that Trotsky's framework is based on the idea that "the mainspring of human progress is man's command of the forces of production," but that these forces progress at different rates. These uneven social formations then combine and "provide the basis for the emergence of something of a new and higher quality."[25] Backward elements are propelled forward, surpassing those that are more advanced, resulting in more cooperative forms of labour and social organization.

One example of the process of uneven and combined development is in the area of creative culture. Early expression of the artistic impulse is found in decorative treatments of functional objects and as a solicitation of spiritual favour. This impulse was accelerated by the development of technology, which allowed for originality and experimentation, presenting new and exciting vistas for artistic expression. The unevenness of the development of various peoples, due to their circumstances, meant that their eventual contact allowed for mutual influence in their artistic forms. It is a long and rich journey from the use of the drum as a telecommunication device to complex jazz and other forms of contemporary music. The carvings of neolithic times became the sculpture of tribal peoples today only upon the combination with cultures that had evolved to the stage of creating art for its own sake. The Arctic administrator James Houston, for example, was the initiator of the current market for "Inuit art." Houston, upon seeing carvings of small amulets, lamps, and other implements, encouraged the carving of large-scale representative works in the character of European sculpture.[26]

Today, the technology of modern sculpture, steel chisels, electric grinders, and polishers, is used extensively by native carvers, and were it not for the insistence on racial authenticity in "Inuit art" by dealers, galleries, and the territorial government tourism departments, Inuit artists would be able to experiment and work in a wider variety of materials and genres. The territorial governments even "authenticate" artworks with a tag ensuring that a "real Eskimo" produced them. A major portion of aboriginal art is produced under governmental control, warehoused, and marketed to dealers and galleries in Canada and internationally. Much of the output is aimed at the tourism market and is available in airports and department stores. Native carvings and paintings are considered an industry, and consistency of form is important to assure buyers that the product is genuine. With few exceptions, native artists are identified with their community and the style of carving associated with it.

The focus on racial authenticity rather than socially determined artistic quality as the central feature reduces much native art to repetitious carvings of seals and Inuit hunters poised over breathing holes. Undoubtedly many fine works exist in spite of the circumstances, but they too must subscribe to the strictures of authenticity, one of which is that the medium be stone from the area where the artist lives. An Inuvialuit friend, Angus Cockney, experienced reactionary cultural imposition when his attempts to broaden his style met with the response from dealers that his work was "not native enough." Such strictures on native artists preclude individual creative development and participation in the universal art world.

While teaching at Arctic College in Yellowknife, one of us (Howard) initiated discussions on opening an art school that might bring guest instructors from other parts of Canada and other countries. Meetings with the associated government departments made it clear that native art was simply viewed as part of the tourism industry, and any changes in style were opposed. The response to any suggestions that the merchandising of repetitious carvings in craft shops and airports trivialized the medium was that these outlets were "pretty lucrative." This reflects the insistence on characterizing native sculptors as "carvers" instead of artists.

An understanding of the process of uneven and combined development indicates that the problems facing aboriginal peoples today are due to an unprecedented circumstance. The cultural gap between two peoples coming into contact has never been wider, and the developmental process that resulted has taken place over a relatively short space of time. In spite of the relativist claims often made about the "sophistication" and "complexity" of pre-contact aboriginal cultures, it cannot be denied that the bow and arrow had to contend with the iron sword, the musket, and the cannon. The plough and draught animals far out-performed the hoe and the digging stick; transportation and much else was transformed by the introduction of the wheel. It must be clarified here that the huge developmental gap is not associated with any genetic difference. The differences between two different routes of social evolution – the invaders from Western Europe and the inhabitants of the Americas – were based on the environmental factors involved in securing the necessities of life.

Rather than integrating the social formations enabled by their developed technology, the Europeans embarked upon a course of appropriation contingent on regarding aboriginal people as sub-human. Native people in North America were generally ignored beyond their relationship as suppliers of furs to be sold in Europe. Although many aboriginals were able to overcome these obstacles and have subsequently integrated with modern culture, the short time period over which contact occurred has meant that the residue of tribal, kinship-based culture persists. This has resulted in the continuation of extreme dislocation for many aboriginal peoples, as well as frustration within modern society about the supposed "inability" of native people to participate in industrial social formations. Consequently, a number of half-hearted schemes have been devised that never seriously and sensitively provided aboriginal peoples with the intensive programs and services that were required for them to become full citizens and economic participants in the modern world. Today this schism between aboriginal people and other Canadians is encouraged by the Aboriginal Industry, which proposes initiatives that retain neolithic cultural features.

The more recent response to this historical injustice has been to deny the theory of cultural evolution itself. Over the last century Morgan's theory has been gradually usurped by the postmodern theory of cultural relativism, which now is the main framework for attempting to explain the problems currently facing aboriginal peoples. Its most significant proponent was Franz Boas (1858–1942), a German anthropologist who extensively studied the Indians of North America and the Inuit. In contrast to Morgan's approach, which maintained that culture, like life more generally, evolves from the simple to the complex, and that certain cultures are at a more advanced stage of development than others (determined by their ability to control nature to satisfy their needs), Boas argued that all cultures surviving today have "evolved equally" but in "different ways," and therefore they must be "judged on their own terms."[27] He characterized observing the existence of different evolutionary stages as "ethnocentric" – the interpretation or evaluation of other cultures in terms of the standards of one's own (which cultural relativists assume to be "arbitrary").

But his accusations of "ethnocentrism" were not based on a careful analysis of cultural evolution;[28] instead, they largely were a response to the concern that the cultural evolutionist framework could be used to justify racist policies. Boas's book *Anthropology and Modern Life*, for example, was written with an agenda, specifically to refute the racist assumptions behind American immigration policies.[29] Perceiving different cultures as being "equally evolved" became a way to challenge proposals that different cultures/races should be cleared from the land to make way for "genetically superior" conquerors. As a result, it became politically incorrect to describe cultures in developmental terms, since it was assumed that this implied that a particular group did not have the *capacity* to develop.

These arguments rely on a profound misunderstanding of cultural evolution and are a misguided attempt to oppose racism – the wrong method for the right reason. Morgan's theory of cultural evolution does *not* envision variances in cultural development as being caused by innate (i.e., racial) differences. Instead, as he argued, "human necessities in similar conditions have been substantially the same" and rational capacity has been "uniform in virtue of the specific identity of the brain of all the races of mankind."[30] In opposition to racist theories, Morgan maintained that environmental factors such as the differential distribution of domesticable plant and animal species were the important determinants of the uneven rates of cultural evolution in the Old and New Worlds.[31]

The rejection of cultural evolution denies the reasonable observation that environment influences social groupings. This especially has been the case in two fields that are instrumental in generating theories about human development: archaeology and anthropology. In archaeology, the rejection of cultural evolution is most clearly manifested in studies of the New World, where there is a tendency to exaggerate the development of the ancient Aztecs, Mayas, and Incas.[32] Population counts climb higher with each telling,[33] and it is asserted that "civilizations" existed in the Amazon rainforest before contact.[34] Massive empires are now claimed to have existed despite the absence of draught animals and the necessary technology to sustain large, integrated populations (e.g., the wheel, iron, the plough, alphabetic writing). A number of inventions have been "discovered" recently, in an attempt to give credence to this exaggeration of development. Included are claims about the existence of pre-contact wheels (attached to toys, not as transport), phonetic hieroglyphs, the zero, and a calendar and road system similar to those of ancient Rome. All these "findings," however, either rely on a failure to rule out post-contact influences, or are made possible by huge interpretive leaps unsupported by convincing evidence.

Two of the best examples of such questionable claims can be seen in the uncritical acceptance of the existence of wheeled toys and the invention of the zero in the Americas before contact. Unlike in the Old World, where the wheel is considered to have gradually evolved through the increase in understanding made possible through the practical use of moving large objects with sledges and rollers,[35] it is claimed that the Olmec invented wheels and axles abstractly without such practical experimentation. They did not possess carts, water wheels, potter's wheels, or millstone wheels, and so the invention of wheeled toys, if it were to have occurred, would have been purely for amusement, not to obtain a survival advantage over other groups through the saving of labour time. This is a highly unlikely scenario, but the fame and interest generated from "discovering" the existence of wheels in the pre-contact Americas appears to have prevented a rigorous evaluation of the archaeological evidence.[36]

More implausible than the existence of wheeled toys is the claim that the Maya had invented the zero before contact. Although the Maya had a number system that was comparatively primitive to those existing in Ancient Greece, Egypt, and India, with dots for the numbers one through four and a bar for the number five (and two bars for ten and three bars for fifteen), it is claimed that this culture had developed a concept that was invented to aid advanced mathematical calculations. It is even asserted that the Maya had an "astonishing array of zero-symbols," including faces, full figures, half a flower, snail shells and "at times nothing we can name."[37] But how is it known that these symbols represent zero, and not some other number or a non-numeric concept entirely? To accept that these various symbols actually represent the idea of zero, or the existence of place value notation, we have to rely on the interpretation of various Mayanists whose careers are enhanced by making such a discovery. Even more disturbing, Mayanists often express hostility toward those who question their assumptions, and evaluations of glyph decipherment are sought not from an independent peer review process but an insular group of self-proclaimed experts.[38] There is no evidence that these glyphs represent the concept of zero outside of these Mayanist interpretations.

Similar dubious claims also have been enthusiastically welcomed in the field of anthropology. As well as the connection between many anthropologists and the Aboriginal Industry, this reflects the tendency of anthropologists to be concerned about "cultural loss" within the groups that they study. As Margaret Mead pointed out over forty years ago, there is a "general occupational preference of anthropologists for the preservation of the past when it comes to the culture of native peoples, but a preference which is transmuted, by all too familiar psychological mechanisms, into an ardent espousal of any kind of change – called 'progress' – in other social areas with which they are not themselves concerned. Thus, measures which will stabilize an aboriginal people in a subsistence economy and therefore prevent them from any participation in world culture can be defended as 'preserving their culture.'"[39]

Mead attributed this tendency to researchers observing the dislocation that occurred when primitive cultures came into contact with advanced civilizations. Witnessing the social disintegration that inevitably followed, Mead says, led these anthropologists to "conjure up past functional felicities" and propose a return to the "optimally functioning system" that they hypothesized existed in the past.[40]

What Mead did not realize was how such an attitude was related to the discipline of anthropology as a whole. Anthropologists are concerned with studying the whole history of human cultural development, and so the integration of a tribe under observation into a more advanced society would mean the destruction of a particular piece of "data" for their research. The loss of primitive cultural characteristics ("cultural loss") means the disappearance of evidence, causing many anthropologists to react to cultural development in the same way as an archaeologist would if ancient artifacts were destroyed. Calls to "celebrate cultural diversity," therefore, act to perpetually preserve aboriginal peoples in a jar so they can continue to provide a living laboratory for anthropological research.

These anthropological considerations are also supported by a more general celebration of "diversity" in society as a whole. Any trip to the local library or bookstore will provide ample evidence that "different world views" and tolerance of diverse "political identities" are now the rallying cries of the global intelligentsia. Throughout the industrialized world, governments are rethinking their support of common rights and obligations within their territorial borders. Instead, the concept of "differentiated citizenship," in which certain groups obtain various legal privileges in relation to others, is gaining popularity. Furthermore, disciplines in the social sciences have now spawned separate departments catering to different genders, ethnicities, and sexual orientations. This is a rejection of the assumptions of the Enlightenment; there is no longer the promotion of the idea of progress – economic, political, and intellectual developments from which everyone can benefit. The idea that there can be common political and intellectual goals is sneered at.

## POSTMODERNISM MAKES THE CONTRADICTIONS
## GO AWAY

Many people confess that, while they are familiar with the term "post-modernism," they do not have a clear understanding of what it means. This is not surprising, since postmodernism embraces eclecticism; it proudly advocates "radical scepticism" or anti-authoritarianism, claiming to reject all "grand theories" or "metanarratives" attempting to explain the world. All assumptions upon which the Enlightenment was based are to be rejected not only because they are supposedly ethnocentric but on the basis that they are oppressive. Postmodernism argues for "celebrating differences" in opposition to focusing on common principles, claiming that they suppress human freedom and creativity.[41]

Although postmodernism has invaded all aspects of contemporary life, the most significant influences pertain to the realms of science and politics. Scientific methods are portrayed as being "socially constructed" and just "one way" among many to perceive the world. The debunking of science is then used to support postmodernism's main project – undermining those political struggles that are striving for universal human emancipation. This has had significant implications for politics on the left, since class is no longer held as the fundamental category for determining different interests in society. Instead, class is proposed as just one category among many other sites of "difference." The result has been the assumption that encouraging various "subjective realities" will result in the political liberation of a plethora of oppressed groups: women, "the poor," the mentally handicapped, homosexuals, the transgendered and the transsexual, ethnic, religious, and racial minorities, and indigenous populations. Opposition to the increasing fragmentation inevitably created leads to accusations that opponents of postmodernism must be secretly harbouring sexist, racist, and/or homophobic attitudes.

The dual character of postmodernism – a rejection of science alongside support for political diversity – has seriously damaged the social sciences.[42] Scientific attempts to retain the objectivity of research are now disparaged on the basis that they are oppressive – the acts of Eurocentric, white, heterosexual males attempting to maintain their powerful position in the world. As a result, social science has been transformed from an academic enterprise that attempted to achieve a greater understanding of society to a collection of political advocates who interpret research in a manner that gives credence to the goals of particular groups. Facts are refuted in order to support a predetermined argument. Scientific objectivity is eschewed because it confronts the unscientific nature of "alternate world views." The patronizing encouragement of irrationality is referred to as giving the marginalized "a voice," the professed first step to aboriginal freedom and achievement.

While a number of postmodernism's sophistic tactics have been identified in the literature,[43] and are referred to throughout this book, the most common is what we have referred to elsewhere as "pomospeak."[44] Our identification of this common postmodern move, and its political implications, is borrowed from George Orwell's perceptive novel *Nineteen Eighty-Four*. In that novel the state of Oceania (analogous to the Stalinist bureaucratic dictatorship in the Soviet Union) invents a language to which Orwell gives the name "Newspeak." Examples of Newspeak appear first in the official slogans of the "Ministry of Truth":

*war is peace*
*freedom is slavery*
*ignorance is strength.*

These slogans illustrate the function of pomospeak: denominating a concept by its opposite for the purpose of legitimating an invalid argument or denouncing a valid one. Hearing these slogans, the people of Oceania are encouraged to support war and ignorance, and are opposed to freedom, since the "Ministry of Truth" defines these concepts in contradictory terms. In this way logical argumentation is destroyed because people are encouraged to confuse a concept with something that it is not.

Pomospeak is everywhere in the literature justifying current aboriginal policies. Postmodern academics persist in applying words like "logic," "knowledge," "justice," and "equality" to circumstances where there is actually irrationality, ignorance, discrimination, and privilege. To deal with the problem of identifying a concept as its opposite, readers are told that a spiritual belief is a "different kind of knowledge," or that flawed reasoning is simply "another kind of logic." Various oxymoronic phrases are used with the same effect: descriptions such as "tribal nationalism," "customary law," "oral literature," and "spiritual science" are offered to prevent audiences from understanding how words used as adjectives may actually contradict what they are describing.

The most prominent kind of pomospeak occurs in the context of the confusion of culture and race – one of the main barriers to understanding cultural evolution and the roots of aboriginal deprivation. Race and culture are often used interchangeably, even though the two concepts refer to completely different aspects of human existence. On the one hand for the purpose of obscuring the problems of advocating rights on the basis of ancestry (race), postmodernism insists that aboriginal groups are defining themselves culturally. On the other hand, it regards aboriginal culture as inseparable from race, so that critics of current aboriginal policies can be accused of racism. Obsolete aboriginal traditions and spiritual beliefs are defended, for example, by the postmodern claim that they are "inherent" (i.e., genetically determined). Arguments that these cultural values and practices need to be transformed if aboriginal peoples are to participate in modern nation states are immediately met with more pomospeak – the charge of "cultural genocide." This terminology has been recently transformed into the oxymoron "cultural racism."[45]

The accusation is sustained by the assertion that recognizing the uneven level of evolution in *aboriginal cultures* means one assumes that *aboriginal peoples* are racially "inferior." But while some members of society might be inclined to think such a thing, this would require that they view culture as invariably connected to race, thus resulting in the conclusion that less complex cultures are incapable of integrating into modern society *because* of their race. Accepting that a culture is at a different stage of development, however, only necessitates the recognition that there is a difference in complexity between industrialized nation states and subsistence cultures based on kinship loyalties. When the relative complexity of modern society is linked to the historical availability of resources and not to race, as is the case in the theoretical leanings of Novack, Trotsky, Morgan, Leslie A. White, and Jared Diamond, no culture can be considered "subordinate" since early cultural forms are necessary parts of the whole evolutionary process.

It is interesting that postmodernists do not challenge the idea that *is* actually racist – that cultures at an earlier stage of development are "subordinate" or "inferior." And since they are so adamant in showing that aboriginal cultures are *not* lower, we can reasonably infer that they hold the view that cultures in early evolutionary stages *are* "subordinate"/"inferior." This indicates another contradiction of postmodernism's value system, revealing why relativists are so anxious to prevent an evaluation of the theory of cultural evolution. Instead of attempting to understand the reasons why aboriginal marginalization exists so that it can be overcome, postmodernists are intent on obscuring the developmental gap. Not only does this sentence native peoples to a state of cultural stagnation, but it also encourages the retention of oppressive characteristics. There are a number of cultural practices, both contemporary and ancient, that can be generally accepted as oppressive in one way or another: genital mutilation, bride burning, flogging, human sacrifice, animal torture, religious imposition, sexual enslavement, caste designation, and blood feuds, to name a few. Appeals for the unqualified preservation of culture serve only to prevent the abandonment of some odious traditions.

In addition to justifying the retention of obsolete and oppressive cultural practices, postmodernism has had another harmful social consequence. Its promotion of "difference" has led to the acceptance that aboriginal peoples have a completely different understanding of the world than non-aboriginals, an understanding that cannot be evaluated by scientific methods. The result has been the proliferation of a highly dubious body of research on aboriginal "methodologies" and "epistemologies." The lack of content in these perspectives is ignored in all discussions of "native studies" because of the assertion that respect for native "world views" is the key to aboriginal liberation. So even if these claims are invalid, political sympathies for the plight of the native population makes Canadians eager to support them.

## "NATIVE STUDIES" AND THE CREATION OF PRETENTIOUS ARROGANCE

The year 1969 marked the emergence of the career of one of the most prolific and well-known members of the aboriginal intelligentsia, the late Vine Deloria Jr. Deloria began his scholarly career with the publication of *Custer Died for Your Sins: An Indian Manifesto*. After this publication, he wrote or edited sixteen books and was the author of an extensive number of articles and publications. But Deloria's first book was especially influential in the field of anthropology. The fourth chapter, "Anthropologists and Other Friends," was a sneering attack on scientific anthropology, and as a result, his highly subjective criticisms were enthusiastically embraced by postmodern academics. So influential was this book that the eighty-eighth annual meeting of the American Anthropological Association held a session entitled "Custer Died for Your Sins: A Twenty-Year Retrospective on Relations between Anthropologists and

American Indians." At the conference, fourteen social scientists (mostly anthropologists) presented papers on Deloria's influence, which led to the eventual publication of a book entitled *Indians and Anthropologists: Vine Deloria Jr. and the Critique of Anthropology.*

Although Deloria's critique of anthropology is an indication of the frustration and anger aboriginal peoples undoubtedly feel about the treatment they have received historically, it adds nothing of substance to the debates about the discipline. Instead, it largely consists of personal insults directed at anthropologists and arguments that, taken seriously, would result in a rejection of the discipline itself. For Deloria, scientific research that attempts to obtain abstract knowledge is "useless" and "should be utterly rejected by Indian people." He shares with postmodernism the charge that this knowledge is being used to oppress aboriginal peoples, and encourages the politicization of anthropology. "We should not be objects of observation for those who do nothing to help us," he maintains.[46] Ridiculing the idea of objective scientific research of aboriginal culture, in its stead Deloria proposes that "each anthro desiring to study a tribe should be made to apply to the tribal council for permission to do his study. He would be given such permission only if he raised as a contribution to the tribal budget an amount of money equal to the amount he proposed to spend in his study."[47]

So, anthropological research should proceed only if findings support the political agenda of the tribe being studied and sufficient bribes are offered to the aboriginal leadership to obtain their cooperation. Both these recommendations are hostile to the fundamental aim of scientific anthropology: understanding the nature of culture and its development. However, as was shown in the last chapter, anthropology's unscientific preoccupation with "decolonizing the discipline" has meant that Deloria's self-serving assertions are still being taken seriously. Deloria, after all, represented the "voice" of an oppressed group, and postmodernism dictates that his views must be considered "equally valid" in comparison to "Eurocentric" (i.e., scientific) scholarship.

Attempts like Deloria's to politicize anthropology can also be seen in a number of other disciplines. Some archaeologists, for example, now claim that the "world views" of the aboriginal groups whose remains they study are "just as valid as the archaeological viewpoint of what prehistory is about."[48] While archaeology was once one of the more rigorous social sciences, scholars like Michael Shanks, Christopher Tilley, and Ian Hodder are advocating that studies of the past support the political aspirations of marginalized groups. Hodder, for example, shows himself to be an extreme supporter of archaeological relativism by maintaining that "archaeologists should aid subordinate peoples in interpreting the past the way they want it interpreted."[49]

Concern about including the "newly heard voices of descendants of those whose lives archaeologists try to illuminate" has resulted in significant changes to the discipline of archaeology.[50] As Bruce Trigger explains, "many Native groups now routinely regulate the anthropological research that can be done in their communities and are quick to take issue with conclusions that they find objectionable."[51] Although Trigger maintains that such a circumstance has not undermined the discipline, a number of incidents suggest otherwise. One concerns aboriginal opposition to any archaeological findings that support the Bering Strait theory (that aboriginal peoples migrated from the Old World over the land bridge in the Bering Sea, and possibly by boat, during or before the last Ice Age) since this has been perceived as "weakening the land claims of aboriginal peoples."[52] So strong is native opposition to this hypothesis that museum exhibits examining it have either been eliminated or reduced in "size, impact, and clarity of message." Robert McGhee explains that the marginalization of this exhibit in the Canadian Museum of Civilization was due to "the unwillingness of Native consultants to deal with their more adamant constituents who demanded that the 'Bering Strait hypothesis' be removed or drastically downgraded; pressure from our ethnologist colleagues who feared that the expression of archaeological views would cause problems between them and their Native clients; and lack of support from a management which recognized that Natives can arouse more public concern than can archaeologists."[53]

Another disturbing development concerns the study of aboriginal remains. Although one can understand opposition to the excavation of burial sites where archeologists are dealing with deceased people actually known to families living today, opposition to the study of aboriginal remains occurs in cases that are hundreds or even thousands of years old. The controversy surrounding the study of Kennewick Man in Washington State, for example, involved a skeleton that was 8,400 years old.[54] In the "Long Ago Person Found" case in northern British Columbia in 1999, although the skeleton was 560 years old, the Champagne and Aishihik First Nations insisted that the remains be "repatriated" to them. The skeleton was "cremated" during a "spiritual ceremony" in 2002, destroying an archeological find that potentially could have continuously contributed to the knowledge base of all humanity.

Restrictions on the study of aboriginal gravesites out of "respect" for aboriginal traditions have seriously diminished Canadian archaeology. As Ian Dyck, a curator at the Canadian Museum of Civilization notes, indigenous archaeology in Canada now is largely the study of camp-sites, not of burial sites. This means that many of the most important archaeological artifacts are inaccessible, since often the best weapons were buried with those who died. This is very different from what occurs in studies of indigenous remains in Russia, where aboriginal "spirituality" has not been promoted as it has in Canada. Dyck notes that digging in graves there is not taboo, and instead "people in Russia are thrilled to know about their ancestors."[55]

The political pressure on archaeology has been so intense in North America that a subfield of "Indigenous Archaeology" has been formed to accommodate "the special needs and desires of indigenous communities." But why are the "needs and desires of indigenous communities" different from any other? Why, as Robert McGhee asks, "would anyone think that Indigenous Archaeology would or should differ from any other kind of archeology – Canadian or American, German or Chinese Archeology?"[56] The "difference" is required because Indigenous Archaeology is unscientific; it has been created to satisfy the political aspirations of aboriginal organizations, not to more accurately understand the past.

Similar pressures have been documented in the discipline of history. The Australian historian Keith Windschuttle, for example, notes that the assumption "that there are facts about history is no longer accepted as the starting point for debate, but is itself seen merely as one ideological position among several."[57] Instead of accepting that it is the "obligation [of] historians ... to try to shake off their own values and pursue the truth," there is a tendency to see history as *nothing more* than a form of literature" serving the personal and ideological agenda of its authors just as legitimately as a novel.[58] As Windschuttle explains, "most historians over the last two hundred years have accepted the view that the truth about the past is something independent of themselves," but "quite a few historians today ... believe that the past is not something we discover but something that each age invents for its own purposes." Such relativist tendencies encourage, as Windschuttle describes it, "perspectives that differ radically from the literary traditions borne by the main nineteenth century imperial powers."[59] One of the most significant "perspectives" put forward is, once again, the aboriginal view that they did not evolve out of Africa but were placed on their territories by "the Creator" at "the beginning of time."

In Canada such developments in the discipline of history have resulted in Georges Sioui's *For an Amerindian Autohistory* (1995). On the publisher's homepage, two excerpts from reviews of the book appear:[60]

> It was with great pleasure that I received Sioui's book, and I read it with as much interest as profit. Nothing is more important for the future of our studies than to know that our Amerindian colleagues are ready and determined to take on their own anthropology and their own history. Sioui's work is a brilliant demonstration of this undertaking. – Claude Lévi-Strauss
>
> Well written and well presented ... It was with pleasure that I read *For An Amerindian Autohistory*. A literate and well argued plea for a reassessment of Canadian history from the Amerindian point of view ... Sioui's scholarship is very sound ... His most original contribution is his reliance on the traditions of his people and oral testimony ... He is deeply imbued with his Huron culture. – Olive Dickason, Department of History, University of Alberta

These glowing endorsements by a pre-eminent anthropologist and a respected aboriginal historian raise a number of questions. What does it mean for Amerindians to "take on their own anthropology and their own history"?[61] How will Canadian history be "reassessed" from "the Amerindian point of view"? And by what criteria is Sioui's scholarship "very sound" and a "brilliant" undertaking?

Essentially, Sioui's work, like Deloria's, is an attempt to have native spiritual beliefs accepted as historical fact. To do this, Sioui accuses "Euroamerican" historians of practising what he is actually guilty of – confusing mythology with science. He refers to cultural evolution as "a myth" used by Europeans to oppress native people. In its stead he proposes the "Native vision of the sacred circle of life."[62] Essentially, such a "vision" amounts to the spiritual notion that life is "divided into four quarters." This is so, we are told, because of a native numerology that believes that "four is a sacred number" and consequently "there are four sacred directions, four sacred colours, four races of humans, each with its own sacred vision, as well as four ages of human life (childhood, adulthood, old age, then childhood again), four seasons, and four times of day which are also sacred."[63] Sioui uses the highly improbable travel writings of none other than the Baron de Lahontan, the previously discussed originator of the Adario motif of invented dialogue, to support his claim that aboriginal peoples are more environmentally conscious that non-aboriginals. As further support, Sioui points out that aboriginal peoples did not destroy the earth while Europeans did, failing to recognize that aboriginal peoples lacked the technology and economic incentives to have a serious environmental impact.

The most surprising aspect of Sioui's book is Bruce Trigger's foreword. Trigger, unlike many anthropologists studying aboriginal issues, has remained critical of the postmodernist challenge to cultural evolution. His scientific objectivity, however, is seriously lacking in his condescending promotion of Sioui's book. Trigger sidesteps the unscientific nature of Sioui's ideas by substituting the word "spiritually" with "emotionally" in his analysis of Sioui's arguments.[64] He goes on to state that Sioui's use of Baron de Lahontan's work and the natural environmentalism argument are "compelling pieces of evidence."

Yet in his own book *Sociocultural Evolution* (1998), Trigger supports the very theory that Sioui is attempting to refute. He doesn't find it necessary to mention Lahontan except to argue that the Baron's ideas represent "the Rousseauian idealization of the primitive and the rustic."[65] Trigger's arguments about aboriginal environmentalism are even more at odds with Sioui: no longer is Trigger promoting the idea of the "sacred circle of life" but instead he maintains that "it appears profoundly retrograde for some deep ecologists to be urging people to readopt an animist view of the universe."[66]

Why would Trigger oppose these arguments in his own book, yet support them when they were being put forward by Sioui? This difference indicates the double standard existing in universities today and the reluctance of non-aboriginal scholars to criticize the work of their aboriginal colleagues. It also shows that scholars like Trigger are apprehensive about supporting evolutionary theories out of fear of "offending" aboriginal peoples, as indicated by Trigger's introduction to *Sociocultural Evolution*:

> I know that by publishing this book I risk giving pain and moral offence to many people, especially my Wendat clan-brother Georges Sioui, who in his own writings has eloquently exposed the racism and colonialism inherent in so much evolutionary theorizing, and powerfully defended the relevance of the traditional beliefs of his people for the modern world (Sioui, 1992). I do not disagree with

anything Georges has written on this topic and certainly have no wish to deny the negative role that sociocultural evolutionary theory has often played in the past. Yet the skill with which he has adapted his people's cultural traditions to the needs of the modern world provides an example of evolutionary development of a very different kind.

Only by resorting to pomospeak – "evolutionary development of a very different kind"– can Trigger avoid the obvious contradiction between his own and Sioui's work while appeasing the cultural pride of his "Wendat clan-brother." Sioui's work, after all, was attempting to *refute* evolutionary theory and replace it with the spiritually based romanticism that technological development estranges us from our "natural" existence.

The double standard in archaeology, anthropology, and history also has intruded into the discipline of political science. Although describing itself as a "science," this designation does not extend to work undertaken by aboriginal political scientists. Particularly significant is the work of Kiera Ladner, a political scientist recently granted a Canada Research Chair in Indigenous Politics and Governance at the University of Manitoba because she is regarded as "an expert in the field of indigenous politics."[67] But Ladner has made a number of incredible assertions, including statements that Blackfoot governance can be understood by "observing a buffalo herd," that aboriginal peoples' "relationship to Creation" is a key determinant of indigenous political systems,[68] and that a pre-contact "Mi'kmaq constitutional order" would have been analogous to the legal framework currently existing in Britain.[69] These claims are based on the opinions of aboriginal elders and a political manifesto of an aboriginal organization. Ladner, in association with three other aboriginal political scientists, also initiated a prayer at the beginning of the plenary session of the 2004 Annual Meeting of the Canadian Political Science Association,[70] during which all audience members (except us) stood, even though some felt uncomfortable. No political scientist would find the initiation of prayers by any other group acceptable. However, it was condescendingly accepted under the auspices that "aboriginal perspectives" must be accommodated within the discipline.

The tension that arises from allowing such contradictory standards to co-exist within the social sciences has led to pressure for the development of Native Studies programs. These programs have been developed not for any academic purpose but, as Elizabeth Cook-Lynn explains, to support a particular political ideology: the "defense of lands and resources and the sovereign right to nation-to-nation status."[71] This advocacy role can be seen in the case of Dale Turner, a well-known indigenous intellectual in Canada and a professor of Native Studies at Dartmouth College in New Hampshire. The college website states that "Dale's courses reflect the importance of asserting and protecting tribal sovereignty in Indian Country." The next sentence states that "at the same time students are encouraged to develop their critical thinking skills." This raises the question of what happens if these "critical thinking skills" lead students to question "the importance of asserting and protecting tribal sovereignty."

In Canada, pressure for Native Studies programs began in the late 1960s, under the schema of making universities "more relevant to the histories and needs of Native people."[72] In 2006 these programs were present in twelve Canadian universities.[73] The first was developed at Trent University in Ontario. The focus of Trent's program is articulated in *In the Words of the Elders*, edited by professors in the program, where it is explained that in Native Studies "the focus tends to be on Aboriginal peoples described from the cultural 'inside'. This involves a new kind of intellectual project, new forms of teaching strategies, new methods of research and enquiry, and, indeed, new ways of working in a scholarly environment."[74] The writers advocate "a new respect for the thought of Aboriginal cultural, spiritual, artistic, and spiritual leaders," which includes "providing a greater legitimacy" for "teachings" such as the politically motivated belief that aboriginal peoples were given North America by "The Creator."[75]

Another ambitious program in this genre has emerged at the University of Victoria, which offers certificates in the Administration of Indigenous Governments, as well as an M.A., Concurrent M.A./LLB, and PH.D. in Indigenous Governance. The program is headed by Taiaiake Alfred, one of the best-known scholars studying indigenous politics today.[76] This program is largely oriented toward "personal decolonization" and spiritual renewal rather than academic achievement.[77] And although Alfred maintains that "truth is a powerful weapon," the concern of his teachings are the romanticization of aboriginal traditions and a form of racial essentialism that pits indigenous people against "white power."[78]

An even more significant development in the area of Native Studies has occurred with the formation of the First Nations University of

Canada, entirely devoted to "offering post-secondary education in a culturally supportive First Nations' environment."[79] The university's vision statement asserts that "we, the First Nations, are children of the Earth, placed here by the Creator to live in harmony with each other, the land, animals and other living beings." The university also "recognize[s] the spiritual power of knowledge," asserting that in "following the paths given to us by the Creator, the First Nations have a unique vision to contribute to higher education." One aspect of this unique vision lies in involving elders who "use humour, prayer and sweetgrass to assist those in need" and "reinforce our respect for, and understanding of, the Creator's role in our lives." In the indigenous studies program at the university "competencies in the standard of western educational accomplishments are stressed as only one part of balanced personal development," and students are encouraged to "seek cultural growth as a vital part of their education within the more broadly based meaning of university higher education." All these assertions compromise the essential concept of a university: that it exists to encourage the academic study of all subjects, not to engage in political and religious indoctrination.[80]

Why are such irrational and reactionary proposals so enthusiastically promoted for the native population? Such initiatives are very different from the orientation of many other historical movements, where access to scientific education was demanded as a right. Most black leaders in the United States, for example, have been vehemently *opposed* to segregation in education.[81] W.E.B. Du Bois, a respected academic and black protest leader during the first half of the twentieth century, even criticized attempts to politicize the social sciences and romanticize the black population. He argued that such a misguided idealism would jeopardize the capacity to "establish the Truth, on which Right in the future may be built."[82]

The reactionary character of aboriginal politics can partially be explained by the history of aboriginal/non-aboriginal relations. This differed from black struggles in the United States, which were largely rooted in the working class. The position of black people as the most exploited producers in American history began with enslavement, when their ancestors were torn from tribal relationships in Africa and forcibly integrated into a much more developed economy and society. Although they endured extreme exploitation, cultural combination during this process enabled them to acquire the skills necessary for participation in a plantation economy and to become sharecroppers and wage labourers when slavery was overthrown. It was this position of blacks as exploited producers unencumbered by tribal loyalties that has enabled them to become such a strong progressive force in American history and the modern world.

With the exception of the fur trade in Canada and parts of the United States, most aboriginal people were sidelined from economic activity and as a result largely remained stuck in time, enabling many primitive cultural features to persist. Most significant is the continuing existence of subsistence practices and tribal affiliations, which have provided serious obstacles to their integration into the agricultural and industrial workforce. As a result, they were either exterminated in genocidal wars, or forcibly relocated to unproductive reserves when the fur trade declined. Native people were *repressed* by indifference to their uneven development and lack of respect for their humanity, not for their labour power. And although raw materials were extracted from areas inhabited by aboriginal peoples, their neolithic technology had made them previously unable to turn these resources into commodities. Therefore, unlike blacks, nothing of value, in an economic sense, was taken from them.

In his book *Class Counts*, sociologist Erik Olin Wright notes that this historical difference in the treatment of blacks and aboriginals is reflective of two kinds of colonialist relations that occur in the development of capitalism as a global system: exploitative and non-exploitative oppression. According to Wright, exploitative oppression occurs when an invader needs the exploited for their effort (i.e., labour). He notes that in cases of non-exploitative oppression (which occurred with aboriginals in North America), policies of genocide were often adopted as a strategy for social control if indigenous populations could not be used for the purpose of economic development. According to Wright, "it is no accident that culturally we have the abhorrent saying, 'the only good Indian is a dead Indian,' but not the saying 'the only good worker is a dead worker' or 'the only good slave is a dead slave.' It makes sense to say 'the only good worker is an obedient and conscientious worker,' but not 'the only good worker is a dead worker.'"[83]

It is this non-exploitative oppression of aboriginal peoples that has been instrumental to the kind of aboriginal politics that we see today. Lacking the power that comes from being needed for labour, aboriginals have had to rely on the formulation of legal arguments by the Aboriginal Industry. But a reliance on the law to assert political goals is, in the end, ineffective since aboriginal groups must defer to the state's interpretation of what was originally "meant" in various precedents. It also results in a fragmented, as opposed to a cohesive, political movement for aboriginal peoples. Competition for government money and the ownership of resource rights means that aboriginal political alliances constitute marriages of convenience rather than an identification that stems from common interests. This is why governments have been able to divide native groups so easily in their negotiations with them.

## ARROGANCE DRESSED AS SELF-ESTEEM

Poor educational performance, poverty, and the associated conditions of social dysfunction are broadly considered to be the result of low self-esteem among the aboriginal population. The simplistic logic that dysfunction results from low self-esteem – and that some manufactured sense of "cultural pride" will overcome these predicaments – has detrimental effects on many levels of government policy and public attitudes toward native people. The Aboriginal Industry advocates subsistence practices and the retention of tribal values as a remedy for low self-esteem. However, reverting to past practices cannot provide anyone with the resources to meet with present or future challenges; at best, it is a mechanism for avoidance. Furthermore, kinship social values, dominance of powerful families in settling disputes, and imposed "forgiveness" by victims leave no room for the unselfish accomplishment that is the basis for true self-esteem.

Self-esteem is the healthy satisfaction of social contribution, self-control, and the capacity to accept criticism. As described by psychotherapist Nathaniel Branden, it is "the disposition to experience oneself as being competent to cope with the basic challenges of life and of being worthy of happiness."[84] Postmodern reasoning encourages the building of artificial self-esteem by the use of faulty causation: while academic accomplishment may cause self-esteem, self-esteem cannot cause high marks. Heaping undeserved rewards and praise on any person without encouraging the capacity for accomplishment promotes attitudes of superiority, narcissism, and arrogance.[85] In the case of the native population, specific examples of the effects of attempting to build self-esteem by entrenching tribal values in the modern context are given in the following chapters pertaining to self-government. They reveal the arrogance of many aboriginal leaders who reject financial accountability for public funding, trivialize spousal and child sexual abuse, and defend their personal and kinship privileges.

# PART TWO

# Taboos, Fabrications, and Sophistry

# 3

# Land Claims: Dreaming Aboriginal Economic Development

In 1989, audiences around the world were subjected to the spiritualism and sentimentality of the movie *Field of Dreams*, starring Kevin Costner. Adapted from W.P. Kinsella's novel *Shoeless Joe*, the screenplay tells the mythical story of a New Age Iowa farmer, Ray Kinsella (Costner), who listens to a voice that tells him to build a baseball diamond in one of his cornfields. "If you build it, he will come," asserts the voice, and Ray follows these instructions in an attempt to seek some unknown yet somehow spiritually significant benefit. Ray is rewarded when the ghost of "Shoeless Joe" Jackson materializes out of the adjacent cornfield in the hopes of playing baseball once again (Jackson and eight other players from the Chicago White Sox were banned from baseball for life after accepting a bribe to throw the 1919 World Series). Jackson and the other disgraced athletes then all congregate on Kinsella's field to reclaim the purity of the sport.

Whatever one may think of the dewy-eyed mysticism celebrated in the movie, its importance in this instance lies not in its message but in a common error in logic upon which the story is based. This error involves the confusion of cause and effect that is rationalized by the spiritual element in the film. To a person who believes in such mysticism, the coexistence of the two variables – a baseball game being played and a field with bases, a batting cage, an outfield and bleachers – could be incorrectly interpreted as the field *causing* people to come and play baseball on it rather than baseball diamonds gradually emerging to satisfy the requirements of the game. But while Kinsella's story was fictional, the same confusion is being repeated in Canadian aboriginal policy. In all aboriginal policies the same logic is employed: imposing a desired effect artificially in the hopes that its cause will miraculously emerge. By putting in place economic and administrative structures that are present in productive and self-determining nation-states, it is expected that marginal aboriginal communities will eventually throw off their dependency and social dysfunction. It is assumed that if economic, political, and social structures are "built," self-determination and economic development "will come."

The most prominent example of this flawed logic is land claims initiatives. Land claims constitute the most significant and costly of all aboriginal projects, and they therefore require the greatest amount of historical revision and legal justification from the Aboriginal Industry. At great expense to the Canadian public (it is estimated that land claims could cost as much as $200 billion to settle),[1] federal, provincial, and territorial governments pursue these initiatives under the principle that it will create an "economic base" in aboriginal communities and "economic certainty" and prosperity for all Canadians. By giving aboriginal groups large cash settlements, rights to land, resource revenues and harvesting, subsidies, participation in environmental management programs, and guarantees of jobs and government contracts, it is argued that aboriginal groups will become self-reliant, and the dependency and political unrest that has characterized aboriginal–non-aboriginal relations will be a thing of the past. As Harry Swain, a previous deputy minister of the Department of Indian and Northern Affairs,[2] puts it: "If you add 5 or 10 percent to the amount of money that is going to be spent anyway through dependency payments and so on, you can actually solve a problem instead of just swimming alongside of it. If we do this right, if we create economic as well as political self-reliance in Indian country, we will be a lot better off." According to Swain, there is "very good evidence" from initial land claims settlements "that even from the narrowest accountant's point of view, this stuff is darn near free in public finance terms ... If you put money in people's hands in that fashion it does two things: one, it reduces the demand for dependency payments, and second, it gives a powerful kick to economic development – it involves people in a larger economy who have not otherwise been involved ... putting resources into the hands of Indian and Inuit people in big lumps after negotiation is in fact darn near free, because what it does is reduce the cost of dependency payments to the [Indian and Northern Affairs] department."[3]

These arguments are no different than the claims made by the voice in Ray Kinsella's head. Infusions of money, grants disguised as native "economic development corporations," or various "rights" do not create a viable economy or aboriginal self-sufficiency: it is a viable economy – that is, the production of needed goods and a market to purchase them – that requires institutions to manage and distribute resources. All economies, to be viable, must produce as much as they consume; aboriginal communities, because they are isolated from global markets and sparsely populated, are unable to become viable in the modern context. And because these remote areas have an uneducated, unskilled, and socially dysfunctional population, most of their aboriginal residents lack the prerequisites to be involved in the extraction of these resources.

## THE NEGOTIATIONS THAT NEVER END

The federal government's formal declaration of the start of negotiation of land claims began in 1973, when it announced that "in all cases where traditional interest in land has not been formally dealt with, the government affirms its willingness to do so and accepts in principle that the loss and relinquishment of that interest ought to be compensated."[4] The initiative was largely a response to the policy vacuum that was created in the aftermath of the rejection of the Trudeau government's White Paper by the aboriginal leadership and the dispersal of funds to native organizations.[5]

In the federal government policy, land claims are divided into two basic types: comprehensive and specific.[6] Comprehensive claims concern those aboriginal groups that have "continuing Aboriginal title to lands and natural resources," because they have not signed treaties.[7] The objective of these claims is to settle title over the area, since British law required that treaties must be signed before the Crown could assert ownership over previously occupied lands. Specific claims, on the other hand, are grievances that result from treaties already in existence for a period of time.[8] While the amounts being demanded by specific claims are less than comprehensive claims, there are far more of them.[9] Settled comprehensive claims also have the potential of becoming specific claims, if aboriginal groups believe that the government has not lived up to its legal commitments.

Present-day land claims have evolved through stealth. Originally, the federal government's land claims policy was not envisioned to involve large sums since the focus was on aboriginal groups' "traditional interest in land" (i.e., the use of the land for subsistence purposes), and lawyers like Thomas Berger asserted that that the aboriginal groups they were representing were not seeking compensation.[10] Today, "traditional interest" is only a small part of settlements, since land claims are now about trying to secure benefits from capitalist developments so as to "build" a modern economy in aboriginal communities. Even more significantly, the government has been gradually pressured to abandon its demands that aboriginal groups relinquish "aboriginal title." The federal government supports this change to its policy on the basis that it has "contributed to the achievement of settlements in recent years."[11]

The stealthful gains made in influencing government policy also have been buttressed by an increasingly activist judiciary.[12] The most significant court decision in this regard was the 1997 Delgamuukw Supreme Court of Canada decision, which maintained that aboriginal title was a specific aboriginal right, implying ownership of land.[13] According to the Supreme Court decision, "Aboriginal title encompasses the right to use the land held pursuant to that title for a variety of purposes, which need not be aspects of those aboriginal practices, cultures and traditions which are integral to distinctive aboriginal cultures."[14] This decision, therefore, mirrors the developments in government policy, where aboriginal title is seen not merely as involving "traditional use" but also as the capitalist concept of owning resources as property for the purpose of increasing profits.

Despite growing acceptance of these stealthful demands in both judicial and political arenas, as well as the spending of untold millions over thirty years, there has been surprisingly little progress in the settlement of claims. It cannot be said that existing policies have "contributed to the achievement of settlements in recent years," as the federal government maintains, since after thirty years of negotiations, only 10 comprehensive claims have been settled.[15] In the meantime, numerous other claims have been asserted, many challenging the legitimacy of existing settlements.

Specific claims settlements are also proceeding slowly. The Department of Indian Affairs pointed out in 2006 that, since 1973, Canada had settled 275 specific claims and 123 were in negotiations.[16] This figure does not include the number that are "under review" (632), "in active litigation" (74) and "in the ISCC [Indian Specific Claim Commission] process" (32).[17] This situation had actually worsened since 2002, when 232 had been settled, 117 were under negotiation, 491 were under review and 15 were in litigation.[18] And even when a specific claim is rejected (86 claims have been classified as "No Lawful Obligation found" and 80 as "File Closed"), aboriginal groups can always resubmit a claim, petition for the decision to be reviewed, or pursue litigation at a later date. The number of these claims is bound to increase in the future since, according to the Department of Indian Affairs, "technical defences such as laches and limitations are not considered; nor are strict rules of evidence."[19]

The difficulties being experienced can be explained by all the parties involved having an interest in keeping the negotiations going. Calvin Helin points out that $550 million in debts have been incurred by aboriginal groups negotiating treaties, and a few negotiation loans of native bands are so large that they are approaching 50 per cent of the expected settlement. According to Helin, "community members complain that many Aboriginal negotiators ... have made profitable careers largely through negotiating one treaty. Youth view many of these negotiators as elitists not wishing to bring an end to the 'ongoing banquet' but instead are sucking the assets out of a treaty settlement before it is even made. Ordinary Aboriginal folk wonder where the incentive for their negotiators to settle their treaties is, when they are profiting handsomely from the process."[20]

Lawyers also benefit if the negotiations end up in court, a possibility that is becoming more and more likely when one considers the impact of the 1997 Supreme Court decision on aboriginal title. This decision did not really settle anything, because although it recognized that aboriginal title could exist if an aboriginal group occupied their lands before British sovereignty was asserted, it "did not specify the type and density of occupation necessary to validate aboriginal title."[21] As Tom Flanagan points out, "all one can say with certainty is that aboriginal-title litigation will be a bonanza for lawyers, historians, and anthropologists because such cases demand huge amounts of evidence about past land use. Also, there is bound to be an increasing tendency for multiple Indian nations to launch overlapping and conflicting claims to aboriginal title."[22] The Supreme Court also states that there must be compensation if aboriginal title is infringed, but maintains that "the amount of compensation payable will vary with the nature of the particular aboriginal title affected and with the nature and severity of the infringement and the extent to which aboriginal interests were accommodated."[23] The Supreme Court, in fact, "leaves most of the pressing practical issues unsettled" so that "the only answer to ... vital questions is that the courts will have to decide through further litigation."[24]

One of the most revealing examples of the land claims quagmire can be seen in the B.C. Treaty Process – the framework that has been set up by the federal and British Columbia governments and aboriginal organizations to negotiate comprehensive claims in the province.[25] As of January 2007, fifty-seven claimant groups (representing 116 of 197 eligible aboriginal groups) have submitted "Statements of Intent," and organized themselves into forty-seven "negotiation tables."[26] Only a few agreements,[27] however, have been signed in sixteen years despite the millions of dollars that have been spent each year.[28] An attempt has even been made to disguise this lack of progress by dividing the treaty talks into stages and then reporting how various groups have "advanced" to the next level of negotiations.[29]

One reason for the slow progress might be that the organization set up to facilitate the talks, the British Columbia Treaty Commission (BCTC), benefits financially from prolonging these processes. The operating budget for 2005–06 was $2.19 million, and $26.42 million has been spent since 1993.[30] This expense includes the salaries for four part-time commissioners, a full-time chief commissioner, and thirteen staff. Since the BCTC has no authority to make decisions with respect to land claims settlements, most of its efforts are devoted to trying to obtain more money from the government for negotiations.[31]

A body similar to the BCTC is present in the settlement of specific claims – the Indian Claims Commission. At fifty-one people, it has a larger staff than the BCTC. Its expenditures for 2005–06 were $6.876 million, an amount that has been rising since its inception in 1991 when the budget was $1.184 million.[32] Chief commissioners have included Jim Prentice, a lawyer who represented aboriginal groups (who also has been a minister of Indian and Northern Affairs), Phil Fontaine, the present grand chief of the Assembly of First Nations, and Renée Dupuis, another aboriginal rights lawyer. Like the BCTC, the Indian Claims Commission does not have any authority to make decisions, and only makes recommendations to the federal government while helping aboriginal groups mediate their claims. Furthermore, the commission lobbies for increases in funding for land claims negotiations to deal with the fact that the system is "gridlocked."[33]

Although the commission currently prides itself on being "an independent body that provides an effective alternative to lengthy and costly court cases," its mediation approach has only led to "the negotiation or settlement" of seventeen claims.[34] It also notes that "for many years, First Nation and government negotiators have attempted to put an end to deadlocked land claims, but there has been little progress. Negotiations have been slow and difficult, and relatively few settlements have been reached."[35]

The gridlock that exists in the settlement of both comprehensive and specific claims is being exacerbated by the increasing uncritical acceptance of "oral histories" as a legitimate basis for aboriginal demands – an acceptance promoted by both the Indian Claims Commission and the BCTC.[36] The Royal Commission on Aboriginal Peoples even advocated the renegotiation of all treaties whose written texts differed from the oral histories of aboriginal elders.[37] And because of the resistance to having elders' memories evaluated alongside other sources, there would be no way to stop vast numbers of politically motivated grievances from dramatically increasing the number of claims.

Bernard Schulmann, a Lilloet-based public policy analyst who has been extensively involved in the B.C. Treaty Process, maintains that land claims agreements will not provide any certainty because "the documents are becoming so complex they are bound to cause large-scale disputes in the future."[38] He argues that "modern treaties have become understandable only to a tiny elite group of lawyers, bureaucrats and ... consultants," and sometimes even judges cannot comprehend them. According to Schulmann, "it seems clear that treaties have become a public make-work project for lawyers" and that more basic agreements should be signed through province-wide negotiations rather than with processes tailored to each group.[39] He notes that "this idea is very unpopular with the First Nations, as they are extremely reluctant to give any real power to a province-wide organization."[40]

## BRINGING HOME THE SINECURES
## AND SUBSIDIES

In 1963 the Hawthorn Report noted "the growing danger that a majority of Indians ... may become a more-or-less permanently isolated, displaced, unemployed or under-employed and dependent group who can find no useful or meaningful role in an increasingly complex urban industrial economy."[41] Although these comments were made over forty years ago, they are just as applicable today. Aboriginal people still remain the most disadvantaged group in Canada, despite billions of dollars being spent on economic development programs. Aboriginal communities remain heavily dependent on federal transfers, and unemployment rates continue to be far higher than the Canadian average.[42] Such a circumstance has led Pauline Comeau and Aldo Santin to ask: "How could billions of dollars be spent with nothing more accomplished than the realization of Hawthorn's nightmare?"[43]

The dominant explanation for the continuation of aboriginal marginalization is "colonialism."[44] Aboriginal people, the argument goes, lack the land, capital, and control over their affairs needed to build a viable economy.[45] It is maintained that governments have thwarted this process by not providing aboriginal groups with what they require to develop their economies, the most significant prerequisite being a "land base."[46] Aboriginal leaders have also stressed the need to acquire political control over these resources, including any social assistance provided by the government. Some claim that this is necessary so that they can determine the pace and character of development to suit aboriginal cultures, enabling them to balance industrial development with "traditional lifestyles."[47] Others maintain that they need to free themselves from government intervention because this is what has created native dependency. Harold Cardinal, for example, recounts a conversation with a young chief from an isolated community who maintains that the government provided aboriginal peoples with welfare to break down their historical self-reliance so that "they would have us where they wanted us."[48] For Cardinal, "there is one way the whites can help, a way so simple that it generally is rejected out of hand. As the old comedian said, 'Don't just applaud, send money.' I would add, money without strings attached."[49]

Cardinal's view has been echoed by Louis Stevenson, chief of the Peguis band. Complaining that the government allocated only $52,000 for economic development while $2.7 million was being spent on welfare, Stevenson argued that money should be spent on "economic development" so that jobs could be created, businesses promoted, and an economic base established instead of "pissing [the money] down the drain on welfare."[50] And since it is assumed that providing aboriginal people with "land and resources" will create viable economies, the Canadian public has been led to believe that social assistance payments and other subsidies will decrease once land claims are settled.[51] This viewpoint is also expressed by critics of the existing system like Calvin Helin, who maintain that welfare is a "trap," while the ownership of land and cash payments brought by land claims "results in an unprecedented opportunity to forge a new era of self-reliance."[52]

But if the increased aboriginal control over lands and resources is supposed to create aboriginal economies, why hasn't there been a decrease in federal transfers where land claims have been settled? Aboriginal leaders, in fact, argue that the settlement of land claims should not be used by the government to avoid its "fiduciary responsibility." In the case of

Nunavut, where one of the largest land claims was settled, there was even the demand that federal funding must be increased because of the need to build more infrastructure in the territory.[53]

This is because, as one aboriginal commentator has put it, "the vast majority of First Nations reserves and Aboriginal communities are small and of marginal economic value."[54] To understand why this is the case, one has to look at the history of the development of aboriginal communities. They did not arise out of the development of capitalism, as occurred in the rest of Canada, where certain areas produced commodities for the home market or for export. Instead, aboriginal reserves "were given to Indians usually in the expectation that such land areas possessed limited economic value for the white men and hence when resources were located in these areas it was a consequence of accident."[55] Therefore, the possibility of aboriginal economic development will be confined to a few reserves that, because of chance, happen to be situated on top of resources that can be profitably extracted. The rest will continue to be reliant on transfers, whether in the form of "economic development" funds, "treaty payments," or welfare. This circumstance was recognized by Bill Knight, a minister of Indian and Northern Affairs in the 1980s. Responding to criticisms about the continuing welfare dependency in many aboriginal communities, he replied, "What would you suggest in an isolated locale, without markets, without resources, without an industrial base, without economic opportunities. You try as best you can to provide a social safety net, as we do to all Canadians."[56]

Even when aboriginal communities are fortunate enough to be sitting on a reserve that has resources that can be profitably extracted, they have not become self-reliant. This is because resource extraction is not labour intensive; it hires relatively few people, and those who are hired must have skills, values, and attitudes of a kind not possessed by most aboriginal people who are isolated from the mainstream. "Economic development" on these reserves, therefore, largely consists of collecting resource royalties, which does not generate long term prosperity. As Tom Flanagan points out with respect to the oil-rich Morley and Hobbema reserves in Alberta, "these reserves have earned huge royalties, and some residents have become well off; but large majorities on the reserves are still dependent on welfare and suffer from all the attendant social pathologies. Cash flow is not the same as prosperity. Royalties bought new houses and pick-up trucks for residents, but few ever became self-supporting wage-earners."[57] These circumstances are

compounded by the fact that any money-making ventures are monopo-
lized by powerful families (a circumstance discussed in the next
chapter) who use their influence to distribute resources to their kin.

Problems occur even when aboriginal communities are close to urban
centres where they can potentially access Canadian markets. The
Musqueam band, for example, is situated on lands in an affluent area of
Vancouver. From 1966 to 1980 the Crown on behalf of the band leased
some of this land to non-natives in ninety-nine year terms. In an
attempt to give the band more control over its affairs, the federal government transferred the leases back to the band in 1980, and in 1991
gave them authority to collect taxes from residents. Since property values had increased substantially in Vancouver by this time, the band
maintained that rents should be increased to reflect market values, and
residents were subjected to rent hikes of more than 7,000 per cent (an
increase from $400/year to $28,000–$38,000). Taxes on the land were
also doubled.[58]

A legal battled ensued, culminating in a ruling of the Supreme Court
of Canada that argued that "it does not follow that the freehold value
of land outside the reserve should be used to determine the rent ... The
capital asset here is reserve land surrendered for leasing, not land surrendered for sale." The Supreme Court maintained that the value of
reserve lands was about half that of the surrounding area, and as a
result, the band could only charge $10,000 per year instead of
$28,000–$38,000. It argued that "since [the Musqueam band] has
chosen not to surrender the land for sale, the band holds reserve land
and must accept the realities of the market for this capital asset."
Although the aboriginal leadership insinuated that the decision was
racist,[59] it actually reflected that economic value in capitalism is determined by what the market will bear. Leasehold lands on aboriginal
reserves, because they are governed by more restrictive laws that stip-
ulate that land can be sold only to the Crown, are worth less than freehold lands off reserve. This circumstance is noted by Tom Flanagan
when he explains that "land is most valuable when it can be put to its
most profitable use," and that additional legal restrictions on the use
of aboriginal lands "cannot help but detract from economic value by
introducing uncertainty."[60]

The value of these lands will be lowered further if a tribally exclusive
government administers them. In the case of tenants leasing land from
the Musqueam band, decisions were being made by an authority over
which they had no popular control. As a result, meetings were held by

the band to discuss the tax and lease increases, but only Musqueam members were allowed to attend. There were even discussions about drafting legislation that would exempt Musequeam members from having to pay the same rents as non-natives (it was thought that Musqueam members might be able to take advantage of the plight of tenants who would have to sell their houses for a low price when they were unable to afford their re-evaluated leases).[61] Knowledge of the existence of such a discriminatory regime would surely lower what prospective tenants would pay.[62]

What land claims and other economic development initiatives do is hide the problems that aboriginal communities have in integrating into modern economies. A façade is created by the government providing a vast array of direct and indirect subsidies to shelter aboriginal economic initiatives from competition. Then, the fabricated infrastructure is pointed to as evidence that current policies are working.[63]

The most extensive subsidies are provided in comprehensive land claims settlements. In each settlement, millions of dollars are allocated to aboriginal groups as "capital" for newly formed "economic development corporations." The expectation is that the money will be invested in the local economy, and businesses will form and hire aboriginal workers to produce commodities for global markets. But because of the unviable character of the areas where these claims are settled, the agreements generally result in two scenarios: 1) the land claims capital is invested responsibly in profitable enterprises outside the community, and then small payments are distributed to aboriginal shareholders in the form of dividends; or 2) money is invested irresponsibly because of political pressure exerted by those aboriginal leaders who control the economic development corporations.[64] Most of the employment that comes from land claims, in fact, consists of the positions that are created in the bureaucratic structures negotiated as part of the settlement. As one commentator has pointed out, "over the past 20 years, the people of the North have become what observers call 'board junkies'. In an economy with few job opportunities for the minimally educated, board appointments are a way to earn good per diems, frequent travel opportunities, and direct political influence."[65] "Board junkies" do not just exist in the North; they constitute a common source of employment for many aboriginal leaders across Canada.

In addition to land claims settlements, many government departments – especially Human Resources Development Canada, Indian and Northern Affairs, and Industry Canada and their provincial equivalents

– have put in place a number of institutions, programs, and services to give the illusion that viable aboriginal economies exist.[66] The most extensive of these initiatives concerns the growth of the aboriginal "business sector." In 2001 there were over twenty thousand native businesses in Canada, about 50 per cent of which were on reserves, and their numbers have been increasing at a rate faster than the national average. Aboriginal Business Canada, a division within Industry Canada, maintains that this growth rate was about 170 per cent between 1981 and 1996, and continues to increase.[67]

But the growth has been made possible by the fact that the government has continually increased the subsidies it allocates to aboriginal businesses. The federal government has now created numerous aboriginal financial institutions to provide "capital" to these businesses. In 2001 these institutions lent between $50 million and $60 million, an increase in $10 million to $20 million from previous years. As well, the Department of Indian Affairs and Northern Development has "boosted its $25-million investment in business development to $100-million and is establishing a venture capital fund."[68] Aboriginal Business Canada asserts that special financial institutions were created for aboriginal people to "allow for services to be provided which take into account different local market conditions and economic environment" in native communities.[69]

But what are the "different local market conditions and economic environment" found in aboriginal communities? Essentially, what is meant by these euphemisms is that these communities are unproductive and reliant on federal transfers, and so the only market is the community itself or the government. As a result, the private sector will not invest in these businesses because "on reserves with little economic activity, every business venture becomes high risk."[70] The government must provide the loans; hence the need for these "aboriginal financial institutions."

The number of businesses that need constant infusions of federal government money to stay afloat is unknown, because there is little analysis of their profitability. Instead, many discussions merely assume that the increasing number of native businesses is indicative of success.[71] Without providing any data to be evaluated, it is stated that "Indian business success stories across the country grow in number every year, becoming models for the community and offering proof that native people can survive in the business world."[72] Discussions of these enterprises revolve around the anecdotes of native "entrepreneurs," who maintain that they are successful.

The unviability of these businesses is also obscured because analysis of them is usually undertaken by advocates. Take, for example, the case of the "northlands agreements" that Ottawa and Alberta, Saskatchewan, and Manitoba signed between 1974 and 1989 to develop the northern communities largely inhabited by aboriginal peoples. Total funding spent on these agreements exceeded $460 million, and although they were promoted as "innovative and successful" by the governments involved, "a review of the independent studies shows that all of the programs, regardless of when or where they were introduced, failed to accomplish their goals. However, the consultants' reports of the government-funded analysts repeatedly glossed over the findings with an overly positive, generalized introduction that often misled the reader: 'Agreement represents a good application of public funds,' noted the consultants who evaluated one of the three Saskatchewan agreements. The analysis then went on to outline in great detail the program's massive failings."[73]

Other attempts to disguise the unviability of aboriginal economic development initiatives include "culturally sensitive" evaluations that examine "socio-economic development from a First Nations perspective."[74] This includes looking at "not just the 'economic' aspect," but spiritual, cultural, and political factors.[75] Because these indicators are "very difficult to define,"[76] they can be used to show that almost any initiative is "successful."

One of the only things produced in aboriginal communities that can be exported are those items that fall within the rubric of "cultural tourism" and "native crafts." But the demand for these is limited, and so almost all aboriginal economic activity needs constant sheltering from competition. Tax breaks, interest free loans, and grants, as well as preferential contracts, are some additional mechanisms.[77] Aboriginal peoples are also allowed to engage in economic activities that exclude non-aboriginals by law, such as the operating of casinos and putting up billboards on their lands.[78] This approach is often used to legitimate an activity that aboriginal groups were already pursuing illegally.[79] Smuggling and other black market activities, in fact, are among the main non-subsidized forms of "economic development" in aboriginal communities. Devolution of control over law enforcement means that aboriginal communities can become lawless areas where tax-free cigarettes and alcohol can be obtained,[80] or where illegal immigrants are transported without detection.[81] The most disturbing development is occurring in the weapons trade. While weapons were originally sold to a fringe element in the native population engaged in illegal activities, guns are now being sold to biker gangs.[82]

All these initiatives raise questions about why it is expected that a large number of aboriginal people will become entrepreneurs or power brokers in the capitalist system in the first place. Capitalism is a late development, after all, and before European contact, there was no knowledge in the New World of capitalist principles – the extraction of large surpluses through the exploitation of wage labour and the sale of commodities. Instead, aboriginal tribes produced little surplus, and everything was distributed through a system of kinship reciprocity. Yet despite this continuing gap in cultural development, the idea that solutions to aboriginal problems will come from their ability to accumulate profits is constantly promoted.[83] This also ignores the fact that most people in society, even if their cultural background is one that has evolved within a capitalist framework, do not become the owners of businesses or capitalists. Instead, capitalism requires that the majority become wage labourers.

## HAVING YOUR CAKE AND EATING IT TOO

Central to the problems of aboriginal people is their entrenched dependency. Native unemployment is much higher than the Canadian average. This is especially true for reserves and the isolated communities in the North, but natives in urban centres also experience high unemployment rates.[84] Aboriginals are also far more likely than most Canadians to receive social assistance, and when employment is obtained, it is often in the form of seasonal or part-time work.[85] High native population growth will exacerbate this problem unless drastic measures are taken. It is estimated that 300,000 jobs will have to be created over the next fifteen years to bring native employment levels up to Canadian standards.[86]

These circumstances are attributed to a number of causes, among them racism, low education and skill levels, and problems of social dysfunction.[87] While, from an elementary point of view, these are all contributors, a deeper look into the nature of labour itself reveals the fundamental reasons for the lack of aboriginal participation in the workforce.

Labour, in one form or another, is as old as humankind.[88] The need to toil in supplying human needs is apparent from the earliest times. Searching for food, by climbing or by constant foraging, and then hunting, fishing, and gathering, required the discipline to complete the tasks at hand in order to satisfy the most basic needs of survival. This form of labour directly answered immediate needs, and it was used accordingly. Eventually, as technological efficiency increased, allowing more coordination of effort and the formation of larger groups, humans developed the capacity to accumulate surplus food and other life-supporting goods, and new forms of labour came into being: the production of goods with indentured, tributary, or compensated labour, so that now the overly productive majority could support the idle few.

In the modern European or industrial context, there has been a continuous increase in productivity through a greater division of labour and the development of externally controlled and disciplined labour processes.[89] This culminated in the nineteenth century with the factory system, which continues today. The factory system organizes the workers' labour power and, paying directly for it by the hour or day, controls it under strict supervision. Workers in the factory system use labour to produce only a part of the product, and own none of it. They sell their labour. This cultural history of modern workers applies, of course, to a range of services outside the area of manufacturing goods. The increased efficiency of the division of labour and sophisticated technology creates surplus to pay for functions from teaching to garbage collection, mail delivery, and health services.

This development of the labour process occurred over hundreds of years in Europe. And working for wages, which seems so self-evident today, took a lot of getting used to. For the vast majority of humanity's history, labour was directed toward the completion of a task. With wage labour, workers were expected to engage in continual production, regardless of the number of tasks completed, for the amount of time they had sold their labour. This necessitated a dramatic change in the way people related to the labour process. As the historian Paul Phillips points out, this change, which occurred in the development of the capitalist labour market, "required a remaking of the behaviour and attitudes of the workers themselves, a remaking that constituted a cultural as well as an economic transformation – a replacement of the habits of irregularity, ill-discipline and sloth and a preoccupation with the immediate, with habits of punctuality, regularity and order and a longer-term view, all of which were necessary to the working of an emerging capitalist order with its new scientific technology."[90]

These problems encountered by all workers in the transition to capitalism have been much more pronounced and long lasting with the Canadian indigenous population. This is because, unlike most social groupings in other areas of the world, aboriginal cultures in what is now Canada had not progressed into indentured or compensated labour when capitalism was thrust upon them. Their hunting and gathering and horticultural economies before contact were at an earlier stage than that which involved the production of commodities – goods produced to be sold on the market. This extensively developed form of production was completely unknown.

Hunters and gatherers and neolithic horticultural societies are characterized by the fact that they exert much less control over nature than was the case in feudal economies. Their simple technology and division of labour resulted in their following the rhythms of nature, instead of developing the abstract conceptions needed for a more coordinated and productive economy. A lack of surplus means that once a requirement is met, the fruits of that labour are consumed or used, and the effort is repeated only when the need arises and natural circumstances permit. This is the reason behind anthropologists' conclusions that "hunter-gatherers focus on the present. People make decisions based on what they can find, kill, or gather now, not at some later time or as a result of long-term strategic planning."[91]

Carried into the disciplines of the modern workplace, this attitude results in high rates of tardiness and absenteeism. Often referred to as "unreliability,"[92] the phenomenon is explained by anthropologist Hugh Brody thusly: "Hunter-gatherers tend not to plan and manage surplus. They need food or money now, not in several weeks' time. In the modern world, the hunter-gatherer often appears to be restless as well as poor."[93] This situation is compounded by the kinship orientation of aboriginal culture.[94] Cooperative work with others outside of their kinship group is difficult for people who place a strong emphasis on the value of tribal loyalties. Aboriginal people retaining tribal cultural characteristics feel uncomfortable when they must leave their communities to look for work or to get an education, even though there are few opportunities on reserves, and late capitalism requires that workers become increasingly mobile.[95] It is also important to point out that one of the "changes in attitude and belief" needed for development in modern economies is "impersonality," or the "judgement of merit and performance, not social background or irrelevant qualities."[96] Tribalism prevents this kind of judgment from taking place, because it is kinship reciprocity, not "merit and performance," that shapes economic decisions in aboriginal cultures. This results in nepotistic hiring practices rather than selection of those best qualified for the job.[97]

By not having the generational experience of the transition from a precapitalist to a capitalist economy, native people face a perplexing future. While working people in the rest of the world adapted to the productive character of their own and other cultures, the large gap in development between hunting and gathering and/or horticulture made it difficult for aboriginal people to participate in emerging capitalist relations. In addition, the economic processes that were occurring in Europe had already produced workers who were "the finished products of the most advanced school of industrial capitalism in the world" where "the pain of transition had all been suffered, and the cost of training had all been paid for, in another country."[98] This made governments in Canada reluctant to devote the resources necessary to develop the aboriginal population or to coercively integrate them into the labour force. Instead, it was easier and cheaper in the short term to warehouse aboriginal people on reserves and offload the responsibility for them onto the churches.

The unfortunate result of the problems certain cultures have faced in becoming workers in modern society is derogatory references to particular "races." This is because it can seem apparent to some that the absence of participation in work is a character fault. Most people tend to evaluate others by the standards they apply to themselves; if they work hard and someone else doesn't, this must be an indication of the latter's "laziness." And if that characteristic can be identified with a particular ethnicity, it must be racially determined. Ignorance seeks simple answers, and racism is one of the easiest. Then, the effects of racial oppression are ironically the basis for more racism. People denied jobs because of their race are then thought lazy because they aren't working. There is no attempt to understand the social circumstances that prevent certain groups of people from entering into the workforce.

The underrepresentation of aboriginal people in the workforce, however, is not, for the most part, racially inspired. Government incentives to hire native people are abundant. Aboriginals are given priority in government hiring, and firms doing business with government are given extra consideration for having aboriginal employees. Even unions are being pressured to encourage corporations to hire more natives through the collective bargaining process.[99] In fact, it is now good public relations to hire natives. The problem is in finding those with appropriate skills, values, and attitudes.

These incentives have caused a distorted view of the labour process within the native population – one that sees jobs in the context of sinecures.[100] This is most evident in the public sector, because the cultural obstacles to aboriginal peoples' entrance into the workforce can be hidden by creating superfluous positions within the bureaucracy. Thus "compared with the Canadian economy as a whole ... the aboriginal working class is overly concentrated in employment which is directly or indirectly funded by the state."[101] As well, a significant number of aboriginal public sector employees work in areas where they provide services only to the native population.[102] The Northwest Territories and Nunavut, which both have large aboriginal populations, further exemplify the use of sinecures for native people in their bloated bureaucracies.[103]

A number of influences have implanted this false sense of entitlement. First is the encouragement of a grievance mentality: aboriginal peoples are constantly told that they are "owed" for the abuses suffered at the hands of the colonizers.[104] Compensation, not earnings, becomes the principal concept of acquisition in native communities. The leadership created by the Aboriginal Industry has bought the loyalty of native people with promises of wealth without working for it. Government is seen merely in terms of the amount of money that it can provide, and no attention is given to the quality of the effort to implement programs. A proliferation of associations and boards ensues as a means of distributing the spoils. This environment provides no appreciation of the productive process. It also leads to a negative attitude toward labour, and the complaint that, despite low skill levels, native people can only obtain "menial jobs";[105] much preferred are "office jobs" – the euphemism for sinecures.[106]

The anti-labour attitude that exists within the native population also has the disadvantage of entrenching aboriginal dependency. Aboriginal people with low educational and skill levels will not be able to become professionals or office workers unless "culturally sensitive" standards are applied. By refusing unskilled work, they are left only with the option of remaining on social assistance. An avenue to aboriginal political and economic development is denied when natives are encouraged to believe that socially necessary "menial jobs" are beneath them.

The process of political and economic development has been documented in the case of the Irish by the Canadian labour historian H. Clare Pentland. According to Pentland, the Irish were culturally backward and unskilled in comparison with English labourers when they arrived in Canada, because the Irish economy was far behind capitalist developments in England. As Pentland points out, "the Irish peasants came to Canada as strong and willing labourers, but men profoundly untutored in the ways of an industrial economy. They brought many troubles on themselves by their own ignorance and lack of self-discipline, and many more were thrust upon them as the predatory and unscrupulous sought to exploit them."[107] Pentland, however, goes on to argue that the Irish immigrants developed through their struggles as workers.[108] Even more significantly, they learned to overcome their tribal tendencies by learning that "unity, to be very effective, had to encompass all labourers."[109] As a result, there is no longer an "Irish problem." By taking on menial jobs, the Irish were able to acquire the skills and attitudes needed for full participation in Canadian society.

## DISGUISING THE UNPRODUCTIVE CHARACTER OF NATIVE SUBSISTENCE

In addition to the sense of entitlement encouraged by the Aboriginal Industry, the development of skills and attitudes needed for participation in the modern world is being impeded by the continuation of aboriginal peoples' "traditional way of life." This situation, however, is being obscured by the current scholarship on the nature of aboriginal economies. While there used to be a general recognition in political economy that societies had become larger, more productive, and complex over the course of history, with the emergence of postmodernism this understanding of the past has been challenged.[110]

The challenge began in anthropology with the works of James Woodburn, Richard Lee, and Marshall Sahlins. These anthropologists claim that hunting and gathering economies are not "simple" or "primitive" as was once thought, since they have more "leisure time" than many agricultural societies.[111] Sahlins even argues that hunters and gatherers constitute the "original affluent society." Hugh Brody interprets the evidence provided in the work of Sahlins et al. thusly: "with small populations, low levels of need, and expertise in a particular landscape, human beings could eat well, enjoy much leisure, and evidence great health of body and mind. The central stereotype of human social evolution was more than contested and undermined: it was turned on its head."[112] Brody maintains that such findings "offered a fundamental challenge to the depiction of hunter-gatherers as people without achievements. The most telling example centers on attitudes toward material goods and monuments: hunter-gatherers eschew these in order to maintain their highly effective systems of harvesting, yet those who consider material goods and monuments to be indicators of progress and civilization have taken their absence among hunter-gatherers as evidence of the primitive."[113]

These arguments are flawed by a postmodernist misrepresentation of common terms. First, leisure is confused with idleness, so that idleness can be linked to affluence. In fact, the two are at opposite ends of the spectrum of social wealth. The leisure that emanates from affluence is the time consciously taken off work for alternative pursuits; it is made possible by surplus accumulation. Idleness, on the other hand, is imposed by circumstances usually beyond the control of the subject and is used for resting and sleeping. This certainly was the case in neolithic times when life was dependent upon the vicissitudes of nature. Availability of vegetation or prey and suitability of weather conditions determined the activities of Stone Age peoples. When circumstances imposed inactivity, the result had as much to do with leisure as being unemployed does in modern society.

"Low levels of need" is one reason Brody provides for neolithic peoples being able to enjoy so much leisure. The improbable inference is that they enjoyed, in abundance, the very things that modern society values – to "eat well, enjoy much leisure" and have "great health of body and mind." But lacking control over nature meant that the fortunes of hunter-gatherers were not in their hands, resulting in continuous uncertainty about obtaining food and a proliferation of spiritual beliefs instead of scientific thought.

This accounts for the absence of material goods and "monuments" that Sahlins et al. claim were "eschewed" by hunter-gatherers. As there were no means to avail themselves of the "indicators of progress and civilization," they hardly could be eschewed. Indicators of progress like iron tools, the wheel, draught animals, and so on would have greatly improved the lives of hunter-gatherers and horticulturalists – by enabling them to move beyond the Stone Age. But hunting and gathering is very limited in its ability to increase the productivity of the resources that these groups relied on; consequently, they also needed to travel over a large area, or their food supply would be depleted. This is what prevented them from acquiring material goods or building monuments. To attribute this to their "highly effective systems of harvesting" is deceptive.

Besides the confusion of leisure with idleness, there are many distortions elsewhere in the literature that attempt to keep the unproductive character of pre-agricultural societies hidden. The Royal Commission on Aboriginal Peoples, for example, distorts terms like "nomadism" and "subsistence."[114] Instead of "nomadic," the Royal Commission prefers "mobile" since it claims that aboriginal groups "systematically harvested" land to conserve natural resources. The commission also objects to the use of the word "subsistence" to describe aboriginal economies because it "is a western concept, which carries with it the negative connotation of a hand-to-mouth existence." It maintains that "many of the resources [aboriginal peoples] used were extraordinarily productive, even by modern standards," and therefore it is incorrect to assume that aboriginal economies were "unspecialized, inefficient and unproductive."[115] To show this, the Royal Commission uses the example of nineteenth century aboriginal fisheries on the West Coast – which had already undergone a hundred years of exposure to European technologies.

Such distortions have also has been perpetrated by activist court decisions extending aboriginal rights, influencing scholarship on aboriginal peoples. In the case of the Heiltsuk in British Columbia, for example, economists Ian Keay and Cherie Metcalf use the Supreme Court decision *R. v. Gladstone* to argue that, for this aboriginal group, "the commercial trade of herring spawn on kelp was a central, significant and defining feature of their culture in the pre-contact period."[116] Examination of the court decision, however, reveals that this conclusion was not reached from careful evaluation of the evidence. Instead, the court was unduly influenced by arguments from defence lawyers who were pursuing the political agenda of establishing Heiltsuk rights to commercial harvesting. The arguments relied on excerpts from the journals of Alexander Mackenzie (1793) and Dr William Tolmie (1834), written many years after the Heiltsuk were introduced to European Iron Age technology and trade (thus undermining the claim that these practices were significant before contact).[117] The court decision also relied exclusively on the testimony of an anthropologist commissioned by the defence,[118] while ignoring opposing arguments, such as that of the anthropologist Sheila Robinson, for example, who asserted that the rareness of references in the accounts of explorers, government officials, and missionaries to Heiltsuk trade meant that the activity was not a "transaction based on necessity or exclusivity" and therefore not one of commerce. Robinson has also noted that Heiltsuk exchange did not constitute commerce since it was "driven by kin-based considerations" and "did not involve wage labour, standardized currencies, or markets removed in any way from a kin-based matrix."[119]

So prevalent has been the influence of political advocacy that it is now maintained that assertions about the primitive nature of aboriginal economies are a "myth."[120] These arguments either rely on the dubious suggestion that pre-contact aboriginal technology was "sophisticated," or simply assume that recognizing the historical evolution from hunting and gathering to industrial society must be due to some kind of biased thinking or moral failure.[121] Such opinions are generally supported by the beliefs of aboriginal peoples rather than an analysis of the objective requirements of modern economics. A common device is to refer to hunting and gathering as a "spiritual" activity, thereby transforming wage labour into a form of apostasy.[122] It is maintained that the developmental gap between wage labour and hunting and trapping should not be identified as a problem because it will lower the self-esteem of aboriginal persons, further entrenching their dependency.[123] This is another version of the "field of dreams" logic. Unproductive aboriginal workers or unviable native economies should be described as productive and viable so that they will miraculously *become* productive and viable.

The most significant distortion of present aboriginal circumstances has come in works that describe productive processes in aboriginal communities as a "mixed economy" – terminology generally used to refer to modern economies with both private and public forms of ownership.[124] Peter Usher, for example, claims that this form of production in aboriginal communities "integrates two spheres of activity, institutions and practices: market and subsistence, brought together, not simply side by side in a class-divided village, but directly within the household. Production and consumption are combined in one basic unit, the household, which functions in effect as a micro-enterprise."[125] Usher, in fact, provides a diagram (see figure 3.1) of this type of economy (originally developed with Martin Weinstein).[126] According to Usher, the diagram shows "how the household organizes productive activity and allocates the factors of production (land, labour and capital) so as to optimize income flows form both the market and subsistence spheres of the economy." These "income flows" include "cash income" from wages, the sale of commodities, or transfer payments, and "income in kind" from subsistence production. Usher maintains that such an economy explains why aboriginal peoples remain in areas "that by conventional economic measures do not have much going for them." He points out that this form of economy does not require a reliance on grocery stores or the payment of mortgages, and "the kinship-based social support network ensures that everyone's basic needs

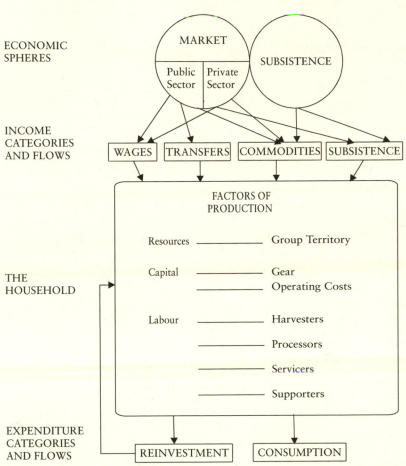

ECONOMIC
SPHERES

MARKET

Public | Private
Sector | Sector

SUBSISTENCE

INCOME
CATEGORIES
AND FLOWS

WAGES | TRANSFERS | COMMODITIES | SUBSISTENCE

FACTORS OF
PRODUCTION

Resources ——————— Group Territory

Capital ——————— Gear
——————— Operating Costs

THE
HOUSEHOLD

Labour ——————— Harvesters

——————— Processors

——————— Servicers

——————— Supporters

EXPENDITURE
CATEGORIES
AND FLOWS

REINVESTMENT | CONSUMPTION

Figure 3.1    The "Mixed Economy."

SOURCE: Peter Usher, "Environment, Race and Nation Reconsidered," *Canadian Geographer* 47, no. 4 (2003): 373.

are covered by the exchange of food, labour, equipment and personal care." It also "shows how the collective title in land and resources is essential to the viability of this economy," and therefore the dispossession of aboriginal lands is "not simply a matter of culture change or loss of tradition" but "is a violation of a property right with measurable economic consequences."[127]

This characterization of aboriginal communities, however, is a serious misrepresentation of the actual nature of the economies in these areas. In the above diagram, for example, the market and subsistence "economic spheres" are shown to have equal importance, as are the "income flows" from wages, transfers, commodities, and subsistence. But what such a diagram fails to acknowledge is that the whole "economy" is only made possible by transfers.[128] Although the "subsistence" economic sphere provides food, firewood, and other materials for household and community use, this represents a very small portion of the total cost of maintaining aboriginal communities. Hundreds of millions of dollars are needed for infrastructure as well as for advanced educational and medical services. Almost all of this "income flow" is derived from productive processes occurring outside of aboriginal communities.[129]

It is these externally produced surpluses, not the "subsistence economic sphere," that make it possible for aboriginal peoples to remain in these areas. Aboriginal "subsistence," in fact, is only possible because external economic processes provide cash for snowmobiles, powerboats, rifles, and all the other technologically advanced equipment needed for hunting today. Money for mortgages is not needed only because the government covers these costs. It is government funding that "ensures that everyone's basic needs are covered," since without transfers, aboriginal communities – or even whole territories like Nunavut – would not exist.

## THE WITHERING AWAY OF ABORIGINAL COMMUNITIES

Once the unviability of aboriginal economies is recognized, there will be a tendency to shift ground from a denial of the lower productivity of aboriginal cultures to questions as to why the standards of "white society" or "Europeans" must prevail. Why, it will be asked, should aboriginal people have to accommodate themselves to "European ways," and not the other way round? The answer to this question is that aboriginal people want to share in the benefits of modern society. They want pickup trucks, indoor plumbing and heating, snowmobiles and rifles, and modern services. Yet the low productivity of hunting and gathering means that they cannot be participants in the economic system that produces these items.

Land claims initiatives, however, are often supported by those on the political left because they are seen as opposing capitalism. But, as David Newhouse points out, there is not an "outright rejection of capitalism by Aboriginal people," only a "desire to adapt this particular political-economic system to work in accordance with Aboriginal belief systems."[130] This generally involves either becoming rentiers in resource-rich areas or attempting to preserve an unviable economic form by extracting transfers from productive members of society.[131] Neither of these "adaptations" addresses current problems.

Dependency and social dysfunction are the norm in aboriginal communities because these areas were developed to warehouse people who lacked the requirements to engage in the developing economy.[132] But this problem cannot be solved simply by encouraging aboriginal peoples to leave the reserves, as some have suggested.[133] The reserves exist because aboriginal people who retain neolithic cultural characteristics are *unable* to participate in the wider society. To phase out the reserves before this problem is addressed would be to deprive these people of what they currently need to survive. Providing them with intensive social services so that they can acquire the skills and attitudes to participate in actual economic processes, on the other hand, will gradually make the reserves less necessary as the native population is able to make the transition to modern life. The reserves will wither away when they are no longer necessary to sustain the dependent and dysfunctional native population. But such a circumstance is resisted by lawyers working for aboriginal organizations on the grounds that vacating reserve lands will jeopardize future aboriginal rights claims.[134]

Transitional programs oriented toward the eventual phasing out of unviable areas, however, are impossible in the context of the current promotion of self-government. Proposals for self-government do not attempt to bridge the developmental gap; instead, they devolve responsibility to aboriginal organizations to hide it. The incorporation of "traditional knowledge" and the involvement of elders in various programs are promoted, which does nothing to develop the native population. Even more disturbing, the devolution of control to aboriginal communities is resulting in the entrenchment of tribalism, making it difficult for most native people to access even the basic resources needed for survival.

# 4

# Self-Government: An Inherent Right to Tribal Dictatorships

Throughout history, taboos have existed against miscegenation – the intermarriage of people of different races – many becoming integrated into modern legal systems. In South Africa, for example, the policy of apartheid prevented miscegenation between blacks and whites,[1] and German laws developed during the Nazi era criminalized "race-mixing."[2] This was also the case in the United States, where a number of states' laws prohibited interracial marriage. These laws were claimed to serve legitimate purposes, including preserving "racial integrity," as well as preventing "the corruption of blood," "a mongrel breed of citizens," and "the obliteration of racial pride." The laws were also supported by various religious beliefs. In a famous case in the state of Virginia, for example, the judge stated that "Almighty God created the races white, black, yellow, Malay and red, and he placed them on separate continents. And but for the interference with his arrangement there would be no cause for such marriages. The fact that he separated the races shows that he did not intend for the races to mix."[3]

With the defeat of European facism, the end of apartheid in South Africa, and the declaration of anti-miscegenation laws as unconstitutional by the United States Supreme Court in 1967, such pernicious ideas have come to be rejected in modern multi-ethnic societies. Although still espoused by fringe elements, the promotion of "racial integrity" and "racial pride" is absent from current debates on human development. Rather, racial interaction is recognized as inevitable, with the positive effects of extending the gene pool and lessening social conflict. It testifies to global political and cultural progress that no regime today officially promotes the segregation of different races – that is, except when it comes to various self-government initiatives concerning aboriginal peoples. Because of their focus on ethnic isolation, these initiatives embrace a philosophy not unlike those promoted in Nazi Germany, South Africa, and the southern United States.[4] The tactics of confusing physical differences with species differentiation, the concern with the preservation of culture through racial segregation, and the linking of racial hierarchies to some kind of dictate from "the Creator" become disturbingly familiar when one views a number of arguments put forth to justify self-government. In an attempt to channel the resentment that already exists in aboriginal communities toward the "white man," some aboriginal leaders have argued that natives should remain spiritually and culturally "pure" by developing separate institutions and "ways of life" (cf. the "Record of the Two Row Wampum Belt" ).

An extreme example of this reasoning emerged in a court case in 1993 where three Alberta Indian bands sued the federal government to prevent members who had been historically deprived of their Indian status from rejoining the band. To justify this exclusion, the bands maintained that giving status to others would destroy the cultural integrity of their communities. Chief Wayne Roan of the Ermineskin Band explained: "The moose and elk do not mate, that is the natural law ... Our elders have always said Cree should marry Cree to preserve the culture and way of life."[5]

The similarity of this argument to fascist doctrine was not lost on the judge who heard the case. At the time, Federal Court Justice Frank Muldoon maintained that Roan's statements embodied "racism and apartheid." He argued that societies everywhere experience a loss of culture when they come in contact with others and that an attempt to exclude people on the basis of blood was indicative of fascist politics.[6]

Judge Muldoon's articulation of the political implications of Roan's arguments, however, was not appreciated by his superiors. The Canadian Judicial Council criticized him for using "unnecessarily disparaging and offensive language about aboriginal peoples." It then went on to state that "your use of needlessly inflammatory, derogatory and culturally insensitive language ... leaves the impression that you used your judicial office inappropriately to express your personal opinion in relation to aboriginal rights." According to the council, Muldoon's "references to such emotive terms as 'fascism', 'racism' and 'apartheid'" were unacceptable because they "have the effect of further alienating aboriginal peoples from the Canadian judiciary."[7]

That the Canadian Judicial Council was more concerned about "alienating aboriginal peoples from the Canadian judiciary" than in rejecting fascist, racist, and segregationist attitudes is indicative of the acceptance of the Eleventh Commandment and the presence of the racism accusation taboo in discussions of self-government in Canada. Such a climate assumes that all criticism of aboriginal policy, no matter how justified, is "colonialist" or "culturally insensitive." The ideas expressed by Roan would be intolerable if a non-aboriginal person were expressing them. But because of Roan's aboriginal identity, the Eleventh Commandment leads to an acceptance of his rationale, since to do otherwise would be interpreted as a rejection of aboriginal aspirations.

Supporters of self-government also attempt to evade the racially exclusionary character of the aboriginal leadership's demands by maintaining that aboriginal groups constitute a cultural identification that is not based on race.[8] But such a view ignores that aboriginal culture is rooted in the kinship group, where blood ties bind a community together, making it fundamentally exclusive.[9] In the words of the Royal Commission on Aboriginal Peoples, "political life has always been closely connected with the family, the land and a strong sense of spirituality" existing "thousands of years" before European contact.[10] This means that aboriginal politics shares a fundamental characteristic with racist world views – it actively excludes those who not share a biological relationship with the group. This characteristic of self-government was recognized by the Canadian philosopher Charles Taylor even when he was trying to refute the charge that aboriginal politics are racist. According to Taylor, an important characteristic of self-government is that "certain powers ... will be given to a group that is defined by descent; that is, a group that others can't join at will."[11]

Although Chief Roan expressed his opinions more candidly than most aboriginal leaders would dare, the pervasive attempts at connecting "ancestry" with "land" comes very close to the fascist conception of *Blut und Boden* (blood and soil). All claims to aboriginal self-government, like all ethnically based forms of nationalism, have racist tendencies because they oppose forms of political mobilization that find common ground among groups that are ethnically different, and grant privileges on the basis of ancestral connections. This is contrary to the modern understanding of democracy and human rights upon which countries such as Canada are based. Unlike ethnic-based conceptions of nationalism, Canada grants citizenship to people regardless of ancestry.

The tribal basis of politics in aboriginal communities, therefore, is incompatible with modern values because it is exclusive rather than inclusive, concerned with ancestral privilege rather than equal citizenship under the law, and reactionary rather than progressive. Although the Canadian public is supportive of the aboriginal movement because it purports to represent marginalized members of society, it is important to recognize that, as anthropologist John Price pointed out, "the demands made by activists on behalf of Indians often conflict with general Canadian values and cultural features. The fundamentals of democratic life, the separation of religion and politics, industrialization, urbanization, and policies universally applicable to the whole citizenry are among the particular points of friction."[12]

## CONSOLIDATING THE LAWYERS' RETIREMENT FUND

Arguments promoting self-government for aboriginal peoples in Canada centre around the idea that it is a right that is "inherent." Although pressure for aboriginal control over government-funded programs and services emerged in the 1960s, claims about the "inherent right of self-government" came later. This development occurred alongside efforts to elevate aboriginal and treaty rights to the highest level possible. Claiming that the right to self-government is inherent creates an uncontestable rationale that aboriginal peoples can never have this right taken away or regulated by any other authority.

But what makes the aboriginal right to self-government inherent? Generally when we think of rights, we look to various legal documents to show that a particular entitlement or protection exists. The Charter of Rights and Freedoms, for example, gives citizens the right to free speech, to practise their religion, to travel around the country, and so on. Section 35 of the Constitution Act of 1982 also tells us that the Canadian state recognizes "existing aboriginal and treaty rights." However, this makes these rights flow from the Canadian constitution – a legal document – not from any claim to "inherency." The legal recognition of inherency contradicts its purported transcendental character.

Aside from pointing to the Royal Proclamation of 1763 and international law (a tactic that again undermines the concept of inherency), and relying on religious mythology (the claims that "the Creator" placed aboriginal peoples in North America so that they could be its custodians), aboriginal leaders argue that the inherent nature of their rights is due to the fact that they were the original occupants of what is now Canada. But doesn't this mean that all previous occupiers of territories have an inherent right to govern themselves on what used to be their "ancestral lands"? Shouldn't the ancestors of the Huron govern what used to be Huronia, or the Cree give up some of the land they came to control in the course of the fur trade, since they used arms acquired from the Hudson's Bay Company to displace other tribes? And if we all go back in history to our original ancestry, doesn't this mean that all of us, including aboriginal peoples, have a right to land and governance in our original "homeland" – Africa?

The fact that human history has been a complex process of migration, conquest, displacement, genetic (i.e., racial) mixing, and cultural development makes any idea of inherent rights untenable.[13] Rights to land and self-governance have only come about when there has been social agreement that such entitlements exist and there is a legitimate authority that ensures that they are respected. Canadian society might decide to grant rights to various aboriginal groups for reasons of expediency or out of a particular conception of justice, but these rights do not exist as some kind of transcendental principle. Whether aboriginal leaders like it or not, aboriginal rights exist only in laws that are enforced by a state apparatus. And since aboriginal tribes in North America had not developed states before contact, it always has been French, British, or Canadian law that determined the nature and existence of their rights. This is why so much time and resources were spent attempting to have the "inherent right" to self-government recognized in the Constitution Act of 1982.

The Canadian Constitution has been the focal point of demands for self-government precisely because it is the highest law of the land. As such, entrenching the "inherent right" in the constitution would mean that various self-government agreements could be revoked by the Canadian populace only with great difficulty. It would require a constitutional amendment, and as any student of the constitutional struggles of the 1980s and 1990s will testify, finding agreement between the federal government and the provinces for even minor constitutional changes is very difficult. Gaining constitutional status for self-government, therefore, would increase the likelihood that Canadians would be stuck with an expensive and cumbersome "third order of government" for a long period of time, even if they wanted to change the policy.

Besides the legal leverage that would come with entrenching the inherent right to self-government in the constitution, the process also has been embarked upon because of the lucrative character of the negotiations themselves. After stealthily managing to get an evasive reference to "existing aboriginal and treaty rights" in the constitution, lawyers were hired to define them. Although the constitutional meetings to define these rights focused almost exclusively on developing an amendment concerning self-government, none ever materialized. Aboriginal organizations were demanding sovereignty in the sense that aboriginal peoples should be allowed to determine their own membership and forms of governance in isolation from Canadian law,[14] while Ottawa wanted self-government to be delegated from either federal or provincial authorities so that there would be some accountability for public funds allocated. This put the aspirations of aboriginal leaders in direct conflict with the mandate of federal and provincial governments, who as representatives of all people in Canada, were understandably reluctant to allow more than six hundred publicly funded regimes to operate independently of popularly elected institutions. As a result, every proposal put forward by the federal government was rejected by the aboriginal leadership.[15]

Despite the fact that the "inherent right" was never entrenched in the constitution during the 1980s, and even though further attempts at entrenchment in the Charlottetown Accord were defeated politically, the Liberal government declared that self-government was a constitutional right and began negotiations on this basis.[16] In 1993 it developed a "Self-Government Policy Guide" and began consultation processes with various aboriginal groups.

These negotiations, however, have not been very effective in achieving results. An internal audit by the Department of Indian and Northern Affairs in 2002 found that the $75 million in government funds spent on thirty-nine sets of negotiations involving 327 communities had only resulted in five deals. (By the end of 2006, a total of eight final agreements had been signed.)[17] The audit also found that the money was poorly tracked, and so it was difficult to determine where it went or what was achieved.[18] But these costs are not surprising when just one Agreement in Principle can contain seventy-seven pages of legalese.[19] And even when these agreements are finalized, it doesn't mean that they are settled. Agreements are seen as just being the framework upon which further negotiations will be based. Then, with the "settlement" of these agreements, comes "implementation."

The negotiations surrounding the "inherent right" to self-government have been supplemented with parallel consultations to amend the Indian Act. Enacted in 1876, the act defines the special guardianship or "fiduciary" relationship between aboriginals and the Crown. It stipulates who legally is an "Indian," and the entitlements that come with this designation. It regulates all aspects of reserve life, including band elections and the powers of the chief and council. It gives Indian lands a special legal designation and determines the government's role in managing and selling the resources on these lands. Finally, it allows certain exemptions from taxation. More generally, the Indian Act ensures that it is the federal government, not provincial authorities, that is legally responsible for providing services to Indians on reserves.[20]

Although the government originally intended the Indian Act to be a stop-gap measure to be phased out as the native population developed and assimilated into the wider society, and has toyed with its elimination since the 1940s on the grounds that it is discriminatory and/or paternalistic, these efforts have not gone far. The act, except for a few amendments in 1927, 1951, and 1960, is very similar to what existed in the nineteenth century, despite decades of consultations. The first attempt to eliminate it occurred in 1968, culminating with the 1969 White Paper. At the time, the Liberal government assumed that the White Paper's proposal to get rid of the act would be supported by the aboriginal leadership.[21] Although the vehement opposition to this proposal made the government reluctant to embark upon further attempts at amendment, the continuing dependency and political dysfunction on reserves reactivated reform efforts. Both Liberal and Conservative governments have tried repeatedly to enact changes, both to free up ownership restrictions on reserves and to make band councils more accountable. Despite the constant infusions of funds for more consultations,[22] and even proposals that aboriginal bands could opt out if they opposed the new legislation,[23] all the efforts have been unsuccessful.[24]

A common feature of these ventures is that regardless of the native leadership's constant complaints that the act needs revision, there is a great reluctance to change it.[25] The argument inevitably arises that any change should be opposed because of the possibility that aboriginal and treaty rights will be infringed. Furthermore, no matter how lengthy and expensive the consultations, there never seem to be enough of them.[26] The result is perpetual negotiations without hope of resolution. According to Fred Fenwick, this circumstance is due to a "disconnect" between aboriginal leaders and the government about the inherent right to self-government. According to Fenwick, these different conceptions lead aboriginal groups to perceive consultation as "meaningful dialogue with all affected First Nations and maybe a de facto veto," while the government wants to embark upon a "traveling road show with hand-picked participants whose suggestions may or may not be actually put into effect."[27]

But while aboriginal leaders say that their resistance to reform of the Indian Act is because the proposed changes embody "racism" and/or "colonialism" and the government's attempt to thwart aboriginal self-determination,[28] this avoids the reality of how aboriginal leaders are generally opposed to accountability as a principle. Aboriginal politics is fundamentally at odds with modern governance because it is tribal, not national, in character. Consequently, common rights based on citizenship in a geographical area – what the proposed changes to the Indian Act were trying to bring about – are strongly resisted.

## THE CONFUSION OF TRIBALISM WITH NATIONHOOD

In 1981 the National Indian Brotherhood put forward a "Declaration of First Nations" intended as a political manifesto, outlining the basis of aboriginal demands for self-government. Amongst other things, the declaration claimed that "we the Original Peoples of this Land know the Creator put us here"; "the Creator has given us the right to govern ourselves and the right to self-determination"; and "the rights and responsibilities given to us by the Creator cannot be altered or taken away by any other Nation."[29]

Besides revealing the religious mythology and romanticism upon which aboriginal claims to self-government are based, the declaration is an interesting document in that it marked a shift in thinking about the character of aboriginal politics. Until the late 1970s, aboriginal groups were commonly described as "bands" or "tribes," not "nations."[30] Even the original aboriginal organizations referred to themselves as "Indian Brotherhoods," and it was not until 1982 that the Assembly of First Nations came into existence.

Essentially, this change in strategy is an attempt to inflate the legitimacy of aboriginal demands for self-government. It was prompted in large part by a statement in the United Nations' Charter that "all peoples have the right to self-determination."[31] Although the United Nations did not define what it meant by "peoples," it is generally understood to refer to *national* groups that share a common territory, language, and history,[32] not *tribes* or *bands*, which are generally much smaller and organized on the basis of kinship, not geography.

The same motivation is behind claims that aboriginal people were "sovereign" before contact. It is thus argued that natives should be able to reassert their pre-contact sovereignty through a process of decolonization. Patrick Macklem, a prominent legal scholar and advocate for aboriginal rights, for example, maintains that "four complex social facts lie at the heart of the relationship between aboriginal people and the Canadian state. First, Aboriginal people belong to distinctive cultures that were and continue to be threatened by non-Aboriginal beliefs, philosophies, and ways of life. Second, prior to European contact, Aboriginal people lived in and occupied vast portions of North America. Third, before European contact, Aboriginal people not only occupied North America, they exercised sovereign authority over persons and territory. Fourth, Aboriginal people participated and continue to participate in a treaty process with the Crown."[33] Macklem then goes on to assert that "the complexity of these social facts does not lie in their factual accuracy. Although some might take issue with their precise formulation, few deny their basic truth."[34]

What Macklem has done is to present three accurate "social facts" with one that is erroneous. Although aboriginal people do have "distinctive cultures" that are "threatened," and they did "occup[y]" North America before Europeans arrived and continue to sign treaties with the Crown, they did not exercise "sovereign authority" before contact. Sovereign authority requires the development of laws and the existence of a state apparatus to ensure that they are enforced. Macklem does not undertake an analysis of this circumstance; it is sufficient for him to state that it is a "social fact," deploying this "basic truth" to claim that aboriginal self-government should be protected by the Canadian Constitution because "Aboriginal and European nations were formal equals at the time of contact."[35]

The erroneous characterization of aboriginal groups as "sovereign nations" is obscured further by claiming that they were "organized societies" before contact. All social groupings are organized to some extent; this does not make them nations exercising sovereignty. An organized society, to be a nation, would require a viable economy so that a state apparatus *could* exercise jurisdiction over a particular territory. This is not the case for aboriginal "nations," since even wealthy aboriginal groups cannot exist without the infrastructure made possible by the economies of scale present in Canadian society. In other words, a group's assertion of sovereignty and self-determination is dependent on its material capacity. It requires a level of economic and cultural development that is not present in aboriginal bands or tribes.

This makes aboriginal nationalism very different from Quebec's claims to self-determination.[36] The Canadian state's attempts to thwart Quebec sovereignty, however, has resulted in a number of legal initiatives causing deceptive comparisons between the two. Whatever one's political views on Quebec sovereignty, there is one fact that cannot be denied – Quebec, unlike any of the six-hundred-plus aboriginal "First Nations" now in existence, has the *capacity* to assert independent statehood if it so chooses. References to aboriginal peoples having lived for a longer period of time in the area, "inherent rights to self-determination," and other legal or religious arguments obscure this fundamental difference. Quebec has a viable economy, a distinct territory, and a state to manage it. It has a language and an intellectual history that is shared by several other countries in the modern world. And although a population of six million is small by modern standards, a number of nation-states in the world today are able to participate in global economic and political processes with the same resource base. And, most importantly, Quebec sovereigntists are not demanding that the realization of self-determination be accompanied by perpetual transfers from the federal government.

This is in contrast to aboriginal peoples in Canada. Unlike the Québécois, who have made the transition from feudalism to capitalism and participate fully in the modern world, over six hundred bands stretch across the entire Canadian land mass in isolated pockets that are completely dependent on federal funds. Even if all these bands were lumped together, they would not have the prerequisites to become "self-determining." All the talk about aboriginal nationhood and sovereignty are merely fallacious legal arguments made for the purpose of obtaining compensation from the government. And since the realization of these demands will create obstacles for Quebec sovereignty by increasing the legal ties between the Canadian state and aboriginal groups in Quebec, they are now enthusiastically entertained by the federal government.

In addition to being tribal rather than national, governance in aboriginal communities differs substantially from modern political processes since it is determined by a *traditional* as opposed to a *legal-rational* form of authority.[37] In systems based on legal-rational principles, "authority is attached to offices rather than to the individuals occupying them," and there is "a formal and abstract conception of legal order existing and having significance apart from the interests of individual persons."[38] In such a political system, "written rules govern conduct in almost all settings, decisions are made consistent with rules rather than on a case-by-case basis, and exceptions to rules require formal justification, sometimes in new rules."[39] With systems based on traditional authority, on the other hand, "there is no requirement that rules be consistent, and appeals made to those exercising traditional authority are made personally, not as matters of principle."[40]

Because the appeals that are made personally in aboriginal societies are rooted in kinship relations,[41] there is no basis for the liberal democratic principles that have evolved to accommodate different interests between rival factions, such as equality under the law, freedom of speech, or the separation of church and state. Aboriginal communities exercising traditional forms of self-government, therefore, provide no overarching authority to protect those without family connections or to ensure that all citizens receive access to publicly funded social services. As is shown in the next chapter, conventional policing services are opposed by native leaders who demand the prerogative of "handling their own affairs."

The lack of institutional mechanisms for distributing public resources in aboriginal culture is disguised by claims that aboriginal communities govern by consensus. The Royal Commission on Aboriginal Peoples, for example, maintains that many aboriginal people want to return to "decision making by consensus" instead of "majority-based electoral systems" because it is consistent with their culture. It is maintained that electoral systems are flawed because they are "susceptible to domination by numerically powerful families in the community," while consensual processes "will incorporate broader and more balanced systems of accountability."[42]

What is not explained, however, is how "decision making by consensus" will work when there are conflicting interests within the community. Despite vague statements such as "consensus ... is more quality of life than a distinct process, structure or outcome," and "decision making by consensus, often referred to as coming to one mind, is gradual, and the resolution of issues is built piece by piece, without confrontation," how can "coming to one mind" be achieved if the community contains different factions, each wanting to control the distribution of resources to benefit family members? The Royal Commission even acknowledges that consensus government "presuppose[s] a basic political unit having strong continuing ties, such as those found in the extended family." How will such a system be compatible with national principles that expect public officials to distribute resources to citizens regardless of their familial relationships?

Although these problems have been downplayed by the federal government for a number of years, they are beginning to be flushed out into the open,[43] as more and more instances of tribal corruption (otherwise euphemized as "mismanagement," "mistakes," or "growing pains") have received media coverage.[44] "Accounting discrepancies" across the country have been uncovered, and it was estimated in 2000 that 183 out of 609 aboriginal communities were in financial trouble.[45] These circumstances might explain why only 37 per cent of aboriginal people on reserves were satisfied with their band government's performance in 2003, while 51 per cent supported the federal government's attempts to improve accountability. Calvin Helin even notes that the 37 per cent approval rating of band governments "accords roughly with the number of family members that Chief and Councils are likely to have in a community."[46]

Despite increasing concerns, there is still no recognition of the serious obstacles to any attempt to institute accountability in these areas. Although a few aboriginal organizations have formed to fight corruption, much of this opposition simply reflects the efforts of rival factions to obtain power to control funding in their own interests.[47] Many aboriginal leaders are so tribal in their outlook that they do not think that distributing public money on the basis of kinship is wrong. This explains the astonishing arrogance of a number of aboriginal leaders when their unethical practices have been discovered and publicized.[48] Exposure of the endemic corruption that exists on reserves is met with aggressive assertions that this is merely a racist attempt "to discredit First Nations and put into question their ability to govern themselves."[49] Leaders who pay themselves huge salaries while "their people" live in poverty refuse to answer questions from the media, stating that they do not have to explain their behaviour to non-aboriginal people.[50] Those aboriginal people who raise questions about the spending of funds are accused of disloyalty, since native leaders belligerently declare that all problems should only be discussed "behind closed doors" within the community.[51]

But self-government is a way for the government to delay culpability for the mess that it has created, and so there is a tendency to concede to the demands of aboriginal leaders. Jean Allard, for example, has noted that "Indian Affairs has effectively escaped public criticism [for the lack of accountability on reserves] by handing over authority to make decisions to chiefs and councils who, if pressed, cry racism."[52] This offloading of responsibility has been reinforced by the federal government's fears that it will face lawsuits from aboriginal organizations if it continues to act as a trustee of native peoples and their resources.[53]

Although declarations of aboriginal nationhood, self-determination, and sovereignty are largely promoted by governmental and Aboriginal Industry interests, there is a more general reluctance by non-aboriginals to recognize that self-government is not consistent with the objective interests of native people. Aside from sympathy for their plight, public support for self-government exists because of the assumption that aboriginal tribes were socialistic or egalitarian before contact, and that the oppressive character of native communities is exclusively due to European influence. Preventing European interference in "aboriginal ways," as well as revitalizing "traditional governance," is the proposed remedy for native marginalization and deprivation.

### DEBUNKING THE MYTH OF NATURAL SOCIALISM

The influence of the Eleventh Commandment has led to the general acceptance of the idea that the claims of aboriginal leaders should be supported regardless of content. As a result, descriptions of native leaders tend to be filled with effusive references to their "eloquence," "sophistication" and "savvy" or self-sacrifice. There have, however, been a few more realistic appraisals of native leadership. Some of these accounts observe that aboriginal organizations are completely funded by the Canadian government, an entity they supposedly contest. As a result, they have a tendency to shape their "opposition" in a way that maintains the funding they receive, even if this ends up perpetuating native deprivation.[54]

The most uncompromising version of this argument has been put forward by Howard Adams, a Métis activist and academic. In *Prison of Grass* and *A Tortured People*, Adams lambastes the aboriginal leadership as "collaborators" and "compradors." According to Adams, the money flowing into aboriginal communities from the government has created an aboriginal elite completely unrepresentative of the marginalized aboriginal population. He argues that because these leaders are free of accountability to the government, the current system "is inclined to attract persons who are opportunists, drifters, hucksters, uncommitted and non-political workers. The flow of easy money and its unaccountability generate a basic rip-off philosophy. Because there is no real direction or purpose in the jobs, a 'free loading' philosophy develops."[55]

But in Adams's view, the problems currently experienced with the native leadership have been entirely created by European influence. This is because he believes that "sharing was a natural characteristic of [the aboriginal] way of life" before contact, making coercive forms of social control unnecessary. For him, therefore, the solutions lie in restoring traditional political institutions, spirituality, and the "indigenous lifestyle." He also argues that it is necessary to reject "eurocentric historians' and anthropologists' distorted interpretations of our economy and culture. To us, these eurocentric academics were mere apologists for the colonizers's oppression and its corrupt imperialist state."[56]

It is often implied that a return to traditional forms of "governance" will form part of the solution to aboriginal problems. The general view is similar to that expressed by Adams – that corruption has been caused by European influence, since pre-contact aboriginal societies shared resources and individuals did not accumulate material wealth. These theorists maintain that the problem lies with what is referred to as "neo-colonialism" – the imposition of "colonial institutional structures, philosophies, and norms" on aboriginal political systems.[57] Again like Adams, they maintain that the key to solving the current leadership problems is for aboriginal peoples to reject "European" values and revert to their traditional conceptions of political organization.[58]

These views rely on a misunderstanding of historical development and the erroneous assumption that aboriginal societies embody socialist principles. Socialism is an advanced form of political organization that comes about through overcoming the class contradictions of capitalism; it occurs when private ownership of the means of production is replaced by social control of the factories, natural resources, and technology used to produce goods and services. Because the interests of the working class are universal regardless of where their labour is performed, socialism is international in character; the individual's role in the productive process surmounts concepts of national identity. And although no socialist society has ever been completely achieved, this does not negate the fact that socialized forms of production have evolved out of, not preceded, private ownership.

While aboriginal societies before contact were without class divisions, not all classless societies are socialistic. Aboriginal societies were actually pre-class, with distribution determined by kinship relations. In all human societies characterized by neolithic technology and hunting and gathering/horticultural practices, extended kinship groups have shared resources communally. This did not come about because of some "philosophy" or "spirituality" separate from material circumstances but because production was too meagre for wealth to be accumulated. As soon as aboriginal peoples acquired Iron Age technology and participated in a market economy, economic differentiation and "hierarchies" began to form.[59] Currently what exists in aboriginal communities is what Elizabeth Rata has called "neotraditionalism" or "neotribal capitalism," in which "traditional leaders of a revived communal tribe" enjoy privileged access to capitalized resources and compensation packages.[60]

Myths about the existence of "natural socialist" philosophies before contact also fail to consider that "consensus" and "sharing" occurred *within*, not *between*, kinship groupings. Throughout human history the survival instinct entailed the sharing of all kinds of resources within nuclear and extended families. This sharing, however, in no way indicates socialistic cooperation, or that non-kin will be treated the same way as family members. Institutionalized cooperation with non-kin only emerged with the development of civilization. While all societies have a particular concern for their own children as part of the impetus for the propagation of their genes, societies with an extensive division of labour require the expansion of cooperation to include civic or non-kin elements. The capacity for such universalism is the result of our evolving culturally past the challenges of immediate personal survival to a broader, more inclusive orientation toward commonality rather than difference.

In addition to misguided assumptions about the "natural socialism" of aboriginal peoples, another argument, which is somewhat in contradiction to the former, is put forward in support of aboriginal claims to self-government. This is that aboriginal self-government should be recognized because it has *similar* principles and processes to those found in modern systems of governance. Numerous claims are made that aboriginal societies had sophisticated and democratic forms of governance before contact, but no convincing evidence is produced to support these arguments. One of the most prominent of these concerns the relationship between the Iroquois Confederacy and the American Constitution.

## FABRICATING POLITICAL DEVELOPMENT: THE
## IROQUOIS CONFEDERACY

Seldom has the revision of history in support of self-government demands occurred more blatantly than in the case of the Iroquois Confederacy and its relationship to constitutional development in the United States. In many texts on aboriginal politics, it is claimed that the constitution of the United States (and by extension, the one in Canada) was derived in varying degrees from the political system of the Iroquois. For example, David Ahenakew, a former grand chief of the Assembly of First Nations, maintains that "Benjamin Franklin, and others wrote lengthy treatises on the political structure of First Nations, particularly the one closest to them, namely, the Iroquois Confederacy."[61] Kiera Ladner maintains in an introductory political science text that "a growing body of literature shows that Indigenous ideas and practices contributed to how concepts such as rights, liberty, happiness, equality, democracy, and federalism were understood by American founding fathers" and that "there is much evidence to suggest that these leaders emulated the Haudenosaunee political system of he [sic] Iroquois confederacy."[62] And although Ladner cites only Bruce Johansen's *Debating Democracy: Native American Legacy of Freedom* as the example of the "much evidence" in existence, a number of works make similar claims: Johansen's previous work, *Forgotten Founders*, Jack Weatherford's *Indian Givers*, Oren Lyons's *Exiled in the Land of the Free*, and Donald Grinde's *The Iroquois and the Founding of the American Nation*, to name a few.[63]

It turns out, however, that despite the "growing body of literature" asserting a connection between the American founding fathers and aboriginal politics, no framer of the Declaration of Independence or the Bill of Rights ever wrote any treatise (never mind one that was "lengthy") on the "political structure of First Nations." One of the benefits of a literate culture is that the evidence for this claim can be evaluated, and there are no references to the Iroquois in the debates of those who concerned themselves with constitutional development – Alexander Hamilton, James Madison, John Jay, John Adams, Thomas Jefferson, Tom Paine, and Benjamin Franklin. According to Elisabeth Tooker, a prominent anthropologist in the United States, only three documents connect the Iroquois Confederacy to the American Constitution.[64] Two of these concern a speech by Canasatego, an Iroquois chief and spokesman, which was made at a treaty conference in 1744. In this speech

Canasatego urges the colonies to form a union so that the American colonists, like the Iroquois, "will become stronger." This speech was then referred to by the commissioners of Indian Affairs in 1775 during another meeting with the Iroquois. In this meeting the commissioners mentioned that "advice was given about thirty years ago, by your wise forefathers, in a great council ... when Cannassateego spoke to us, the white people." The words of Canasatego are then repeated for the benefit of the people at the meeting.

The third document is a passage written by Benjamin Franklin in 1751, responding to some musings of Archibald Kennedy. Kennedy had written a pamphlet favouring the union of the colonies, which he also thought would "encourage our Indians." Franklin agreed, adding that "it would be a very strange thing if six Nations of ignorant Savages should be capable of forming a Scheme for such an Union, and be able to execute it in such a Manner, as that it has subsisted [for] Ages, and appears indissoluble; and yet that a like Union should be impracticable for Ten or a Dozen Colonies, to whom it is more necessary, and must be more advantageous; and who cannot be supposed to want an equal Understanding of their Interest."[65]

Tooker points out that the two documents pertaining to Canasatego's speech are not very convincing pieces of evidence for the claim that the American Constitution was based on the Iroquois Confederacy because they only confirm that "at least some whites and some Indians in the eighteenth century realized the advantages of confederation." They do not show that the American constitution was based on the Iroquois Confederacy. The passage from Franklin cannot be considered to support this claim at all, since Franklin uses the success of the system of "ignorant Savages" only to support his argument that a "like Union" would work for the politically aware colonists. It is obvious that Franklin thought that the Iroquois' political system was too primitive to be used by the colonists. Franklin's biographer, Francis Jennings, is amazed that this statement has been used as "proof" for the Iroquoian origins of the American Constitution, calling the people who make this claim "Iroquois propagandists." In Jennings's words, "How [Franklin's] contempt for 'ignorant Savages' can be twisted into praise for them is beyond my comprehension."[66]

Bruce E. Johansen, professor of Communication and Native Studies at the University of Nebraska at Omaha (and the source used by Ladner), however, is not deterred by Jennings's rebuke. The problem, according to Johansen, is that Jennings "reads Franklin without nuance."[67]

Although Johansen does not explain how one reads "with nuance," presumably it involves a postmodernist strategy whereby words like "ignorant" and "savage" are given the alternate meanings "sophisticated" and "civilized."

The fact that grandiose claims are made on such shaky foundations illustrates the extent to which the motivations of aboriginal rights advocates have usurped the standards of evidence in social science. Drawing parallels between the Iroquois Confederacy and American institutional development is important to them, since it gives credence to claims for self-government. After all, if the traditions of the Iroquois are similar to those espoused in the American constitution, how can anyone be opposed to granting them rights?

Citing numerous "authoritative" sources claiming that the Iroquois Confederacy formed such an influence is usually enough to stop people from questioning this claim. The "founding fathers" were grappling with much more complex issues than those found in an extended kinship group attempting to protect its access to fur-bearers and European trade goods. Theorists developing the American Constitution were considering issues such as states' rights, freedom from British monarchical control, the extent of democracy that would be allowed (i.e., there were arguments over suffrage and whether the presidency and senate should be life terms), separation of powers, federal versus unitary political systems, bicameral versus unicameral legislatures, and the separation of church and state. None of these matters was of concern to the Iroquois. Their "confederacy" was essentially an indeterminate military alliance, not an attempt to reconcile the competing interests brought about by the incorporation of an economic powerhouse into the world capitalist system.

And one does not have to look very far to find the actual intellectual influences on the framing of the American Constitution: the writings of John Locke and Montesquieu. Both political theorists were interested in the separation of powers (executive, legislative, and judicial), and Locke especially was interested in the boundaries between public authority and private property. Although Montesquieu had nothing to say about the Iroquois, since he concerned himself with Roman and British law, readers of the *Report of the Royal Commission on Aboriginal Peoples* will know that John Locke (like other contract theorists such as Thomas Hobbes and Jean Jacques Rousseau) maintained that aboriginal peoples were in a "state of nature" without laws or government.[68] It is likely that the "founding fathers" had a similar opinion. If they considered the matter at all, they would have seen the confederacy as too primitive a political system to address the requirements of a constitution for the United States.

"Iroquois thesis" advocates, however, are not even content to limit themselves to the unsupportable claim that the Iroquois confederacy was the basis of the American Constitution. They go further and establish the Iroquois Confederacy as the "oldest constitution in the world." This has been achieved through the use of oral histories and Adarios such as Deganawidah (The Peacemaker), Hiawatha, Atotarho, and Jingosaseh. According to Iroquois beliefs, the Iroquois Constitution – otherwise known as "The Great Law of Peace" – was adopted in 1451. Although the Iroquois had no numbers, the "founding date" was proposed by Paul A.W. Wallace (author of *White Roots of Peace*) because Iroquoian oral histories claimed that an eclipse supposedly occurred at the time the "Great Law" was being ratified, and an eclipse occurred in the area in 1451.[69]

The founding date has been pushed back even further by Barbara Mann and Jerry Fields.[70] Relying once again on eclipse tables, they maintain that in 1451 this particular eclipse's shadow fell over Pennsylvania, not over Iroquois territory. In 1142, however, according to Mann and Shields, there was an eclipse that would have been visible to the Iroquois, and this date is supported by family lineages and by counting the number of people who have allegedly held the office of the Tadadaho (speaker) of the Confederacy. Using the works of contemporary "Iroquois oral historian" Paula Underwood and the anthropologist William N. Fenton, Mann, and Shields estimate the founding of the Confederacy/League to 1090, a date that they argue "compares roughly" to the 1142 date indicated by the eclipse.

As noted earlier, however, oral histories are notoriously unreliable, and the contention that facts about political processes and the timing of eclipses can be accurately passed down orally over many hundreds of years is beyond reason. The Royal Commission, however, evades these problems with assertions that "the Haudenosaunee [Iroquois] have quite a different test for the authenticity and authority of the traditions that have been passed down orally and that they practise today." Yet the material provided by the Royal Commission provides no evidence of "standards" or "means of validating knowledge"; aboriginal "historians" simply expect that everything that they say should be accepted no matter how improbable the claim. This is clear when the Royal Commission provides the following statement from Chief Jake Thomas, a "highly esteemed historian and ceremonialist,"[71] in support of its assertions about "standards": "peace is supposed to work. It's the power of the words of the Creator where they come from, of unity, being of one mind, a good mind. That's what makes power."[72] The Royal Commission quotes Thomas again on the origins of the Iroquois clan system. The "means of validating knowledge" is the following: "we talk about the clan system. That's where it originated, from the time of the Creation." The commission then points out that Thomas "did not place a date on the origin of the practices sanctioned by the Creator and the Great Law [the constitution of the Iroquois confederacy], except to say that they existed long before the arrival of Europeans."[73]

And what of the Adarios who have been given the role of "founding fathers and mothers" of the Iroquois Confederacy? Although there is no evidence to support the existence of these people, they are now referred to as if they were akin to Thomas Jefferson and Benjamin Franklin. The mythological nature of these figures is inadvertently exposed by Johansen, who argues, "The story of how Jingosaseh joined with Deganawidah and Hiawatha is one part of an indigenous American epic that has been compared to the Greeks' Homer, the Mayans' Popul Vu, and the Tibetan Book of the Dead."[74] But these works are viewed as mythological, so why are the aboriginal Adarios considered historical figures?[75]

Those sceptical of the validity of oral histories are subjected to various *ad hominem* attacks. Since many claims about the viability and benefits of self-governance are tied tenuously to these accounts, taboos must be constructed to stop any questioning of them. Those who demand written or archeological evidence are accused of being Eurocentric. It is no surprise, then, when Barbara Mann comes to the conclusion that: "it is capricious, and most probably racial, of scholars to continue dismissing the [Iroquois] Keepers [oral historians] as incompetent witnesses on their own behalf."[76]

Elisabeth Tooker has been subjected to just such a personal attack from Vine Deloria Jr. In a sneering review of her analysis of claims about the Iroquois Confederacy, Deloria characterizes Tooker as a "bitter [person] eager to criticize Indians at the drop of a hat." He claims that "Tooker's argument is so wonderfully naive and anthrocentric that it makes the informed observer of the debate weep for her inability to free herself from the blinders which adherence to anthro doctrine has required she wear."[77] He comes to the perplexing conclusion that "the real debate ... is over authority: to whom shall we listen

– about anything? Here the credentials of the past, no matter how valiantly won, are just not enough to dominate or close debate on a subject – period."[78]

Determining the actual relationship between the Iroquois League and the American Constitution cannot be based on appeals to "authority"; it must come from an objective analysis of the evidence that is presented to support various claims. The first account of the nature of the Iroquois Confederacy was put forth by Lewis Henry Morgan. Although these observations were made in the late nineteenth century, after extensive contact with European institutions and economic imperatives, Morgan described a form of organization that was matrilineal and custom based. It had neither the complexity nor the democratic values that are required in a modern society.[79]

## COMING TO TERMS WITH TRIBALISM

On 28 August 1963, Martin Luther King Jr. stood on the steps at the Lincoln Memorial in Washington and gave one of the most visionary speeches of all time. Known simply by its title, "I Have a Dream," King's address inspired many with the hope that "the sons of former slaves and the sons of former slaveowners will be able to sit down together at a table of brotherhood" and that his children would "one day live in a nation where they will not be judged by the color of their skin but by the content of their character."

King's speech remains inspirational to all people, regardless of their race, sex, or culture, because it imagined a future where we would live together on the basis of our common humanity. No one listening could ask the question, "How does all this apply to me?" since no one was asked to accept something at the expense of another. It was this ability of King, to bring out shared aspirations, that enabled him to point the way forward to a truly progressive understanding of what the future could be.

Such a vision, however, is not reflected in the speeches of aboriginal leaders. Instead, there are constant arguments about special legal "rights" and how "more funding" is the number one priority. Non-aboriginals are never included in the demands made because they are "spiritually different" and unable to understand aboriginal peoples' special needs. Instead, the native leadership asserts that non-aboriginal people are in perpetual debt to the entire native population, since "white people" stole their land, took away their languages and culture, and subjected them to all sorts of abuse. As the main beneficiaries of the perpetuation of these irreconcilable conflicts, these leaders have no interest in promoting a more inclusive and cooperative vision of the future.

In liberal democracies, the mediation between diverse interests and values has been made possible by the development of individualism. Although individualism is often dismissed in discussions of self-government because it is argued that aboriginal peoples "possess an irreducible core" that is threatened by the promotion of individual autonomy,[80] this argument obscures the progressive character of individual rights. Individualism makes the notion of human rights possible because it recognizes that all people (individuals) are entitled to respect on the basis of their common humanity. As Elizabeth Rata explains, the "idea of the individual as someone who can be simultaneously attached and separated from the group makes possible the concept of a common universal humanity. This enables people to belong to and identify with non-kin groups as well as with members of their kin or ethnic group." She goes on to point out that "however closely involved the individual is in the private world of family and friends, in the public sphere the individual has rights because of his or her status as a citizen, whose political rights are derived not from kinship or ethnic group rights, but from universal human rights."[81] The universalism of individualism is completely different from "group rights" such as the inherent right of self-government, which excludes those members of society whose ancestors were not the original occupants of what is now Canada.

Aboriginal insistence upon ancestry, rather than economic circumstances, as the determinant of their relationship to others also is an obstruction to their involvement in radical, class-conscious organizations, especially unions. Unions exist to consolidate workers' political power in struggles against their exploitation by owners and employers. As such, unions represent workers, not a particular race, sex, or culture. To maintain solidarity, they encourage workers to look beyond their diverse characteristics to their common role as producers of economic value. The necessity to fight against the various kinds of discrimination in the workplace does not override the central function of representing all workers. Tribal identities, on the other hand, conflict directly with the purpose of unions. A change in native leadership often results in mass firings of existing personnel, who are then replaced by cronies of the incoming chief and council. Unions pose a threat to these tribal dictatorships, and so leaders discourage their formation on the basis that "unions aren't Native," or that they are an "instrument of White control."[82] It is also difficult to maintain solidarity within a union when its membership consists of large numbers of aboriginal employees, because of the lack of working-class consciousness in native culture.[83]

Finding a way forward where we can build a world that is acceptable to everyone means coming to terms with tribalism – an obsolete form of political organization belonging to all peoples at one time, albeit in different historical periods.[84] But, as the following chapters show, various initiatives – justice, child welfare, health, and education – try to keep aboriginals isolated from Canadian society, entrenching the tribal character of aboriginal culture, preventing the native population from acquiring the attitudes, skills, and values needed to work and participate in a national political system. As is especially evident in the case of aboriginal "justice" initiatives discussed in the next chapter, this will forever prevent aboriginals from becoming a part of an inclusive society such as the one that Martin Luther King Jr. envisioned.

# 5

# Justice: Rewarding Friends and Punishing Enemies

During the 1990s two murder cases involving aboriginal peoples in Ontario received prominent coverage in the *Globe and Mail*. One story concerned the case of Martin Blackwind, an aboriginal homeless person in Toronto, who smashed in the head of "his lover," Kathleen Hart, killing her while she slept. The second murder occurred during the summer of 1995, when Leon Jacko, an Ojibway from the Sheguiandah Reserve near Sudbury, bludgeoned another community member, Ron Thompson, to death.

Blackwind was eventually convicted of manslaughter because prosecutors felt that his inebriated state at the time of the killing would have made it difficult to prove intent – a necessity for sustaining a murder conviction. Although the killing of Hart followed a long list of violent crimes, including a previous attempt on Hart's life and a murder of another aboriginal woman in 1976, Blackwind's lawyer argued for a shorter sentence that would allow him to receive treatment for alcoholism. More significantly, she also asked the judge to consider Blackwind's native background when sentencing. To support this position, she cited statistics that show natives make up 15 per cent of inmates in federal penitentiaries, yet comprise only 3 per cent of the population.[1]

In Leon Jacko's murder trial, the Ontario Court judge hearing the case considered the accused's professed belief that his victim was "a bearwalker" – a mythical demon that uses sorcery to trigger sickness in people and even kills them – to be a legitimate basis for self-defence. According to Basil Johnston, an Ojibway author and lecturer who supplied information at the trial, it is acceptable in Jacko's culture to use force against people like Thompson who are "reputed to be bearwalkers." Because Johnston argued that "the fear is real" and "a person so believing in it and who may be harmed is allowed to resist,"[2] the judge acquitted Jacko of the murder charge – this in spite of the concern expressed by a number of members of the community that it provided a dangerous precedent for future cases involving aboriginal people where a person's spiritual beliefs could provide a ready excuse for perpetrating violent crimes.[3]

Although different in many respects, the cases of Blackwind and Jacko share a feature increasingly prominent in discussions about aboriginal self-government – that aboriginal peoples should be treated differently from non-aboriginals in the Canadian justice system. This idea has come out of thirty years of contemplating aboriginal peoples' marginalized position in modern society and the recognition that natives have suffered terrible injustices at the hands of the Canadian state. Because of aboriginal peoples' tragic history, it is argued that they should control justice in their communities. This respect for aboriginal "difference" has resulted in a "cultural defence" for aboriginal people who commit crimes. The defence first arose in an attempt to mitigate situations where crimes of property were to be settled in a manner consistent with native custom. Anyone who has lived in a small community where a sense of sharing is prevalent will understand the benefit of borrowing a cup of sugar or some firewood. An axe or other tools can be shared with ease; and if they're not returned promptly, the owner can just retrieve them. Problems arise, of course, when snowmobiles, trucks, and powerboats also become the objects of such "sharing" practices, often being "borrowed" by a person who damages them beyond repair.[4] But these circumstances still raise important questions about applying laws when they are not understood. Should the courts apply the law equally even if accused persons, because of their culture, are not cognizant of committing a crime?

This question is especially pertinent since such a "cultural defence" has been recently extended to deal with the high level of violence in aboriginal communities. As the cases of Blackwind and Jacko illustrate, aboriginal peoples, because of their culture, are given leeway not available to non-aboriginal Canadian citizens. In the case of Blackwind, charges of murder were reduced to manslaughter despite his violent history, because of the commonly held assumption that aboriginal persons cannot control their impulses if they are drunk (alcohol, after all, was introduced by colonizers, and so aboriginal peoples should not be held responsible if violent incidents involve it). The cultural defence in Jacko's case was even more apparent. Jacko's professed spiritual beliefs gave him a licence to kill other people. Both of these individuals would have received much more severe penalties if they had not been aboriginal persons, since Canadian courts have determined that neither drunkenness nor a person's spiritual beliefs can be used as an excuse for criminal activity.[5]

Accommodating aboriginal practices and beliefs in the Canadian justice system, therefore, contains a disturbing contradiction. It is one view that the accommodation of aboriginal cultures is needed to reduce the number of offences in the native population. But in another view, attempts to accommodate aboriginal culture in the system always involve demands that aboriginal offenders should be given leniency for the crimes they do commit. This means that accommodating aboriginal cultures could actually result in an increase in the number of offences perpetrated, as there are fewer deterrents against native criminality.

As was seen in the arguments made by Blackwind's lawyer, one of the main justifications for leniency is that the justice system is prejudicial toward natives, singling them out in comparison with other Canadian citizens.[6] The reasoning for this view is the high incarceration rates in the native population in comparison to that of non-aboriginals. What goes unmentioned is the vastly greater incidence of violations in the native communities, much involving violence against women and children. Reducing incarceration rates without first addressing these rates of violence only exacerbates the dangers faced by the most vulnerable members of society.

Those who acknowledge the high rates of violence try to assuage concerns about its persistence by rooting it in colonialism. Aboriginal peoples, the argument goes, lived a harmonious existence for thousands of years with their own justice systems before Europeans arrived. They respected individual autonomy, and aboriginal women in particular had high social status. Attempts to assimilate the native population destroyed aboriginal cultures, and the resulting dislocation led to increased criminal activity. Because assimilationist policies are believed to be responsible for high native incarceration rates, reversing them – accommodating the values and practices that were destroyed by colonialism – is the proposed mechanism for decreasing crime.[7] It follows, then, that aboriginal societies should free themselves from the influence of European culture so that the traditional status of native women can be regained.

But does it really make sense to imply that European culture is responsible for the current rates of violence endured by women and children in aboriginal communities, when these incidences of abuse are obviously much *higher* within the native population? Although it is impossible to know exactly what aboriginal culture was like before contact, early accounts from missionaries and explorers relate numerous instances of violence against women – violence that they claimed was much more pronounced than in the non-native population.[8] These accounts also noted that the sexual autonomy of women was not respected, and wife stealing, wife lending, and other forms of sexual coercion were common practices.[9] This is not to say that there is anything "naturally" violent in the aboriginal character, only that there is a pragmatic cultural sanction for the use of force to aid survival in pre-civilized modes of life.[10] In hunting and gathering societies, no laws existed to protect the group collectively, and as Mirianne O. Nielsen points out, "justice did not exist, at least not in the legal sense conceived by European-based Canadian society."[11] There were no police, courts, or judges before contact nor universally applied forms of punishment such as jails, fines, or "community service" for people who inflicted harm upon others. Order was based on retribution by the offended, and that could only occur if the victim had the physical resources to carry it out.

The stress imposed on aboriginal culture by contact with Europeans caused a deviation from the role of violence as a practical means to its exercise in new situations. Fuelled by the frustrations of dislocation from a subsistence lifestyle caused by the leap to the Iron Age without experiencing its developmental stages, violence became the response to drastic social change. Traditional mechanisms for maintaining order broke down as nomadic kinship societies were transformed into much larger settled communities dependent on a more economically and politically developed society. Artificially created aboriginal settlements with no economic base resulted in a native population frozen in time.

Aboriginal peoples today live in modern conditions, yet the view persists that the mechanisms of social control once used in kinship-based hunting and gathering groups can still be applied. This means that instead of the enforcement and protection of rights being carried out by the state, on behalf of all members of society, aboriginal peoples' well-being will still depend on their position within the community. The current initiatives being promoted under the rubric of self-government, therefore, do not constitute "justice" at all; they are actually attempts to prevent justice from being served. Those in power will be able to use their newly acquired control over the justice system to avoid being held accountable for oppressive practices that Canadian society as a whole has rejected.

## DOING THE CRIME, BUT NOT THE TIME

Since 1967 there have been numerous studies of aboriginal peoples and the justice system, including ten major reports in the last decade. These reports encompass specific public inquiries, reviews, and task forces held in Nova Scotia, Manitoba, Saskatchewan, and Alberta, as well as national studies looking at aboriginal peoples and criminal justice more generally.[12] Many of these studies were sparked by specific incidents, such as the police shooting of J.J. Harper, the negligent police investigation of Helen Betty Osborne's murder, and the wrongful conviction of Donald Marshall Jr. As a result of a number of these troubling incidents and the high incarceration rates of native peoples, it has been concluded that the Canadian justice system unfairly discriminates against the aboriginal population.

In an attempt to deal with the charges of discrimination, two distinctly different approaches for accommodating aboriginals have been proposed. One concerns "indigenizing" the existing system by making it more sensitive to the native population through affirmative action programs, measures to improve communication with aboriginal offenders and victims, the inclusion of aboriginal traditions (using sweat lodges and pipe ceremonies in prisons, for example), and cultural awareness training for non-aboriginal personnel.[13] The other is to push for a separate justice system for aboriginal people, where laws would be made, applied, and enforced by special native institutions in different communities.[14]

Although numerous areas of the justice system have been targets for reform, high native incarceration rates have made sentencing the most obvious focus. Demands for a separate justice system have led to a greater accommodation of native values and practices through "sentencing circles" and other forms of community sentencing.[15] In these initiatives, members of the community are brought together under the supervision of a judge, Crown representative, and other selected court officials to decide what sentences should be handed down. The particular values attributed to aboriginal culture are the reasons given to support separate sentencing arrangements for native offenders. It is argued that the integration of these values and practices will make the system more just toward natives and reduce their recidivism rates.

But linking jail to recidivism is a weak argument, considering that the native population is already being treated more leniently than non-aboriginals who commit violent offences.[16] Contrary to the prevailing wisdom about aboriginal incarceration, aboriginal peoples are *more* likely to receive probation for aggravated assaults and to be convicted of manslaughter rather than first or second degree murder.[17] They also generally receive shorter periods of detention than non-aboriginals with the same criminal history and are less likely to receive life sentences for committing a homicide. Such leniency is even greater in the case of aboriginal offenders who are female; 29 per cent received probation or suspended sentences in comparison with only 10 per cent of non-aboriginal offenders.[18]

Although these lighter sentences often reflect an emerging trend within the justice system to give consideration to the poor socioeconomic conditions of offenders,[19] leniency toward aboriginal offenders is also the result of judges applying the "cultural defence" claim.[20] This is particularly evident in cases involving sexual offences, where alcohol and native "attitudes toward sex" are taken into consideration during sentencing. A Territorial Court judge, Michel Bourassa, for example, noted that rape cases in southern Canada generally involved violent acts by a stranger, while "the majority of rapes in the Northwest Territories occur when the woman is drunk and passed out" and a drunk man "comes along and sees a pair of hips and helps himself."[21] Although Judge Bourassa uses references to the "Northwest Territories" and "down south," these are euphemisms for aboriginal versus non-aboriginal rape cases. It is apparent that Bourassa is implying two things with respect to differentiating rape involving aboriginal peoples from that in mainstream society. The first is that rape is less serious in aboriginal communities because it is not violent and merely reflects a primitive view of sex (i.e., a man "sees a pair of hips and helps himself"). Secondly, the fact that alcohol is involved is seen to lessen the crime's effect on the victim and to excuse the offender.

The alcohol defence for sexual assault appears routinely in cases involving aboriginal offenders. In her analysis of sexual assault cases involving natives, Margo L. Nightingale maintains that "a finding that a Native offender was intoxicated will always be noted and discussed, while non-Native offenders who have consumed a degree of alcohol may not have any intoxication noted." Alcohol is also perceived as being the "root cause" of violent acts.[22] On the other hand, aboriginal women who drink are blamed for "foolishly expos[ing] themselves to attack" when they are raped.[23]

Even more disturbing is the leniency shown toward aboriginal leaders who have been convicted of violence against women and children. Instead of making an example out of these men because they are expected to adhere to a *higher* standard of behaviour than ordinary citizens, consideration is given to the "stress" of holding a leadership position. In the case a of member of the NWT Legislative Assembly who was charged with fondling his stepdaughter's breasts and vaginal area on three separate occasions, for example, Judge Bourassa described the assault as "inappropriate cuddling" and sentenced the man to five days in jail and probation. He justified the lenient sentence: "He was stressed out; he wasn't liked by his peers; he was having trouble with his relationship with his wife and trouble with drink, and rightly or wrongly, he fondled his ... stepdaughter."[24] In a particularly horrific crime of rape, a Métis leader was given the lenient sentence of two years less a day because he had "kept himself out of trouble" since the assault and was seeking treatment for his alcohol problems. According to Supreme Court Justice de Weert who presided over the case, "he's a person who could ... make a very good life for himself. He's obviously a capable person who's respected by his community. A long time has passed since the offence, relatively speaking, and I consider that in mitigation ... [as] time appears to heal most wounds."[25]

The concern of judges toward aboriginal offenders to the detriment of their victims has been mirrored by a similar trend with Crown attorneys. These attorneys are increasingly taking on an advocacy role, which is having disastrous consequences for criminal justice in aboriginal communities. Because the Canadian justice system is based on adversarial procedures – i.e., both the prosecution and defence conduct their own investigations and present only information beneficial to their case – a Crown attorney who is sympathetic to the accused causes the system to break down. The victims, whose interests should be represented by the Crown, are marginalized, while the accused essentially have two defence attorneys (and a judge who is "sensitive" to their needs).

Results of this kind of "justice" often go unseen because many of the victims do not occupy a prominent position in aboriginal communities. Once in a while, however, a glimpse of what is actually going on appears. This was the case with two aboriginal men in the northern Quebec community of Kuujjuaq who were charged with sexual assault against young children in 1999. Although both cases resulted in serious injuries and the victims had identified the perpetrators, the charges were dropped because no witnesses were available to testify.[26]

These two cases were referred to us by a long time resident of Nunavut, who claimed that similar acquittals had also occurred there because of Crown incompetence. The backlog of cases that exists in dysfunctional aboriginal communities means that prosecutors are prevented from spending the time needed for investigations and gathering the evidence required for a conviction. This circumstance is exacerbated in communities when court officers must be flown in, since special trips must be made to gather evidence.

But placing the blame on overstressed court workers disregards the lack of cooperation that they receive from aboriginal communities. It is a common argument that aboriginal peoples interpret the Canadian criminal law as "non-Aboriginal interference,"[27] and therefore a separate, aboriginally controlled, system is necessary. Attitudes like these create serious difficulties for authorities attempting to investigate and prosecute crimes. What does a prosecutor do if no witnesses come forward? How do judges respond when people in the community reject their authority and refuse to participate in court proceedings?[28] These problems have created pressure to offload government responsibility for aboriginal criminality under the guise of restoring "traditional justice."

## CUSTOMARY JUSTICE: THE RIGHTS OF THE STRONGER

In the voluminous literature promoting aboriginal justice, typologies are presented to emphasize the differences between aboriginal and European practices. Usually taking the form of two columns, where the alleged traits of each are presented as opposites,[29] they point out that aboriginal practices tend to be informal and immediate, involve unwritten rules, value group cohesion, rely on consensual forms of decision making, and so on. The argument is thus made that the social control mechanisms of hunting and gathering societies have similar functions to those of industrialized nation-states; aboriginal peoples may have different ways of doing things, it is conceded, but they still have a system to administer justice.

Although it is not explicitly stated in these typologies, the language used harbours the assumption that aboriginal practices are somehow superior to those used by European systems. European justice is concerned with "punishment," while aboriginal societies prefer "healing." The Canadian system relies on "impersonal rules" instead of being concerned with "relationships" and "harmony"; offences are dealt with by the courts in a "strictly legal" fashion, not in the "holistic context" that is valued by native communities. This is also the case with the different values believed to inform each system. It is assumed, for example, that "peace, kindness, sharing and trust" or "respect, responsibility, obligation, compassion, balance, wisdom, caring, sharing and love" are fundamental aboriginal "legal inheritances."[30] The impression given is that European forms of justice are mechanistic, inhumane, and vengeful, while justice employed by aboriginals is forgiving, people-centred, and concerned with rehabilitation. By giving aboriginal peoples control over sentencing in their communities, it is implied, the conflict-ridden "adversarialism" found in Canadian courts can be replaced with peaceful and consensual "reconciliation."[31]

What is not considered, however, is the extent to which those favourable characteristics pointed to as aboriginal also exist within Canadian society as a whole. They are the processes by which most people use to decide matters not prescribed by law. A group of friends trying to decide which restaurant they want to go to, for example, uses a number of the same processes assumed to be particular to aboriginal groups. The same goes for disagreements within families. If two children are having an argument with one another, the parents may choose to hold a "sentencing circle" to determine how "group harmony" can be restored. The offending child may even be "banished" for a period of time or "shunned" (i.e., sent for a time-out) until "restitution" is made to the victimized. These matters are all determined by the customs of the people involved.

But while there are many different informal processes used to mediate disputes between people in Canadian society, there is a qualitative difference between the situations referred to above and those governed by law. Laws are used to regulate serious disputes such as property offences or those involving physical harm to another person. Because these matters are deemed to be more pertinent to public order and safety, the state is obligated to impose penalties on behalf of the whole of society if a law is violated.

The actual distinction between aboriginal and European forms of justice is that the former is based on kinship relations, while the latter is determined by laws, enforced by the authority of the state on behalf of all members of the political community regardless of their family status.

This is indicated in that historically in aboriginal societies "personal offences were viewed as transgressions against the individual rather than the community," and so sanctions were meted out by the individual and/or his or her family, not the collective.[32] Response to the offence of murder, for example, could either be the pursuit of blood vengeance or the acceptance of gifts, depending on the status of the victim and the relative strength of the family.[33] Essentially, three options were available for families when one of their members was murdered: killing the offender, accepting payment from the offender's family, or chasing the offender away from the camp. But these options depended on the resources of the families involved. If the victim's family was relatively powerless, there would be nothing they could do except move away from the camp, since there were no laws to hold the offender accountable and the family lacked the military capacity to exact blood vengeance or tribute.

Blood vengeance, in fact, was an important form of social control in all societies organized according to kinship. As the anthropologist Leslie A. White has pointed out,

> In primitive society an injury or a death was avenged by the injured party or by his kinsmen. And in case the actual culprit could not be found for punishment, revenge could be inflicted upon members of his family. In short, in tribal society, vengeance was an affair among kin groups, a private right rather than a public, tribal prerogative. On higher cultural levels, where property is more abundant and is coming to be more significant in social relations, the rule of a life for a life, an eye for an eye, becomes commuted into money, and the wergild [blood money] is established in a series of gradations corresponding to the seriousness of the offense ... with the advent of civil society private vengeance becomes outlawed, and the state assumes an exclusive right to kill.[34]

White's reference to *wergild* indicates that it was not just aboriginal societies in the New World that used this primitive mechanism of reparation. Wergild was used by the Vikings and neolithic Anglo-Saxons. Its existence also has been documented in the histories of many other European countries, including Ireland, Wales, Russia, and Poland (where the practice was called *ericfine, galanas, vira (βupa)*, and *główczyzna*, respectively).

It was the transition from kinship forms of organization to larger, geographically based social relations that made the concept of justice possible in the first place. Discussions about the concept's meaning have been at the forefront of many of the debates in the history of political theory, the most famous being Socrates's dialogue in Plato's *Republic*. Central to all the literature is the recognition of a need to equalize the treatment of members of society to eliminate conflict. The universal symbol of justice has been the blindfolded figure holding a set of balance scales, signifying the ideal of equality of the application of the law. She is blindfolded to show impartiality and a singular concern for the scales to balance: whatever injury has occurred must be balanced by reparation, and justice will be achieved.

Aboriginal "justice," on the other hand, is often emphasized by anthropologists as being "intensely personal." Although lauded for considering "the holistic context of an offence,"[35] personalization means that the social power of an offender determines the community's response to criminal acts. "Intensely personal" is a euphemism for subjectivity, where powerful members of society receive preferential treatment.[36] It is for this reason that Roberts and LaPrairie maintain that sentencing circles violate a number of principles in the existing Canadian system, including proportionality – "the severity of punishments should be directly proportional to the seriousness of the crimes for which they are imposed" – and equity, whereby "a sentence should be similar to sentences imposed on similar offenders for similar offences committed in similar circumstances." Therefore, they maintain that this "return to highly individualized punishments" constitutes a "retrograde rather than a progressive step."[37]

The problems with tribal forms of social control in the modern context are obscured by arguments that maintain that aboriginal groups are "egalitarian," their survival having depended on the sharing of resources, while Canadian laws act to maintain the rich to the detriment of the poor. This simplification fails to recognize the distinction between economic systems and the law. Modern economics involves large surpluses, their redistribution varying depending upon ownership regimes. The state, however, is delegated to treat all members equally – within the law, not in economic distribution. The reality that the economically privileged can use their financial resources to access *better* services (i.e., more skilled legal help) does not negate the principle of legal equality; they are subject to the same procedures as everyone else if they are in violation of the law. Modern laws, at the outset, serve the interests of society in common, and so, have the general support of all citizens. Equal, objective, and impersonal application of the law makes sexual assault of anyone and everyone illegal, regardless of social position.[38]

Despite the unsubstantiated claims about idyllic pre-contact societies, evidence from the present generally indicates a complete disregard for the well-being of vulnerable members of the native population.[39] Aboriginal communities today are dominated by powerful men, and many use their control over community politics to support male abusers and intimidate their victims.[40] These men also are protected by organizations like the Assembly of First Nations and its provincial equivalents, which derive their mandates from the heads of powerful families. Those who question self-government's impact on women and children are merely told that these are the risks that must be accepted.[41]

## KEEPING ABUSE IN THE FAMILY

It is an indication of social progress in the history of human civilization that the rights of women and children have come under the protection of the state. Until very recently women and children were regarded as the property of men, and violence perpetrated against them was seen as being similar to the abuse of animals. It was acknowledged that a certain amount of violence was necessary if a wife or child "got out of line." Vicious beatings were subject to social disapproval, but rarely resulted in state intervention. At a particular time in the history of British law, attempts were made to curb violence against women by limiting the size of the stick that a man could use to legally beat his wife. Today, of course, violence against women is illegal in Canada and other politically advanced countries. Children, on the other hand, are still governed partially by custom. Causing injury is child abuse, but spanking is left up to the "traditions" of the household.

Although we still have a long way to go before domestic violence is eliminated, the legal protection of vulnerable members of society is much stronger today than in the past. One important aspect of progress in legal culture is that victims cannot approve of a criminal act. Police officers or others who have evidence of, for instance, a beating, can press charges without the victim's consent. This was put in place to overcome the reluctance of women to press charges against their spouse because of possible reprisals.

But while these improvements are being made for women and children in Canadian society as a whole, they are actually being taken away from those who need them most. In aboriginal justice proposals, it is maintained that victims, offenders, and their respective families should all sit down together in an attempt to achieve "reconciliation" and "community harmony." After hearing what the offender and his family have to say, the victim is expected to "forgive" the transgression. The community then decides how restitution should be made. Banishment, providing meat to the victim's parents, giving money to a women's shelter, and entering into alcohol treatment are just a few of the ways offenders have been able to "reconcile" with the victim and restore "harmony" in the community.[42]

Although one can see how the offender would prefer this process, how does it benefit the victim? How would non-aboriginal Canadian women feel about sitting down with the man who raped them while his family told them how they should "forgive" their abuser for the terrible crime he has committed? Then, how would they respond if, instead of being sent to jail, the rapist was sentenced to live in a cabin for a year?

This actually happened in the case of Billy Taylor, a member of the Lac La Ronge Cree Band in Saskatchewan. Taylor had raped and threatened to kill his former wife, Maxine Clinton. Although the doctor who examined Clinton found multiple bruises and evidence of sexual cruelty, Taylor maintained she had consented. When he was convicted, however, Taylor admitted his guilt (although he blamed his behaviour on alcohol) so that a sentencing circle could determine his punishment. The circle recommended that he be banished to a cabin for one year, even though concern was expressed that the location of the cabin was easily accessible to members of the community. Clinton also was not happy with the result because she claimed that she had been pressured to agree to the circle.[43] Her experiences indicate a disturbing possibility of "community justice" – that the community has the potential to coerce "forgiveness." Despite all the rhetoric concerning healing and reconciliation, it is obvious that the possibility of avoiding jail makes sentencing circles desirable to offenders.[44] And since offenders are often members of powerful families, victims who attempt to press charges rather than agree to a "culturally sensitive" alternative can be subject to extreme social pressure.[45]

Besides being exposed to the direct threat of reprisals, aboriginal peoples are often discouraged from speaking out about the problems of community justice through fear of being seen as a traitor to the aborigi-

nal cause. Emma LaRocque, a professor in the Department of Native
Studies at the University of Manitoba, for example, discusses this problem in her analysis of a sentencing circle in Hollow Water, Manitoba. In
this case, a couple who had repeatedly raped their two daughters
received three years probation. Many aboriginal women were unhappy
with this decision, but were afraid to speak out against it because
"when Aboriginal women demand justice in a contemporary context,
they are accused of betraying 'solidarity'"; therefore "'tradition,' 'culture,' and 'history' are political handles with many twists that result in
continued oppression and silencing of women."[46] According to
LaRocque, a number of non-aboriginal journalists contacted her about
the Manitoba case and urged her to speak out against it because they
were not "politically free" to do so themselves.[47]

Despite aboriginal communities' isolation from Canadian society as
a whole, and the likelihood that both overt and subtle pressures prevent many violent crimes from being reported, a number of incidents
concerning community justice initiatives in British Columbia, the
Northwest Territories, Manitoba, and Ontario have made it into the
media. In many of these cases there is a complete lack of concern for
the victim since the purpose is to stop the offender from being sent to
jail. Victims are pressured to go along with the process, and in the
most extreme cases, women and children have had to leave the community when they ignored aboriginal leaders and attempted to hold
their abusers accountable.[48]

Advocates of community justice maintain that these circumstances
merely indicate a capacity for "forgiveness" in aboriginal culture.[49] To
support this view, it is pointed out that many women, even victims and
their families, do not want offenders to go to jail. Under the auspices of
valuing "community harmony" over individual rights, sexual predators
and spousal abusers are welcomed back into the community after they
get out of jail. But such situations can be partially explained by the fact
that women who do not share the community's capacity for "forgiveness" and demand the incarceration of abusers often suffer the traditional punishment of being banished or shunned.

Attempts by advocates to explain why aboriginal peoples "regularly
tolerate degrees and frequencies of criminal misbehaviour which in our
eyes seem extreme"[50] are more intent on providing excuses for aboriginal
dysfunction than in offering realistic solutions for stopping the violence
plaguing native communities. It is generally accepted that one of the
important factors for addressing the problem of abuse against women

and children is for the perpetrators of the violence to recognize that it is wrong. How will this ever occur if aboriginal offenders deny responsibility for their oppressive attitudes by blaming external factors?

The most common excuse given for aboriginal violence is that it is caused by alcohol. But if alcohol is directly linked to violence in aboriginal communities, why don't all aboriginal men who drink assault their wives and abuse their children? And if alcohol is a major factor in incidents of abuse, why are some aboriginal abusers men who are "sober"?

The first circumstance – that some men of aboriginal ancestry are *not* abusive when drunk – indicates that violence against women is related to cultural values, not to alcohol per se. Although people may decide to act out their attitudes when drunk because alcohol has disinhibited their aggression by diminishing the controlling effect of fear (fear of the consequences of acting violently), it is impossible for alcohol to be the direct cause of violence against women because different cultures respond differently to alcohol intoxication. The Addiction Research Foundation, for example, states that a huge body of research has been gathered that shows that "in different cultures, people's conduct when drunk was somewhat uniform within the culture, but varied greatly between cultures. Drunks would tend to be sleepy in one culture and wide awake in another, friendly in one culture and hostile in another, noisy in one culture and subdued in another."[51]

According to the Foundation's article, such varying reactions support the "expectancy theory" that maintains that "beliefs about alcohol effect how one behaves while intoxicated; therefore, if a culture holds to the belief that alcohol causes violence, people will be more likely to be violent while intoxicated, and the society will tend to forgive, or assign less blame to, this behaviour."[52] This has extremely serious consequences for aboriginal communities, since the constant linking of alcohol and abuse indicates that this expectancy certainly exists. It also encourages denial of the problem when the perpetrator does not drink. Since it is thought that drunkenness causes violence, a sober person, according to this view, cannot be abusive.

## ARE THE LUNATICS RUNNING THE ASYLUM?

The acceptance of violence in aboriginal societies can be illustrated by comparing their leaders with those selected throughout Canada as a whole. Although violence against women and pedophilia are present in

Canadian society, being convicted of these offences would be considered to be a career ender in politics. Federally, provincially, or municipally, no candidate would be endorsed who had a history of violence against women or children.[53] When it is discovered that such a past does exist, as was the case of Reform Party MP Jack Ramsey, the individual is thrown out of the party. And although Ramsey did run in the next election as an independent, he was soundly defeated.

This response of political parties and the Canadian electorate indicates how repugnant our society finds the abuse of women and children. The selection of leaders is a barometer of this sentiment, since we hold those who make public decisions up to a higher standard than other members of society. Although it is recognized that rapists or pedophiles can pay their debt to society and eventually be released into the community, they can never meet the standards required of an elected representative.

In aboriginal politics, however, a candidate's abusive behaviour is not an issue.[54] Abusers can be supported as leaders without even acknowledging that the violence that they have perpetrated against women and children was wrong. This is especially noticeable in the North, where a high percentage of the population is native. Over the years, several politicians sitting in the NWT Legislative Assembly have had criminal records for violent offences, and in community politics the situation is even worse. In one NWT community, a native leader was actually re-elected while serving time for sexually assaulting a child.[55]

The problem of leaders being implicated in abuse is even greater in Nunavut, the area of Canada where modern cultural influences are the weakest. With a violent crime rate that is five times higher than the Canadian average, finding men who do not have a criminal record becomes a challenge. Since the territory was formed in April 1999, already there have been several scandals involving Nunavut MLAs who were responsible for violent acts against women. One involved the speaker of the Assembly, Levi Barnabas, who was convicted of sexually assaulting a woman while she slept. When Barnabas was charged, his fellow MLAs showed their support by giving him a standing ovation. Barnabas resigned when he was convicted and given a twelve-month conditional sentence with 240 hours of community service (he was also required to donate $1,500 to a women's shelter). This evidently surprised Barnabas's victim, who "thought for sure he was going to go to jail."[56]

A second scandal involved the minister of education, James Arvaluk, who was charged in two separate cases of assaulting women. When

Arvaluk resigned from cabinet after he was charged in the second case, the premier of Nunavut, Paul Okalik, incensed women's organizations when he referred to assault causing bodily harm as "an incident," and stated that Arvaluk's input would be "miss[ed] ... during our cabinet deliberations."[57] Veronica Dewar, the president of Pauktuutit, responded to these comments:

> As Inuit, we are very tolerant and forgiving, placing much value on a person's well being and personal integrity. However, our values of tolerance and forgiveness must not compromise the rights of the victim. We must show victims at least the same support and respect as is too often only given to offenders. When we see that the justice system appears to have again favoured the offender over the victim, and that those whom we have elected in good faith to represent our interests in government are not willing to act in our best interests by stating that crimes of violence against women will not be tolerated, our faith in our leadership and our belief that we are entitled to equal protection under the law are destroyed.[58]

It is this fundamental principle of the rule of law, however, that is most resisted by the aboriginal leadership and the advocates for community justice.

Because of the "culturally sensitive" courts in Nunavut and the judicial leniency shown to native leaders, even Canadian law couldn't help the woman Arvaluk had assaulted. Arvaluk was acquitted of assaulting her in June 2001, despite the fact that "a drunken fight" left her "with a bloodied face and two gashes requiring 14 stitches to close." Justice Howard Irving, who was presiding over the case, acquitted Arvaluk because he wasn't sure if he had intended harm. "Was this a case of domestic abuse against a woman?" asked Irving. He then went on to state that he was "not persuaded that it was" since "the brawl may well have been a drunken, mutually consensual one."[59]

Even more disturbing than the developments in the Nunavut government is the sequence of events involving Paul Quassa, a previous president of Nunavut Tunngavik Incorporated, the Inuit-controlled organization that administers the Nunavut Land Claims Agreement. Quassa was president of the organization when the agreement was signed in 1993, even though he had been convicted of sexual assault in 1992 (for which he received an absolute discharge because the judge thought public opinion had punished him enough). Quassa was forced to resign from NTI in 1994, however, after he was arrested for leaving his child unattended while drinking in a bar.

Even after another brush with the law – this time for assaulting his wife in 1998 – Quassa was again elected president of Nunavut Tunngavik Incorporated by a wide margin. Throughout his campaign, no one even mentioned that he beat his wife. One Iqaluit resident is quoted as stating that Quassa "made a mistake but everybody makes mistakes, the people have forgiven him for one mistake in 20 years."[60] And when Quassa's electoral victory was mentioned on the discussion board associated with the Nunavut newspaper *Nunatsiaq News*, several people sent their heartfelt congratulations, some even declaring "You deserve it!" and "We can't wait to see what you can do."

## IF THEY CATCH YOU, GIVE
## IT BACK

With Paul Quassa's election to the helm of Nunavut Tunngavik Incorporated in 1999, it was only a matter of time before the organization would be plagued by scandal once again. This time it did not concern abusive or neglectful behaviour; it was the small matter of $36,000 that Quassa ran on the organization's credit card during his first ten months in office, $13,000 of it in cash withdrawals from bank machines around the country. This incident was not the first; it followed two previous warnings about "irregularities" in Quassa's use of the organization's money. The organization had also paid off two credit card bills that exceeded their $15,000 limit in early May and September.

Although Quassa had used the organization's credit card for numerous personal expenses, and the $13,000 in cash was completely unaccounted for, he maintained that the scandal could have been avoided if he had just done the required "paperwork." He refused to recognize any wrongdoing on his part. Instead he claimed that he would be able to meet the organization's future expectations by being "humble and [knowing] there is someone who is greater than all of us, and that is our Creator."[61] And when the *Nunatsiaq News* did not buy Quassa's new-found "humility" and dared to question him about the details of his spending spree, the Inuit leader maintained that he was being persecuted and that the media had exaggerated what he had done. To the newspaper's attempts to get Quassa to explain what the $13,000 was spent on, he responded: "I've already given [the money] to the board, it's a done deal and I've got no more comments. I'm not accountable to you."[62]

Both Quassa's arrogance and the reluctance of a pseudo-government agency to hold him accountable spring from the same roots – the acceptance of stealing in aboriginal culture. As was explained earlier, traditional aboriginal societies had no understanding of theft because the kinship relations and low productivity of hunting and gathering economies necessitated sharing for group survival.[63] What worked for hunters and gatherers, however, is inappropriate in technologically advanced nation-states where large surpluses are produced. Various government programs exist to ensure that these surpluses are distributed in a manner that benefits society. When people use their authority to distribute public money to themselves or their friends and relatives, it is considered fraud, not "sharing." This perception of stealing as sharing occurred in the case of Quassa. The incident was treated as if he was merely "borrowing" the money, so that when the matter was brought into the open, Nunavut Tunngavik thought that it was appropriate that he be allowed to keep his position if he paid the money back. This circumstance raises the question of what would have happened if Quassa had not been caught. Obviously he would have continued to "borrow," deriving a personal benefit from government funding that was intended for the benefit all Inuit residents of Nunavut.

It is apparently not understood that "giving the money back" is not an acceptable response to the "misuse of public funds" because it provides no deterrent against theft. If such an option were available to all citizens, everyone would steal constantly, hoping their acts would remained undetected. The obvious consequences of dealing with property crimes in this way are never addressed, however, because all the evaluations of aboriginal justice initiatives are done by advocates.

An example of such an analysis has been provided by the late Joan Ryan, a former consultant and professor emeritus of anthropology at the University of Calgary. In *Doing Things the Right Way*, a book widely in use as a "'how to' text on conceptualizing, funding and operating PAR [participatory action research] projects,"[64] two cases of theft are examined in a chapter entitled "Taking back Control." In one instance, Ryan examines the theft of two marten pelts at a school "because it is an example of how Dogrib rules can work very well on their own."[65] To show this, Ryan recounts how the Community Education Committee (CEC) decided to resolve "the issue" (i.e., the theft). Since the pelts were stolen from the gym, it was declared that this area of the school would be closed to all users, including those in regular classes, until the pelts were returned. After a few weeks of the gym being closed, the person who had taken the pelts was pressured to come forward. He admitted to selling the pelts, and a group of his friends decided that they would collect money to buy other pelts to replace the ones that had been stolen.

When the pelts were bought, the elders maintained that they were of a lower value than those that were stolen. The CEC, however, was "prepared to accept them anyway." Ryan then explains that "the young men went back to playing basketball; the school children got back to classes. The matter had been closed." In conclusion, Ryan informs us that the "Dogrib ways of dealing with things" had "worked" since "harmony was restored ... the matter was closed. There was no court record of the theft."[66]

The second case concerns the case of Mary Rose Moosenose, a postal employee in Lac La Martre (a small community in the NWT, now called Wha Ti), who was charged with stealing $27,000 from Canada Post. Although many people in the community thought it would be unfair if Moosenose was exempted from jail since others had been incarcerated for less serious offences, it was decided to allow the elders to determine her fate. They gave her "harsh words" and directed her not to gamble, drink, or play bingo. She was also supposed to listen to the elders about "how to behave properly" and pay back the money.

Problems began immediately. Moosenose did not visit the elders or start paying back "her debt," and she continued to play cards and go to bingo. People in the community began to criticize her, suggesting that she go to jail, but after a meeting it was decided that she could remain in the community. In order for her to do so, the elders decided that she would have to meet three conditions: abide by a curfew, stay in the community, and provide one day of community service per week. It was also decided that she should not have to pay back the money she stole because "that would be punishing family members."[67] The judge presiding over the case did not accept these recommendations entirely and also directed that Moosenose be prohibited from gambling and pay back $5,000 of the stolen money. To ensure that she abided by these conditions, she was to be supervised by the chief and council.

In her evaluation of the case, Ryan informs us that "although there have been a few glitches and considerable community mumbling, MRM [Mary Rose Moosenose] has honoured the conditions of her probation and, in fact, has given more than the required number of days for community service. The payment of $5,000 has not been addressed. The only time MRM has been out of the community was to go to hospital for surgery." Ryan also explains that the "strict conditions" of MRM's probation had quieted critics. To indicate the severity of the "sentence," Ryan quotes an unidentified woman as saying "I'd rather go to jail than not be allowed to play bingo or cards."[68] The case study is concluded with the comment that this sequence of events shows that "the community does not accept theft as appropriate behaviour, that the elders are prepared to provide guidance and harsh words, and that there are culturally appropriate ways of balancing things so reconciliation, restitution, and restoration of harmony is possible."[69]

Two footnotes, however, indicate that the enthusiastic conclusion Ryan reaches is a sham. We learn that MRM was walking around the streets of Yellowknife "when she went to town for surgery," that she had been allowed by the chief to attend a dance where there was drinking, that she had gone to Yellowknife with the chief's permission to "pick up her income tax cheque and to shop," and that she had "allegedly" been seen at the Gold Range Bar during this visit. We are then told that "the Crown and the RCMP decided not to charge MRM with breach of probation because she had permission from the chief to go to the dance and to town."[70]

Under what standards can it possibly be said that the case of the marten pelts and Mary Rose Moosenose had "worked"? In the case of the marten pelts, even if we leave aside the "if they catch you, give it back" approach to stealing, the pelts that were eventually returned were of *lower* value than the ones stolen. This means that "harmony was restored" by enabling the thief to benefit from his criminal activity. Mary Rose Moosenose's case is even more problematic. How had "reconciliation, restitution, and restoration of harmony" occurred? She had not paid back the money or abided by any of the "strict conditions" of her probation (except for the questionable claim about the community service component). In fact, she continuously showed a flagrant disregard for the "community justice" procedures that had enabled her to avoid going to jail.

These cases do not show that "the community does not accept theft as appropriate behaviour," as Ryan claims. They show just the reverse, that stealing is acceptable (particularly so, if the money comes from "the government"). This kind of behaviour is obviously a remnant of a kinship-based hunting and gathering culture, but when it is applied in the modern context and large amounts of money are involved – $36,000 in the case of Quassa and $27,000 for Moosenose – one can see the kinds of problems that will arise.[71]

Reciprocity and sharing are admirable qualities since they make human cooperation possible and reduce conflict. But this holds true today only if it occurs *across* kinship groups in a society. When we investigated the Moosenose case, it turned out that "hamlet insurance" had paid back the $27,000 to Canada Post.[72] This raises a number of questions; first, there is no provision in Canadian law for insurance against criminal behaviour; crime involving the mail carries particular penalties. Our attempts to find the origin of this "hamlet insurance" were stonewalled with the view that it was the exclusive concern of the native community. The money, however, comes from the productive members of Canadian society who make federal government transfers to Lac La Martre and Nunavut possible. Although Quassa and Moosenose think that it is appropriate for them to "share" these large sums of money, what reciprocity are they providing to the rest of Canadian society? Maintaining kinship-based justice in the modern context can only increase conflict between native communities and the Canadian mainstream. This is especially true for cases when kinship relations inhibit the investigation of serious crimes such as murder.

## OMÈRTA AND THE TRAGIC CASE OF CAROLINE BONIFACE

The word *omèrta* can roughly be translated into the phrase "code of silence" in English. Although applied to the Mafia, *omèrta* can be seen at work to a lesser extent in various ethnic enclaves across Canada. In these communities, members of a particular ethnic group are often dependent upon a small number of wealthy individuals for all the necessities of life: jobs, shelter, loans, and so on. Consequently, when the police do try to investigate crimes in these communities, no cooperation is forthcoming because ethnic support networks will evaporate if people are "disloyal" to one of their benefactors.

A most famous instance of *omèrta* was the horrific murder of Helen Betty Osborne in The Pas, Manitoba. In 1971, four men abducted, raped, and stabbed Osborne fifty-six times with a screwdriver. The men were white and Osborne was native. Racist attitudes in The Pas led to a conspiracy of silence, where information about the murder was withheld from the police in an effort to "protect their own." This, as well as the bungling of the police investigation, meant that it took sixteen years for the case to be brought to trial. Ultimately only one of the four men involved in the abduction and murder of Osborne was convicted of the crime.

Osborne's family and native leaders were understandably outraged by the outcome of the case. Her sister stated that the murder "has haunted our family for over 25 years knowing that those involved in her death escaped justice."[73] Phil Fontaine, as the grand chief of the Assembly of Manitoba Chiefs, argued that the other three men should be punished to the full extent of the law "to ensure that justice is done."[74] With this circumstance, therefore, aboriginal people were opposing *omèrta* in their attempt to have an overarching authority – the Manitoba justice system – hold non-aboriginals accountable for a crime perpetrated against someone considered to be an "outsider." Increasing pressure from natives and concerned non-aboriginal citizens led to an overhaul of the Manitoba justice system to prevent such an injustice from recurring.

Despite the native leadership's worthy opposition to *omèrta* in this case, it is not its usual response to similar injustices occurring between natives in aboriginal communities. This is because kinship loyalty is one of the defining characteristics of native culture, an orientation that is exacerbated by rhetoric blaming "white people" for land theft and for perpetrating "cultural genocide." Under these conditions the job of the police becomes very difficult. People are afraid of the social repercussions of pressing charges, while xenophobia toward "whites" creates an entrenched resistance to any outside intervention.

We first became painfully aware of this while living in Yellowknife, when one of us (Howard) witnessed a native woman being assaulted by a native man. Howard tried to hold the man and told the woman to call the police, but before the authorities arrived, the perpetrator had escaped. When a policeman arrived at the scene (he too was native), Howard asked the woman if she knew the man who had assaulted her. In front of the policeman, she said "Sure," and stated his name. She then went on to explain that he was from her community. The policeman asked Howard if the people involved were drunk. Howard replied that he didn't know and that the only thing he was sure of was that he had definitely witnessed an assault. Without showing any interest in Howard's story, the policeman forced the victim to go to the police station against her will. Howard insisted that they both take his card so that he could be called as a witness.

The next morning Howard called the police to inquire about the incident and was informed that the woman had been released. When he repeated that the woman was an assault victim, he was told that this sort of thing happened all the time and the woman would inevitably refuse to testify against the perpetrator. Howard protested that he was a witness, sober, and prepared to testify and identify the assaulter. He was then assured that the woman would inevitably state that the assaulter was not responsible and that the police did not want to be "embarrassed in court" by witnesses refusing to testify.

After complaining about the incident to a local women's organization, we were told that this was a common circumstance in the North. Assaults against women were rampant in native communities but rarely went to trial because women were reluctant to come forward. Living in the North, we often saw this view confirmed by police sources in the media. These stories are still common in northern newspapers.[75]

It was this understanding that made a story in News/North jump out at us. The article, "In Mourning: Death Attributed to Alcohol, Not Assault," appeared on 30 August 1999 after we had moved to Toronto. Glen Korstrom, a journalist employed by Northern News Services, reported that the community of Fort Good Hope was in mourning because one of its residents, Caroline Boniface, had died after being "medevaced to Edmonton with severe brain injuries earlier this month." Although Korstrom noted that "family in Fort Good Hope declined to comment more on her condition," Fort Good Hope RCMP Cpl. Marion Lemothe confirmed that "there was an allegation of an assault against Boniface on Aug. 13 and that investigation is continuing." Lemothe, however, assured Korstrom that RCMP members in Edmonton had found that Boniface's death had nothing to do with any assault that "she may have been a victim of." Instead, according to Lemothe, "her death was related to the extreme intoxication level she was in when she was admitted." The article concludes with the following comment from Lemothe: "I'm not sure what the cause of death will be but it will be as a result of the drinking and not from any assault."[76]

We were immediately suspicious of this article because Boniface's death had occurred so soon after an "alleged assault" was reported, yet everyone seemed very anxious to confirm that alcohol was the cause of death, even though the autopsy results had yet to be received. Our suspicions seemed to be justified when two more articles on the subject appeared a week later. The first follow-up article, "An Unsettling Death: Initial Finding Supported by RCMP" (also written by Glen Korstrom) opened with this sentence: "Though the death of Fort Good Hope's Caroline Boniface was initially pegged on long-term alcohol abuse, an autopsy was ordered because there were bruises on her body." The article went on to quote Yellowknife's G division Staff Sgt

Wylie Grimm, the police officer who handled the investigation. According to Grimm, "this lady was a long-time abuser of alcohol. She had bruises, but that's an indication of using alcohol to excess. Just to be sure, we had an autopsy done in Edmonton to make sure that there was no foul play." The autopsy was performed by Dr Graeme Dowling in Edmonton, but he could not comment because the matter was still under police investigation. The NWT coroner, Percy Kinney, also asserted that Boniface's alcohol levels were "not high enough to cause death in one sitting, but the long-term prolonged use damages the organs of the body and her official cause of death is acute alcohol abuse."[77]

The second follow-up article, once again written by Glen Korstrom, appeared on the same page. Entitled "Stopping Violence: Alcohol Can Be a Mask," the article states that "according to women's advocate Arlene Hache, though doctors have determined that Boniface's death was the result of excessive alcohol consumption, the real cause lies much deeper." Hache is then quoted as saying, "There was violence long before that girl ever ended up in the hospital dead because of alcohol. There was tons of violence before that ever happened." The rest of the article confirms that there was an assault complaint involving Boniface on 13 August and that this confirmation has resulted in other women "speaking out about how rampant violence is in the North and how victims need support." Hache also comments that people in the North often find it easier to accept that someone is a drunk than that they are victims of abuse.[78]

The three articles taken together present a very strange story and a number of questions arise from the "facts." Was Boniface's "severe brain injury" one of the "damaged organs" related to her "acute alcohol abuse"? How could her death be caused by both an "extreme level of intoxication" and the effects of long-term alcohol abuse not acquired at one sitting? Was she assaulted? If so, why was it being assumed that the bruises on her body were due to "using alcohol to excess"? And if the "alleged assault" had nothing to do with her death, why did Glen Korstrom write an article pertaining to Boniface that talked about the rampant abuse in the North and how people found it easier to accept that a person is a drunk rather than a victim of abuse?

Obviously, more information was needed to determine what had happened. We contacted a number of people: Korstrom, RCMP Cpl Marion Lemothe, the Fort Good Hope Health Centre, NWT coroner Percy Kinney, Dr Graeme Dowling, Ray Scott (chief executive officer of the

Inuvik Regional Health Board), the Fort Good Hope Health Centre, a CBC journalist who wished to remain anonymous, and finally, Inspector Alex Popovic, the officer in charge for the Commercial Crime Section of the Toronto RCMP.[79]

Glen Korstrom said that it was his impression that Boniface had been "beaten pretty badly," although he couldn't say whether or not this was related to her death. RCMP Cpl Marion Lemothe confirmed that the assault complaint regarding Boniface had been investigated, but no one admitted to knowing anything about it when the police asked questions in the community. NWT coroner Percy Kinney was not sure how Boniface's "severe brain injuries" were related to her death or what organs were involved because he had not yet received the autopsy report. He maintained, however, that she was initially admitted into hospital because of conditions relating to her long-term alcoholism. An autopsy was ordered only after bruises were discovered on the corpse.

Dr Graeme Dowling stated that Boniface's death was "definitely not a result of the alleged beating" and that the bruising could be due to falls she sustained while under the influence of alcohol. When we wrote to Dave Hancock, minister of justice and attorney general for the province of Alberta, attempting to get more information on the case, the reply came from Dr Dowling, informing us that only the next-of-kin were entitled to receive Boniface's autopsy report. The only information he relayed was that the "cause of death was determined to be complications of long-standing alcohol abuse."

Ray Scott, the CEO of the Inuvik Regional Health Board, gave out the information that Boniface had first been sent to Inuvik on 17 August and after being sent back and forth between Inuvik and Edmonton, she was eventually medevaced to the University of Alberta Hospital on 22 August when her "condition could not be stabilized." Scott stated that he could not comment as to why she was initially sent to Inuvik, because this information was confidential. When asked about the "alleged assault," he said he believed that the allegation had been looked into and eliminated.

The Fort Good Hope Health Centre said it could not release any information about why Boniface was medevaced to Inuvik. However, it gave us the name of a journalist who worked for CBC North who had been investigating the Boniface case. This resulted in a very interesting conversation[80] lasting almost two hours. After about fifteen minutes of questions, the journalist expressed concern that the "higher-ups" at CBC North would not appreciate that this information was being given out.

At this point, Widdowson agreed not to identify the person by name. During the conversation it was apparent that the journalist was familiar with the community of Fort Good Hope. The information relayed was obtained from the journalist's conversations with Boniface's family and friends.

According to the journalist, Boniface had been abused by her spouse for some time. He was convicted of assaulting her with a flashlight in 1996, for which he served ninety days on weekends. He was also convicted of sexual assault involving another woman in Fort Good Hope in 1998 and sentenced to two years less a day, but was released in the spring of 1999. When he arrived home in the community, he began assaulting Boniface again. A few days before Boniface was sent to the Inuvik hospital in August, she called her mother to come and pick her up because she was tired of being beaten. She evidently had been drinking for two weeks and had bruises on her arms, legs, and breasts and claimed that her spouse had assaulted her. She also was having difficulties bending over (a probable mis-translation of "straightening up"), and was eventually sent to the Inuvik hospital. Her family were told by hospital authorities that she had low sodium levels because of her drinking, and when she was treated for this, she developed seizures. As a result of these seizures, she was medevaced to Edmonton and eventually put on life support.

The journalist claimed that the abuse Boniface was enduring had been brought to the attention of two professionals from the Department of Health and Social Services in Fort Good Hope. These professionals reportedly did nothing about the assaults since they were friends of Boniface's spouse and felt that Boniface annoyed him by getting drunk all the time (he was known for being "sober"). Other people in the community also found it hard to believe that Boniface's spouse would assault anyone, because he had quit drinking. The fact that it was Boniface who had the serious drinking problem led many people in the community to think that she was the person at fault.

We stress that all this information is second and even third hand, and so must be viewed accordingly. However, the fact that Boniface's spouse had a previous conviction for assaulting her, the vague and contradictory information obtained from government and police sources, the fact that everyone involved seemed so eager to find that it was alcohol abuse and not an assault that had caused Boniface's death even before the investigation had been completed, and the bruises found on Boniface's body all indicated to us that the matter should be reopened. This opinion was further solidified during Widdowson's experiences on the Political Discussion Forum associated with *Nunatsiaq News*. When Boniface's case was used as an example to illustrate the problem of blaming violence against women on alcohol, an irate message was received from a person who was identified only as "Fortgoodhoper." The following is this posting in its entirety:

## FW'S REFERENCE TO FORT GOOD HOPE

Posted by Fortgoodhoper on January 01, 19100 at 10:20:24:

Being from Fort Good Hope, I want to take exception to FW's interpretation in the following excerpt of her Dec. 27th posting:

"Such attitudes have particularly disasterous implications for cases of spousal assault where the perpetrator does not drink. This circumstance recently occurred in Fort Good Hope where a woman who had been abused for a number of years by her spouse was medevaced to Edmonton because of a 'brain injury' and then later mysteriously died because of 'alcohol abuse.' Because the woman was an alcoholic and her spouse was allegedly 'sober,' many members of the community and some health authorities could not accept the fact that she was a victim of abuse."

FW's reference and interpretation of this particular incident again demonstrates how weak her research skills really are. She fails to mention that the husband was away for a full year and a half during which time, the 'victim' was physically assaulted by others (male and female) at many drinking parties; and that when she finally went into a coma shortly after his return, the health authorities in Edmonton expressly did not seek his advise [*sic*] nor permission to "pull the plug." Evidently, they believed that he was responsible for her ultimate condition. Her immediate family thought so as well. But in hindsight and after much soul-cleansing grief, the community rallied around the thematic areas of "individual rights & choices" and "collective rights & responsibilities." In the final analysis, it comes down to the old adage "Am I my brother's keeper?"

There is no argument that she was a victim of abuse – this community, like so many others, is trying to deal with the negative effects of rapid social and cultural change. If you had seen and experienced violence from an early age, you might be inclined to think that this is the norm. Like others in similar circumstances, Fort Good Hope has been trying to change common attitudes about acceptable and unacceptable types of behaviour for a long time. It's not easy to change things overnight but with the help of the School Board, Band Council, and other local institutions (especially the extended family), positive change might occur within this present and future generations.

I knew the "victim" and the "perpetrator" and the entire community and so it seems to me that FW's misguided interpretation of this incident – is, to be kind simply "out to lunch" and self-serving. FW's inference that the community has and continues to condone acts of spousal assault because of the "expectancy syndrone" [sic] creates an image of her that I will keep for a long time: looking into a glass cage ... treating us northerners as if we were some kind of guinea pigs in a laboratory experiment for her "future book on northern culture and politics."

This internet thing is wonderful! Did FW think that she can get away with making wild statements about communities in the western Arctic – on the NPDF? What gall!

Fortgoodhoper

The response is noteworthy for two reasons. The first concerns the downplaying of the abuse perpetrated by Boniface's spouse, because he was not the only one abusing her and had just recently returned to the community. (It is not mentioned that the spouse had been away from the community for "a full year and a half" because he was serving time for sexual assault.) Secondly, despite the outrage expressed at our "self-serving" and "out-to-lunch" research, the author does not seem to be disagreeing with our analysis. It is acknowledged that both the authorities in Edmonton and Boniface's family thought that the spouse was responsible for her death, and the person makes no attempt to refute this view.

Following this exchange with "Fortgoodhoper," we decided to take the matter outside the North. After many telephone calls to determine what senior officer would be able to investigate the situation from a federal perspective, we were referred to RCMP inspector Alex Popovic. Howard met with Popovic and gave him the file that we had accumulated, including the interviews. He informed Howard that he would investigate the matter and get back to us. The calls we have made to him subsequently have not been returned.

We also inquired as to the RCMP's policy on assaults against women. The RCMP's Communications Office informed us that there is no option but to lay charges where there are reasonable and probable grounds of abuse. It is up to the courts to determine guilt or innocence. Investigating officers must look at all avenues related to the violation. It is obvious, therefore, that this policy was not followed in the case of Caroline Boniface. If Boniface had not died, the media would not have covered the incident, and it would have been just another case where no one came forward. This indicates that the rates of violence recorded in the North and in aboriginal communities are grossly under-reported. As long as *omèrta* and anti-white xenophobia persist as a way to avoid the consequences of violent crime, these problems will worsen.

### POISON AS THE ANTIDOTE

In the introduction to the "Incarceration" section of *Aboriginal Peoples and Canadian Criminal Justice*, the book's editors, Robert A. Silverman and Marianne O. Nielsen, argue that "it is in the best interests of the criminal justice system, Canadian society, and Native people themselves that they be encouraged to maintain their own culture."[81] As a result of this assumption, Silverman and Nielsen advocate that prisons institute programs and hire personnel to ensure this end.

But what if the various values, beliefs, and practices making up native culture actually encourage the criminal behaviour they are supposed to prevent? As we have seen throughout this chapter, some values and beliefs that are identified as "aboriginal" have actually excused and entrenched the violence existing in aboriginal communities. In these circumstances the proposed antidote – aboriginal culture – is actually turning out to be the poison.

Fears about accusations of racism, however, have prevented the development of any understanding of the cultural basis of crime in aboriginal communities. Although academics have attempted to draw attention to some of the problems with aboriginal "justice," their accounts are constrained by a tendency to romanticize aboriginal culture and blame colonialism for the dysfunction in aboriginal communities. Anne McGillivray and Brenda Comasky in their book *Black Eyes All of the Time*, for example, show how a number of aboriginal women are opposed to diverting their abusers from the criminal justice system. At the same time, the book contains a foreword romanticizing aboriginal traditions where the solution to domestic violence is seen in terms of encouraging aboriginal men to regain "contact with their cultures."

The authors resort to the theme of European cultural domination as the cause of aboriginal violence.[82]

But it is not racist in any way to understand that when cultures come together, there are differences that can contribute positively to all concerned, and there can be conflicts so distinct, so alien, that they cannot be reconciled. These differences tend to be practices that the other culture has consciously rejected. People raised in cultures that condone violence against women will accept it, unlike those raised in cultures where it is deplored. But more socially positive attitudes can only be instilled if oppressive ones are recognized and rejected and the perpetrators condemned by society.

# 6

# Child Welfare: Strengthening the Abusive Circle

On 18 April 1998 the *Montreal Gazette* recalled a horrific incident that had occurred eight years earlier in Montreal.[1] While visiting the city, an Inuit woman from northern Quebec went home with a Montagnais man after drinking with him and his Gwich'in roommate, Michel, at the Mont Bar on Ste Catherine Street. Although the woman was too drunk to have sexual relations with the man, and passed out on his couch, she woke up some time later to find her wrists and ankles taped and Michel sodomizing her. The ordeal ended hours later when she was blindfolded and shoved into an elevator.

The above would be just another terrible story of aboriginal dysfunction if it weren't for one small detail – the man named Michel had the family name of Chrétien. The person who committed these unspeakably oppressive acts against another human being had been raised by the man who was to become the prime minister of Canada. Jean and Aline Chrétien adopted Michel from an Inuvik orphanage when he was eighteen months old. The Chrétiens were doubtlessly motivated in part by compassion for the conditions of many native children in the North, and by concern that so few Canadian families were willing to adopt them.

In the *Gazette* article describing the above events, writer Brad Evenson speculates that Michel Chrétien's problems stem from the fact that he was raised outside his own culture in a "white home." After making the vague statement that Michel Chrétien "has led a deeply troubled life, quite possibly in part because his Indian identity was denied," Evenson goes on to inform us that "Michel is part of a lost generation of people whose lives are torn between two cultures." While acknowledging that the Chrétien family tried to provide a loving and supportive environment for Michel, the writer concludes that their generosity was "based on a belief in the myth of one road for red and white."

In a nutshell, the argument put forward was that aboriginal peoples have a culture that is inseparable from their race. Raising aboriginal children outside of their culture, therefore, causes a longing to be back "with their own kind," resulting in all sorts of social problems. Only by ensuring that aboriginal children remain in aboriginal homes will they be able to discover "who they are" and feel comfortable with themselves. Preventing the two cultures (races?) from sharing "one road" becomes the justified objective.

Evenson chose his sources to support his own position. He cites Tom Dore, a Mohawk lawyer who taught introductory Indian studies at Saskatchewan Federated Indian College in Regina, who refers to aboriginal people adopted by white families as "born-again Indians" or "apples – red on the outside, white on the inside." A quote from Edwin Kimelman, a Manitoba judge who conducted an exhaustive review of aboriginal adoptions in the early 1980s, also follows this logic by referring to the non-aboriginal adoption of aboriginal children as "cultural genocide" since there was a "planned placement of children without having any regard for their background." John Cashore, a former minister of Aboriginal Affairs in British Columbia, sympathizes with the Chrétiens because he too adopted an aboriginal child and she, like Michel, also experienced "anger" and sometimes "blamed it on her identity crisis."[2] Michel's aboriginal friends and his birth mother, Anne Kendi, also point to a loss of identity as the cause of his problems. Kendi even encouraged Michel to visit the North to "discover who he was."

But is the conclusion reached by Evenson and his sources – that Michel's problems were due to the fact that he was adopted by non-aboriginal parents – plausible?[3] Do we really think that a "white" person has to live in a particular culture, and one that is "red" another, and never the twain shall meet? And what about the children of mixed marriages? Will the child who is three-quarters aboriginal have more of a "spiritual connection with the land" and require more sweat lodges, pipe ceremonies, and "guidance from the elders" than one with one-quarter aboriginal blood? Besides, there are many cases of non-aboriginal cross-cultural adoptions that have not been plagued by the same difficulties.[4] An example is the many successful adoptions of Chinese children by non-oriental parents. There is virtually no recognition of cultural loss dysfunction in this group of adoptees, in spite of the extreme cultural difference. Yet the inherently racist claim of cultural loss in aboriginal babies as a root cause of social dysfunction persists.

Scrutinizing the *Gazette* article closely reveals a more credible hypothesis for Michel's dysfunction. It appears that when he was in jail in 1995, a report noted that "Attention Deficit Disorder and Fetal Alcohol Effect cannot be entirely ruled out at this time but if present, have not been clinically significant in the past, or currently." After disclosing this analysis, Evenson points out that "Fetal Alcohol Effect is a condition far more common than the better-known Fetal Alcohol Syndrome. Both are irreversible brain disorders caused by exposure to alcohol while in the womb. Children with the disorders learn slowly, become easily frustrated and can often turn violent. They often cannot distinguish between right and wrong or understand the consequences of their actions." After this brief explanation, we are told that "Alcohol syndromes are familiar to adoptive parents of native children," and that Michel is one of the "many adults ... who are affected because of abuse of alcohol by the mother while they were being carried."

If it is likely that Michel, like many other native children adopted by non-aboriginal parents, has FAS/FAE, why did the media downplay this explanation?[5] Why was the emphasis on the colour of Michel's adoptive parents' skin rather than on the brain damage he probably sustained from his mother's "hard living" while he was in the womb?[6] The reason is that a recognition of this circumstance would expose the dysfunctional child-rearing in aboriginal communities.

### SACRIFICING FUTURE GENERATIONS TO AVOID STIGMATIZATION

FAS/FAE is an extremely serious problem, because unlike many other afflictions that affect Canadian children, there is no "healing" available. The brain damage caused by exposure to alcohol in the womb lasts a lifetime, entailing special care and assistance for victims until they die. FAS/FAE children will also face extreme difficulties if they have children themselves, which means the problem will continue for generations.[7]

But addressing FAS/FAE is very difficult; while its incidence is low in the Canadian population, it is a serious problem in aboriginal communities. FAS/FAE is estimated to occur between one to three births per thousand in European countries, but rates for aboriginal children can range anywhere from one hundred to four hundred per thousand of the school-aged population.[8] When hospitals track FAS/FAE cases, up to 75 per cent involve aboriginal children, even though they make up approximately 6 per cent of births in Canada.[9]

But despite the implications that high FAS/FAE rates have for aboriginal communities, there has been no attempt to systematically document the extent of the syndromes in the aboriginal population across Canada.[10] All estimates are based on the records of particular hospitals, studies in selected communities, or the anecdotes of health care professionals. In the *Report of the Royal Commission on Aboriginal Peoples*, only three sources concerning FAS/FAE in Canadian aboriginal communities are cited, and one is a report requisitioned by the Commission itself.[11] Even more disturbing, the most comprehensive study of aboriginal health problems in Canada – *Aboriginal Health in Canada* (Waldram et al., 1995) – does not even mention FAE or FAS.

The severity of the FAS/FAE problem was identified by the government as early as 1992, when a House of Commons standing committee recommended "aggressive public information campaigns" targeted at the aboriginal population and "more effective and appropriate community-based ways of dealing with learning disabilities, of which FAS is the major portion of demand."[12] The minister of health at the time rejected this recommendation, maintaining that current health programs were sufficient to combat FAS/FAE in aboriginal communities.[13] It was asserted that aboriginal peoples were not at greater risk and that programs targeting natives would only stigmatize them.[14]

But why would the government take it upon itself to see "stigma" as the overriding concern? Isn't health the more important issue here, not public perceptions? The government had targeted the aboriginal population concerning a number of health problems in the past. Why was it now choosing to avoid addressing a much more serious health risk?

There has even been an attempt to discourage a linkage between FAS and the aboriginal population on the grounds that this constitutes a stereotype. Dr Jack Armstrong, former president of the Canadian Medical Association, for example, stresses that "the white population cannot point smugly at aboriginals and claim fetal alcohol syndrome is just a native problem." Diane Malbin, a co-founder of the FAS/Drug Effects Clinical Programs in Portland, Oregon, actually denies the seriousness of the problem within the aboriginal population.[15] She argues that it is not poor and uneducated aboriginals who are the most at risk but white, middle-class, and educated women. According to Malbin, "the stereotype exists in part to meet the need of the dominant culture – uncomfortable professionals and the general population – to have a focus for the problem, an identifiable group on whom to focus the considerable anger, frustration and moral indignation generated by this hot topic."[16] In fact, few FAS/FAE babies are born to white, middle-class, educated women.

This reluctance to recognize FAS/FAE as a serious native problem can be traced to the political pressure coming from the aboriginal leadership and its coterie of consultants and advisors. As Suzanne Fournier and Ernie Crey point out in their book about aboriginal child welfare, *Stolen from Our Embrace*, a number of studies were started in aboriginal communities to determine the extent and severity of FAS and FAE, but they were shelved when "early results led to sensational headlines."[17] One study involving the Ktunaxa-Kinbasket in British Columbia even became the subject of litigation. Evidently, "Ktunaxa- Kinbasket leaders felt the study put scientific goals ahead of the needs of their community and would cause more harm than good. Instead the community elected to move towards intervention and prevention rather than gathering statistics."[18] Fournier and Crey see this opposition as indicative of the desire of many aboriginal groups to retain "ownership and control of FAS/FAE research" so that it will "meet their needs first."[19] The result of these kinds of considerations is an assortment of ineffectual but politically acceptable non-interventionist initiatives relying on "community involvement," promotion of spiritual practices such as smudging ceremonies,[20] labelling liquor bottles, and banning "lifestyle advertising" associated with alcohol.[21] Obviously, in communities characterized by high rates of alcoholism, social dysfunction, and illiteracy, such programs will not be able to address the problem.

The non-interventionist approach for addressing FAS/FAE is similar to all aboriginal child welfare policies in that it maintains that solutions must be developed by aboriginal peoples themselves. It is assumed that because aboriginal peoples are racially and culturally distinct from non-aboriginals, they should determine child welfare policies without outside interference. This assumption is not, however, based on any understanding of the current reality of children's lives in aboriginal communities.

## STOLEN FROM THE EMBRACE OF ABUSIVE ALCOHOLISM

The year 1959 marked the beginning of a policy coined as the "Sixties Scoop."[22] Child welfare authorities began an accelerated removal of aboriginal children from their families, placing them with non-aboriginal adoptive parents or in foster homes. By the end of the decade, it is estimated that between 30 to 40 per cent of aboriginal children were under the state's care.[23] The government's initiative was one of the most hated ever undertaken: in the view of aboriginal leaders and their advocates, these children were "stolen" from their parents by "overzealous social workers"[24] attempting to perpetrate "cultural genocide."[25] The actions of child welfare authorities were seen as part of a larger agenda to expropriate aboriginal lands and resources, assimilate aboriginal peoples into the dominant society, and destroy aboriginal culture.[26] They were viewed as stemming from a "culturally biased perception of native families and communities as impoverished, primitive, socially disorganized, and as generally unsuitable environments for children."[27]

Arguments like this have become even more strident in recent years. The most comprehensive are found in the aforementioned *Stolen from Our Embrace*. Glowingly reviewed in Canada,[28] the book takes claims of cultural genocide to new heights by arguing that social workers were part of a conscious conspiracy to steal aboriginal babies.[29] Without any evidence except a few anecdotes from native adoptees, they assert that private adoption agencies sold aboriginal children to the United States for thousands of dollars, and that social workers accepted bribes in exchange for finding adoptable children. Fournier and Crey cite Edwin Kimelman, a judge investigating the adoptions, who ends up concluding that "cultural genocide has been taking place in a systematic routine manner. One gets an image of children stacked in foster homes as used cars are stacked on corner lots, just waiting for the right 'buyer' to stroll by." To support the idea of the aboriginal "trade in babies," Fournier and Crey provide the following statistic: "55 per cent of native children in Manitoba's care were sent out of the province for adoption, compared to only 7 per cent of Caucasian children." They fail to consider that this could be due to the fact that there were far more aboriginal children being apprehended, and/or fewer requests to adopt them in Manitoba.

The opposition to the adoption of native children is based on a revision of history that does not properly describe the circumstances of the 1950s or of the present. In the 1950s the government became aware of the dysfunctional character of aboriginal communities, with high rates of child neglect, pedophilia, and incest.[30] With the level of drunkenness that existed in these communities at this time, many families were unable to provide a safe and loving home for children and it was the government's responsibility to intervene. While the intervention may not have been carried out appropriately, the fact remains that the conditions in aboriginal communities were intolerable for many children. Clearly, the poor implementation of the intervention must be examined and criticized separately from the conditions in the communities that the government was attempting to address.

Fournier and Crey obscure this distinction, however, in their effort to downplay the reality of the abuse and neglect. We are told stories of parents who "were neglectful only when they were drinking" and aboriginal homes that were "stable and loving, except on weekends when ... parents drank."[31] There is the case of Mary Longman, a Plains Cree artist, whose painting entitled "Separation" shows "seven tiny weeping faces silhouetted in the back window of a social worker's car." This image glosses over the fact that Longman was often left hungry while her parents "went to town" on a drinking binge.[32] Through selective reporting, the impression is given that aboriginal children were taken away solely because their parents were poor or had cultural traits judged to be inferior by Eurocentric authorities.[33] While alcoholism, neglect, and abuse were obviously major reasons for the removal of children, the opposite is usually argued – that the dysfunction in native communities today is the result of government intervention.[34] This view fails to account for the fact that the majority of native children were *not* taken out of their communities, even though poverty was prevalent.[35] There is neither reason or evidence to support the view that the children of sober, caring parents were removed from their families.

Developing the dichotomy between aboriginal homes that are "loving," "stable," "happy" and "cozy," and abusive non-aboriginal foster and adoptive families is consistent with the advocacy aims of books being written in support of aboriginal control over child welfare. It also reinforces the disturbing logic that the answer to current problems of child abuse cannot be solved by removing pedophiles from the community. As Brian Chromko, a N'laka'pamux paralegal worker and executive director of the Native Courtworker and Counselling Association of B.C., argues, "if you removed all the sex offenders from our communities and put them in jail, the reserves would be emptied out. Our children would be abandoned all over again."[36]

## LEGITIMIZING ABUSE AND NEGLECT

With a recognition of the "failure" of placing aboriginal children in "non-aboriginal homes" and the increasing demands for self-government, both provincial and federal governments decided to take the path of least resistance – devolving the responsibility for child welfare to aboriginal communities. In 1981 the federal government, along with provincial authorities, began entering into agreements with aboriginal groups to give native communities more control over child welfare.[37] As a result, extensive aboriginal child welfare programs are in place in Nova Scotia, Ontario, and Manitoba, while at least eleven aboriginal groups in British Columbia are in the process of negotiating a variety of agreements. Devolution of authority is also being initiated in Quebec and the Northwest Territories.[38] In the early 1990s, the Department of Indian and Northern Affairs was allocating $160 million each year to aboriginal child and family services, and an additional $1.5 million was disbursed to aboriginal organizations to help them develop their own standards.[39] Five provinces – British Columbia, Nova Scotia, Manitoba, Saskatchewan, and Alberta – have also either proposed or implemented legislation that greatly restricts non-aboriginal adoption of native children.[40] As a result, there now are complaints that many native children will never be adopted, perpetually remaining in foster care.[41]

Although serious problems of child abuse and neglect continue to plague aboriginal communities in Canada,[42] the government is devolving control over child welfare policies because of the perceived importance of revitalizing traditional child-rearing practices that are alleged to have protected children in the past. The child abuse that exists today did not exist historically, the argument goes, and so it can be inferred that restoring these practices will also bring back functional family relationships.[43] Aboriginal traditions with respect to raising children essentially comprise the following: a lack of corporal punishment, teaching by example, imparting spiritual mythology through storytelling or ceremony, and instituting various taboos against incest.[44]

As in other self-government initiatives, however, restoring traditional values and practices involves ignoring the fact that the circumstances that gave rise to them no longer exist. Traditional values, practices, and taboos existed in a time when aboriginal peoples lived in small kinship groups. Children learned by example rather than from formal instruction, and the natural world was believed to be infused with spiritual forces. Although useful for survival in a hunting and gathering tribal existence, this kind of child-rearing is not sufficient to meet the requirements of an ethnically diverse and technologically advanced society. Nor does it encourage the capacity for sceptical thinking, rational judgment, and abstraction. Many aboriginal children are under-stimulated at home and arrive at school ill equipped to adjust to the demands of modern education.[45] It has been noted that, in aboriginal communities, the parenting style often borders on neglect and that children "don't have any coping skills to deal with any kind of adversity ... the direct result of lack of parental limit setting and boundaries."[46] Rupert Ross attributes this to a traditional "ethic of non-interference," where parents are "forbid[den] ... from telling their children when to go to school, what to eat, when to come home, that they must see the dentist, etc ... It goes without saying that we interpret the absence of parental direction and control as signs of a lack of concern. I suspect that in fact most Native parents now wish they could interfere, but struggle with the force of traditional prohibition."[47]

The problems of unstructured environments in aboriginal communities are obscured by arguments that equate discipline with abuse. In traditional societies, discipline was not required because subsistence economies and kinship relations meant that children did not have to be socialized to coordinate their activities with large numbers of people, or to learn complex rules and procedures. As societies develop, however, much more information must be relayed to the young. Also, rules must be imposed to ensure that children become civilized and learn to get along with non-relatives and function in modern institutions. There is a long history of corporal punishment in developed societies, but the trend now is to reject it as a cause of adult violence and spousal abuse. Unlike previous generations, many parents today raise their children to be inquisitive, self-disciplined, and socially functional people without resorting to assault.

### LESTER DESJARLAIS: A GLIMPSE OF SELF-GOVERNMENT

In response to public pressure over the number of native children being removed from reserves and the mainstream system's "insensitivity to aboriginal culture," Manitoba became the first province to negotiate the devolution of child welfare responsibility to aboriginal groups. The first agency to take over these responsibilities was Dakota-Ojibway Child and Family Services (DOCFS). Established in 1981 with the mandate to stop the "loss of children to the white child-welfare system" and "provide a full range of culturally sensitive child-welfare services,"[48] it was perceived as a model for aboriginal self-government in the area of child welfare.

A glowing review of the program was produced in 1984.[49] As the review was undertaken by consultants hired by DOCFS (in conjunction with the Evaluation Branch of the Department of Indian Affairs and Northern Development), it is not surprising that it found that the agency had been successful "in building community competence for the return and maintenance of Indian children in Indian communities."[50] But as is the case with aboriginal "justice" initiatives that focus on reducing incarceration rather than eliminating abusive behaviour, the measure of "success" for this child welfare program was "halting the removal of children" and "repatriating children who had been previously removed to non-native substitute care."[51]

Soothing terms like "success," "partnership relationship," and "communal resources," however, concealed a darker reality, and concerns began to emerge about the program at the same time the evaluation was being undertaken. An internal provincial review in 1983 discovered that only nine cases of child abuse had been reported, even though many more allegations had been made. The review team "raised concerns about the inconsistent follow-up and reporting of abuse cases," noting that "within the relatively close network of relationships in a small community there can be a tendency to undervalue the seriousness of these incidents and protect those responsible for such abuse."[52]

These comments turned out to be just the beginning of the revelations of instances of child abuse in the region. At a 1990 inquest held for Lester Desjarlais, a thirteen-year-old boy from Sandy Bay who had committed suicide, it was discovered that political interference was endemic in the community's child welfare system.[53] Although Lester had made allegations to several people that his step-uncle, Joe Desjarlais, had tied him to a tree and raped him, the child welfare agency had done nothing about it. Because chiefs and band councillors often sat on the boards of child welfare agencies and school boards, they were able to exert great pressure on social workers, teachers, and other members of the community who tried to report cases of child abuse. Children who were being abused by powerful members of the community would not be taken into care, and "overzealous" childcare workers would find themselves isolated from the power structure and soon out of a job. One child was threatened and physically assaulted until she recanted her testimony.

Brian Giesbrecht, the judge who presided over the inquest, was not hesitant to state that these problems were not particular to Sandy Bay. He referred to Lester's suicide as "unremarkable" since similar cases were emerging around Manitoba. According to Giesbrecht, "women and children have no choice but to accept dangerous living environments that would not be tolerated by non-aboriginal people," since the reserves were being "overseen by an Indian leadership that in too many cases is more concerned with allegiance to family and friends and the pursuit of political goals than with the welfare of the community."[54] Ellen Cook, a former teacher at Sandy Bay, confirmed Giesbrecht's opinion, saying, "it all boils down to politics. If you step on that person's toes and that person has umpteen family members on the reserve, you aren't going to get in in the next election."[55]

In the case of Sandy Bay, the RCMP and the Manitoba government took a hands-off approach with the reserve's agency. There were instances of sexual assault charges not being filed when reports of abuse were made. The Manitoba government department that was responsible for monitoring aboriginal child welfare agencies would not investigate alleged cover-ups of abuse cases if family members refused to cooperate.[56] Part of the inaction was clearly caused by fears of being accused of racism for linking child abuse to aboriginal communities. The provincial authorities also did not want to have to deal with the political fallout of exposing the extent of native child abuse.

Lester Desjarlais's abuser, Joe Desjarlais, was the nephew of the chief and brother of Cecil Desjarlais, a powerful band councillor (Lester was Cecil's stepson, not a blood relative). Although Joe was a notorious abuser in the community and had been nicknamed "the bogeyman of Sandy Bay,"[57] no charges were ever laid against him, and he was even employed as a janitor in the community's elementary school. Marion Glover, the social worker in charge of Lester's case, repeatedly attempted to remove the boy from the community and away from his abusive step-uncle, but her efforts were always thwarted by the powerful Desjarlais family.[58]

In response to the disturbing details that emerged as a result of the inquest, a task force was set up to examine aboriginal child welfare in Manitoba, and hearings were held across the province.[59] The task force, however, ignored the inquest recommendations aimed at preventing political interference and improving accountability. Instead, it argued that "fast-tracking" self-government would solve the problems existing in the system,[60] and many members of the task force expressed the opinion that political interference was a "non issue" for them.[61] When they met with Judge Giesbrecht, the task force chairman dismissed his call for improved provincial monitoring of aboriginal child welfare agencies with the following comment: "I suspect that had you been on the voyage of discovery we have been on, your report would have been much different."[62] This "voyage of discovery" led the task force to recommend that the "adoption of traditional methods" should be the main focus of aboriginal child welfare agencies.[63]

The inquest, however, did give Lester's sisters – Nancy, Sherry, and Annette – the courage to pursue charges against Joe for the abuse that they had themselves endured at his hands. He was eventually convicted and sentenced to eight years in prison. The three women, however, were not supported in their decision to lay charges against their uncle. The new chief, Angus Starr, using a variant of the "stigma" excuse, was "especially annoyed" since "he was afraid that if more things were said about the reserve, it would crush whatever spirit there was left."[64] At the trial a group of relatives showed up – not to support the victims, but their abuser. For years the sisters were ostracized by their family and the community, since they were perceived as participating in a "witch hunt" and breaking the "unwritten rule" in tribal politics that "protecting family and community took precedence over airing problems in the outside world."[65]

## THE NEED TO PUT CHILDREN FIRST

In his report, *Inquest Respecting the Death of Lester Norman Desjarlais*, Brian Giesbrecht argued that if aboriginal child welfare agencies were incapable or unwilling to protect children under their care, then the government must intervene.[66] That recommendation has fallen upon deaf ears. In fact, it was vehemently rejected by the Assembly of Manitoba Chiefs and ignored by the federal and Manitoba governments.[67]

Aboriginal leaders are in complete denial about the extent and severity of the abuse that exists in native communities. They either attribute these problems to the "growing pains" of aboriginal organizations, or continuously recount the cases of abuse perpetrated by "white people." Louis Stevenson, chief of the Peguis band in Manitoba, characterizes the situation thusly: "Let an Indian have one problem and it's all blown out of proportion and the whole system is labelled. But I know better now than to let people convince me that is the case. So what if we have a few problems, it's not going to be as great as many problems that we've been subject to ever since someone else controlled our lives."[68]

The high incidence of child abuse in aboriginal communities also can be used to justify demands for more funds to hire native counsellors, social workers, and "traditional healers." Because of the horrendous problems that exist and the vulnerability of the victims, claims are made that large amounts of money will be needed.[69] These demands are accompanied with the usual references to the "greater need for individuals attuned to the native culture and lifestyle,"[70] and these "culturally sensitive" positions often provide substantial salaries for community members.

Many "aboriginal families, communities and nations" are in such a dysfunctional state that they are incapable of making responsible decisions about the welfare of their children. All parents, no matter how abusive, are understandably resistant to having their children removed from the family unit, and as a result, they will put pressure on aboriginal agencies that attempt to intervene.[71] This means that the very things prized in "culturally sensitive" programs – non-interference – will actually maintain the abuse and neglect that is occurring.

Undoubtedly the festering problems in aboriginal communities can only be addressed through widespread social change, with aboriginal peoples given access to the health care, education, and housing that they need. Then, with the necessary social supports, they will have the confidence and skills to integrate with the wider population at their own pace. In the meantime, intermediate measures must be instituted to protect those at risk. This means sensitive government intervention with qualified professionals. In other words, it means putting children, not tribal loyalties, first.

# 7

# Health Care: A Superstitious Alternative

In Angus Graham's 1935 biographical story *The Golden Grindstone*, a Toronto-born insurance adjuster named Mitchell has his knee operated on by two Dene women in a northern camp. Graham recounts Mitchell's ordeal:

> Flora made her first cut, about three inches long, inside the knee and upwards: this didn't bleed freely and what blood there was came out clotted, but it gave a feeling of relief and I urged them to press the blood out. Then she made another cut cross-ways below the knee and a third like the first, up the outer side of the leg, and after these cuts the blood came much more freely. Then she seized the u-shaped flap of skin and flesh that she had just released on the two sides and bottom and flayed it up and back, exposing the knee-cap; and just as old Jane had said, it was split right across from side to side with the two halves drawing away from one another upwards and downwards.
>
> Old Jane had evidently known what she was going to find and had set some men to make a lot of little pins out of caribou bone. Now she forced the two halves of the knee-cap together and the other little bird drove in the pins below the base of the lower half and above the top of the upper half, and then wound them very firmly together, figure-of-eight, with strong sinews taken from the back of a caribou and pulled out to about the thickness of the coarsest sewing-thread. Then they put back the flap of skin and bound it into place with thongs, without any stitching.
>
> I don't know how long all this process took: it may have been two or three hours – anyhow, it was dark all the time except for the fire-

light. I tried to carry off the first part of the game with a high head – had my cutty pipe and tried to pretend there was nothing wrong. But I must have passed out more than once, as I would waken up to find little bags of moose skin with hot ashes in them in the palms of my hands, which they used to revive me when they thought I had been out too long and perhaps might not come back otherwise.[1]

Graham then maintains that when Mitchell finally left the Dene camp, "doctors found his knee-cap perfectly knit" and his leg was brought back to a "perfectly sound condition."[2]

A story like this would have remained largely unknown were it not for Randy Freeman, a Yellowknife historian. Freeman read the account on CBC Radio on 2 November 1998 because he felt that it was evidence of the sophistication of Dene traditional medicine. According to Freeman, "To me, it's evidence that the people living here 100 years ago could do this sort of thing ... People don't REALIZE that people, primarily women, were conducting surgeries on the land. This traditional knowledge, traditional medicine ... not a lot of it is written down. And traditional surgeries aren't being used to the extent they once were used."[3]

Freeman's views were supported by orthopedic surgeon Roger Purnell, who stated that "it would be possible to fix [a knee-cap] without modern equipment." Such a process, in Purnell's view, would be aided by the fact that aboriginal peoples had extensive knowledge of anatomy through butchering animals. Dr Purnell also pointed out that the techniques used in Graham's account were "not too dissimilar from what we do today."

Despite the propensity of Freeman and Purnell to believe such an account, we remain unconvinced. Consider, for example, the following realities:

- the insertion of any kind of "pins" would require a drill; the logistics of "pounding" caribou bone into the top and bottom of a kneecap defies common sense;
- an "extensive knowledge of anatomy" is learned through the dissection of human bodies, not butchering animals;
- no mention is made of a method for stopping the flow of blood;
- it is likely the body's immune system would react to the introduction of caribou sinew, reportedly used as a "figure-of-eight" wrapped around bone pins protruding from the kneecap;

- the problem of pulling a "flap of skin" over the protruding pins and "figure-of-eight" caribou sinew;
- placing small bags filled with hot ashes on Mitchell's palms to combat shock, when a blood transfusion would be necessary;
- the difficulty of performing delicate surgery in the dark with only the light of a fire to see;
- the quick healing of three large unstitched cuts without any sign of infection in the context of the sanitary conditions that would be present at a 1898 hunting camp; and
- Mitchell's ability to endure the pain of such a procedure without intoxicants.

The most amazing aspect of the story is that anyone would take it seriously; surgeons in the eighteenth and nineteenth centuries encountered major problems, even when using much more advanced medical equipment and procedures than those available at the Dene camp. It is far more likely that "Flora" and "Old Jane" were Adarios. Angus Graham, after all, was trying to sell an adventure story to the Canadian public of the day, while George Mitchell was a man who liked to impress his friends with far-fetched stories.

The unlikely case of the "Dene surgery," and the ease with which such an improbable story was taken in, are very similar to the other claims that are currently made about aboriginal traditional medicine. A much more prominent example – ethnobotany – will be examined later in the chapter. This revision of history has one purpose: it is an attempt to justify the devolution of health care responsibilities to native organizations. For if aboriginal peoples were engaging in medical practices that were just as sophisticated as western scientific bio-medicine, how could anyone object to the devolution of health care responsibilities to aboriginal communities?

## MAKING THE CASE FOR COMPENSATION

Whenever aboriginal health care is discussed, an extensive overview of aboriginal health problems is provided with alarming statistics: high rates of suicides, addictions, and disease in comparison to non-aboriginal Canadians.[4] And despite the billions of dollars spent on these problems, not much improvement has been made.[5] The persistence of the huge gap between the quality of life for aboriginals and the rest of

Canadian society underlines the urgency to "do something" about these problems. If action is not taken to combat FAS, teenage pregnancy, substance abuse, sexually transmitted diseases, and violence, the problems can only become much worse.

The dominant explanation for the continuance of poor aboriginal health in the wake of increased spending is, once again, colonialism.[6] Aboriginal people, the argument goes, were healthy before European contact. This degree of wellness deteriorated as European intervention in aboriginal affairs increased. Aboriginal economies and societies were destroyed, and they became dependent and impoverished – major factors in causing poor health.[7] The native population also increasingly relied upon the decisions of outside authorities instead of determining what was best for themselves, resulting in low self-esteem and additional health problems. The mechanisms proposed for restoring the level of wellness existing before contact are land claims and self-government, because it is thought that they will reinvigorate aboriginal economies and cultural pride.[8]

Self-government is also justified by the argument that aboriginal peoples used culturally specific "healing systems" to "avoid sickness" in the past.[9] But this is based on the spurious argument that because aboriginal people before contact did not suffer from the diseases they do today, they must have had some kind of "healing system" that was effective.[10] The argument fails to consider that the diseases brought by densely populated countries with domesticated animals were unknown to native tribes. North America was sparsely populated, and most tribes did not domesticate animals. As a result, there were no problems with waste disposal, increasing migrations of people from distant lands, or acquiring diseases from pigs, chickens, cows, and the like.[11] Aboriginal peoples were observed to be in good physical condition in comparison to the Europeans who arrived because subsistence practices were incompatible with frailty. In aboriginal societies there was not enough surplus to keep the decrepit alive, and only the strongest survived.[12] Much more significant are the statistics that determine the general health of a population – life expectancy and infant mortality. The former was much lower and the latter much higher in hunting and gathering societies.[13] Today we expect to live longer than our ancestors did. How will aboriginal traditions facilitate this improvement over the past?

Although words like "balance," "harmony," and "integration" are used to describe aboriginal healing systems, their main differentiating feature is spiritualism. Unlike western bio-medicine, which is concerned with the material causes of illness (both physical and psychological), aboriginal cultures assume that spiritual forces influence disease. Essentially, this means that aboriginal cultures believe that people can fall ill because they have been affected by evil spirits or have failed to propitiate good ones. In response to such beliefs, it is maintained that various rituals are needed to bring about a cure.[14] The spiritual aspect of aboriginal "healing systems" is epitomized by the role of the shaman or "medicine man." This person is believed to have a special connection to the spirit world, and thus conducts the rituals that are required. A medicine man is also thought to be able to put curses on people through the use of "bad spirits." Sorcerers or supernatural beings are believed to cause disease by projecting their spirit or by otherwise "throwing bad medicine" to cause illness or bad luck.[15]

While spiritual beliefs undoubtedly distinguish aboriginal healing systems from western medicine, it is hard to fathom how these differences will improve the health of the native population. Describing them as forms of healing or medicine legitimizes what has been discarded by modern medicine as quackery. The aboriginal understanding of health and disease comes from the neolithic period or before, when there was little knowledge of material processes. Almost all medicine then was what we would now call "magic."[16] While basic procedures for mending broken bones and the treatment of wounds were used, along with the ingestion of various plants to alleviate aches and pains, there was little understanding of human physiology or the pharmacological properties of plants.

Modern medicine, in fact, has only recently shed itself of similar superstitions. In European societies, illness was attributed to mysterious bodily "humours," sorcerers, witches, and the like as late as the Middle Ages.[17] Chinese traditional medicine retains superstitious elements, with unsubstantiated claims that Yin and Yang interactions and the "five elements of nature" (wood, fire, earth, metal, and water) are the foundations of healing.[18] The same is the case for the East Indian Ayurveda, where three "body energies" of Vata, Pitta, and Kapha are thought to be derived from another perception of the five elements (air, fire, water, earth, and space).[19] With the recording of various scientific discoveries and controlled experimentation, however, more and more diseases previously attributed to spiritual forces came to be understood as having natural causes. This knowledge developed gradually with the increasing specialization and advances in technology that isolated specific material processes.

A number of tactics, however, prevent the primitive character of aboriginal healing systems from being understood. The most common is simply to accuse critics of having some kind of moral failing. They are decried for being prejudiced, biased, or paternalistic,[20] while supporters are "tolerant" and "open." Thus an article by John O'Neil and Brian Postl claims that "traditional medicine has been, and continues to be, misunderstood and underestimated by mainstream health care providers. Indeed, for a period of time, one might describe the interaction as systematically condescending and discriminatory toward the traditional healing methods employed by Aboriginal healers."[21] They even refer to modern medicine as "colonial" because it has the "insidious" effect of "convinc[ing] the subordinate population that their own values and beliefs are no longer valid."[22]

Proposals to maintain these traditions for aboriginal people are also sustained through postmodern arguments, where subjective and objective factors are blurred. An example of this kind of argumentation is put forward by Waldram et al., who claim in their 1995 book, *Aboriginal Health in Canada*, that

> the efficacy of traditional medicine must be seen within its proper social and cultural context. What constitutes an illness differs from society to society (with intrasocietal variation as well), and it is best to think of "illness" as socially and culturally defined. Therefore, what constitutes an effective treatment for an "illness" will also be socially and culturally defined. To use an Aboriginal example, victims of "bad medicine" are "ill" as defined by their Aboriginal cultures; whether biomedical science can discern any disease is not relevant. The culturally appropriate means of dealing with "bad medicine" is to seek out a traditional healer, who will perform the necessary healing ceremonies. The patient is healed insofar as the patient, and his or her significant others, subjectively believe that the "bad medicine" has been removed.[23]

In "aboriginal systems," what constitutes an illness and its effective treatment is solely based on the unsubstantiated beliefs of the people involved and their faith that a shaman can heal them. Although it is true that aboriginal people who believe in "bad medicine" can be "healed" when they think it has been withdrawn, they would never have become sick in the first place if they had not been socialized by their culture to accept this belief. The legitimation of aboriginal spiritual beliefs by health professionals like O'Neil and Postl and Waldram et al. actually constitute a form of malpractice. Such condescension makes believers vulnerable to manipulation and the stress and illness caused by it. In exchange for "curing" people who have become victims of another person's "bad medicine," the shaman can demand gifts or practice other forms of extortion.[24] He can then increase the demand for his services by claiming to "throw bad medicine" himself. These beliefs can also lead to legitimate (i.e., biomedical) cures being neglected. In a case referred to by O'Neil, a traditional healer insisted all other treatments be stopped before providing his services.[25] One of the unfortunate results of the celebration of medicine men/shamans is that they are able to use their influence to discourage people from being treated scientifically.[26] They obtain their power from the superstitious beliefs they impart, and so they resist the "intrusion" and "meddling" of modern medicine.

The acceptance of native healing becomes especially problematic when an aboriginal culture's perception of a health problem conflicts with medical knowledge. According to Waldram et al., the Ojibwa in Ontario, for example, do not accept the view that hypertension is chronic and that treatment must be constant to manage the condition. The authors point out that "hypertension is conceived by the Ojibwa as episodic in nature accompanied by perceptible symptoms, and treatment is needed only when symptoms are present."[27] But is hypertension a chronic condition, or not? If it is chronic, what will be the effect of promoting how "hypertension is conceived by the Ojibwa?" Waldram et al. evade discussion of this problem with the ambiguous conclusion that "hypertension control [for Ojibwa] is considerably more complex than recalling patients for blood-pressure checks and pill counts."

Besides, if we are going to take a "culturally relativist" approach to aboriginal health and healing, and if illness is "socially and culturally" defined, why don't we determine health in the same way? Alethea Kewayosh, for example, notes that, contrary to biomedical knowledge that obesity leads to diseases such as diabetes, in aboriginal societies there are "strong cultural beliefs that equate health and prosperity with being overweight."[28] Moreover, tobacco is considered to be "spiritually significant" for aboriginal people.[29] An aboriginal school in Saskatchewan even posts a sign declaring that tobacco is one of the sacred plants, encouraging students to use their cigarette butts in spiritual ceremonies.[30] The perception that aboriginal peoples are racially/culturally different with respect to illness and health, therefore, could be partially responsible for the high rates of smoking in the native population.[31]

## LOWERING STANDARDS TO FUND QUACKERY

Throughout the 1970s, initial attempts were made to transfer responsibility for health care to aboriginal communities with the establishment of aboriginal health and social services boards.[32] In 1979 the federal government developed an Indian health policy that "established both traditional medicine and community control as important components of an Aboriginal health system."[33] To this end the Royal Commission on Aboriginal Peoples recommended that two fundamental changes be enacted: the establishment of healing institutions that "would operate under Aboriginal control to deliver integrated health and social services," and a human resource strategy that incorporates traditional knowledge and trains aboriginal people.[34]

Essentially, then, demands for self-determination in the health-care field involve both separate health-care services run by aboriginal people and processes that attempt to integrate the native population into modern heath professions. The separate system's purpose is to be as autonomous as possible, so that aboriginal communities can decide health-care priorities and the allocation of funds. Integration into the mainstream system, on the other hand, involves increasing aboriginal representation. Numerous programs are in place to try to encourage more aboriginal people to become nurses, doctors, social workers, and the like. Despite these efforts, however, there has been little improvement in this regard. As Comeau and Santin point out, "unlike the growth in the number of aboriginal lawyers, the numbers of native doctors, nurses, and other health care professionals have almost remained stagnant."[35]

This lack of representation can be explained by the low educational levels in aboriginal communities. Unlike the training of lawyers, where aboriginal law degrees are granted to native people, the government is more hesitant to lower standards for health-care professionals. Lives are on the line, and an improperly trained doctor or nurse would risk malpractice suits. As a result, most of the pressure has come for integration into the Canadian mainstream of traditional healers, where no educational prerequisites are needed and no professional standards apply. For this reason, the Royal Commission on Aboriginal Peoples recommends a health strategy based on a "diversity of approaches that respond to cultural priorities and community needs."[36]

It maintains that this will be achieved largely by "traditional healers and healing methods."[37]

The implications of having lower standards for the native population are obscured by postmodern euphemisms such as a "more tolerant regulatory environment" and "self-regulation."[38] Although it is maintained that "traditional healers generally object to the application of external controls,"[39] there is the perception that they have their own "culturally sensitive methods" or "authority structure" for evaluating traditional medicine.[40] John O'Neil, for example, speaks of an "evaluation process" undertaken by "experts in traditional medicine" where "censure of questionable practices among medicine people must rely on subtle communication of information within the Indian community."[41] Nowhere in the literature is the nature of this "evaluation process" specified.

What all these claims disguise is the fact that no objective evaluation of traditional healing exists. It all relies on "faith" in the healer. Native healer Renée Thomas-Hill, for example, maintains that assessments are "not so much based solely on physical indicators, but on a more comprehensive diagnosis," which includes whether or not the patient believes in a higher power and has unconditional love for the healer.[42] This is why aboriginal healers are so opposed to any outside evaluation of their treatments. References to the spirituality of native healers are used to stop evaluations from taking place. One study states that healers cannot disclose their treatments because their "medicine bundles" are sacred.[43]

Evaluation is also discouraged on the grounds that these "healing systems" are "holistic." Although it is usually difficult to determine exactly what this term means, and it often ends up just being another word for "spiritual,"[44] "holism" is also a buzzword used within a larger area known as "complementary and alternative medicine" (CAM). It is reasoned that a holistic system "tends to work from a broad philosophical perspective towards an increasing precision," where "integrated systems" are used instead of "detailed parts."[45] This is often expressed as "the mind and body must be treated as an integrated system,"[46] or that patients should be more involved in their own health care.[47] On the basis of this difference, it is argued that "it would be utterly inappropriate to measure traditional, holistic healing and its results using reductionist bio-medical methods," and therefore "standards of evaluation" should be developed by aboriginal communities.[48]

Such attempts to use assertions of holism to avoid evaluation have led John Ruscio, a psychologist at Elizabethtown College in Pennsylvania, to characterize the method as "a scientists' curse and a charlatan's dream." This is because, according to Ruscio, human beings can only compare a few variables at one time, and as a result, statistical techniques are more effective for understanding complex phenomena than intuitive judgments made from diverse information sources. Ruscio points out that "holists imply an ability to 'take into account' all relevant factors which they cannot, and shield their lack of knowledge or skills with linguistic evasions while steadfastly refusing to state, define, assess, or integrate any specific variables at all." For Ruscio, "holism is an empty retreat from reality, a method by which pseudoscientists muddy rational thought, avoid clear and concise communication, and follow their own idiosyncratic beliefs to justify doing whatever they please in the name of all that sounds nice and feels good."[49]

While holism is often advanced as an indication of sophistication and complexity of aboriginal healing systems,[50] it actually indicates the opposite. A shaman or traditional healer does not spend many years learning about complex bio-chemical processes since no objective criteria can determine their spiritual ability to heal. It is this belief in the spiritual that has led to the expectation in aboriginal cultures that one person should be able to "holistically" look after all ailments. A vague conception of causation makes it possible to claim that just a few techniques and remedies can "cure" everything.[51] The "reductionist" or "mechanistic" character of western scientific bio-medicine, on the other hand, exists because of the need to understand these processes. This does not mean that modern medical research is ignorant of the truism much vaunted by "holists" – that material processes are interconnected. Once medical research has come to an understanding of the parts, it is necessary to figure out how they interact with one another. Going back to traditional medicine cannot in any way aid this task.

The problems with aboriginal healing are kept hidden because the evaluations always come from advocates intent on showing that these systems work and have just as much to offer as scientific medicine.[52] Such assertions, however, are instead what Kimball C. Atwood IV, a contributing editor of the *Scientific Review of Alternative Medicine*, has identified as "the confusion of popularity with validity."[53] Vague and implausible anecdotes are offered as evidence of traditional healing's efficacy,[54] without any attempt to determine if patients' recovery is due to administration of the "medicine," the placebo effect, or getting well on their own accord.[55]

The main difference between traditional healing and modern medicine – that the former relies on faith in the practitioner, while the latter must be objectively evaluated – is never addressed. Attempts to justify the use of traditional medicine and increasing aboriginal control of health care rely on flawed reasoning, poor analysis, and postmodern sophistry. Although these tactics are present in all discussions of aboriginal health practices, nowhere are they more pronounced than in claims about aboriginal people's knowledge of the pharmacological properties of plants. This area has generated an entire "discipline" called ethnobotany.

## LIES THE ETHNOBOTANY INDUSTRY TOLD US

On 12 June 1999 we began one of our innumerable Internet debates on a discussion group associated with the Nunavut newspaper *Nunatsiaq News*. In the course of these heated arguments, a huge initiative of which we had been previously unaware was revealed. The area is called "ethnobotany" and involves "the study of human evaluation and manipulation of plant materials, substances, and phenomena, including relevant concepts, in primitive or unlettered societies."[56] Ethnobotany is argued to be an essential aspect of aboriginal traditional healing since it is claimed that much of modern pharmacology is based on aboriginal peoples' knowledge of the medicinal properties of numerous plants.[57]

In the discussion, a person writing under the pseudonym "Karl Popper" maintained that he had worked with Costa Rican aboriginal elders on a range of "ethnobotanical projects" and argued that there was "nothing vague about their knowledge of the pharmacological properties of plants in their neighbourhood." Aboriginal elders, Popper wrote, "do not have a theory of molecular biology, nor do they conduct double blind experiments. Their approach is unscientific. But researchers like Richard Schultes, John Arnason and others have built entire careers on ethnobotanical research that builds on the database provided by TK." Popper also maintained that "thousands" of pharmaceuticals in use today had been derived from aboriginal peoples' "pharmacological knowledge," which had "saved science many, many years of initial research in identification of potentially useful medicinal plants."

When we requested clarification about the organization of the "database" of plants, the names of the "thousands" of pharmaceuticals that had been discovered, and the exact nature of the pharmacological properties understood by the elders, we were referred again to the ethnobotanists Schultes and Arnason (as well as "Awang" and "Wade"). When we refused to accept a deferral to these "experts" on the grounds that it was evasive, and demanded actual data to support such assertions, none were provided.

The tactic of making grandiose claims without substantiation and then referring critics to "the literature" is common in the discipline of ethnobotany. E. Wade Davis (presumably the "Wade" we were referred to in the above discussion) argues that "between 25 and 50 percent of the modern drug armamentarium is derived from natural products, and most of these compounds were first used as medicines or poisons in a folk context."[58] Although Davis references two sources as "evidence," he identifies only twelve drugs that have been developed in this way (four were from the Americas).[59] This approach is also used by the Royal Commission on Aboriginal Peoples, which quotes historian Olive Dickason to support the contention that aboriginal peoples' good health before contact was due to the fact that they "had knowledge of herbs and other therapies for treating injury and disease."[60] In the quote Dickason states that "the process by which the Amerindians acquired their herbal lore is not clearly understood, but there is no doubt about the results. More than 500 drugs used in the medical pharmacopoeia today were originally used by Amerindians."[61] Consulting Dickason's book, one finds a reference to a note where four sources are cited.[62]

Waldram et al. use the same approach when they state that "it is virtually impossible to present a coherent and comprehensive discussion of the many botanical medicines which are known to have been used by Aboriginal peoples." They direct readers to the works of six other authors. They then argue that although there have been "relatively few pharmacological studies" of the properties of these plants, the usefulness of aboriginal botanical knowledge is supported by the fact that Europeans often used the herbal remedies of aboriginal peoples and because "more than 170 drugs which have been or still are listed in the Pharmacopeia of the United States of America owe their original to Aboriginal usage."[63] Waldram et al. point out that while aboriginal people would have had a different understanding of how and why these plants worked, "through thousands of years of adaptation to their environments, and through experimentation, they had developed an impressive array of botanical medicines and preparation techniques."[64]

With just four commentators on ethnobotany, we have gone from "thousands" of drugs currently in use to 170 that may or may not be currently listed in the *Pharmacopoeia of the United States of America.* And when one looks at the major source provided by Waldram et al. and Dickason – Virgil J. Vogel's *American Indian Medicine* – it appears that Dickason's statement about "500 drugs used in the medical pharmacopoeia today" is not true. First, it is not correct to imply that folk remedies and pharmaceuticals are the same. Secondly, far fewer that 500 drugs "in the medical pharmacopoeia" today were originally used by Amerindians. Even Waldram et al.'s figure of 170 is a gross exaggeration. Many of the "remedies" derived from these plants include flavourings, colourings, bandages, latex products, and suspensions; they can hardly be considered "drugs." And of the remaining herbal remedies originally used by Europeans, almost all were dropped from the *Pharmacopoeia* in the nineteenth and early twentieth centuries. In Vogel's compilation, only the following fourteen were still listed as of 1970:[65]

- May Apple (*podophyllum peltatum* L.): used directly as a purgative;
- Mint Family – Horse Mint (*Monarda punctata* L. ) and Wild Mint (*Mentha arvensis*, var. *canadensis* L.): from which pulegone and thymol/carvacrol were derived and used for hookworm;
- Pine oil and tar (*Pinus* species): pyrethins and rotenone were derived and used as an antibacterial or expectorant;
- Sweet Gum (*Liquidambar styraciflua* L.): led to the development of American Storax, which has stimulant, expectorant, and antiseptic purposes;
- Wild Cherry bark (*Prunus virginiana* L.or *Prunus serotina* L.): used as a sedative and pectoral [this is not defined by Vogel, but the dictionary defines it as "good for chest disease"];
- Willow bark (*Salix* species): aspirin was developed from its main ingredient, salicin;
- Witch Hazel (*Hamamelis virginiana* L.): an astringent to relieve congestion, bruises, and hemorrhoids;
- Yerba Santa (*Eriodictyon californicum*, syn.: E. *glutinosum*): marketed by Parke-Davis & Co. as a stimulating expectorant;
- Balsam of Tolu (*myroxylon balsamum*): used as an expectorant;
- Cinchona bark (from several species): originally a febrifuge (for reduction of fever) before contact, but its use by Europeans eventually led to the development of the anti-malarial drug quinine;
- Coca leaves (*Erythroxylon coca*): resulted in the isolation of cocaine, which is used as an anesthetic;

- Curare and the derivative tubocurarine chloride (from several species of *Strychnos* and the family *Solanaceae*): originally used as an arrow poison but later became an antiparalytic drug and anesthetic;
- Ipecac (from the roots of *Cephaelis species*): led to the derivation of emetine, which is used to treat amebic dysentery and hepatitis; and
- Vanilla bean (fruit of *V. Planifolia*): an element of the pharmaceutical product kaomin.

So, from the "thousands of drugs," we have very few that are significant to modern pharmacology. With the exception of quinine, cocaine, curare, and ipecac, the other remedies have only a very general application. They relieve aches, pains, and coughs or act to purge unwanted substances from the body. And with the exception of coca leaves, all other plants were used to treat much more general conditions than the drugs that were eventually synthesized from them. Cinchona bark, for example, from which quinine was eventually derived, was originally used to reduce fever (a very general symptom). It was not used by the South American Indians to combat malaria, because this was an African disease (since malaria is accompanied by a fever, the bark was first used just to combat this symptom; its anti-malarial qualities were discovered accidentally). Before contact none of the plants listed above was used to fight a specific disease.

The vagueness of these remedies is in contrast to the specificity of modern pharmaceuticals. This can be explained by the fact that drugs are now developed using a much more sophisticated methodology. In the case of "traditional aboriginal medicine," plants came into use either through trial and error or superstition. In the case of superstition, plants used in the shaman's rituals would work because of unsubstantiated beliefs in his ability to extract "spiritually curative" properties (i.e., the placebo effect mentioned earlier). The large number of substances used as expectorants and purges also had a superstitious basis. This phenomenon was noted by the archaeologist V. Gordon Childe in his studies of Egypt and Mesopotamia, where he points out that medicine "consisted essentially in the expulsion of the evil spirit by incantations and ritual acts" and "the nastier the potion, the sooner the demon would take flight."[66] Many of the plants pointed to by ethnobotanists, therefore, were not consumed because they cured disease; ignorance of material causes led to their prescription by traditional healers.

The process of trial and error, however, did enable those who ate plants with beneficial results to thrive and pass on this experience to their offspring. Through the operation of this mechanism over a number of generations, aboriginal peoples learned to use various plants as remedies for general ailments. But this did not mean that they had knowledge of the pharmacological properties of plants. They had discovered a connection between the ingestion or application of a particular plant and the resulting effect (usually relief from general pain), but there was no understanding of *why* a particular plant had the effect that it did. It was only with the scientific methodology of controlled experimentation that diseases came to be understood as the result of specific material causes. And by using this same methodology, the actual pharmacological properties of different plants came to be known. As a result of this knowledge, a number of alkaloid compounds were isolated from plants in the nineteenth century – narcotine (1803), morphine (1806), emetine and strychnine (1817), brucine and piperine (1819), colchicine and quinine (1820), nicotine (1828), atropine (1833), cocaine (1860), and physostigmine (1867) – and the pharmaceutical industry was born.

Today science has gone one step further. From an understanding of the chemical basis of disease and human physiology, most drugs are now synthesized without the use of plants. Scientists working for pharmaceutical companies either analyze particular bio-chemical processes in the human body and investigate how specifically developed substances act on them, or they examine the chemical properties of a disease and construct molecules in a laboratory that they hypothesize will have a neutralizing or disabling effect on specific illnesses. Both processes have the benefit of using the large body of knowledge accumulated about the character of matter to target their investigation. They do not have to examine thousands of plants in the hopes that a cure for a specific disease will be found. Because of this proactive approach, of the sixty-six most valuable drugs introduced since 1899, fifty-seven were discovered and then produced in industrial laboratories. Therefore, despite Richard Schultes's lament that 90 per cent of Amazonian plants have not been subjected to chemical analysis,[67] it is unlikely that undertaking such a monumental project would be a wise use of resources.

The greater efficacy of scientific methodology explains why so much progress has been made in the development of drugs in the last two hundred years, while aboriginal herbal medicine has remained the same. Although the early settlers evidently did use a number of remedies discovered by the aboriginal population, as Waldram et al. assert, most of these substances were abandoned when more effective and standardized remedies became available in the nineteenth century. Unlike aboriginal traditions, the scientific process enables us to separate out substances that work from those that are merely placebos. In this way, we have largely rid ourselves of various quack medicines, many of which are undoubtedly still being flogged today by various "traditional healers."

The ability of scientific methodology to continuously advance our understanding of disease has been followed by a huge increase in the number of medicines available to treat all sorts of specific ailments. Instead of eating plants for "stomach aches" or "female problems," we now can prescribe specific amounts of a particular chemical to cure thousands of identified diseases and health problems. In contrast to the fourteen aboriginal remedies that still have a place in modern medicine (albeit in a more refined form), modern pharmaceuticals now cover a huge range of functions. The major categories currently existing include autonomic and central nervous system pharmacology, cardiovascular system pharmacology, drugs affecting blood, drugs affecting muscle, digestive system pharmacology, reproductive system pharmacology, kidney pharmacology, dermatological pharmacology, endocrine pharmacology, histamine and antihistamines, chemotherapy and immunosuppressants.[68]

Because ethnobotanists have not produced any knowledge of the pharmacological properties of plants and no new drugs have been developed since the nineteenth century from the "database" collected from aboriginal peoples, no mainstream pharmaceutical company has funded research involving traditional healers.[69] Only Shaman Pharmaceuticals Inc., a company based in California that is essentially a non-profit conservancy foundation (i.e., a charity), has made any financial commitment to ethnobotanical research. Financial support for the company has steadily increased from government departments and government-funded agencies and institutions.[70] This "research," however, only consists of endless accounts of aboriginal uses of plants and their cultural or spiritual significance to various tribes; they have not been shown to objectively enhance human health in any way. As Schultes and Von Reis point out, "the discovery, enumeration, and evaluations of uses of plants in primitive societies ... is often not considered 'scientific enough.' It is nevertheless, the basis of any and all types of ethnobotany and will continue to be of both academic and practical value."[71] But if this information is not systematically tested to determine whether or not it improves human health and cures disease, what practical value can it have?

Despite the dubious value of this research, a huge number of academic departments, journals, and government agencies are involved in the documentation of ethnobotany. Aboriginal leaders also are becoming increasingly vocal in their support for ethnobotany because they hope to receive a share of the government grants by asserting their intellectual property rights over this "knowledge."[72] The fact that aboriginal peoples only used these plants, and did not develop any knowledge pertaining to their effects on health, is not a concern.

## SCIENTIFIC HEALTH SERVICES INSTEAD OF SINECURES

Despite the huge waste of funds occurring with initiatives like ethnobotany, the orthodoxy is that aboriginal control over health care will actually result in cost savings. The Royal Commission on Aboriginal Peoples, for example, argues that "a more active role for traditional healing could lower the cost of bio-medical care, thus freeing resources to improve other determinants of health such as economic status, environmental conditions, child and maternal health, and so on."[73] This is also the view of Priscilla George and Barbra Nahwegahbow, the president and executive director, respectively, of Anishnawbe Health in Toronto, who point out that "traditional healing is certainly cost-effective because it does not entail hospital stays, surgery, costly prescription drugs, costly and invasive tests, or referrals to high-priced specialists." The support for this statement is that the organization's budget for physicians is $300,000, while their "traditional healing program" only costs $45,000.[74]

But such arguments assume that increasing funds to "traditional healing" will result in a corresponding decrease in demands for scientific medicine. Of course, this is not the case. Aboriginal "healing systems" are merely extraneous services that are used while aboriginal people continue to access the benefits of the mainstream system. Aboriginal leaders actually argue for increases in the numbers of doctors and nurses in aboriginal communities, as well as hospitals and modern equipment.[75] The $45,000 pointed to by Aninishnawbe Health, therefore, is an additional expense, not an indication of a cost reduction. Aboriginal people, like all other Canadians, use scientific medicine because it actually works. This is why so much of a society's resources are needed for a modern medical system. Large amounts of funding are required to ensure that treatments are effective. Doctors and nurses must be properly trained, drugs tested, and medical techniques evaluated according to measurable criteria. Contrast this to "traditional medicine," where no resources are spent on evaluations because there is no method for estimating the effectiveness of aboriginal healing systems.

Although much of the promotion of aboriginal healing is due to taboos that prevent an understanding of its undeveloped character, there is also a more disturbing reason. The increasing acceptance of aboriginal medicine (and traditional healing more generally) is related to the two major threats facing modern health care today. The first is the whittling away of universal programs and services that were fought for and won in Canada during the second half of the twentieth century. The idea of "another kind of medicine" with "different" but "equally valid" standards amounts to laying the philosophical groundwork for providing inferior care to poorer segments of the population. This, of course, is related to the second threat – the increasing acceptance of unscientific health practices. When scientific methodology is not used to evaluate health care, there is no way of documenting inferior levels of care.

# 8

# Education: Honouring the Ignorance
# of Our Ancestors

When we abandon the hunter/gatherer life we abandon the childhood of
our species.

– Carl Sagan[1]

Carl Sagan – scientist, writer, and educator – was one of the great progressive minds of the twentieth century. His death on 20 December
1996 at the age of sixty-two was a sad day for all who value rational
thought. Through various books, articles, and television programs,
Sagan was able to inform non-experts about the importance of scientific thinking in humanity's development. He also used these public
forums to warn us about the intellectually corrosive consequences of
New Age pseudo-science and mysticism.

It is this sentiment that drives one of his most engrossing books, *The
Dragons of Eden: Speculations on the Evolution of Human Intelligence*, for which he won the Pulitzer Prize. In this book Sagan traces the
evolution of the human brain from its reptilian origins to the intellectual achievements of our modern technological age. To accomplish this
end, he focuses on the distinctly human feature of our brains – an
increased capacity for learning. Human beings have the longest period
of nurturing in the whole animal kingdom, Sagan points out, because so
much of our behaviour is determined by what we learn.

This great capacity for learning has evolved alongside our ability to
control nature. Initially, changes in technology and an increasing division of labour occurred very slowly, so much so that the past was not
discernibly different from what followed it. People survived in this relatively static state by observing their kin and engaging in the same pursuits that had sustained them over numerous generations. In times of
rapid technological and cultural change, however, "traditional ways"

often come to be incompatible with the requirements of a more complex social order. Sagan identifies the uneasy co-existence between looking to the past and preparing for the future when he explains that "the traditionalism of societies in a static state is generally adaptive: the cultural forms have been evolved painfully over many generations and are known to serve well. Like mutations, any random change is apt to serve less well. But also like mutations, changes are necessary if adaptation to new environmental circumstances is to be achieved."[2]

Sagan also points out that while our ancestors' resistance to change came out of the development of the human brain, it appears that we are irreversibly set on the path of a high-technology culture. Human survival today is dependent upon becoming more adaptive to the changes occurring in the world. Following in the footsteps of our ancestors, on the other hand, is becoming less useful because we live in increasingly complex and constantly changing societies; what worked in the past will not necessarily enable us to thrive today.

Increasing complexity and dynamism necessitated advancements to relay a greater amount of knowledge to the young. Progressive specialization and formalization of the education process ensued. The rapidly increasing information being discovered about the material world also required general theorizing to link different branches of knowledge. These educational developments are absent in aboriginal societies since their cultures are at an earlier stage of development. To promote educational initiatives that "honour the wisdom" of native ancestors, therefore, is to promote an entrenchment of the ignorance that existed in all societies historically. This denies to aboriginal peoples the fundamental features of human intellectual development, preventing them from ever becoming self-determining today.

## HOW INTELLECTUAL DEVELOPMENT BECOMES COGNITIVE IMPERIALISM[3]

Over the last thirty years the low levels of education in the native population have been consistently documented.[4] According to the 2001 Aboriginal Peoples Survey, 52.0 per cent of aboriginal peoples graduate from high school in contrast to 69.2 per cent of non-aboriginal Canadians.[5] More disturbing is the fact that there does not appear to be a convergence of aboriginal and non-aboriginal educational achievement, and a substantial gap between the two continues.[6] Michael Mendelson has noted that "an astonishing 43 percent of Aboriginal people aged 20 through 24 reported in 2001 having less than high school education" and that this cohort "would have been in high school in the 1990s, not in some distant past of discredited old policies and old programs."[7]

These statistics, however, do not tell the whole story, since the actual level of native educational achievement might not necessarily correlate with graduation rates. Political pressure to increase the number of aboriginal peoples with credentials has created a fertile ground for disguising low educational levels. While there certainly is much lip-service paid to the cause of educating native people, in practice deeply entrenched checks mean that the "educated" native will still need lots of help. The demand of native control over curriculum assures that traditional cultural practices have precedence over modern communication requirements so that students remain unprepared for the disciplines of secondary education. The secondary schools are then adjusted to allow aboriginal peoples to graduate artificially. And why stop there? Many undergraduate programs are now specifically designed for natives, where the application of "Aboriginal" signifies the lower standard of the degree.[8]

The further extension of this trend is the employment contrived for semi-educated graduates. Sinecures, sometimes thinly disguised but often blatant, absorb native people ground out by the system. Government departments concerned with aboriginal affairs, as well as the territorial political systems, are prominent repositories. Aboriginal organizations offer many job opportunities for privileged native individuals, and law offices and banks appoint token native people as a means of securing business from aboriginal organizations enriched by land claims. In all cases the obligatory "consultants" are hovering nearby.

The obscuring of real achievement levels is ignored in current discussions of aboriginal control over educational programs. Instead it is argued that control over education is needed to restore aboriginal pride and self-esteem.[9] It is also common to hear that aboriginal peoples have different and inherent "ways of knowing" and "teaching styles" that must be accommodated in a separate educational system if aboriginal people are to achieve self-sufficiency.[10] These arguments can be found in all the demands for self-government over education, beginning with the National Indian Brotherhood's *Indian Control of Indian Education* in 1972. Eventually accepted by the Department of Indian and Northern Affairs as official government policy, the proposal advocated that "the Federal Government must take the required steps to transfer to local Bands the authority and the *funds* which are allotted for Indian education [emphasis added]." Specific recommendations included hiring more native teachers and counsellors, making the curriculum "more sensitive" to native values, and developing facilities and services in accordance with the wishes of the various communities. It was maintained that these different initiatives would lead to the realization of two fundamental goals: reinforcing aboriginal identity and enabling native people to make a "good living" in modern society.[11]

Although this policy originally focused on increasing aboriginal representation in the mainstream system (i.e., hiring more native personnel), more recent initiatives advocate a transformation of the educational system to be completely controlled by aboriginal communities. Aboriginal students, it is argued, are discriminated against by the Canadian educational system because "Eurocentric" standards prevail.[12] To rectify this, a number of reforms have been advocated to address what are perceived as the special needs of aboriginal students. The most significant reform proposed is the incorporation of "spirituality" into all facets of aboriginal school programs.[13] Sharilyn Calliou, for example, explains that one of the major aspects of native education programs is "promoting acceptance that spiritual teachings are legitimate in the public sphere." She applauds the Dene Kede Curriculum in the Northwest Territories that "seeks to replace Eurocentric programs of study with a curriculum based on spiritual teachings." According to Calliou, "the goal is not to produce citizens with critical thinking skills who are able to participate in the global economy," but to socialize children as "'citizens' in a sacred relationship with self, the traditional territory ... and other people. Such open spirituality challenges the highly secularized late twentieth century world."[14]

The assumption of native spirituality also forms the basis of the much lauded use of the "medicine wheel" in many aboriginal educational programs.[15] The medicine wheel essentially uses the belief in the spiritual significance of the number four to divide up all subjects – directions, seasons, the human lifespan (infancy, adolescence, adulthood, and old age), and races of mankind (white, black, yellow, and red). It is also assumed that spirituality is one of the four aspects of a person (along with the body, mind, and emotions), and therefore educational processes should be made spiritually relevant. As Lillian Dyck explains, "in aboriginal culture there is no debate [about the existence] of a spiritual world."[16]

In addition to promoting native spirituality, self-government over aboriginal education involves incorporating native teaching styles or "pedagogy." This argument maintains that mainstream educational institutions need to recognize that aboriginal peoples traditionally have developed their own methods for teaching their children.[17] It is pointed out that aboriginal people lived in small closely related groups, so that teachers were related to their students. Because aboriginal people lived according to an "oral tradition," knowledge was not disseminated with the written word but through storytelling, ceremony, and allowing children to "learn by example." We are also told that teaching was "task oriented." There were no abstract principles that had to be learned; education was concerned with helping children to understand their place in the community and giving them the skills to hunt or gather and be a member of the group.[18]

These different "educational methods," the argument goes, make Canadian institutions alienating for aboriginal students, causing them to drop out and perform poorly in comparison with non-aboriginals. The solution to this problem, self-government advocates reason, is to incorporate the above forms of "aboriginal pedagogy" into the curriculum. Teachers who are familiar to aboriginal students should be hired, and if outsiders are brought in, they must become socially active in the community. Aboriginal students are encouraged to apply abstract concepts, instead of completing assignments involving "number-based mathematics."[19] There are also recommendations that the curriculum should not be organized according to abstract categories, but in the "context of the children's daily lives."[20] Paul Nadasdy notes that aboriginal learning is experiential, not formal, and that experience on the land is more important than the classroom. He even argues that direct instruction is regarded as a "disservice to the learner," since the animals are the "greatest teachers." [21]

As well as alternative curricula, "different" forms of communication are advocated for aboriginal students. It should not be expected that students will be able to structure information in terms of arguments and evidence. Instead, they should listen to stories where a "multifaceted conversation" and "narration ... presenting accounts of many experiences" result in a "conceptualization of ever-increasing completeness, without a stated conclusion."[22] This is partially attributed to the influence of aboriginal languages, which "do not necessarily organize reasoning according to a linear sequence of cause-and-effect, or axioms-theorems-corollaries, as do speakers of European languages."[23] It is also explained in terms of differences between "high-context" and "low-context" cultures. Low-context cultures are those, like European societies, where precise forms of communication are relayed through the spoken word. High-context cultures, on the other hand, are common to native communities. In these cultures communication is not explicit and "a great deal is left unsaid and situational factors deliver the greater part of an intended meaning."[24] In addition, teaching critical thinking skills becomes problematic since it "may be viewed as challenging the traditional etiquette of respectful listening."[25] It is argued, for example, that the "sacredness" and "fundamental truth" of myths should be honoured while also developing skills to "discover native knowledge and values."[26] This concern with promoting "respectful listening" has even led the University of Victoria to change teaching methods and curricula to "accommodate aboriginal traditions and values."[27]

What all these examples fail to explain, however, is how making educational systems more "culturally sensitive" toward the native population will help with the second goal initially stated by the National Indian Brotherhood: enabling aboriginal peoples to make a "good living" in modern society. If aboriginal peoples are not able to master "number-based mathematics" or must rely on "non-explicit" forms of communication, how will they ever be able to become the "engineers, managers, business people, natural resource specialists, and all the other experts" that self-government advocates maintain are needed in native communities?[28] Demands for self-government over education are fundamentally contradictory – proposals for maintaining "aboriginal identity" actually prevent aboriginal people from acquiring the necessary knowledge and skills for meaningful participation today.

The fact is that the various skills, values, and attitudes that maintain "aboriginal identity" belong to the neolithic period, where small kinship groups were organized around subsistence activities. Today the world is a much more complicated place. Nation-states require elaborate and universalized educational systems to transmit the vast knowledge areas of a technologically advanced global economy and society. Reading, writing, and arithmetic require abstract thought and more formal methods of instruction. Traditional aboriginal societies did not even have what we call education, since there were no formal processes developed to instruct the young. Rather, as anthropologist Margaret Mead has pointed out, it was the much more general process of *enculturation*, where children learned through empathy, identification, and imitation.[29]

This unfamiliarity with the disciplines required for education continues today. Many native children growing up in isolated communities live in a relatively unstructured environment where waking up and going to sleep at regular hours and having a quiet area to complete homework or even the presence of reading materials at home is not part of their life experience.[30] As an editorial in a northern newspaper explains, "the practise of early rising to a schedule is a cultural characteristic of Europeans, believed necessary for making money and getting a job done. In the North, less than 100 years ago, waking when necessary was not a problem but it was not necessary to wake up at 7:00 every morning ... The weather, seasons and animals ruled, so time management is a relatively new tradition for the North."[31] The retention of such traditional practices, according to another editorial, is why far fewer Inuit graduate from high school.[32]

But education is not only important because it enables people to make a "good living" in modern society. Education is worthy in its own right as it enables us to develop critical thinking and independent thought to further our understanding of the universe and our place in it. Aboriginal people, like all other human beings, need to acquire this understanding in order to fully self-actualize in the contemporary world. Regression to the teaching of primitive survival skills denies aboriginal children a fundamental prerequisite to their development.

## MAKING MOUNTAINS OUT OF MOLEHILLS

Pointing to traditional aboriginal enculturation mechanisms as just a "different kind of education" obscures the fact that all educational systems developed out of these processes, and they still form much of the informal learning that takes place in modern society. Children often learn to cook or to fix things by watching others. The same is true for storytelling: it is common for parents to recount tales and anecdotes that they enjoyed hearing as a child. This creates a common cultural experience between generations, aiding the process of socialization.

But learning through observation and storytelling alone constrains the development of abstract thought. This is because, as is discussed in detail by Maryanne Wolf in *Proust and the Squid,* "educated members of an oral culture had to depend entirely on personal memorization and meta-cognitive strategies to preserve their collective knowledge," and this limited "what could be said, remembered, and created." Wolf points out that "as humans learned to use written language more and more precisely to convey their thoughts, their capacity for abstract thought and novel ideas accelerated."[33]

Imagine, for example, trying to learn calculus through informal processes and unsystematic observation or by having a math teacher tell the class a story about how algebra was discovered. This would be impossible since the principles are abstract, and learning them depends upon understanding a chain of complex numerical relationships. These mathematical axioms must be formally taught over several years since the information is just too complex to be absorbed through more basic forms of learning.

This also applies to all the other subjects in modern educational curricula. The humanities and sciences contain far too much detail to be learned in accordance with the methods attributed to aboriginal culture in the current literature on aboriginal self-government. Hard sciences, for example, are not just categorized into physical and biological sciences; the physical sciences are further subdivided into physics, chemistry, and astronomy (each with many different specializations), while biological sciences include the study of biological structure and function as well as types of living organisms (again, each with numerous specific areas of study). This specialization is necessary to deal with the enormous amount of knowledge that is developed in modern society.[34]

Beside the different levels of complexity between aboriginal and modern conceptions of the universe, there are also developmental differences in socialization. In modern society, children are socialized to be citizens of a country, and in more progressive environments, members of the human species. Although there may be close family bonds, "growing up" means leaving the warmth of kinship ties and entering into the wider world. This movement is facilitated by first going to school and meeting other children; then there is enrolment in secondary and often tertiary levels of education with people of different backgrounds. After graduation, young people seek employment, often in another city. Some learn new languages and travel to live in a different country. Despite the discomfort or homesickness they may initially feel with the disruption of familiar routines, a broader understanding of the world overcomes parochial insecurities. This gives rise to feelings of confidence at being able to adapt to new situations.

Although the maintenance of strong kinship ties was necessary for survival before contact, it is maladaptive in the modern context. To become an educated and productive member of society, it is necessary to interact with large numbers of people to whom one is not related. "Aboriginal only" programs and attempts to have all services provided by aboriginal people in the communities, however, isolate them from these processes. The hiring of aboriginal teachers ensures that aboriginal children will not be exposed to "outsiders." Curriculum is increasingly focused on aboriginal traditions, so that new ideas are minimal. There is even a movement today to develop special post-secondary programs to be taught in aboriginal communities. This trend is clearly seen in Nunavut. As a result of serious educational deficiencies in the territory, a number of special educational programs are being offered that are not available to non-Inuit. One is the new Akitsiraq Law School, developed in association with the University of Victoria, where Inuit lawyers will be trained to interpret the Nunavut land claims agreement and to work in the burgeoning bureaucracy. The Inuit-only program will not charge students tuition, but will give them each a $50,000/year living allowance. The objective is to allow Inuit to study law at a reputable university without experiencing the discomfort of leaving home.

The program was the subject of a scathing criticism by Alison Blackduck, a Dogrib writer. In a column entitled "Reality Check on Nunavut Law School," Blackduck maintains that the program was developed because Inuit who want to be lawyers "are concerned that they won't be able to make a successful transition to attending university full-time in southern Canada." Blackduck explains that although living in an urban environment and suffering financial hardship can be difficult, such feelings of discomfort are common to many students, both aboriginal and non-aboriginal. Sheltering Inuit people from these experiences undermines the educational process because it "turns post-secondary education into little more than a technical training ground."[35]

What Blackduck doesn't mention, however, is the main purpose for constructing a separate law school for Inuit students – accommodating the lower standard of educational achievement amongst the Inuit population. Like the aboriginal teacher educational programs, nursing programs, and Native Studies departments across the country, native law programs give degrees to students who have not met the requirements expected from non-aboriginals.[36] The low quality of education in primary and secondary school is thus hidden by a post-secondary law program.

But these graduates will not be qualified to work anywhere other than Nunavut. Inuit leader Paul Quassa offers a solution: even with the huge number of sinecures already in the Nunavut government, more should be created. To justify this, Quassa argues that "[the Nunavut] government thinks that when you talk about education, you're talking about the larger Canadian society's way of interpreting education. In our territory that interpretation has to change." He recommends hiring unilingual Inuktitut-speaking elders "steeped in traditional knowledge" instead of college or university educated applicants.[37]

The ignorance and insularity being perpetuated by self-governance of education has yet to be understood, as native education programs are reviewed by advocates.[38] In these evaluations, the most common manoeuvre is the usual confusion of culture and race, and the charge of racism that meets anyone who recognizes the developmental gap between aboriginal teaching methods and modern educational processes. There is also the accusation that acknowledging this gap will be harmful to aboriginal peoples' self-esteem and that a critical analysis of native spirituality is disrespectful.

In order to evaluate the effect of various native education programs on academic achievement, it is necessary to do two things: first, to develop objective criteria to measure the knowledge and skills that are required by the "white man's educational system" so that aboriginal peoples can participate effectively and make a "good living,"and second, to conduct tests so that academic achievement (or the lack of it) can be mapped over time.[39] Evaluations that rely on the anecdotes of teachers and students, such as those that are found in all the assessments of current native education initiatives, are compromised because the people interviewed have a stake in the outcome of the study.

Objective forms of evaluation, however, are resisted by supporters of self-government.[40] One of the proposals made by the National Indian Brotherhood, for example, is "eliminating the use of I.Q. and standardized tests for Indian children."[41] Deborah L. Begoray, an associate professor and graduate adviser in the Faculty of Education at the University of Victoria, also maintains that reading tests are flawed and should not be applied because they will reveal that aboriginal students are lagging behind non-aboriginals. Instead, she recommends "construct[ing] a picture of literacy abilities in B.C. which has depth and breadth" by "learn[ing] from our aboriginal community about the strengths of their children (for example, oral storytelling and reading the land) which are not revealed on any large-scale reading test."[42]

Although standardized tests are opposed on the grounds that they "do not truly reflect the intelligence of children belonging to minority, ethnic or other cultural backgrounds," eliminating their use also inhibits an assessment of the current claims about self-government's "success" in educating aboriginal students.[43] This way, the negative impacts of spiritualism, the use of storytelling, and the reliance on unqualified teachers and elders remain hidden.[44]

As a result of the dearth of objective forms of evaluation, another area of self-government over education – the revitalization of aboriginal languages – has not been adequately studied. The promotion of these languages has become a *cause célèbre*, with organizations in several countries promoting their use. But as will be shown below, these languages are pre-literate and poorly suited for modern communication requirements. Such a reality, however, is being obscured by another major player in the global Aboriginal Industry – the linguist.

## PRESERVING "ORAL TRADITIONS" OR PROMOTING ILLITERACY?

In 1993, one of the most extensive works on the teaching of aboriginal languages in the Canadian context was published. Edited by three university professors and containing seven articles from experts, *Aboriginal Languages and Education* is strident in its promotion of aboriginal culture, especially the preservation of pre-literate languages. To justify its goal of preventing further "language loss," the book's introduction claims that "in the expression of a deeply-reflective Weltanschauung, and in the codification of a rich tradition, these languages constitute precious verbal media for conveying and institutionalizing ideas, concepts, and emotions that relate to the experience of Canada in its ecological totality."[45]

But what are these "ideas, concepts, and emotions" and "Weltanschauung" (philosophy of life)? We have already seen how aboriginal peoples' animistic spiritual beliefs inhibit a scientific understanding of the universe. Does the promotion of aboriginal languages constitute another method of retaining neolithic cultural characteristics in the modern context? Answering this question requires an analysis of the nature of language development and an understanding of how aboriginal languages differ from others spoken and written in the world today.

In order to cooperate in production and social life, people have to inform each other about what they have seen and heard, share their impressions and feelings, and store and communicate knowledge through language. As history unfolded, peoples of different languages came into contact, and their need to communicate changed their languages. This process was not a one-sided overtaking, but a sifting of the better parts of both tongues, resulting in a richer, more meaningful language. In the process, even the dominant language culture abandoned words in favour of others that seemed to more accurately indicate meaning. Social integration also brought pairs of words with similar meanings into continued use. This is due to the slight shades of difference their respective cultures required. Each remains in use because of a slightly different nuance that allows for complexity and detail. The expression of ideas depends upon the clarity, precision, and subtlety of the language used.

The development and extension of language stem directly from the requirements of the culture that uses it. This includes not only new words like *computer* and *neutron*, but abstract words that help to convey concepts, emotions, and minute, subtle details. Concepts also need language to be expressed; thus limitations in vocabulary equate to limitations in ideas. Language is a technology, and the more versatile, functional, and adaptable it is, the more effective the resulting product – ideas – will be. This also means that different languages will respond to the particular needs of the societies that use them. Human social evolution requires language to facilitate the process – to describe, discuss, and record its progress.

One of the most significant aspects in the evolution of language has been the relatively recent invention of writing approximately six thousand years ago. Carl Sagan describes the relationship between writing and the development of human intelligence by placing it in the context of three different kinds of information: genetic pre-programming, commonly referred to as instinct; extra-genetic information, which is learned; and, finally, extra-somatic knowledge, which is unique to humans and stored outside the body – primarily in writing.[46] It follows that the absence of writing precludes any kind of historical recording. Writing came about due to the need for more reliable communication than could be expected from a messenger's memory or relying on the oral transmission through a series of individuals.[47] Records could be kept and referred to at a date in the future. And although written documents may be influenced by the biases of their authors, just like all forms of communication, as Alexander von Gernet points out, "a written document, while often biased in its original formulation, at least becomes permanent as it is archived and 'subtracted from time.'"[48] The introduction of writing opened a floodgate to human development, allowing a huge increase in the creative use of intelligence since the ability to store information externally increases access to knowledge and ideas across both space and time. As Maryanne Wolf puts it, "while reading, we can leave our own consciousness, and pass over into the consciousness of another person, another age, another culture."[49]

Postmodernists attempt to disguise this gap in development by describing aboriginal recollections as "oral literature," even going so far as to claim that "when an elder dies, a library burns."[50] It is also asserted that oral traditions contain numerous philosophical insights.[51] But "oral histories" are told by way of general stories that capture only the history's essence so that the retelling allows for embellishment to meet the expectations of the audience or purpose of the teller. Clearly, this form of knowledge transmission does not accommodate complex organization of information. The development of history, logic, science, and philosophy requires that observations and arguments be recorded so that they can be analyzed.[52] Without writing, the verification and refutation of assertions become impossible, because there is no mechanism to determine what was originally said.

As in the evolution from oral cultures to written ones, there is a discernable sequence in the development of writing itself. This sequence is articulately expressed by Ignace Gelb in his book *The History of Writing*.[53] Gelb shows the development from pictograms (where a character is directly representative of an object), to ideograms (where words are represented by an abstract symbol), to phonetic syllabics, and finally, the alphabet. Syllabics were developed gradually as rebus forms replaced pictograms and ideograms,[54] while the creation of the alphabet required a further step – spelling out the sounds of syllabics into their respective vowels and consonants. Once this was accomplished, a number of interchangeable letters could be used to accurately correlate written words with their spoken sounds, and alphabetic writing systems were born.[55]

This understanding of the progression of writing explains why languages like Chinese, which are largely based on the ideographic principle, are less efficient than those with alphabetic scripts. But aboriginal languages represent a much earlier stage of development than pre-alphabetic languages like Chinese. Vocabulary is one of the greatest indicators of this developmental gap. While the Chinese vocabulary is limited by its script (it has, at most, fifty thousand words)[56] in comparison to alphabetic languages,[57] the sparse vocabularies of pre-literate languages provide a much larger problem for their expressive power. All written languages have far more words than those that are pre-literate, which must store their entire vocabulary in the memory of the living generation. A 1925 Inuktitut-English dictionary, for example, documents only 2,600 Inuktitut words, and some of these would be concepts brought by literate Europeans (these words were being *written* in a dictionary, after all).[58]

The obvious gap in development between pre-literate and written languages has resulted in attempts to modernize aboriginal languages in two ways: first, by developing new writing systems; and secondly, by "aboriginalizing" modern concepts. These attempts were first made by missionaries so that they could bring Christianity to the aboriginal population. Words like "sin" and "hell," for example, had to be developed in order to indoctrinate the natives. The missionary James Evans even created a new script of syllabics so that the Bible could be translated into Cree. This script was later revised by another missionary, Edmund Peck, for the Inuktitut syllabic system.[59] Although the characters of the Roman alphabet are also used in some of the scripts for aboriginal languages, syllabics are still the most dominant form of writing.

The current native use of syllabics, however, presents serious obstacles to aboriginal participation in the modern world. First of all, these systems are only spoken by aboriginals and small numbers of non-aboriginals (mostly linguists), discouraging native familiarity with a script that would allow them to access ideas from much larger numbers of the world's population. Secondly, as was explained above, syllabics were the precursors of the alphabet, and as such, their meaning is dependent upon context. This makes the language much less specific than those that use an alphabetic script.[60]

An even greater problem than the primitive nature of the script is that new words have been grafted on to what is still basically a pre-literate culture. The values, attitudes, concepts, and knowledge needed to become fully literate today did not exist historically in native cultures; thus even though a new word might be created in an aboriginal language, there is no concept that exists in the culture to give it meaning. This leads to much less specific ideas being applied to new concepts. Domestic animals, for example, are described in Inuktitut as *nujuattaittut*, or "animals that do not run away,"[61] thereby including injured animals, a turtle hiding in its shell, or a snake that has become too cold to move. The identification of a grocery store in Yellowknife resulted in the even vaguer description of "the place across from where you get chicken." This description resulted from the fact that the supermarket was on the opposite side of the street from the Kentucky Fried Chicken outlet. This understanding, however, is dependent upon people being familiar with this establishment and would be incomprehensible to anyone who was not a participant in the local culture.

The pre-literate character of aboriginal languages makes them less precise than those that have evolved with the development of writing and all the cultural advancements that come with it. This became apparent when one of us (Howard) was hired to construct a poster for the Nunavut Heritage Trust. The poster contained a number of pictures of various archaeological sites in Nunavut, including one for a cache of food, and another a burial site. To appeal to as wide an audience as possible, the poster was to have captions for these different sites in four languages – English, French, German, and Inuktitut. But while the translations for the three European languages were completed effortlessly, the Inuktitut captions became fraught with problems when they were accidentally mixed up. It became necessary to seek an Inuktitut speaker to identify what inscription went with each picture. All the speaker was able to say was "this says buried," which did not help at all since both pictures involved burials – one with respect to food (a cache) and the other to a person (a grave). Moreover, different Inuktitut speakers, when asked for assistance, disagreed about the identification of the captions.

These difficulties with a very simple use of Inuktitut made us wonder about all the documents that the government translates into aboriginal languages. If these languages do not have the same concepts as those used by European ones, what is the quality of information being relayed to unilingual aboriginal language speakers? To investigate the discrepancies that might exist, we decided to have a few paragraphs of a government document that had been translated into French, Dogrib, and Inuktitut translated back into English. In this way, we could compare the back translations to the English and see if there was a difference in specificity between a European language such as French and two aboriginal languages.

The document we used was the Government of the Northwest Territories' *Report of the Traditional Knowledge Working Group*.[62] The report includes an executive summary in English that is translated into eight other languages. We chose three to be translated back into English – French, Dogrib, and Inuktitut. The French was translated by Suzanne Desfossés, a territorial government employee who had previously done translations for the Canada Mortgage and Housing Corporation. The aboriginal languages were translated by two professional firms recommended by the territorial government, Tindee Interpreting Services for

Figure 8.1

| English | French | Dogrib | Inuktitut |
|---|---|---|---|
| The survival of northern aboriginal peoples depended for thousand [sic] of years on their knowledge, special relationship with their environment, their ways of organizing themselves and their values. Traditional knowledge was passed on from one generation to the next. It was based on thousands of years of observation and testing. | For thousands of years the survival of the Northern Autochthonous [Aboriginal] people was dependent on their knowledge, their special relationship with the environment, their ability to adapt and prioritize their values. Their customs were passed on from generation to generation. These [customs] were based on thousands of years of observation and experience. | In the Northwest Territories and also the people of down south, wants [sic] to re-learn their traditional way of life. If the Government of the Northwest Territories provided and implemented traditional skill [sic] to people they would lead a healthier and meaningful life. | The people of the Northwest Territories survived for many years, they survived by using their own traditons [sic], they knew their surroundings well, they have been taught their tradition well. For thousands of years the traditonal [sic] values of the people were practiced. |
| In the relatively recent history of the Northwest Territories, the assumptions, values and knowledge of Euro-Canadians have come to form the basis for most of the institutions, laws, programs, activities and policies of both government and non-government institutions. | It is only in the fairly recent history of the Northwest Territories that Euro-Canadian assumptions, values and culture have been used to form the basis of most institutions (agencies), laws, programs, enterprises and the politics of government and non-government institutions. | The people want to maintain their traditional way of life, and in today's world there are not a lot of elders living with us. The aboriginal people say that if people practice their traditional way of life and also speak their language they would be able to maintain it. The white people say in order to protect and keep this land and the tradition is to start talking about it now. | Today, and as we look into our future we are drifting towards Eureopeon [sic] lifestyles, our employment is based on the Eureopeon [sic] style, as well as our legislation and justice system. The economy and the way our governement [sic] operates, and the private industry they all are based on the Eurepeon [sic] life style. |

Northern aboriginal peoples are increasingly aware that integrating their traditional knowledge into the institutions which serve them is a key to their cultural survival as distinct peoples and to determining a place for themselves in the modern world. They are demanding that culturally appropriate systems be available in which to work out their problems. Traditional knowledge must be the foundation on which to build appropriate systems and reverse the cycle of dependency within aboriginal communities. Rapid social change and the death of more aboriginal elders each year add to the urgency of documenting and increasing the use of traditional knowledge.

The Indigenous People of the north realize more and more that by integrating their customs in the "Social Establishment" that they will survive as a distinct people and determine their place in the modern world. They ask that culturally sensitive systems be put in place in order for them to work out their problems. Traditional methods [knowledge] must be the foundation of any system [plan] developed that will stop the cycle of dependency in the Indigenous communities. There is an ever increasing urgency to document and intensify the use of customs due to a rapidly changing society and the ever growing number of aboriginal elders that die each year.

The people of the Northwest Territories know that there will be a lot of changes, so they want to maintain their cultural [sic] and language and also to live the modern way of life. They want to keep their traditional way of life so that they can learn how to be self sufficient. Each year our society is changing, and also our elders are slowing [sic] passing on, so we should work on this issue as soon as possible.

The aboriginal people of the Northwest Territories are more aware of using their traditonal [sic] culture, as well they want to preserve their culture if possible.

If their culture can be recognized officially and survive, the aboriginal people want to strengthen their culture in order to find answers to problems arising due to cultural shock.

Today we face rapid changes, that we are not able to cope with, our elders are dying rapidly, we have an urgency, whereby we have to get their traditional knowledge on paper before we lose it all, by doing this their tradition[sic] can be passed down and carried on by the next generation.

the Dogrib, and Puulik Translations for the Inuktitut. The results of this back translation are documented in Figure 8.1.

As the reader can see, the French back translation is very similar to the English. Although there are a few differences in the way the ideas are expressed and the words that are used (traditional knowledge, for example, is translated into "customs"), the essential ideas expressed in the three paragraphs are almost identical in meaning to the original. The story is very different for the Dogrib and Inuktitut translations. The Dogrib is the worst and really bears only the faintest similarity to what was intended by the English text. The Inuktitut is somewhat better, presumably because the preparations for Nunavut have resulted in greater efforts to modernize the language. Much of the meaning of the original, however, has been lost. In the first paragraph, none of the specifics about traditional knowledge depending on a "special relationship" to the environment is mentioned, or the fact that it is passed from "one generation to the next." The second paragraph does not relay the point that it is only relatively recently that the "Euro-Canadian assumptions, values and knowledge" have formed the basis of "laws, programs, activities and policies" of "government and non-government institutions." Instead, it is maintained that "we" are "drifting towards European lifestyles." The third paragraph's main point – that preserving traditional knowledge is the key to ensuring cultural survival and ending the cycle of dependency in aboriginal communities – is not clearly expressed, as it is with the French translation.[63]

It is significant that these discrepancies are large even in the context of a government document about something pertaining to aboriginal culture – traditional knowledge. One can imagine the result if the text concerned the engineering requirements for building skyscrapers, organic chemistry experiments, Renaissance paintings, or Hegel's *Philosophy of Right*. In these cases, few concepts would be present in aboriginal culture to make any kind of meaningful translation possible; aboriginal culture has not gone through the developmental stages in art, science, or philosophy that have occurred in other parts of the world.

Nowhere is the gap between pre-literate and written cultures more evident than in the recent attempts to "aboriginalize" the Canadian legal system. These problems arise because "oral tradition" is inconsistent with the formal laws of modern societies. Aboriginal languages that did not evolve to the writing stage lack the detail and structure required in the complexity of legal procedure, and therefore legal terminology is not translatable into aboriginal languages. For example, a trial in the Northwest Territories was interrupted because a lawyer wanted to know how the judge's instructions had been translated for the jury. When the Inuktitut words informing the jury were translated back into English, "reasonable doubt" was translated as "exactly what happened without the aid of magic."[64] Similar problems have been encountered with "Do you plead guilty or not guilty," which has been translated into "Did you do it or not?"[65]

The lack of modern concepts in aboriginal culture also means that native languages tend to use the same term for a range of different meanings. The verb "to lie" is used to describe being misinformed or wrong as well as misrepresenting the truth. The distinction is particularly important in the courtroom. In one case, a lawyer moved to discredit a witness for inconsistency when, she said the liquor in question was vodka, then later referred to it as whiskey. Further inquiry determined that the language she used simply made no distinction between the two. In a sexual assault trial in Yellowknife we listened to a woman testify, via translator, that the accused (her nephew, and band chief at the time) had maintained penetration for two hours. Increasing the scepticism of all concerned, the whole episode, from meeting him on the street, going to his hotel room, and then to the women's centre for lunch, took only an hour and fifteen minutes. Everyone accepted that she must mean two minutes, but the communication level of her language was insufficient to meet the specificity required by the courts, that is, there appeared to be no distinction between "minute" and "hour" in her language.

The vast difference in complexity between pre-literate languages and those that are written is completely disregarded by most anthropologists and linguists studying aboriginal groups.[66] This occurs even in the writings of Diamond Jenness, a Canadian anthropologist who is often criticized for his "assimilationist" views on aboriginal education. In a chapter on aboriginal languages, Jenness warns us against a "widely-spread error" and maintains that "simplicity in culture does *not* entail a simple language." According to Jenness, "English or French appears comparatively simple beside the intricacies of Eskimo."[67] However, he does not support this claim, except to say that aboriginal languages are difficult to pronounce. The examples that he uses – that the Inuit numbering system consists of differentiating between "one," "two" and "many,"[68] that only three or four colours are distinguished by Indians,[69] and that there are few abstract nouns and sparse vocabularies in native languages – actually show the opposite.

But Jenness maintains that this is because an aboriginal person "will differentiate, in matters that are important to him, where Europeans may make no distinction. Thus Eskimo has one term for falling snow, another for granular snow, a third for a snow-drift, and several others; whereas English possesses but the one word 'snow,' and must employ descriptive phrases to separate its varieties or manifestations."[70] Although Jenness attributes the lower level of abstraction in aboriginal languages to "primitive economic conditions and to the absence of a leisured class devoted to intellectual pursuits," he argues that "there were Indian philosophers who pondered deeply and spent much time in silent meditation; but they seldom revealed their thoughts to others or sought the stimulus and discipline that come from open discussion and debate. So their meditations tended to revolve around concrete things and their languages reflected the concreteness of their thoughts."[71] But if these "philosophers" did not "reveal their thoughts to others," how does Jenness know that they "pondered deeply"? And if there were few abstract terms in aboriginal languages, how was philosophy possible in the first place?

Jenness was failing to make a distinction between the complexity that comes with being highly organized and that which is associated with irregularity. The fact that something is difficult to understand does not mean that it is "complex" in the first sense. As languages progressed, rules were developed so that they could be learned more easily. In other words, languages became more organized as they evolved. This is why the verb "to be" is irregular in almost all European languages. It is the oldest and therefore the most primitive (i.e., the closest to its ancestral roots).

The example given by Jenness, regarding the Inuit words for snow, is also inept. We are familiar with the cliché of Inuit languages having "hundreds" of words for snow, the intent of which is to demonstrate that aboriginal languages are "just as complex" as modern languages, only concerned with different matters. The number of words describing different snow conditions could more realistically be attributed to the absence of adjectives in the language; the "complexity" lies in the need to use separate words for each of the many forms of snow.

There are really only about a dozen words for snow, referring to it in different contexts – not different words for snow itself.[72] As can be seen by the list of these words compiled by Anthony C. Woodbury,[73] verbs like *qanir* ("to snow") are included, as well as descriptions of where snow is located, such as *qanikcaq* ("snow on the ground") and *nevluk* ("clinging debris"). Words are also listed that refer to human uses of snow (*utvak,* "snow carved in a block"), dangers pertaining to snow (*navcite,* or to "get caught in an avalanche"), and qualitative or quantitative descriptions of snow (*pirrelvag,* "to blizzard severely," and *nutaryuk,* "fresh snow"). The fact that a completely different word is used instead of just applying an adverb or adjective to "snow," as occurs in the English translation, actually implies that the language is less, rather than more, complex. It is the language's incapacity for abstraction that makes all these variations a necessity. Instead of being internally differentiated and specialized, as has occurred with the development of different parts of speech in modern languages, aboriginal languages are made up of an assortment of words that have developed in response to the day-to-day survival needs of small, pre-literate societies organized on the basis of kinship.[74]

A list compiled by Scott Heron shows that English has forty-four words for the same types of descriptions of snow, plus a few others.[75] And although extensive, this list of Herron's doesn't even begin to get into the terms used in the scientific analysis of snow. Snow crystals are classified into seven different types, according to the internal arrangement of their oxygen atoms: plates, stellars, columns, needles, spatial dendrites, capped columns, and irregular crystals. There is also an understanding of the different types of clouds that are constituted by snow particles, as well as various kinds of hail. The scientific understanding and classification of ice and ice formations is even more complex.

Regardless of the number of words for snow used by the Inuit, discussions about this aspect of aboriginal languages misses the most important point: this sort of "complexity" is relatively unimportant in the modern context. Much more important are the various abstractions that are used to understand developments in engineering, chemistry, logic, history, art, social relations and philosophy, as well as the specificity in meanings that are required for clear communication with large numbers of people. It is these skills, not different words for snow, that must be acquired if aboriginal peoples are going to participate in and contribute to the wider society.

Yet the increasing influence of postmodern relativism in the field of linguistics propagates the myth of aboriginal languages having the same communication capacity as modern European languages. While linguists were originally scientists who devoted themselves to the study of languages, they now function as advocates promoting aboriginal language preservation, and demand funding on this basis. Such a concern about "language loss" has led to the development of the Endangered Languages Fund and a number of other charitable initiatives to aid language documentation and "revitalization."[76] In Canada the post-modern movement toward "applied" or "conservation" linguistics is manifest in the Canadian Linguistics Association. As part of its ongoing development, the organization has created a Committee on Aboriginal Languages whose mandate is "to share information among linguists and communities working in the area of maintenance and revitalization of aboriginal languages in Canada."[77] This includes sharing information with the Linguistic Society of America's Committee on Endangered Languages and Their Preservation (CELP), as well as various native groups. These organizations are not only present in Canada but throughout the world.[78]

But the *study* of various languages is not the same thing as advocating their preservation and revitalization; theories about the nature and development of languages can still be formulated by analyzing the voluminous data that currently exist. There is also no evidence to support the commonly made assertion put forward to support language preservation – that the disappearance of languages is detrimental to the survival of humanity.[79] The argument relies on a confusion of cultural and biological diversity, as well as a denial of cultural evolution. It is erroneously assumed that linguistic diversity is similar to biological diversity. The comparison is faulty, since languages are a part of culture and can be dramatically transformed even within a single generation. This means that it is not necessary to maintain a variety of cultural characteristics "on hand" so that they can be selected to aid survival. The retention of linguistic diversity, in fact, creates communication barriers *within* our species, thwarting human understanding and cooperation. True language preservation occurs according to its utility in meeting the needs of its speakers. But dependence on exogenously imposed efforts is artificial, and illustrates the redundancy of pre-literate languages. The attempts to preserve aboriginal languages only serve the interests of the linguists of the Aboriginal Industry; they are a disservice to native people.

## IN DEFENCE OF EUROCENTRISM

Of all the initiatives of the Aboriginal Industry, the research that is intent on justifying self-government over education is the most disturbing, as education is the area where solutions to the aboriginal question lie. Lack of education is at the heart of aboriginal peoples' cultural underdevelopment and their inability to participate in the Canadian workforce. Improvements in education, therefore, are directly linked to solving other problems that are symptoms of a marginalized existence – poverty, poor health, violence against women, suicides, child abuse, and so on – caused by the gap in cultural development.

Proper identification of the problem, however, is being impeded by misguided efforts to improve aboriginal peoples' "low self-esteem." Many Canadians believe it is inappropriate to criticize aboriginal educational initiatives because of the terrible injustices that have been perpetrated in that area in the past. They argue that aboriginal peoples should be allowed to "make their own mistakes" and it is inappropriate for "white people" to "tell them what to do." But if there is no debate about educational goals and methods, how will aboriginal people have access to the ideas and knowledge that exist around the world? How will they be able to evaluate their beliefs and cultural practices if they are expected to uncritically defer to the "wisdom" of their ancestors? And on what basis will they even know what mistakes are if standards are continuously lowered and their lives kept artificially separate from the Canadian mainstream?

It is actually exciting to see the acceptance of rational thought that can occur when non-aboriginal scientists honestly evaluate aboriginal viewpoints in discussions with native people themselves. This was seen in the 2003 Public Broadcasting Service/National Geographic Channel documentary *The Journey of Man*, which chronicles the work of Spencer Wells, a geneticist who has traced the DNA markers that show that human beings migrated out of Africa to all parts of the world. In one episode of the documentary Wells has a discussion with Phil Blue-nose and other members of a Navajo tribe located near Canyon de Chelly in the United States. In this meeting Wells counters the Navajo contention that they were "created" in the Americas by stating that mutations on male chromosomes sampled around the world show that everyone is related to the San Bushpeople in Africa, and that human beings travelled to North America across the Bering Strait about fifteen thousand years ago. He then pulls out a number of pictures of the San, and explains how their facial features exhibit the diverse characteristics that can be seen in all peoples today. Rather than being offended, Blue-nose and the other Navajo people in the group express surprise, and then appear to appreciate and accept the scientific explanation. The division that was created by "different ways of knowing" was replaced with common understanding and the idea that we all have common interests as members of the human family.

The non-aboriginal attitudes that support aboriginal education come down to one word – condescension. Condescension means that a person thinks that there should be one standard for them and another for those to whom they condescend. Condescending persons expect honesty from others, and feel betrayed and manipulated when they are lied to; yet they feel withholding the truth from others is acceptable, because they believe those others do not have the capacity to accept it. Sometimes they even justify their condescension by saying that people are happier when they are deprived of the truth, that "ignorance is bliss."

Keeping people blissfully ignorant, however, has a downside. It leaves them open to manipulation. Taboos against truth-telling enable charlatans to take advantage of those who have been shielded from reality. While this role was exploited in pre-contact times by the various shamans who used magic tricks to extort gifts, the modern deceivers are the Aboriginal Industry. Linguists, anthropologists, and other consultants encourage substandard methods and practices so that contracts can be obtained to develop, run, and evaluate a separate "culturally sensitive" aboriginal educational system.

# 9

## Environmental Management:
## The Spiritual Sell-Out of "Mother Earth"

When one of us (Widdowson) began her doctoral studies, she participated in a First Nations and Public Policy discussion group organized
by York University graduate students. The group, moderated by Michael
Posluns, promised to enable students from all disciplines to engage in
debates about First Nations issues. Posluns had initiated the group
because of his historical involvement in aboriginal politics. A co-author
of the glorified account of George Manuel's life,[1] Posluns had also
worked as the editor of *Akwasasne News*, a native advocacy newspaper, and as a consultant for the Native Brotherhood.[2]

The most heated debates on the listserv concerned aboriginal peoples'
jurisdiction over environmental management. Commonplace in the literature is the claim that aboriginal people have a particular spirituality
leading them to be natural stewards of the environment, and most discussions aggressively supported this position. For example, when we
posted an article that we had written for the *Globe and Mail* challenging the existence of innate aboriginal stewardship,[3] the response from
Paul, a graduate student in political science, was merely the following:
"I trust that this audience is in agreement that [Widdowson's] recent
posting ... is so full of mean-spiritedness and factual distortion as to
make it not worth refuting in detail."[4]

We were again to encounter the wrath of Paul, along with another
graduate student from Carleton University, William, when we responded
to an article posted by Posluns. The article concerned a Circle of Wisdom Native Peoples/Native Homelands Climate Change Workshop in
which NASA had supposedly consulted with aboriginal elders about
global warming to "merge the knowing and wisdom of people who
understand the responsibilities that humans have to the Earth with the

knowledge of non-native scientists."[5] In his posting, Posluns asked the following question: "Will NASA act on the elders' teachings?" We responded by stating that of course NASA would not act, since there were no teachings that would pertain to global warming. Obviously, NASA was just engaging in a public relations exercise that provided a distraction from actually addressing the environmental problems facing the planet.

Although William and Paul's responses were largely a postmodern attack on the validity of science (a stance discussed in the next chapter), our interest here concerns the tactics used to justify aboriginal control over environmental management. Paul again dismissed our arguments, stating that "my comments are brief since I just don't have the will-power to patiently wade through the venom." William, while he did offer some criticisms of our arguments, concluded that our "crass and idiotic writing is strangely reminiscent of recent Reform Party and resource-industry rhetoric. It was disappointing to see it appear on this list, and worrysome that it might in any way represent current thinking in the York University student body." He sent an article to Widdowson's personal email account entitled "Native Band Approves Selective Logging" with the following explanation: "I have decided to make your re-education a part-time personal project."

William, however, was the person soon to be "re-educated." This process began with a posting from Posluns, who upon finding a website featuring the works of Nova Scotia environmentalist David Orton, remarked that it was "appalling to learn that these papers which I considered too pretentious to qualify as hate propaganda but too hateful to represent significant scholarship ... are continuously republished in cyberspace." Posluns's remarks prompted a response from Jamie, another consultant with ties to aboriginal organizations: "I thought David Orton had sufficiently discredited himself with his 'left bio-centric' critique of aboriginal peoples and aboriginal rights already. Given that this discussion has already occurred ... I won't bother exhuming it; I would just advise anyone reading this material that it is not necessary to take it seriously." But William *did* find that the material warranted a serious analysis, pointing out that "name-calling without analysis is hardly the path to better understanding." He went on to state that "for all its shortcomings, Orton's piece raises several extremely important issues. And he's right, there is an alarming unwillingness to discuss these issues within the activist community."

Essentially, Orton came to the somewhat banal conclusion that environmentalists should not unconditionally support the devolution of environmental management responsibilities to aboriginal groups since some
were engaging in ecologically destructive activities. According to
Orton, "there must be a commitment to social justice for Aboriginals
within contemporary Canadian society. Progressive people should support and help initiate whatever social changes are necessary for this to
be achieved, as long as such changes are just to non-Native Canadians
and do not negatively impact upon what remains of the natural
world."[6] This argument sparked outrage because it was seen to be in
opposition to claims for absolute aboriginal sovereignty, thus racist and
reflective of a "colonial allegiance." According to Paul, "if what is
implied is a sort of environmental trump card which can be played to
undermine aboriginal rights then we are indeed entering the terrain on
which charges of racism and colonialism are appropriate." After many
more such accusations, William ended his subscription to the list. As a
parting contribution he asked the question: "Am I beginning to detect a
pattern here where anyone who dares to disagree with any part of pro-
grammatic statements on sovereignty is immediately accused of racism,
support for genocide, hate propaganda, etc.?"

The exchange is instructive because it shows how unconditional support is demanded in all discussions about aboriginal control over the
environment. Even mild criticism results in accusations of racism, colonialism, or hate propaganda. Although Orton's work contains a number of bizarre notions – one being that animal and plant communities
are "nations" – it is difficult to see how his arguments are hateful
towards aboriginal people. In fact, Orton is much less critical of the
current claims about aboriginal peoples' innate environmentalism than
a historical and materialist analysis warrants.[7]

## TURNING TECHNOLOGICAL ABSENCE INTO A
## SPIRITUAL PRESENCE

In many books on the history of aboriginal people, two premises are
constant. The first is that they lived in harmony with their environment
for thousands of years. The second is that spiritual teachings of aboriginal elders enabled this "balance with nature" to be maintained. Unlike
Europeans raised in the Judeo-Christian tradition and encouraged
to exploit nature for their own ends, it is argued, aboriginal people's

spiritual beliefs taught them to respect non-human elements, preventing them from destroying the earth.[8] To "fulfil the role of steward assigned to them by the Creator," aboriginal peoples developed customs, rules, laws, and even institutions that ensured environmental sustainability.[9] Winona LaDuke maintains that "cyclical" thinking in aboriginal spiritual beliefs that spiritual forces will hold them to account in the future for any transgressions made against nature today – imparts an ecological consciousness.[10]

Although most commentators do not attempt to explain how these beliefs translate into daily activities, a few advocates of aboriginal control over environmental management have attempted to detail the various practices used to this end. We are told about the rituals and taboos practised to show respect for various animals.[11] Harvey Feit and Fikret Berkes imply that aboriginal peoples have always had the environmental management techniques present in modern society – harvesting sustainable yields determined through the representative sampling of various animal populations.[12]

Any examination of *how* aboriginal people happened to develop an environmental sensitivity while Europeans did not, however, is usually avoided. The assumption is that aboriginal people, because their ancestors developed a special "covenant" with God when he gave them North America, will "naturally" look after the environment. Since aboriginal people did not destroy the environment, while whites did, it *must* be the former's ancestrally (racially) determined philosophy that ensured environmental sustainability.

The argument that aboriginal people were assigned the position of environmental custodians or stewards by the Creator is an attempt to give a "deep ecology"[13] twist to land claims and self-government demands. Flowing from this argument is the idea that the environmental crisis is a direct result of aboriginal peoples' loss of land and political autonomy. The expropriation of their lands has meant that they can no longer exercise their spiritually assigned role of managing the environment. Therefore, it is necessary to return control over development to aboriginal groups so that they can resume their spiritual role as environmental custodians.

Support for this political agenda depends on an ahistorical and decontextualized interpretation of aboriginal culture. Attributing environmental management practices to various aboriginal tribes fails to consider the effects of European influence. European societies had managed harvesting for centuries before they arrived in North America, and there are many instances of priests, traders, and government officials attempting to impart this knowledge to the native population.[14] The need for conservation in European history came into being with population growth and technological development, both of which put a strain on natural resources. Aboriginal peoples in North America, on the other hand, had sparse populations and primitive technology. They had domesticated only the dog and so did not have the control over animal stocks that would be necessary to manage them. Nor had they developed numbers or methods of counting, making it impossible for them to determine sustainable yields. Therefore, there is no basis for environmental management practices in pre-literate and nomadic hunting and gathering societies. The anthropologist Marc Stevenson even argues that conceptions of "management" are not an aspect of aboriginal traditions, although these ideas are often articulated by younger native people influenced by the "Whiteman's way."[15]

Assertions about aboriginal peoples' ecological consciousness also require a decontextualized understanding of their relationship to the environment. What is promoted as a spiritual connection to the land is actually a result of the *absence* of ecological understanding. Animistic beliefs are a reflection of the neolithic period's lack of technological development and a lower capacity to control nature. Cultures at this level of development reacted to scarcity by trying to appease animal spirits through various taboos and rituals.[16] The Montagnais, for example, blamed lack of success at hunting beaver on feeding beaver bones to dogs instead of hanging them on trees or throwing them into the water, while the southwestern Ojibwa thought "speaking ill of a beaver" would have the same effect.[17] It is such taboos and rituals that are referred to when anthropologists maintain that aboriginal peoples are respectful toward animals.[18]

Rather than methods of "managing" wildlife populations, taboos and rituals were simply attempts to increase the numbers of animals that could be killed and eaten. "Management" of wildlife merely consisted of depleting resources until the carrying capacity of the area had been exceeded, and then moving to another location. It was the abundance of wildlife that placed limits on aboriginal hunting practices, not any conscious attempt to conserve animal populations. Hunting and gathering differs from horticulture or agriculture in that yields cannot be increased with human effort; consequently, when an increase in population puts pressure on a resource, an alternate resource must be exploited, or the population will correspondingly decrease.[19]

Claims about aboriginal peoples' environmental management philosophies are discredited even further when the implications of adopting these various taboos and rituals in the modern context are considered. If one assumes that following particular procedures in killing, butchering, and disposing of wildlife will increase the availability of animal populations, regardless of the number harvested,[20] how will this aid environmental sustainability? Aboriginal beliefs can even result in opposition to environmental management. One example is the belief in reincarnation; killing *more* animals becomes one answer to wildlife scarcity, since a greater number are believed to be "reborn." This concept has led some aboriginal people to resist the implementation of wildlife management practices on the grounds that animal spirits would be offended.[21] Another example is the idea that animals "choose" to be hunted, and therefore imposing limits on harvesting "is denying the animal's right of choice and hence exhibits not only extreme disrespect towards the animal, but also endangers the continuation of everybody's survival as the animals may refrain from offering themselves in the future."[22] With this logic, even the mass slaughter of endangered species could be justified by the belief that the sighting of an animal indicates that it "has offered itself to the hunter."

Erroneously asserting that aboriginal beliefs are indicative of a racially based conservation ethic also fails to consider the many historical instances where aboriginal peoples engaged in environmentally destructive activities. The disappearance of thirty-five species of mammals in the Americas coincided with the arrival of humans. These animals included mammoths, mastodons, giant sloths, pampatheres, glyptodonts, camels, capybaras, tapirs, giant beavers, antelopes, horses, oxen, stag-moose, dire wolves, and serrated-toothed cats.[23] Although the cause of these extinctions is disputed – it is not known to what extent climatic factors were involved – the timing of the sudden disappearance of so many animal species indicates that the introduction of weapon-wielding human predators was at least partly responsible. None of these animals had evolved in relation to human beings, and they had no defence against the hunting technology brought over the Beringia land bridge. It is likely that some were exterminated because they were killed at a rate greater than their capacity to reproduce.[24]

Another example that does not fit well with idealized conceptions of aboriginal peoples' role as "natural stewards" concerns events that transpired after Iron Age technology and commerce were introduced in North America. In the space of three hundred years, aboriginal peoples wiped out most of the beaver and buffalo populations.[25] Although these depletions have largely been blamed on the "white man" for initiating the fur trade, there is no evidence that aboriginal peoples reduced their hunting or trapping activities or showed any philosophical opposition to this economic activity.[26]

In order to sustain the argument that it was aboriginal peoples' philosophy that was the determining factor in their "harmonious" relationship with the environment, it would have to be shown that they retained their beliefs and environmentally sensitive practices even when more destructive technologies and economic systems were introduced. Otherwise, aboriginal peoples, like all human beings who have lived on the planet, were only responding to economic and political imperatives. Once more sophisticated technology is developed and the profit motive becomes dominant, people must either participate in the system or change it; they cannot simply "choose" to ignore it and operate according to some kind of transcendental environmental ethic. To do so would result in being squeezed out in the global competition for resources and markets. Such was the circumstance in the development of the fur trade when different aboriginal tribes used guns they acquired to secure a dominant economic position. The idea that environmentalism is inherent within the aboriginal population, however, has been created by transposing concerns over deterioration of the natural world as a result of industrialization onto a romanticized image of aboriginal peoples.

## CHIEF SEATTLE – THE ENVIRONMENTALIST WHO NEVER WAS

On 17 October 1987, an article by Canadian environmental activist David Suzuki appeared in the *Globe and Mail* about the looming environmental crisis facing the planet. In the article Suzuki quotes large sections of a speech made by Chief Seattle (also known as Sea'thl, Seal'th, or Seeathl) in 1854. Calling it an expression of a native world view "that offers a profoundly different vision of the human place in nature," Suzuki reinforced a common assumption that aboriginal philosophy is essential to helping us solve environmental problems. The platitudes in Chief Seattle's speech which we have heard over and over – "all things are connected," "whatever befalls the earth, befalls the sons of the earth," and "the earth does not belong to man; man belongs to the earth" – are used to show how our attitudes must change if we are to save the environment.[27] They also are put forward as evidence that environmentalism is an innate component of the aboriginal mindset. As Rudoph Kaiser points out, "while American Indians are seen by some people as ecologists by birth, Chief Seattle is hailed as the prophet of an ecological sentiment, which is said to be lacking in western industrialized nations."[28]

Suzuki is not the only member of the environmental movement to have used Chief Seattle's speech to promote ecological awareness. The speech has been translated into several languages and many environmental groups have published sections of it in the hopes of increasing the emotional appeal of their agenda. In 1990 the Canadian government even included Seattle's words in its Green Plan, to show how it was concerned about the environment. Several books on environmental management include quotes from the speech to encourage a holistic view of the relationship between humans and the environment. A children's book entitled *Brother Eagle, Sister Sky: A Message from Chief Seattle*, sold 280,000 copies in the year after it was published in 1995.[29] Seattle's words are said to be "the most-quoted single statement by any native American."[30]

What is not mentioned, however, is that the words so often quoted are not Chief Seattle's. The "speech" was actually written thirty-three years after the fact by Dr Henry Smith, a non-aboriginal physician who claimed to have taken notes while listening to Chief Seattle. His rendition appeared in a 1887 article in the *Seattle Sunday Star*. Smith's account was used to develop another version for an ecological film called *Home*, produced in 1972. Ted Perry, the non-aboriginal English professor who wrote the script, "made no bones about the fact that while he used a version of Smith's version of Seattle's speech for inspiration, he came up with his own version which differed markedly from the original."[31] What was originally written by Smith has very little that pertains to any aboriginal "environmental consciousness." It largely concerns Seattle's purported resignation to the "white man's" presence in the area and the inevitable disappearance of the "red man." The only reference to the earth concerns the linkage of the land to the spirits of his ancestors, but this is not about ecological awareness; it concerns the beliefs of Seattle's tribe about ghosts.[32]

But despite the fact that the speeches written by Smith and Perry are conjured evidence for claims about the different environmental world view of aboriginal people, the attribution of these words to Seattle continues to be defended. The arguments take the position that it is the message, not its authorship, that is important. Chief Seattle is seen as providing a metaphor for environmentally sensitive philosophies and actions, a sort of Smokey the Bear for the environmental movement. Whether or not Seattle actually said the things attributed to him is irrelevant to the New Age mindset, since he provides a powerful symbol for promoting a respect for nature and sustainability.

This is now the position taken by David Suzuki in *Wisdom of the Elders*, co-written with Peter Knudtson.[33] Knudtson and Suzuki concede that the words attributed to Seattle are largely fictitious but maintain that questions of the speech's authenticity "need not be taken as serious challenges to the value and validity of traditional Native knowledge about nature, which is amply confirmed in countless other ways." They even argue that awareness of the fabrication will strengthen arguments that native people have an ecological consciousness, because it will encourage people "to look *beyond* the clichés of Chief Seattle – into deeper, more intellectually and spiritually challenging matters."[34]

But if we take away the various environmentalist Adarios – Chief Seattle, Tecumseh, Black Hawk, Black Elk, Standing Bear, Sitting Bull, and, of course, Canada's great fraud, Grey Owl – the evidential support for aboriginal peoples' concern for "Mother Earth" disappears with them. Even the aboriginal reverence for "Mother Earth" is largely a non-aboriginal American invention.[35] At the root of this idea is yet another Adario – Smohalla, a Sahaptin speaker whose words were "interpreted" by J.W. MacMurray in the late nineteenth century. Smohalla was then used as the source to claim that aboriginal people generally shared the belief that "the earth was the mother of mankind" and that agricultural and resource development should be opposed on the basis that it ravishes her body.[36]

Invariably, any "earth-loving" idea put forward by a native person is attributed to teachings connected to their ancestry,[37] even though these same ideas already exist in non-aboriginal traditions. In the eighteenth and nineteenth centuries, for example, English romantic poets like William Wordsworth, Samuel Taylor Coleridge, John Keats, and Percy Bysshe Shelley, as well as American writers Ralph Waldo Emerson and Henry David Thoreau, were espousing a very similar philosophy. Mainstream Christianity also includes people such as Saint Francis and Albert Schweitzer who felt a oneness with the natural world. Rather than originating these ideas, aboriginal culture is reflecting romantic and transcendental philosophies that have been very influential in European, American, and Canadian societies.

It is also apparent that these conceptions of aboriginal "natural environmentalism" overlook the overriding preoccupation of subsistence cultures. Urban dwellers and hunting and gathering cultures have distinctly different relationships to nature. The former ski, canoe, hike, and camp to enjoy the natural wilderness, while native people spend time on the land for reasons of subsistence. Since they have a utilitarian purpose, hunters never return from fruitless hunts with exclamations of the wonders of nature. Aboriginal people pursuing a "traditional lifestyle" much prefer snowmobiles, pickup trucks, and motorboats, all of which enable them to hunt more efficiently.

Despite these observations, many may remain unconvinced that the romanticization of aboriginal culture is a problem; sure, it may be a distortion of history and aboriginal culture, but what is the harm if it makes aboriginal people feel proud of their heritage? After all, aboriginal people are suffering terribly, and the idea that they have a spiritual relationship to the land is one way for them to feel good about themselves. But besides the obvious problem of encouraging aboriginal people to view themselves as spiritually superior to other groups, acceptance of the concept of "natural environmentalism" has two serious consequences. First, it justifies the devolution of responsibility for environmental management to aboriginal groups without ensuring proper regulatory controls. Second, it deters our continued investigation of the economic and political roots of environmental deterioration and the effective pursuit of solutions to a problem that faces all people, aboriginal and non-aboriginal alike.

## PUTTING MOM ON THE AUCTION BLOCK

The fictional character of Adarios like Chief Seattle does not preclude certain aboriginal people having an environmental consciousness. A number of aboriginal groups, after all, are actively involved in resisting polluting industries. Opposition to unrestrained logging, mining, and various other environmentally destructive practices exists in many aboriginal communities. It is for this reason that environmentalists try to make alliances with aboriginal organizations when fighting unsustainable development.

The problems arise when blanket assertions are made about aboriginal peoples' environmental consciousness, where it is assumed that everyone with aboriginal ancestry has a spiritual relationship to the land that ensures that they act in an ecologically responsible manner. David

Suzuki, for example, maintains that recognizing aboriginal cultures' "sacred connections to the land" is important for preserving the environment. To support this unscientific contention, Suzuki offers a number of romanticized accounts from native leaders and points to "enlightened land use" by the Cree and Kayapó. The Kayapó are a tribe of hunters and gatherers living in the Amazonian jungle who resisted the destruction of the rainforest so as to maintain their traditional way of life. Suzuki describes one of their villages as being "like paradise, where people live as they have lived since the beginning of human societies." He also recounts a statement by the renowned leader Paiakan that the Kayapó assume that "the forest is controlled by Nature" and therefore they "would never be so greedy or stupid as to take too much."[38]

But the outcome of this story did not live up to the romantic expectations created by Suzuki in 1992. After British rock star Sting threw his support behind the Kayapó and helped them to gain control over 25,000 square miles of rainforest, the Kayapó began entering into agreements with mining and logging companies. As Sting candidly explained a decade later: "I was very naïve and thought I could save the world selling T-shirts for the Indian cause. In reality, I did little."[39]

Suzuki inadvertently provides another enlightening example of aboriginal peoples' "environmental consciousness." This is the case of the James Bay Crees whose "practices of good conservation and sustainable harvesting," Suzuki maintains, "are at the heart of their traditions." In the early 1990s the Province of Quebec announced that its public utility, Hydro Quebec, would begin a massive extension of a hydroelectric project it began in the 1970s. After an international campaign was mobilized to publicize the havoc that such a project would wreak on Cree hunting grounds, development was put on hold. Suzuki argued that the environmental impacts of the project explained "why the Cree are rejecting all offers of money and compensation and are prepared to fight any further development on their lands" and maintained that "the resolution of their battle with Hydro Quebec will inform us whether we can change our priorities and values."[40]

But Suzuki's romanticism was again to collide with the events of history. The "resolution of their battle with Hydro Quebec" was the Crees signing an agreement to allow logging, mining, and hydroelectric development to take place. In exchange for this assault on their "sacred lands," Quebec agreed to pay the Crees $3.5 billion over fifty years. And although the agreement promised to consult the Crees in how development would proceed so as to protect hunting and trapping, it was well known that the proposed hydroelectric project was going to flood vast areas of the region.[41] The Sierra Club and Révérence Rupert continued to oppose the project, but they maintained that without the support of the Crees it was unlikely that they could be politically successful.[42]

The James Bay case is not unusual. It has been the typical sequence of events for all aboriginal "resistance" to development projects in the 1990s. Challenges to projects are brought forward by aboriginal groups on the grounds that it will destroy sacred fishing areas and hunting grounds. The next thing that occurs, however, is that these groups enter into negotiations with corporations involved in developing the area. After much consultation and legal wrangling, "impact and benefit agreements" are signed, offering construction contracts, hiring targets for aboriginal employees, compensation, board memberships, and research funding.[43] Aboriginal groups also use their opposition to a project as leverage for their land claims, saying that they will not allow development to proceed unless the federal government begins negotiations.[44]

The assumption that aboriginal peoples should play more of a role in environmental management becomes even more problematic when native groups have an interest in development. Unlike the case of the James Bay Crees/Inuit, where development was being promoted by an outside interest, more and more aboriginal groups are becoming partners in various economic initiatives in which aboriginal leaders are lauded for their "business acumen." In the case of the logging and fishing disputes, for example, it is aboriginal groups who profit from cutting trees and selling lobsters and salmon. They constitute what Greg Poelzer has called a "productive interest" in policy development, benefiting financially from resource extraction.[45]

Rather than protecting the environment from destructive practices, a separate, native-controlled regulatory environment will likely lead corporations to target aboriginal lands for development. Aboriginal people constitute the most economically marginalized segment of Canadian society, and as such, they have the least power to resist offers from polluting industries relocating to their jurisdiction. This is already becoming apparent in the case of international whaling,[46] where corporate interests in Norway and Japan are aligning themselves with aboriginal groups in the Pacific Northwest in their attempts to restore commercial whaling. Aboriginal groups in Washington State have gained exemptions from regulations banning whale hunting on the basis that it is a "traditional" or "sacred" activity.[47] Perhaps the right to make "a moderate living" by commercial whaling will be the next step.[48] After all, a legal argument could be made that the commercial sale of whale meat is needed for aboriginal "subsistence."

## MUDDYING THE WATERS WITH SPIRITUAL MYTHOLOGY

In recent years the legal gains of aboriginal groups in the area of self-government and land claims have led to the development of a split personality in native leaders in their attitudes toward industrial development. On the one hand, they want to obtain the economic rewards that can be made from sitting on boards of economic development corporations, acquiring royalties, and getting business contracts, while on the other hand, they express concern over maintaining a "traditional way of life."[49] What is not discussed, however, is how aboriginal leaders plan to reconcile a "traditional economy" (i.e., subsistence) with industrial development. How do they plan to "participate in Canada's industrial economy" while maintaining "the land and life forms that anchor them to their past"? What kind of development do they perceive as being sustainable, and how do they intend to obtain "various modern products," yet live within the earth's carrying capacity?

Aside from nebulous platitudes about being respectful of Mother Earth and engaging in various "spiritual ceremonies," aboriginal leaders are silent about should be done. This is because they have no answers that make sense in the modern context, since native "environmental sustainability" consists of engaging in hunting and gathering practices – practices now largely unviable because aboriginal economies have been transformed by global capitalist imperatives. As will be shown in the next chapter, this circumstance also has implications for the claims being made about the importance of aboriginal "traditional knowledge" for modern policy development.

# PART THREE

# Spheres of Deception

# Traditional Knowledge: Listening to the Silence

It is appropriate that since we started this book with traditional knowledge, we should end with it. Of all the initiatives that we have seen throughout the years of studying aboriginal policy, none equals either in depth or breadth the promotion of traditional knowledge. Because it provides the foundation for all the Aboriginal Industry-inspired claims that are being made, traditional knowledge advocacy goes to the heart of current aboriginal policies. Its essence is the overarching assumption that aboriginal peoples, because of their ancestry (i.e., race), have a special world view or way of understanding reality that makes them intrinsically different from everyone else. This assumption, based on spiritual beliefs about aboriginal peoples' special relationship to "the Creator," justifies the necessity of parallel programs for the native population.

To get a better understanding of what is being perpetrated by traditional knowledge research, we compare it to a well-known parody of postmodern art criticism, a book by Heather Busch and Burton Silver entitled *Why Cats Paint: A Theory of Feline Aesthetics.*[1] In it the authors fabricate museum exhibits, think tanks, journals, testimonials from various "experts," anecdotes from cat owners, and a number of hilarious acronyms to give authenticity to an absurd claim – that cats, like humans, have an artistic sensibility.

The most amusing aspect of the book is the direct evidence of cat painting. Cats are photographed with paint-spattered, outstretched paws in many contexts – in gardens and houses, on sculptures and fences, and so on. Then Busch and Silver provide interpretations of the smudges, classifying them in different aesthetic genres: "formal expressionist," "spontaneous reductionist," "elemental fragmentist." Photographs of "cat paintings" occur throughout the book, usually with the title, year created, medium used, and specific collection in which the "art" is located.

In addition to the witty captions and artistic descriptions, the reader is also treated to deftly wielded postmodern jargon. We are told about cats' "unique way of perceiving the world" and how we may "perhaps derive valuable insights from it."[2] Concern is expressed about the commercialization of "cat art" since it may "diminish the importance of cats' work and tempt us into removing it from the art context." We are informed of the authors' debt to "Specieism": the school of art criticism that "presumes aesthetic intent for the movements, marks or sounds of another species and then sets about interpreting them, without prejudice, in the hope of gaining new insights."[3] The book ends with a substantial "Selective Bibliography" that includes references to journals such as *Cat Art Today.*

The important message behind this clever parody is that even the most improbable idea can be made to seem possible when huge amounts of pseudo-evidential infrastructure are deployed to support it. If readers were unfamiliar with domestic animals or satirical writing, it is quite conceivable that they would perceive the book to be factual. This is because a great deal of material presented in it apparently confirms what the authors are asserting.

But while *Why Cats Paint* is meant as a parody, traditional knowledge research is not. When all the books, articles, conferences, and journals about traditional knowledge are cited, as well as the numerous government departments, international organizations, universities, and institutes that are involved in traditional knowledge research, it is not intended as a joke. The same goes for the postmodern references to aboriginal ways of knowing and cultural context. The intent is to characterize traditional knowledge research as a serious body of scholarly work. Instead of carefully constructed photographs of "cat paintings," it is the observations of "culturally sensitive" researchers, and their vouchsafing of traditional knowledge's importance, that serve as the deceptive infrastructure. These observations form the basis of researchers' interpretations of aboriginal anecdotes and practices. Most readers have no first-hand experience of listening to elders or seeing the kinds of findings that are put forward, and so they can be easily convinced.

As well as the philosophical justification that traditional knowledge research provides for land claims and self-government initiatives, this area is important because of its international dimension. The Aboriginal Industry, of course, is a global phenomenon and many initiatives being undertaken in Canada are duplicated in other countries. The influence of traditional knowledge research is even greater because the assumptions that inform it have implications for all sorts of "development" initiatives around the world, as well as any area of study with an "ethno" or "applied" in front of it.

## IS THERE A THERE, THERE?

The extensive literature promoting the funding and incorporation of traditional knowledge into public policy maintains that traditional knowledge constitutes a "tremendous insight," providing "more and sometimes better information" that is of "greater breadth and depth" than existing scientific data.[4] The information obtained from the documentation of traditional ecological knowledge, its advocates assert, will improve resource management processes, contributing to environmental sustainability.[5] The incorporation of traditional knowledge in the educational system is promoted, both for aboriginal and non-aboriginal students, as offering "valuable insights and teachings in areas such as astronomy, medicine, pharmacology, biology, mathematics, and environmental studies, to name a few."[6]

However, the very term "traditional knowledge" is tendentious, for it purports to decide by terminological fiat precisely the fundamental issue under debate: namely, whether the beliefs in question actually constitute "knowledge." For each element of purported traditional knowledge, we must ask, first of all, whether the belief is true (i.e., a factually accurate representation of the world), and secondly, whether we (or its advocates) have good reason to believe it in the light of the currently available evidence. Let us stress that we are not claiming that traditional knowledge never constitutes actual knowledge; that would be both excessive and false. Rather, each item of purported traditional knowledge – like each item of purported knowledge of any kind – must be evaluated on a case-by-case basis, according to the quantity and quality of the evidence for and against it.

This discussion of the justifiable character of traditional knowledge raises the question of how it differs from the scientific "tradition." This is a difficult question to answer, since there is no consensus on what traditional knowledge actually is or how it relates to science. Some commentators say that it is a "kind of science,"[7] while others maintain that it is fundamentally different from science, or even "superior" to it.[8] These uncertainties mean that any traditional knowledge study begins with a survey of the field, in which researchers weigh the merits of various definitions.[9] The result is never satisfactory, as the definition decided upon is either tautological – traditional knowledge is a "way of knowing," "different knowledge system," "system of understanding," and so forth – or it acts to include elements that are distinct from knowledge, such as values, beliefs, and practices.[10] The *belief* that something is true, for example, does not mean that it *is* true – in particular, that it can be considered knowledge. Some believe that aboriginal peoples were "created" in the Americas[11] ("we have always been here") and that non-human animals were originally people,[12] despite having no evidence to support these assumptions. Therefore, it is erroneous to refer to these beliefs as a form of knowledge. And if only "some" or "many" aboriginal people hold these beliefs (presumably meaning others do not), how can they be considered "knowledge"?

Those who advocate for traditional knowledge, however, resist the evaluation of evidence required for determining the truth or falsity of conflicting knowledge claims. There is even reluctance to state what traditional knowledge is because of the risk that it can be "taken out of the context in which it was generated" and consequently "misinterpreted or misused."[13] But it is never explained precisely how this would occur; nor is there any attempt to describe the difference between "decontextualized knowledge" and knowledge that remains contextually embedded.

### TK: PROTOSCIENTIFIC OBSERVATIONS AND SPIRITUALISM?

Although beliefs, values, and practices are distinct from knowledge, many claims about the importance of traditional knowledge focus on aboriginal peoples' observations concerning plant and animal abundance/scarcity, wildlife behaviour, weather patterns, and ecosystem health. These observations obviously can contribute to our knowledge of the natural world, as they are acquired from close interaction with the environment. But if the observations and experience of aboriginal peoples can increase our knowledge, how does this contribution differ from scientific findings? For if the perceptions of traditional knowledge holders were the same as scientific ones, why would it be necessary to have separate traditional knowledge studies and transform the Canadian educational system? If traditional knowledge really is "replicable, generalizable, incorporating, and to some extent experimental and predictable,"[14] how is it empirically distinguishable from the science of "westerners" (i.e., non-aboriginal people)?

### Traditional Knowledge's Protoscientific Character

One unique feature attributed to the empirical findings of traditional knowledge concerns the fact that they have been accumulated in a local area for the purposes of survival.[15] Aboriginal observations and experience have occurred over generations, the argument goes, instead of in the short period of time used in scientific studies; scientists collect data during a few field trips,[16] unlike aboriginal peoples, who have been "intimately connected" with their environment for "thousands of years." It is for this reason that Peter Usher claims that traditional knowledge can "contribute to environmental assessment by providing a broader and deeper understanding of baseline conditions and a fuller understanding of local environmental processes, at a finer and more detailed geographical scale, than conventional scientific knowledge can offer."[17]

But these assertions distort the nature of science and obscure the fact that its methodology has evolved *out of* "traditional knowledge." Rather than being another "way of knowing," traditional knowledge is a precursor to the scientific method. All peoples, regardless of their culture and location on the planet, survived for thousands of years. They did so by observing patterns in the environment they interacted with, and then using this knowledge to make their lives more secure. By developing an understanding of where animals could be found, what plants were edible or had curative qualities, and how natural materials could be fashioned into effective weapons and other tools, human beings were able to increase their productive and reproductive capacities. This aspect of traditional knowledge is often referred to as "local knowledge" – the knowledge one obtains from residing in a particular area, and observing and interacting with it for an extended period of time. This is basic information that most people (including "westerners") have about where things are located (how to find local landmarks, for example), as well as a practical understanding of general environmental characteristics (i.e., that a particular river's current makes swimming dangerous). It should be distinguished from references to "indigenous knowledge," which maintain that a particular race of people has special knowledge not available to others (generally for "spiritual" reasons).

The concept of traditional knowledge, therefore, is used to refer to both racially/spiritually based "knowledge" and local knowledge, and conflating the two acts to obfuscate direct comparisons with scientific research. When the spiritual component of traditional knowledge is questioned, advocates point to aboriginal peoples' basic knowledge of the flora and fauna. Challenging the capacity of aboriginal peoples' local knowledge to accurately measure wildlife populations, on the other hand, results in the traditional knowledge lobby asserting that aboriginal estimates should be uncritically accepted because native spiritual/racial intuition enables the acquisition of knowledge that is inaccessible to non-aboriginals.

The observations of local knowledge are not systematically measured and recorded, which makes them very different from scientific findings. The scientific method is a significant improvement over previous forms of observation and experience in which the reliance on subjective interpretation allows for the potential misunderstanding of natural processes. The sun appearing to revolve around the earth, flies "spontaneously generating" out of fruit, and heated water transmuting into mysterious substances were all conclusions drawn from human observations and experiences.[18] Only when specific measurements and controlled experiments were undertaken by scientists like Galileo, Redi, and Lavoisier were they shown to be false. Science is an approach designed "to exclude or at least minimize the chance of being misled by an observation."[19] By enabling us to discard those observations that do not stand up to repeated testing, the scientific method increases our understanding over time. The accumulation of more and more accurate observations also enables a body of theory to be developed, which can be continuously tested and refined by further observations. Although Peter Usher claims that the "memory of several generations" can be "preserved" to offer "a broader and deeper understanding of baseline conditions" than scientific records, this view ignores that there are numerous problems with the accuracy of a group's collective memory when it is not recorded.

## The Kinds of Data Obtained from Traditional Knowledge Research

The inconsistent and imprecise character of traditional knowledge observations can be seen in the types of information that are supposed to contribute to baseline studies. One study of the Liard River Basin, for example, includes tables referring to traditional knowledge data concerning the types and numbers of fish, waterfowl, and game species in different areas of the basin,[20] but all that is noted is whether a particular species' abundance is "high," "medium" or "low" in different areas. Similar kinds of data are collected in another study concerning caribou health. Caribou are categorized by aboriginal hunters as "skinny," "not so bad," "fat," "really fat," or "unsure." Butchered caribou are also analyzed and the character of their fat deposits is classified as "none," "some," "quite a bit," or "lots."[21] Because of the inconsistency of subjective terms, the data of both of these traditional knowledge studies would be less useful for monitoring ecosystems in environmental policy than current scientific research. Like other traditional knowledge studies that elicit impressions during meetings, workshops, and "semi-directed interviews" from a variety of aboriginal people (usually elders), the methods of study used are not clearly explained, or even made explicit, to ensure that they are being used consistently.[22] This is very different from scientific research, which ensures that the data collected can be directly compared with other studies, and the methods used publicly evaluated.

These two traditional knowledge studies, however, at least attempt to present data systematically. Most traditional knowledge studies simply provide random recollections from elders. A recent study attempting to use traditional knowledge to understand the environmental impact of climate change, for example, conducted interviews with "16 community members and elders considered to be local experts on sea ice."[23] Their observations are intended to support the assertion that traditional knowledge can be used to "provide a baseline against which to measure change." Although the study maintained that these "observations were remarkably consistent in providing evidence of local change in such variables as multiyear ice distribution, first-year ice thickness, and ice breakup dates," the numerous quotations from elders are vague: "[Ice] goes out quicker now ... It is different"; "Freeze-up is way later. Less [multiyear ice] doesn't make the water as cold"; and "[The weather nowadays is] sometimes cold, but sometimes hot too ... [but at the] wrong time. Way different now." This is in contrast to much more detailed and systematic information that already exists (mentioned in this traditional knowledge study), such as the dates that barges have been able to access northern communities each year, thirty years of documented ice draft measurements from submarine expeditions, and data from satellites.

Even more problematic than studies that provide vague recollections in the form of unsystematic quotations are those that offer "interpretations" from traditional knowledge researchers. As a result, we have claims like "the research team watched and listened to an elder explain in as much detail as any scientist, the effects of permafrost and drainage on the composition and condition of two neighbouring plant communities."[24] We are told that "indigenous people ... can make better predictions about the consequences of any physical changes or stresses they have previously experienced than scientists,"[25] or that the "eyewitness record [of the impact of seasonal floods] was consistent with available physical evidence, such as surficial geology and dendrochronology, but was more precise as to the timing and location of changes and much richer in terms of the number of changes identified."[26] These interpretations are then adopted in actual scientific studies, which treat these highly speculative assertions as fact. Jared Diamond claims that hunter-gatherers and subsistence farmers are "walking encyclopedias of natural history, with individual names (in their local language) for as many as a thousand or more plant and animal species, and with detailed knowledge of those species' biological characteristics, distribution and potential uses."[27] But substantiation of the "detailed explanation" of the effects of permafrost, the nature of the "better predictions," the "more precise" and "much richer" observations, or the specific nature of these "walking encyclopedias" have not been supported by evidence made available for public review.

Claims about traditional knowledge's "precision," in fact, are often contradicted in the same article. Usher, for example, explains that "in TEK, factual observations may be very precise and recalled in extraordinary detail," and then goes on to claim two sentences later that traditional knowledge "tends to be localized and restricted to personal, uninstrumented observations, with little concern for precision in measurement, and it is normally unrecorded."[28]

When specific information is supplied, a researcher's "interpretations" can turn out to be fabrications or distortions. Fikret Berkes, for example, claims in his book *Sacred Ecology* that traditional knowledge has been used to obtain both quantitative and synchronic (simultaneously observed) data, and that "traditional knowledge systems ... use controlled experiments." The "quantitative measures" to which Berkes refers, however, were actually provided by a scientific survey of geese in the region, which just happened to coincide with "an elders' rule of thumb that 'for every goose killed, 20 must leave the Bay.'" Similarly, the "synchronic data collected over large areas" by the "Dene Indian system of monitoring caribou movements" was in fact obtained from two scientific studies that used aerial surveys and tagging studies with radio collars as part of their research and one traditional knowledge study making the dubious interpretation that the Dene occupation of the area "may be viewed as strategically situated reconnaissance patrols for collecting information on caribou movements and intentions."[29] Finally, the "controlled experiments" Berkes claims were undertaken by traditional knowledge holders turns out to be an experiment carried out by Berkes himself (although he alleges to have received the "perfect design" for the experiment from the Cree fisherman accompanying him).[30]

## The Static Character of Traditional Knowledge

It is important to note that local impressions and opinions about ecosystems are only hypotheses that must be subjected to testing before being considered knowledge, and this process cannot be undertaken by local knowledge practitioners, regardless of their experience or "wisdom." This is a question of method, not the particular attributes of individuals. It is incorrect to claim that local knowledge is "systematic," or that it has "confirmed" or "proved that some scientific results were incorrect,"[31] as its observations are a by-product of subsistence activities, and scientific methods must be used to determine if traditional knowledge claims are accurate. A local observation that an area is a "good spot for net fishing," for example, might have been true at one time, but the assumption of the existence of "many fish" will not hold if a chemical spill recently contaminated the area. The value of science is not that its research is always "right," but that the methods used are revised and conclusions discarded if they are shown to be inadequate. In this way, a more comprehensive understanding of the world can gradually emerge over time. Traditional knowledge, on the other hand, does not have this capacity to progress because it involves repeating ancestral patterns. New observations can be made while hunting and gathering, but veneration for "tradition" means that interpretations will be made in a manner that justifies pre-existing conceptual frameworks.

This assertion about the static character of traditional knowledge is contested in the literature, which maintains that it is "adaptable."[32] But if traditional knowledge changes when new information is made available, what is meant by comments about elders being "custodians of traditional knowledge" or that traditional knowledge "is passed down from one generation to another"? In other words, what makes the knowledge "traditional?" It would be unreasonable to say that there are "custodians of science," or that scientific theories are "passed down" through the generations, because scientific theories are revised or abandoned once they are refuted. Thus one of the essential characteristics attributed to science is its deployment of sceptical rigour to understand the material causes of natural phenomena.

Traditional knowledge, however, is immune from questioning and resists its methods being assessed. It is assumed to be "held" by people with revered qualities, usually elders, whose views must be uncritically supported. A common demand is that the spiritual component of traditional knowledge should be "respected,"[33] and accusations of "disrespect" meet any attempt to ask questions about methodology. Public "information sessions" are structured to prevent critical questions from being raised.[34]

## IF THIS IS YOUR SCIENCE, WHERE ARE YOUR THEORIES?

Science has made great advancements in explaining the nature of material forces, from the laws of thermodynamics to the composition of chemical bonding to the theory of evolution, and these insights provide direction to further studies. Traditional knowledge, on the other hand, is not guided by empirically tested theories;[35] it has made no progress in the refinement and advancement of theories or the forming of new ones. Supernatural forces are believed to cause natural occurrences,[36] and as a result, traditional knowledge comes into direct conflict with scientific explanatory frameworks such as the theory of evolution. It is for this reason that concerns have been raised about the incommensurability of the two "knowledge systems."[37]

The theoretical impoverishment of traditional knowledge's observations is obscured by the characterizations of science as "reductionist" and traditional knowledge as "holistic,"[38] disguising the latter's lack of understanding of material processes with references to a nebulous spiritual totality.[39] Similar problems exist with claims that aboriginal peoples have an "intuitive understanding" of the universe,[40] enabling them to make contributions to the theory of relativity and quantum mechanics.[41] Nowhere is it explained how aboriginal cultures, without the aid of measurement, numbers, or mathematics, would have the capacity to develop such a sophisticated theoretical framework,[42] yet advocates vouchsafe that these ideas are indicative of a special kind of "knowledge" not accessible to non-aboriginals.

The absence of a theory to guide traditional knowledge's observations becomes especially apparent in studies of animal behaviour. In contrast to scientific studies, which would be guided by an understanding of empirically tested evolutionary principles, traditional knowledge research provides unsubstantiated opinions from elders. One such study prepared for the West Kitikmeot Slave Study, for example, claims that "caribou migrate to people who live well and behave properly." "Behaving properly" includes using all parts of the animal, not hitting them with sticks and knowing Dogrib caribou terminology.[43] Stephen C. Ellis even complains about the "scientization" of traditional knowledge in animal behaviour studies – the fact that "when traditional knowledge is not substantiated by scientific methods, results, and conclusions, it is commonly ignored or discarded." To illustrate this point, he notes the elders' explanation of a westward shift in muskoxen distribution in terms of their belief that the animals were "following the people because they missed them and wanted their company." Ellis criticizes wildlife biologists for ignoring the elders' interpretation,[44] but how could a "further dialogue" take place in such a context?

The absence of theory is also a deterrent to the use of traditional knowledge's "classification systems" to interpret data. "Ecological insights," it is said, can be gained through the study of "folk taxonomies." Douglas J. Nakashima, for example, maintains that the taxonomy developed by the Inuit "reveals a strong ecological logic" that has the ability "to advance our understanding of arctic ecosystems."[45] This "ecological logic," however, consists of dividing organisms into categories based on considerations of whether or not they "rise to the surface," "walk," or are found on the sea bed. This kind of "classification" appears to reflect the fact that the methods used for hunting these organisms would differ considerably.

A simple description of how a particular culture interacts with its environment does not provide the basis for a system of classification that advances human knowledge. The Linnaean system is a valuable tool for helping us to understand the world because it "reflects the very nature of organisms," by classifying them according to "key" or foundational characteristics, instead of more arbitrary features that vary according to culturally based perceptions.[46] Biological classification has become a complex process whereby scientists use developments in a variety of disciplines, including genetics, biochemistry, molecular biology, embryology, paleontology, and ethology, to learn how various organisms have changed and evolved since life began.

The Linnaean system of classification has itself evolved, showing the progressive character of scientific research. At its inception, Linnaean classification embodied schemes for grouping organisms that in some cases turned out to be misguided from a biological standpoint. The system we have today, in fact, is supplemented by cladistic principles, which stem from a long series of modifications designed to accommodate more precise biological concepts, particularly evolutionary ones. Today, organisms are classified with the help of a "cladogram" – a diagram that "shows the relationship of a group of species based on the fewest number of shared changes that have occurred from generation to generation."[47]

Serious difficulties often arise, therefore, in attempting to incorporate the observations and impressions of traditional knowledge holders into scientific knowledge. Traditional knowledge's interpretations of natural occurrences tend to be incommensurable with scientific theories such as evolution because they are either spiritually based or not applicable outside the confines of aboriginal subsistence. Traditional knowledge's observations are actually what John E. Dodes, the president of the New York Chapter of the National Council against Health Fraud, has referred to as "junk science." According to Dodes, "junk science results when conclusions are drawn using low-quality data such as testimonials, anecdotes, and case reports rather than from randomized, controlled clinical experiments."[48] Dodes notes that junk science is generally used "in support of a political or legislative agenda," which is driven by parties who have an interest in suppressing reliable scientific evidence. It is just such an agenda, in fact, that is causing the exaggerated claims about the importance of traditional knowledge.

## THE MAKING OF A GLOBAL INDUSTRY

Until about twenty years ago, no one had heard about "traditional knowledge"; now it is ubiquitous. It is sought after by governments, studied in universities around the world, recognized in environmental assessment processes, and promoted by international protocols for environmental protection and third world development. It also has received a substantial amount of favourable media attention.[49] How did traditional knowledge suddenly become such a hot commodity?

The phenomenon can be traced back to changes in the discipline of anthropology. Initially, anthropologists studied traditional knowledge in order to document tribal cultures, so that primitive conceptualizations of the world could be compared with those of modern societies.[50] In the 1950s, however, the focus shifted from objective documentation to advocacy as anthropologists took on the role of "validating" aspects of aboriginal cultures that they perceived had been deprecated by the dominant culture. As Stephen Bocking explains, "these trends have led many anthropologists to view indigenous knowledge ... as part of the defining subject matter of their discipline" and to become "intermediaries between Native communities and the rest of society."[51] Anthropological consultant Marc Stevenson, for example, points out that anthropologists can be useful in traditional knowledge research because they are "cognizant of asymmetrical knowledge-power relations in co-management processes" and have the "professional literacy" to create "the space" for aboriginal peoples to "bring their own ways of knowing, thinking, and speaking ... to the co-management table."[52]

This transformation of anthropology coincided with two other developments in the 1960s – a heightened environmental consciousness and increasing activism for the rights of colonized peoples around the world, including aboriginal peoples.[53] The emerging environmental movement at this time was becoming increasingly concerned about environmental degradation, and many environmentalists began to reject science and technology and embrace the romantic idea that adopting aboriginal views toward nature was the key to living harmoniously with nature.[54] These developments congealed in the 1980s "when interest in Indigenous ways of knowing ... and understanding the environment became more widespread and, in particular, was adopted by international development organizations."[55] It has been noted that the growth of traditional knowledge research over the past two decades has been due to "the presence of a dedicated group of core scholars producing not only academic material but also feeding information into international policy circles."[56]

These international developments have legitimized traditional knowledge research in Canada. This was especially the case in the Northwest Territories, where aboriginal peoples comprised the majority of the population. Increasing international recognition of traditional knowledge led the Northwest Territories' government leader to claim during the thirtieth annual meeting of the Canadian Commission for the United Nations Educational Scientific and Cultural Organization (UNESCO) in 1988 that there was a "wide spectrum of areas where traditional knowledge may have an influence on government policy and programs."[57] This was part of the justification for the development of the Government of the Northwest Territories' "Traditional Knowledge Policy." This policy then resulted in a number of federal government departments and agencies pursuing their own traditional knowledge initiatives.[58]

These kinds of government initiatives, however, are more reflective of an attempt to symbolically recognize traditional knowledge than evidence of its incorporation into modern research. It is argued in the traditional knowledge literature, in fact, that government researchers and industry are merely paying lip service to aboriginal peoples' world views rather than giving them a significant role in the policy process.[59] This problem is said to be largely due to "scientific scepticism" concerning "the credibility or reliability of aboriginal information gathered through interviews," leading some scientists to "dismiss Aboriginal knowledge as subjective, anecdotal and unscientific" or "inconsequential and unfounded."[60] Such criticism, however, is rarely made publicly and remains a "hidden discourse" in public policy discussions.[61]

The suspicion of scientists toward traditional knowledge is generally explained in terms of postmodern references to "unequal power relations."[62] From this relativist position, science is believed to have achieved widespread acceptance due to its privileged position in powerful state institutions, not because it is able to offer verifiable explanations of natural processes and has demonstrable value for improving human understanding – a value that is independent of culture or political considerations. What is hard to fathom is not that traditional knowledge has failed to gain acceptance by the scientific community, but that criticism of it remains a "hidden discourse." Incredibly, despite the numerous problems with incorporating traditional knowledge into scientific research, there has been no scholarship that publicly questions its use in public policy. If there is so much scientific opposition to traditional knowledge, what is stopping these concerns from being aired publicly?

The answer is the political climate in which traditional knowledge is currently studied. Scientists are not only required to accommodate traditional knowledge as a condition to pursue their research[63] but there is tremendous pressure within the bureaucracy for public servants to promote traditional knowledge publicly, including the possibility of disciplinary action if traditional knowledge is criticized. For example, all employees working for the Government of the Northwest Territories are required to recognize native spirituality as a legitimate way to explain natural processes, because challenging it would result in their opposition to declared policy and allegedly constitute a breach of the Public Service's "oath of loyalty."[64] Such pressure is largely due to the fact that governments are negotiating land claims and self-government agreements to facilitate resource development in aboriginal traditional territories, and one of the conditions of settlement is that aboriginal peoples' traditional knowledge be considered in scientific studies.[65] Furthermore, the idea of traditional knowledge is used to justify self-government initiatives, as it is argued that aboriginal peoples' distinctive world view can only be protected by a parallel political system for the native population.[66] Political advocacy has even intruded into the scholarly review process so that it is extremely difficult to publish material that is critical of traditional knowledge research.[67]

Moreover, the demand that traditional knowledge be considered involves a continuous dispersal of funds to aboriginal organizations. Traditional knowledge is often used as a lever to extract government transfers, not just for studies to document traditional knowledge but for various "co-management" boards that have been formed to integrate traditional knowledge into environmental management. These funds are distributed to "traditional knowledge holders," aboriginal leaders, and non-aboriginal consultants. This has resulted in millions of dollars being spent on studies that have contributed little to our understanding of northern ecology and the environmental assessment and wildlife management processes based upon it.

Assertions about traditional knowledge's importance are frequently accompanied by appeals for more funding.[68] One traditional knowledge consultant, for example, maintains that "many elders are open to the documentation of their knowledge, but it is a time-consuming and therefore expensive process. Financial resources are rarely made available for the kind of traditional knowledge research which is both appropriate for First Nations and Inuit communities and rigorous enough to earn credibility among western scientists and policy makers."[69] There is increasing preoccupation with "intellectual property rights" with respect to traditional knowledge, even though its value has not been demonstrated. The bizarre scenario is that "knowledge" that is not useful must be obtained and paid for by governments, and then its coerced "use" is heralded as evidence of its necessity.

The uncritical promotion of traditional knowledge not only has the potential to waste government resources; it also has a number of negative consequences for environmental sustainability, as well as for policies pertaining to aboriginal peoples more generally. As was mentioned in the last chapter, many aboriginal people occupy a "productive interest" with respect to environmental management, and this could result in the unconscious distortion of information by traditional knowledge holders.[70] There can also be environmental consequences in the tendency of governments and industry to fund traditional knowledge as an incentive to allow development to proceed. This was the case with the attempts of BHP to develop a diamond mine in the Northwest Territories. Although BHP declared that it did not know what traditional knowledge was or how it could contribute to the environmental assessment of the mining development, it agreed to pay for the research that was being undertaken, presumably to provide a financial incentive for aboriginal groups to go along with the project. In this way projects that have been vetted by traditional knowledge findings could be given an artificial legitimacy.

Shell Oil exploited this tactic in its efforts to portray oil sands as environmentally sustainable. A half-page advertisement in the *Globe and Mail* on 26 January 2002, for example, noted that "an elder from the local community ... is helping us to see the environment from a new perspective. She's teaching us about Traditional Environmental Knowledge ... we're applying what we're learning not just to improve our Athabasca Oil Sands Project, but to ensure we respect the needs of generations to come." But nowhere in Shell's literature is it shown how this "new perspective" will help to "respect the needs of generations to come." The advertisement merely encourages readers to accept environmentally destructive activities such as oil and gas development on the basis that an aboriginal traditional knowledge holder supports it.

The role played by traditional knowledge in legitimating unsustainable development explains why a number of international governmental organizations, including the World Bank, are promoting this "way of knowing."[71] The response of the United Nations to the environmental crisis, for example, has not been to examine its economic and political roots but to stress the importance of aboriginal culture in finding a solution. This gives an outward appearance of concern for the environment, while very little is actually being accomplished in terms of addressing environmental problems. The use of traditional knowledge to "greenwash" unsustainable global economic processes, in fact, has provided part of the justification for the "need for an urgent establishment of a permanent forum for indigenous people within the United Nations system." It also has resulted in the formation of a number of aboriginal "support groups" that have "consultative status" within the international body. These organizations include the International Work Group for Indigenous Affairs (not to be confused with the United Nations Working Group on Indigenous Populations); Indigenous Peoples' Centre for Documentation, Research and Information; and Survival International. The most significant of these support organizations is the International Work Group for Indigenous Affairs, which has produced numerous books advocating aboriginal rights, two that specifically promote the need to recognize traditional knowledge. Founded in 1968 at the Eighth International Congress of Americanists, IWGIA is lauded for the fact that it "spearheaded a radical departure from ... nineteenth-century anthropological interpretations of primitiveness and civilization."[72]

Alongside the United Nations has arisen a huge organizational infrastructure supporting traditional knowledge research around the world. A number of "traditional knowledge centres" have popped up in recent years, as well as institutes associated with universities and aboriginal organizations, such as the Natural Resources Institute (University of Manitoba), the Arctic Institute of North America (University of Alberta), and the Dene Cultural Institute (Northwest Territories), all heavily involved in traditional knowledge research. Then, reminiscent of the constructions in *Why Cats Paint*, there are numerous journals, museum exhibits, university departments, and government programs and policies all engaged in the global enterprise of documenting and "applying" traditional knowledge.

## THE PERILS OF CONTRIVED RESPECT FOR TRADITIONAL KNOWLEDGE

Although our cry "The emperor has no clothes!" was raised with respect to traditional knowledge in 1996,[73] nothing much has changed. Publicly, criticisms of traditional knowledge have been either ignored, casually dismissed as misinformed,[74] or attacked as "racist" or "right wing."[75] Traditional knowledge research has gone on much as before. The huge infrastructure giving it legitimacy, in fact, often results in assertions that its importance has already been determined, so its value to scientific research does not need to be discussed.[76] Mary Simon, Canada's ambassador for Circumpolar Affairs and to the Kingdom of Denmark, even argues that "we would be taking a step backwards if we fell into the debate again of what indigenous knowledge is and does it or does it not have value."[77]

But it is exactly the idea that traditional knowledge does "have value" beyond that obtainable from other sources that has not been substantiated. Instead the relatively modest contribution that the obser-vational component of traditional knowledge has made to scientific research has been taken out of its historical context and tremendously exaggerated. It has been hijacked by different interests that often have little concern with improving the accuracy of information upon which effective policy development relies.

Even amongst those who have no political stake in the issue there is reluctance to critically evaluate traditional knowledge research. Instead, the tendency is for policy analysts and social scientists to *want to believe* that traditional knowledge has value. Behind this lies the confu-sion of culture and race and the fear that accepting the limitations of "traditional knowledge" is equivalent to a racist devaluing of aborigi-nal peoples as inferior.[78] It is also maintained that "recognizing" and "respecting" aboriginal perspectives, regardless of their veracity, is a harmless way to "include" the native population in the policy process. The result is an aggrandizement of basic human observations and unsubstantiated beliefs as another, ethnically determined, way of know-ing that is "just as valid" as scientific research.

Of all the obfuscation going on in the promotion of traditional knowledge, the most destructive effect has been the rejection of science itself. Saying that there are other "ways of knowing" is an encourage-ment to forego the intellectual development that comes with the under-standing of scientific methods and their application. Rejection of science indicates an inability to distinguish between scientific method and the various political and economic interests that have oppressed aboriginal peoples historically. It is not understood that science is a methodology that can enable all cultures, including aboriginal peoples, to understand the material world, and that isolation from it results in ignorance and confusion. Aboriginal peoples' opposition to science, in fact, leaves them open to manipulation from the very interests that are benefiting from their current vulnerability.

# What Is to Be Done?

Throughout the years of writing this book, our conversations with interested parties have invariably turned to the question of solutions. There have been endless accounts of aboriginal problems over the years, such commentators would tell us, but we need to get on with the business of solving the terrible conditions plaguing aboriginal communities. The implication was that if we did not focus on solutions, our book would add nothing to the current discussions about aboriginal policy.

Our answer always has been to state the obvious: that a problem can be solved only when its cause has been properly identified. This cause – the developmental gap between aboriginal culture and the modern world – must be recognized before any meaningful policies can be formulated. But because recognition of this circumstance is so threatening to the interests currently driving aboriginal policies, furtherance of this analysis is opposed. This is why we wrote this book.

Finding a publisher is a case in point. Despite our having numerous articles on aboriginal politics published, receiving a substantial amount of media interest, and even sparking a national debate on the incorporation of traditional knowledge into government policy, the publishing world has been uneasy about our views. Even attempts to find a literary agent were unsuccessful. As one agent put it, "I have read your material with interest and am sympathetic to your thesis, but have concluded that the trade publishers we deal with would demand a radically different editorial approach."

Our difficulties in disrobing the naked emperor were mirrored by the attempts of the late James A. Clifton to put forward similar criticisms. Entitled *The Invented Indian: Cultural Fictions and Government Policies*, Clifton's edited volume (1990) convincingly refutes a number of the myths that currently form the basis of much aboriginal policy and research on native peoples. Various distortions, such as the Iroquois' alleged influence on the American constitution, the exaggerated population numbers of aboriginals inhabiting the Americas before contact, Lahontan's Adario, and Chief Seattle's speech, are some of the areas the book subjects to rigorous analysis and scrutiny. Because of the healthy scepticism employed by all the authors in the volume, we consider it to be one of the best books on aboriginal issues in the last thirty years.

To show the difficulties of publishing these views, Clifton recounted three incidents involving authors who were initially interested in making contributions to the book. One withdrew his essay because of fears that "if it appeared in a book called *The Invented Indian* that researcher's own Indians would be greatly disturbed, blocking further studies of them." Another required that Clifton "provide certification that the other contributors were not 'anti-Indian' or 'racist'" before submitting his piece. Another potential contributor convinced a third party to question Clifton about his motives for publishing the book. Evidently, this author had been warned by the National Congress of American Indians about Clifton's "allegiances" and wanted to proceed only after making further inquiries about the editor's "fidelity."[1]

The concerns of these potential contributors about the book's reception were justified, as was exemplified in the reviews of the book by Vine Deloria Jr. and Ward Churchill. Deloria's review consists of *ad hominem* attacks against the authors, maintaining that they are "not the giants of anthropology, history, and literature, or even the pretty tall people, but ... average if not below average scholars who are not taken seriously by their professional colleagues precisely because their point of view is known and is known to exclude objectivity on many occasions."[2] Deloria argues that Clifton et al. lack objectivity because they "have as their political agenda the rolling back of whatever inroads and changes the authors believe Indians have made in recent decades."[3]

Deloria's response, however, is mild compared to Ward Churchill's critique. Accusations of racism abound; in Churchill's view, "the function of *The Invented Indian* is to attempt a repeal of virtually every glimmer of truth about Native America which has emerged since 1970, reasserting in their stead the full range of reactionary fables long advanced by proponents of the white supremacist colonialism in which Indians are presently engulfed."[4] Allusions to "cultural genocide," Nazi experiments, "Hitlerian" visions, and the "consolidation of a white supremacist empire" discourage readers from objectively analyzing the book's content.

## BACK TO THE FUTURE: CITIZENS PLUS OR THE
## WHITE PAPER?

Although Clifton's book and the attacks mounted against it originated in the United States, two scholarly books critical of Canadian aboriginal policy have also met with a similar response. The first, Tom Flanagan's *First Nations? Second Thoughts* (2000), was an astute examination of the unviable and dysfunctional character of aboriginal communities. Flanagan's analysis was the first scholarly work in the last thirty years to recognize the developmental gap that exists between aboriginal societies and modernity. In spite of its merits, it was immediately branded as racist by aboriginal leaders, even though none of its arguments merited such an accusation. Phil Fontaine, the grand chief of the Assembly of First Nations, for example, describes Flanagan's book as a "rehashing of tired, old, unworkable, discriminatory ideas." And when the *National Post* supported Flanagan's arguments by calling for an end to parallelist aboriginal policies, Fontaine accused the paper of supporting "the cultural genocide and destruction of a race of people."[5] This was also the response of Suzanne Methot in her review for *Quill & Quire*, the trade magazine of Canada's publishing industry. Methot recommends that readers not "waste time" reading Flanagan's book since "it's racist, ethnocentric, and ill thought out." Typically, she presented no evidence in support of these serious charges; her assertions derive from Flanagan's identification of tribes in pre-contact North America as uncivilized – an adjective pertaining to culture, not race, and one that is verified by scientific anthropology.[6]

The second book, *Citizens Plus* (also 2000), written by one of the most respected political scientists in Canada, Alan Cairns, was also widely condemned by the aboriginal leadership, although praised by a number of scholars for raising important questions about aboriginal/non- aboriginal relations.[7] Patricia Monture-Angus, for example, found it "offensive" because it rejected aboriginal leaders' aspirations for parallel institutions.[8] Taiaiake Alfred labelled Cairns a "conservative" and an "old white guy who doesn't know much about Indians," asserting that he was guilty of colonialist impulses for stating that aboriginal peoples are Canadians like everyone else.[9] According to Alfred, *Citizens Plus* was "widely panned (especially by fellow academics who saw through [Cairns's] friendly-sounding jargon),"[10] although this is not shown by the scholarly reviews of the book. The "fellow academics" referred to, but not named, by Alfred are likely to be those whose objectivity is distorted by postmodern romanticism or are compromised by their association with aboriginal organizations.

Although both books' arguments represent significant breakthroughs in challenging the taboos preventing honest discussion of aboriginal issues, they suffer from the fact that they resuscitate a stagnant debate that took place in the 1960s between classical and reform liberalism. This debate was between the proponents of the White Paper, an assimilationist policy direction proposed in 1969 by the Trudeau government arguing for privatization and equal rights for all Canadian citizens (aboriginal and non-aboriginal), and the Hawthorn Report's promotion of differentiated citizenship (special rights for aboriginal citizens). Both positions are flawed because they ignore, or underestimate, the problems of incorporating societies retaining neolithic characteristics into the modern world.

Flanagan, for example, argues that if only aboriginal peoples owned private property and were treated just like other minorities by the Canadian government, they would soon have the incentive to leave the reserves and integrate into the wider social fabric. To facilitate this process, he makes three recommendations: improving accountability requirements on reserves, dispersing the powers of the aboriginal leadership, and introducing a "regime of individual property rights," starting with home-ownership in native communities.[11] Flanagan also promotes transferring funding directly to aboriginal peoples. For Flanagan, "the challenge for self-government is to 'civilize' aboriginal communities in the sense of creating the conditions for civil society to emerge. Above all, that means getting government out of the way – especially the kind of 'self-government' that exercises total control over community affairs."[12] Although "creating the conditions for civil society to emerge" is an important consideration when analyzing the aboriginal question, it is not clear how the remnants of neolithic culture that are inhibiting this development can be addressed without intensive government planning and intervention.

Similar arguments can be found in a self-published book by Calvin Helin, an aboriginal lawyer and businessman. Although Helin makes a number of astute observations about the dysfunction in aboriginal communities and the self-interested character of the Aboriginal Industry, his book provides a very simplistic analysis of aboriginal circumstances. Like Flanagan, he sees aboriginal dependency as being rooted in too much government involvement and the absence of a private sector in aboriginal communities. For Helin, government involvement has resulted in a "welfare trap," where people expect to live indefinitely on government transfers. The solution, in his view, is for aboriginal peoples to regain control over decision-making and focus on "creating an environment conducive to attracting entrepreneurs and investment."[13] Unlike Flanagan, however, Helin has no conception of the historical and material factors influencing cultural evolution and is prone to romanticizing aboriginal peoples. He argues that "there must be a return to the simple tribal and human values that spawned the complex and beautiful indigenous cultures in the first place – in effect, a contemporary reclamation of the lost tribal values and social DNA."

What both writers fail to recognize, however, is that the undeveloped character of aboriginal culture makes it impossible for most aboriginal people in their current state to become productive members of Canadian society. The arguments of Flanagan and Helin actually justify the withdrawal of government funding from aboriginal communities. This would have disastrous consequences for the native population, since intensive government programs and services are needed to develop aboriginal cultures.

Cairns, while justifiably critical of Flanagan's (and presumably Helin's) proposals to reduce state intervention in aboriginal policy, is himself hampered by an uncritical adoption of the assumptions of the postmodern identity politics framework. This is clear when he offers a quotation from Noel Dyck that aboriginal peoples constantly have to listen to the message "that they are unacceptable as they are," and then comes to the following conclusion:

> When they emerge from the sidelines of history, people who have been demeaned, humiliated and stigmatized inevitably construct arguments and reinterpret the past in ways that enhance their dignity. Although the orthodoxies they construct have an instrumental dimension, the psychic gratification they produce is immensely valuable to their believers. Accordingly, destruction of the orthodoxy – in the unlikely event that its believers would agree to renounce it – would not wipe the slate clean. The alienation and resentment which fuelled it would remain, possibly in an exaggerated form, for the comforting respectability and emotional support provided by the vanished orthodoxy would not be quickly replaced.[15]

But there is no evidence that a reinterpretation of the past contributes to the dignity of aboriginal peoples or offers them "psychic gratification." Instead, this conception of aboriginal cultures is being fuelled by non-aboriginal condescension that actually results in an undignified stereotyping of aboriginal cultures that constrains their development as human beings. With the high level of social dysfunction in aboriginal communities, it is also hard to accept that much psychic gratification is taking place. The "comforting respectability and emotional support" provided by the current "respect" and "recognition" of aboriginal cultures actually mystifies native deprivation and marginalization.

Cairns uncritically accepts the need for "a positive recognition of difference,"[16] when this "difference" actually consists of the traditions associated with the remnants of aboriginal peoples' hunting and gathering/horticultural mode of production. "Recognizing" this will not help to address aboriginal dependency, since it encourages the retention of those characteristics that are inhibiting native participation in a larger, more productive, and complex economy and society.

## IN DEFENCE OF "ARROGANCE"

The inevitable response of the Aboriginal Industry to our demands for real education, health care, and housing instead of compensation, sinecures, and bureaucratic and legal processes will be accusations of "arrogance." How can two "southerners," who have spent only fifteen years observing aboriginal politics, claim to know what is best for the native population? And what about democracy? Shouldn't it be aboriginal peoples who are making these decisions, not white people telling them what to do?

While not presuming to tell native people anything, we do want to alert them to the machinations of the Aboriginal Industry. It is also important to raise questions about the extent to which aboriginal peoples really are "deciding for themselves." No one knows what aboriginal peoples themselves think, since the only opinions heard are those of the native leadership. These "leaders" often represent a particular faction and use their power to prevent any opposition from arising. Attempts to communicate directly with community members about important issues are thwarted under the pretence of "respect." Liberal democratic principles like freedom of speech, freedom of religion, and equality under the law are not part of aboriginal culture and are generally lacking in native communities. This means that current initiatives to enable aboriginal peoples to "decide for themselves" actually result in the opposite; civil rights are eroded with the implementation of self-government, enabling powerful families to decide for everyone, distributing resources as they see fit.

It also should be pointed out that there are financial incentives for indigenous cultural preservation, and many aboriginal peoples probably would be less enthusiastic about remaining at a neolithic stage if the funds for promoting this policy direction were no longer forthcoming. It is a matter of speculation as to what the conditions of native people would be today if it were not for the reactionary mechanisms of the Aboriginal Industry, but the retention of pre-literate languages, traditional quackery, animistic superstitions, tribalism, and unviable subsistence activities would likely not persist or would be considerably diminished. This is not to say that there should be an effort to eradicate these beliefs and practices, as forced assimilations number amongst the worst mistakes in Canadian history. It is only to assert that the preservation of traditions, as long as they do not violate universal human rights standards, should be something that is left to aboriginal peoples themselves. When the government provides funds to appease the political demands inspired by the Aboriginal Industry, the result is the artificial retention of an idealized past.

The objective of this book is to provide a realistic assessment of the current situation so that all Canadians including aboriginal peoples can make informed decisions about the future direction of aboriginal policy. At present the public accepts current policies in the belief that they will create viable economies and end the social dysfunction plaguing aboriginal communities. If it is uncritically accepted that land claims and self-government can accomplish this, then debate cannot begin about how things should be changed.

In fact, "arrogance" is a charge we will gladly bear if it will allow everyone to move on to actually examine the arguments being put forward. "Arrogance" is the Aboriginal Industry's catch-all accusation levelled at anyone who opposes its legal and bureaucratic "solutions." And even if we are "arrogant," shouldn't those who are making the accusation still show how we are wrong? What the accusation of arrogance does is discourage those who are sympathetic to the plight of aboriginal peoples from offering any criticisms of current aboriginal policies. The strict dictionary definition of the word  (i.e., being "aggressively assertive or presumptuous"), however, is an attitude the Aboriginal Industry and the native leadership, not we, are guilty of. We have taken great pains to listen to the arguments for land claims and self-government. Aboriginal leaders and their advisors, on the other hand, refuse to listen to any alternative positions, dismissing them without any analysis of their arguments.

Changing the course of aboriginal policy will be enormously difficult. Diverting funding to facilitate aboriginal cultural development will be a huge test for any leader trying to implement this recommendation because of the outcry that will be generated. This outcry can to some extent be muted, however, if more principled members of the aboriginal population recognize the subterfuge being perpetrated. There are a number of aboriginal people out there who have escaped the clutches of the Aboriginal Industry, and it is with them that hope for real change lies.

Because they have been historically excluded from the financial benefits of Aboriginal Industry programs, one of the most promising possibilities for the emergence of a principled leadership is with the Métis. Métis people in Canada, because they have always had more contact with the mainstream, are less tribal in their outlook than more culturally isolated aboriginals. It is a Métis scholar, Ron Bourgeault, who has made the most significant contribution to date to understanding the interaction between aboriginal peoples and the Canadian state. Bourgeault is one of the very few aboriginal people writing today who questions the merits of the "nationalistic" aspirations of the native leadership.[17] He argues that "those who argue the importance of supremacy of the national struggle over all other forms of struggle are prone to difficulties, the least of which are opportunism and manipulation."[18] Bourgeault also correctly identifies postmodernist thought as a form of nihilism and points out that "when [postmodernism] informs the thinking of social movements, which is the intent of some of the Aboriginal intellectuals, it calls for a return to some premodern condition that in reality is untenable."[19] But since he is critical of "aboriginal orthodoxy," his views are largely ignored and reach only a small audience in comparison to people like Harold Cardinal, Taiaiake Alfred, Vine Deloria Jr., Ward Churchill, Matthew Coon Come, and Phil Fontaine.

Another important potential area for political change resides with aboriginal women. A number of female aboriginal academics and activists have challenged reactionary initiatives on the part of male aboriginal leaders, such as attempts to keep reserves exempt from human rights legislation. They also have been the most vocal in opposing aboriginal corruption and violence against women and children.[20] Aboriginal women are more likely to be distrustful of self-government, because they are more likely to be the victims of the patriarchal political systems in aboriginal communities.

The potential for a real, as opposed to comprador, leadership, however, is only undermined by current initiatives to expand "aboriginal identity." In order to stifle Métis political development and draw them into atavistic preoccupations with ancestral rights, lawyers are arguing that this group too should have their historical grievances rectified.[21] One of the main recommendations of the Royal Commission on Aboriginal Peoples, for example, was that a Métis "land base" should be developed.[22] The promise of this kind of financial compensation only inhibits the will to bring about future change. The same can be said for the successful court battle in 1985 to enact Bill C–31, when Indian women who had lost their Indian status had it restored. Although this development had a progressive allure, since it repealed a discriminatory section of the Indian Act, its actual effect has been to encourage native women to more strongly identify with traditional culture. Restoring access to the privileges that come with "status" provides aboriginal women with an incentive to return to unviable "homelands" and obsolete traditions.

## THE NEED FOR A HUMAN DEVELOPMENT STRATEGY

In a television interview in 2001, Tom Flanagan referred to Canadian aboriginal policy as a "failure of socialism."[23] He described aboriginal communities as "socialist ghettos, where everyone works for the government" – referring to the large subsidies that enable these places to exist. Related to his view is the classical liberal idea that the "communistic" world views of aboriginal culture must be destroyed so that natives can become capitalistic profit maximizers, entering into the global economy.

Flanagan's statement about native "socialism" indicates how classical liberal ideology prevents an understanding of the roots of aboriginal problems. Aboriginal communities produce little of economic value and therefore cannot be considered "socialist" or "communistic" in any way. Aboriginal politics actually has more in common with capitalism than socialism. Aboriginal peoples are encouraged to become "businesspeople" and live off royalties from resource development. This is in complete opposition to the real conception of socialism, where resources are collectively owned and everyone participates in production. The capitalistic nature of aboriginal politics can also be seen in the failure of any attempt by the government to evenly distribute the subsidies to native communities. The native leadership opposes all proposals to equalize wealth by helping the poorest first, instead using its power to distribute money to friends and relatives. This is what happens when tribal culture combines with capitalist economics; "socialism" in aboriginal communities is nowhere to be found. The problems faced by aboriginal peoples in countries like Canada and the United States are the product of an advanced capitalist system and how it combined with hunting and gathering and horticultural modes of production.

The strain of interaction between such unevenly disparate cultures is evaded by the reactionary practice of accommodating the very characteristics that impede the universalized social development of aboriginal people. If links are to be made in helping native people to confront the challenges facing all those making their way in the modern world, the policy must change from accommodating traditional, tribal culture to assistance in bridging the gap based on a scientific approach to the future. Essential services – education, health and housing – must be provided by government, rather than transfers to organizations created by the Aboriginal Industry for the purpose of getting control over the funds. Education must be delivered in the context of equality for all Canadians, and those with special or unique needs must be accommodated accordingly, but universal educational standards must apply so that no group is marginalized by the imposition of "traditional knowledge," as occurs when money is transferred to school boards dominated by native elites. The questions of health and poverty must be approached in the same manner. Programs to provide modern health services to native people should be delivered without the influence of "traditional healers" and the constant demand for funding them. The levels of poverty in native communities, and in the urban native population, are largely due to the interrelated features of culture and education, and educational success is dependent upon widespread cultural development. How this development can proceed with the least psychological trauma is a matter for scientific educational professionals to determine.

A few real success stories do exist, and these can be studied and used in future policy development. One such example is the case of Grandview/ʔUuquinak'uuh Elementary School in East Vancouver – a case analyzed by Calvin Helin. In this school, dramatic improvements were made in educational achievement, and this success was largely attributed to the innovations of the former principal, Caroline Krause, and her staff. Interestingly, these improvements were not made by instituting "culturally sensitive" programs, but through a focus on literacy, academics, and objective assessments. Krause notes that "many of the middle-school Aboriginal kids had been put into a segregated program ... long on cultural sensitivity, self-esteem and hugs, but very short on literacy. There were no demands on the kids and they were out of control. Far from feeling self-esteem, they felt like failures."[24] In other words, the academic successes of Krause's students were achieved through careful implementation of "eurocentric" educational methods.

To some extent the dislocation that aboriginal peoples are feeling is inevitable since it is difficult to bridge such a large developmental gap in a few hundred years. Solutions, however, would be much easier to work toward if aboriginal deprivation were seen as a political problem and not a legal one. The pursuit of legal rights always disadvantages the poor and marginal because the law in liberal democratic states is oriented towards protecting private property and limiting the intrusion of the state into the affairs of its citizens. There is no legal guarantee that the state will provide everyone with a decent standard of health care, education, and housing, as is shown by the growing gap between rich and poor and the existence of urban slums in wealthy countries. All social programs exist because they were fought for politically, not because legal rights were respected. And aboriginal peoples, because of their historical isolation from the industrial workforce and relatively small populations, have played only a marginal role in these struggles. This, not "cultural loss" or racism, explains why they continue to be the most disadvantaged members of modern nation states.

### IMAGINE A GLOBAL TRIBE

> You may say I'm a dreamer,
> But I'm not the only one,
> I hope some day you'll join us,
> And the world will live as one.
>                                         – John Lennon

In one incredibly beautiful and poignant song, John Lennon was able to sum up the causes of conflict in human history: religion, nationalism, and economic inequality. While grain is stockpiled in industrialized countries, people in the Third World starve. Under the auspices of maintaining ethnic national integrity, Zionists feel justified in clearing the land of Palestinians. And religion, while not being the cause of these circumstances, is used to justify them. "Chosen people" are entitled to privileged access to land and other resources, while those who are not valued so highly by "the Creator" must comfort themselves by envisioning paradise in an imaginary afterlife. As John Lennon wrote, religion is a substitute for "living for today."

Lennon's idealism is in sharp contrast to our current postmodern preoccupation with "diversity" that is at the heart of the claims for privilege being made by aboriginal organizations. Instead of imagining circumstances where "the world will live as one," postmodernists advocate many parallel worlds. We are encouraged to overlook the oppression being suffered by women and children in aboriginal communities because their culture makes them have "different needs" than those living in "western" societies. Aboriginal peoples' lack of education and their impoverished subsistence is also romanticized under the rubric of postmodernism because they are "children of nature" and should not be contaminated by "linear thinking" and "white greed." These kinds of ideas are constantly disseminated by the mass media, where films like *Dances with Wolves* portray natives as having a natural nobility not possessed by whites.

The media's tendency to romanticize the past was satirized brilliantly in the 2001 television program *History Bites*. The show, developed by Rick Green, used the medium to express an exasperation with people who romanticize the past.[25] To expose the revision of history that is currently being perpetrated by the media, Green imagined that television had been around for the past five thousand years and proceeded to "channel surf" through various historical periods. This way, the values embodied in the television shows of the present could be juxtaposed to how people actually lived in the past. The result was a very humorous exposure of the terrible conditions, brutality, and ignorance endured by our ancestors.

One episode of *History Bites* particularly pertinent to our arguments in this book is "Neolithic Park," which examines the transition from hunting and gathering to agriculture. Green explains that, because there were no written records, all that we know about 6000 B.C. has been determined by archaeologists examining what has been left behind. The result of such archaeological theorizing, according to Green, is that "although no one knows exactly what the past was like, and there's a lot of disagreement over what some things mean, there's also a lot we can say with certainty about Neolithic times. For example, life really sucked!." To show how this is the case, he spoofs the television program *ER*, as a Stone Age doctor invariably recommends trepanning after getting each patient's history ("any curses or demons?"). In a parody of *Speakers Corner*, a man expresses concern about his wife belonging to a skull cult (she is looking longingly at his head); a mock advertisement for a sex manual "Making Love Better," recommends positions that prevent wild animal attacks during copulation.

Green sums up the program by explaining that the agricultural revolution, by giving human beings control over the food supply, created the modern world. He then points out that a number of sceptics claim that surplus food and the resulting leisure time this made possible was actually detrimental to humanity. Green responds to the argument of Daniel Quinn in his book *Ishmael*, that giving up our "natural lifestyle" caused all our modern problems: "You know, 'problems' like living past the age of thirty; like keeping your teeth; like not losing half your infants to disease; like bathing more than once a month; or never suffering natural famines and those great natural plagues. Modern problems like books, eyeglasses, toilet paper. Tell you what, Mr Quinn, move out of your house with the running water and the heating, carve yourself a spear, go in the woods and kill yourself some food and clothing. Live the natural life! Then you'll see that history bites!"[26]

Green's rant pinpoints the most destructive legacy of the Aboriginal Industry's Great Game – rejection of the idea of historical progress. The Aboriginal Industry has accomplished this, first, by painting pre-contact life as some kind of paradise ruined by Europeans and then by establishing the principle that to recognize the great advancements in science, art, politics, justice, and so on is to condone the terrible suffering that aboriginal peoples continue to endure. As a result, instead of recognizing that the tragedy is that aboriginal peoples have been largely excluded from historical progress, we end up condemning progress itself.[27] All scientific discoveries are characterized as oppressive, thus confusing science with the political uses to which it is put.

As we become more frightened about serious environmental problems such as global warming, "the natural life" seems increasingly attractive, while our acceptance of the idea of "scientific progress" diminishes. But it is *because* of the scientific method that we know that problems like global warming exist. These problems are being caused by global economic and political processes, and science is the methodology for helping us to understand this reality. Therefore, it is of the utmost importance to differentiate between the current economic and political system, which is resulting in unprecedented environmental destruction, and the huge increase in knowledge that science has made possible (scientific progress). One does not have to accept the former to recognize that the latter is necessary to improve social communication and human cooperation.

Besides conflating historical progress with aboriginal deprivation, the romanticization of aboriginal culture is also a product of the unrealized aspirations of the Enlightenment. With the philosophy of the Enlightenment there emerged for the first time an understanding of humanity as a whole, instead of particular exclusive national or tribal "identities." This understanding, called "cosmopolitanism" by Immanuel Kant, identified the individual, not the tribe or the nation, as being the most important political unit of humanity.[28] It was a great moment in human progress when it became possible to see that those not part of our immediate social group were human beings just like ourselves, and that, just maybe, some kind of global political system could be developed where all human beings would adopt the golden rule that we should "do unto others" as we would have them "do unto us."

The disintegration of the comfort and nurturing bonds of the kinship group, however, has yet to be succeeded by more universal attitudes of solidarity. The current stage finds social groups divided into classes, where the many toil for the benefit of the few. The conflicts, encouraged by the competition and alienation of modern society, have led to conviction that despite the primitive technology of tribal cultures, "their social systems based upon kinship and characterized by liberty, equality, and fraternity were unquestionably more congenial to the human primate's nature, and more compatible with his psychic needs and aspirations, than any other that has ever been realized in any of the cultures subsequent to the Agricultural Revolution, including our own society today."[29]

However, such statements fail to consider that "liberty, equality, and fraternity" applied only to those within the given social group; those outside it were seen as the enemy. Consider, for example, an anecdote from the same source as the above, by the anthropologist A.R. Radcliffe-Brown, travelling among the native tribes in Australia with a "blackfellow" for a guide. Radcliffe-Brown explains that when he and his guide arrived in a camp, the natives would attempt to determine if a kinship bond existed between them. Only after such a bond had been established could a friendly relationship between the guide and the people in the camp exist. On one occasion, no bond could be established and Radcliffe-Brown remarks that that the guide "refused to sleep in the native camp, as was his usual custom and on talking to him I found that he was frightened. These men were not his relatives and they were therefore his enemies. This represents the real feeling of the natives on the matter. If I am a blackfellow and meet another blackfellow, that other must be either my relative or my enemy. If he is my enemy I shall take the first opportunity of killing him for fear he will kill me."[30]

The explorer Samuel Hearne witnessed a similar circumstance in the eighteenth century. A group of Chipewyans he was travelling with planned the massacre of a group of sleeping Inuit people and, to Hearne's horror, killed them all, men, women, and children, as they tried to escape. This occurred because the Chipewyan and Inuit were not connected by kinship. It is also apparent from Hearne's account that the Chipewyan had genocidal intentions toward all Inuit, since they perceived Inuit women as too alien to entertain intermarriage with them.[31]

Napoleon Chagnon, in his decades of observations of the Yanomamö people – an isolated tribe in the Amazon rainforest that has not been integrated into global economic and political processes – provides another example.[32] In his anthropological research over four decades Chagnon found that the same rules did not apply inside and outside Yanomamö villages; stealing from others and killing people, while unacceptable within the village, were appropriate activities if directed at neighbouring clans perceived to be enemies. Women also could be abducted if their kinsmen were outnumbered, and the life of a woman living in another village could become brutal if she did not have any brothers to protect her. One Yanomamö man who had been trained by missionaries even told Chagnon that he was enamoured with the idea of law because under the kinship-based system in which he lived, he had no protection from retaliation if his brothers killed members of a rival clan.

The Yanomamö were an important case for study because they had not yet been colonized, and therefore the violence that occurred could be directly linked to relations within and between indigenous lineages, clans, and marriage alliance systems. Chagnon points out that these circumstances are unlikely to have been unique to the Yanomamö, and reflect the violent relations that existed between all kinship groups before institutions binding upon the entire population could manage tribally based violence. According to Chagnon, "the Yanomamö stand out because they are one of the few societies that have been studied by an anthropologist at a time that they had warfare. Had anthropologists been around before Columbus in North America, I am sure that levels of violence among native Americans would be strictly comparable to those found among the Yanomamö. And the probability is very high that in our own tribal background violence was very common as well."

The continuing reliance on kinship relations for defence and retaliation in aboriginal cultures has meant that historically there has been a high degree of violence in these societies. According to the anthropologist Lawrence Keeley, the blood vengeance necessitated by kinship-based systems means that primitive societies fight more often, involve a higher proportion of the male population in warfare, and generate greater casualty rates than do the vast majority of wars between modern states.[33] This is also the conclusion of Steven LeBlanc, director of collections at Harvard University's Peabody Museum of Archaeology and Ethnology, who maintains that the perception that primitive peoples were peaceful is merely due to romantic wishful thinking on the part of many academics studying tribal societies.[34]

If we really want to achieve the aspirations of the Enlightenment, the answer does not lie with tribalism. When solidarity is achieved within the kinship group, non-kin are "outsiders" and can become "enemies" if an alliance between families cannot be established. One can imagine how destructive this would be today. Instead of forming relationships with others on the basis of individual personalities or social utility, we would only extend friendship to those connected to our families. There would be no such thing as the public sphere, where everyone is supposedly equal under the law, since kin would be favoured over others in the distribution of goods and services.

While the nurturing of family progeny is a necessary biological function, the widening of the range of social contact is a necessary function of species survival. It was this understanding that Karl Marx had when he coined the term "species being." But as Marx himself realized, such an achievement is not possible until the causes of human conflict are removed. This conflict, elaborated in all of Marx's writings, is the conflict that exists between the few who own the means of production and those who are the producers of all value. It is by eliminating this fundamental "difference" that we can become a global tribe and the "world can live as one."

# Notes

## INTRODUCTION

1 References to "aboriginal," "native," or "indigenous" are uncapitalized throughout, as these terms are used as adjectives or descriptive terms, not proper names.

2 Transcript, Federal Environmental Assessment Panel Review of BHP Diamonds Inc. Northwest Territories Diamonds Project, Yellowknife, Northwest Territories, 13 February 1996, 52.

3 Ibid., 52–3.

4 See, for example, Dave Chatters, cited in Melvin H. Smith, *Our Home or Native Land?* (Victoria: Crown Western, 1995), 41.

5 Molly Raymond Mignon, *Dictionary of Concepts in Archaeology* (Westport: Greenwood Press, 1993), 192–4; Andrew Sherratt, ed., *The Cambridge Encyclopedia of Archaeology* (New York: Crown, 1980), 89–95, 102–9; James Deetz, *Invitation to Archaeology* (New York: Garden City Press, 1967), 121–7; Gordon Childe, *What Happened in History* (Harmondsworth, Middlesex: Penguin, 1942), 33–96.

6 Glyn Daniel, *The First Civilizations: The Archaeology of Their Origins* (New York: Thomas Y. Crowell Co., 1968), 28–9.

7 V. Gordon Childe, *Progress and Archaeology* (Westport: Greenwood Press, 1971) 8.

8 James Mellaart, *Earliest Civilizations of the Near East* (London: Thames & Hudson, 1965), 11–13.

9 Jared Diamond, *Guns, Germs and Steel: The Fates of Human Societies* (New York: Norton, 1999), 17.

CHAPTER ONE

1 A number of other "industries" that either fabricate or maintain problems so
  as to continuously receive funds also have been identified. See, for example,
  Margaret Wente, "Manufacturing Racism: A How-To Guide," *Globe and
  Mail,* 8 November 2001, and Gary Mason, "An Old-Fashioned Approach to
  Drug Addiction," *Globe and Mail,* 24 August 2006. Most significantly, there
  is Norman G. Finkelstein's book, *The Holocaust Industry: Reflections on the
  Exploitation of Jewish Suffering* (New York: Verso, 2000), which details how
  the Holocaust is being constructed to continuously extract funds from various
  sources.

2 The Canadian Aboriginal Industry has been identified by a number of aborig-
  inal and non-aboriginal commentators. These include Melvin H. Smith, *Our
  Home or Native Land?* (Victoria: Crown Western, 1995); "Aboriginal Law
  Becomes Big Business," *Financial Post,* 4 July 1995; "Drive to Native
  Self-Sufficiency Spawns New Industry of Self-Government Consultants," CP
  *Newswire,* 29 December 1995; Douglas Fisher, "Two Solitudes? Make That
  Three," *Toronto Sun,* 28 April 1999; Alison Blackduck, "Indigenous Land-
  scape Is Looking Very Bleak," *Toronto Star,* 12 June 2001; Jeffrey Simpson,
  "Burnt Church Report Cuts to the Chase," *Globe and Mail,* 26 April 2002;
  Jean Allard, "Big Bear's Treaty," *Inroads* 11 (June 2002): 131, 137; "Is There
  an Aboriginal Misery Industry?" *Contact,* Aboriginal Peoples Television Net-
  work, 21 March 2003; Calvin Helin, *Dances with Dependency: Indigenous
  Success through Self-Reliance* (Vancouver: Orca, 2006), 160–1; "Misery
  Money," CBC *Sunday,* 14 January 2007; Tom Flanagan, "Land Claims
  Shouldn't Be an Immortal Industry," *Globe and Mail,* 4 June 2007; and
  Gordon Gibson, "Is Integration the Better Option for Indians?," *Globe and
  Mail,* 22 August 2007. It also has been discussed in the United States in James
  Clifton's edited volume *The Invented Indian: Cultural Fictions and Govern-
  ment Policies* (New Brunswick, N.J.: Transaction Publishers, 1996) and in
  Australia by Philip Batty, "Private Politics, Public Strategies: White Advisors
  and Their Aboriginal Subjects," *Oceania* 75 (2005).

3 See also John McKnight, *The Careless Society: Community and Its
  Conterfeits* (New York: Basic Books, 1995).

4 Allard, "Big Bear's Treaty," 137.

5 Quoted in Dan Smith, *The Seventh Fire: The Struggle for Aboriginal Government* (Toronto: Key Porter, 1993), 62. Robert Nault, a former minister of
  Indian and Northern Affairs, also has been quoted as saying that "We have to
  stop letting lawyers and consultants suck up all our money" (quoted in Helin,
  *Dances with Dependency,* 160).

6 Philip Batty divides the Aboriginal Industry up into four categories. He maintains it includes "committed political activists, dedicated professionals, cynical 'old hands' who have worked in Aboriginal affairs all their lives, and less desirable individuals who regularly engage in corrupt practices, sometimes in cahoots with their aboriginal employers" (Batty, "Private Politics, Public Strategies," 216).

7 This transitional period occurred at different times across the country because the fur trade ended earlier in the East than in the West and the North. Aboriginal peoples were being displaced, and attempts were made to assimilate them as early as 1780 in the Maritimes, partly because of the large influx of Loyalists after the American Revolution; this process did not become dominant in the North until the 1950s.

8 J.R. Miller, *Skyscrapers Hide the Heavens* (Toronto: University of Toronto Press, 1991), 71.

9 Miller, *Skyscrapers Hide the Heavens*, 189.

10 Greg Poelzer and Ken Coates, "Aboriginal Peoples and the Crown in Canada: Completing the Canadian Experiment," in Hans J. Michelmann and Cristine de Clercy, eds., *Continuity and Change in Canadian Politics* (Toronto: University of Toronto Press, 2005), 164.

11 Tom Flanagan, *First Nations? Second Thoughts* (Montreal: McGill-Queen's University Press, 2000), 134–5.

12 Royal Commission on Aboriginal Peoples [RCAP], *The Report of the Royal Commission on Aboriginal Peoples [Final Report]*, Ottawa: Minister of Supply and Services, 1996, vol. 1, 76–82.

13 Roland Chrisjohn and Sherri Young, *The Circle Game* (Penticton: Theytus Books, 1997), 3–4.

14 This view, however, advocated segregation, not integration. See, for example, the perspective put forward by Sir Francis Bond Head, a lieutenant governor of Upper Canada who harboured the *racist* belief that aboriginal peoples could not become civilized and that they should remain segregated until they eventually died out. For a discussion of these views, see John Giokas, "The Indian Act: Evolution, Overview and Options for Amendment and Transition," in RCAP, *For Seven Generations [CD-ROM]*. (Ottawa: Libraxis, 1997).

15 See, for example, R. Gordon Robertson, "The Coming Crisis in the North," *North* 14, no. 2 (March/April 1967), for a discussion of widespread government neglect towards Inuit people.

16 This circumstance is discussed in detail in Allan Moscovitch and Andrew Webster, "Social Assistance and Aboriginal People," in RCAP, *For Seven Generations*.

17  Cited in Olive Dickason, *Canada's First Nations, A History of Founding Peoples from Earliest Times* (Toronto: McClelland & Stewart, 1994), 335; see also RCAP, *Final Report,* vol. 1, 353–65.

18  The most pertinent example of this was the case of William Duncan of the Anglicans' Church Missionary Society. For a discussion see Robin Fisher, *Contact and Conflict* (Vancouver: UBC Press, 1977), 124–36, and Miller, *Skyscrapers Hide the Heavens,* 150–1.

19  This also was the case in the United States. James Clifton, for example, maintains that missionaries formed an integral part of what he calls "Indian Rings" – clusters of advocates for aboriginal peoples. See Clifton, "Introduction: Memoir, Exegesis," in *The Invented Indian,* 15.

20  This occurred at Oka, Quebec, during the nineteenth century. For further discussion, see Miller, *Skyscrapers Hide the Heavens,* 303.

21  This was especially true for the Methodists, who appointed four aboriginal people as clerics, enabling them to make inroads into a number of areas in Canada (Miller, *Skyscrapers Hide the Heavens,* 100, 216).

22  For a discussion of these activities, see Paul Tennant, *Aboriginal Peoples and Politics* (Vancouver: UBC Press, 1990), 87–9, 101–2, 106.

23  Project North, for example, was a coalition of the Roman Catholic, United, and Anglican Churches who opposed the Mackenzie Valley Pipeline and advocated the settlement of land claims in the Northwest Territories. See Robert Page, *Northern Development: The Canadian Dilemma* (Toronto: McClelland & Stewart, 1999), 228–9.

24  See, for example, "Native People, Churches Come Together to Heal," *Windspeaker* 13, no. 9 (January 1996).

25  See, for example, James Wah Shee, quoted in John David Hamilton, *Arctic Revolution: Social Change in the Northwest Territories* (Toronto: Dundurn Press, 1994), 142.

26  Menno Boldt, *Surviving as Indians: The Challenge of Self-Government* (Toronto: University of Toronto Press, 1993), 86; Howard Adams, *A Tortured People: The Politics of Colonization* (Penticton: Theytus Books, 1995), 177–95; and David Bedford and Dan Irving, *The Tragedy of Progress* (Halifax: Fernwood, 2001), 26–7.

27  Bill Curry, "'Too Many Chiefs,' Aboriginal Leader Says," *Globe and Mail,* 7 November 2006.

28  See Boldt, *Surviving as Indians,* 87.

29  William Wuttunee, *Ruffled Feathers* (Calgary: Bell Books, 1971), 148.

30  Sally Weaver, "The Hawthorn Report," in *Anthropology, Public Policy and Native Peoples in Canada,* ed. Noel Dyck and James Waldram (Montreal: McGill-Queen's University Press, 1993), 78.

31 Weaver, "The Hawthorn Report," 77–9.
32 Cited in Dickason, *Canada's First Nations,* 384.
33 See Pauline Comeau and Aldo Santin, *The First Canadians: A Profile of Canada's Native People Today* (Toronto: Lorimer, 1995), chapter 1, for an overview of opposition to the White Paper.
34 Peggy Brizinski, *Knots in a String: An Introduction to Native Studies in Canada,* 2nd ed. (Saskatoon: University Extension Press, University of Saskatchewan, 1993), 216.
35 Chrétien, quoted in Allard, "Big Bear's Treaty," 130. Allard points out that this actually continued in the 1990s, except with "a lateral shift of administrative responsibility from Indian Affairs bureaucrats to Indian administrators," which "gave rise to a vast, absorbent layer of consultants, program officials and administrators, and professionals of all kinds who soaked up a significant percentage of the money filtering down through the system to chiefs and councils."
36 Michael Mandel, *The Charter of Rights and the Legalization of Politics in Canada* (Toronto: Thomson Educational Publishing, 1997), 4.
37 See "Aboriginal Law Becomes Big Business," *Financial Post Daily,* 4 July 1995, and Gordon Pitts, "Native Law Expert Joins Gowlings," *Globe and Mail,* 27 November 2002.
38 Richard C. Daniel, *A History of Native Claims Processes in Canada, 1867–1979.* Ottawa: Research Branch, Department of Indian and Northern Affairs, 1980, 1–122.
39 Ibid., and Tennant, *Aboriginal Peoples and Politics,* 87–9.
40 Charles Stewart, cited in Daniel, *A History of Native Claims Processes in Canada,* 54.
41 Tom Pocklington, "Native Canadians and the Right to Self-Government," *Democracy and Rights in Canada,* ed. Don Carmichael, Tom Pocklington, and Greg Pyrcz (Toronto: Harcourt, 1991), 181–7.
42 Bill Wilson, chairman of the First Nations Congress of British Columbia, speaking in 1990, cited in Mandel, *The Charter of Rights,* 361.
43 This attitude was apparent from two documentaries on the Aboriginal Industry, aired on APTN's *Contact,* 21 March 2003, and CBC *Sunday,* 14 January 2007.
44 "Drive to Native Self-Sufficiency Spawns New Industry of Self-Government Consultants," *Canadian Press Newswire,* 29 December 1995.
45 In the case of the 1973 Nisga'a decision (*Calder et al. v. Attorney General of British Columbia*), for example, the court did not find that aboriginal title in British Columbia existed. Immediately after the decision, however, the federal Liberal government acted as if the court had ruled in favour of the Nisga'a and formed the Office of Native Claims to negotiate land claims anyway. A

similar approach was taken by the B.C. government in the aftermath of the original Gitksan Wet'suwet'en court case (*Delgamuukw v. The Queen*), which dismissed the claims of these aboriginal groups.

46  Mandel, *The Charter of Rights,* 368.

47  John Howard Sissons, *Judge of the Far North* (Toronto: McClelland & Stewart, 1968), and W.H. Morrow, ed., *Northern Justice: The Memoirs of Mr. Justice William G. Morrow* (Toronto: Osgoode Society for Canadian Legal History, 1995).

48  "Northern Justice: The Memoirs of Mr. Justice William G. Morrow – Review," *Beaver* 76, no. 4 (August/September, 1996): 45

49  Alan C. Cairns, *Citizens Plus: Aboriginal Peoples and the Canadian State* (Vancouver: UBC Press, 2000), 177–9.

50  Cited in Wendy Wickwire, "'We Shall Drink from the Stream and So Shall You': James A Teit and Native Resistance in British Columbia, 1908–1922," *Canadian Historical Review* 79, no. 2 (June 1998): 199–236.

51  Ibid.

52  Charles E. Borden, "Wilson Duff (1925–1976): His Contributions to the Growth of Archaeology in British Columbia," in *The World Is as Sharp as a Knife: An Anthology in Honour of Wilson Duff* (Victoria: British Columbia Provincial Museum, 1981), 89

53  Thomas R. Berger, "Wilson Duff and Native Land Claims," in *The World Is as Sharp,* 60–1, and Carolyn Swayze, *Hard Choices: A Life of Tom Berger* (Toronto: Douglas & McIntyre, 1987).

54  Borden, "Wilson Duff," 89 and 92.

55  Marjorie Halpin, *Canadian Ethnic Studies* 29, no. 1 (1997): 184–6. This approach has now intruded upon political science with the works of Kiera Ladner. See, for example, "Decolonizing the Discipline: Indigenous Peoples and Political Science," www.uofaweb.ualberta.ca/polisci/ladner.cfm (accessed 10 March 2007).

56  Noel Dyck, "Telling It Like It Is," in *Anthropology,* ed. Dyck and Waldram, 194–5.

57  Ibid., 196–7.

58  S. Jasonoff, "What Judges Should Know about the Sociology of Science," *Jurimetrics,* 32 (1992): 345–59, cited in John E. Dodes, "Junk Science and the Law," *Skeptical Inquirer* (July 2001): 32.

59  Clifton, "Introduction: Memoir, Exegesis," in *The Invented Indian,* 7.

60  An especially troubling development is the protocols being developed by scholars attempting to study aboriginal peoples and publish with UBC Press, whereby it is agreed that findings can only be released if they are approved by the community being studied (personal communication with UBC Press, July 2004).

61 Bruce Trigger, "The Historians' Indian: Native Americans in Canadian Historical Writing from Charlevoix to the Present," *Canadian Historical Review* 67, no. 3 (1986): 336

62 Mark Whittow, *The Making of Byzantium, 600–1025* (Berkeley: University of California Press, 1996).

63 For examples of advocacy with respect to this case, see Antonia Curtze Mills, *Eagle Down Is Our Law: Witsuwit'en Law, Feasts, and Land Claims* (Vancouver: UBC Press, 1994), and Dara Culhane, *The Pleasure of the Crown: Anthropology, Law and First Nations* (Burnaby: Talon Books, 1998).

64 Flanagan, *First Nations*, 159, 165.

65 Alexander von Gernet, "What My Elders Taught Me," 22, quoted in Flanagan, *First Nations*, 159.

66 "Gitksan, Gitanyow against Treaty," *The Province*, 30 July 1998.

67 Clifton, introduction to *The Invented Indian*, 13–14.

68 Cairns, *Citizens Plus*, 70–3, 117, and 132.

69 Cited in Marc G. Stevenson's "The Possibility of Difference: Rethinking Co-Management," *Human Organization* 65, no. 2 (summer 2006), 167.

70 Sandall, *The Culture Cult*, chapter 1, http://www.rogersandall.com/ Archive_Aboriginal-Policy_The-New-Stone-Age.php (accessed 6 November 2007).

71 See Allard, "Big Bear's Treaty," 145–6, for a discussion of this point.

72 "Misery Money," CBC *Sunday*, 14 January 2007.

## CHAPTER TWO

1 Leland Donald, "Liberty, Equality, Fraternity: Was the Indian Really Egalitarian?," in *The Invented Indian: Cultural Fictions and Government Policies*, ed. James Clifton, 145–7 (New Brunswick, N.J.: Transaction Publishers, 1996).

2 Louis Armand de Lom d'Arce Baron de Lahontan, *New Voyages to North-America*, ed. Reuben Gold Thwaites (London: A.C. McClurg and Co., 1905 [original edition 1703]), 553–4.

3 Ibid.

4 Ter Ellingson, *The Myth of the Noble Savage* (Berkeley: University of California Press, 2001).

5 Robert McGhee, "Between Racism and Romanticism, Scientism and Spiritualism," in *Archaeology on the Edge*, ed. Brian Kooyman and Jane Kelley (Calgary: University of Calgary Press, 2004), 15.

6 Percy Adams, *Travelers and Travel Liars, 1660–1800* (Berkeley: University of California Press, 1962), 1–18.

7  Ellingson, *The Myth of the Noble Savage,* 55, 67–8.

8  Leland, "Liberty, Equality, Fraternity," 164n3.

9  Adams, *Travelers and Travel Liars,* 234–6.

10  Clifton, "The Indian Story: A Cultural Fiction," in *The Invented Indian,* 39.

11  For a more detailed discussion of this see Frances Widdowson, "The Political Economy of Aboriginal Dependency: A Critique of the Royal Commission on Aboriginal Peoples," PH.D. dissertation, York University, April 2006, 135–88.

12  Lewis Henry Morgan, *Ancient Society, or, Researches in the Lines of Human Progress from Savagery, through Barbarism to Civilization* (Gloucester, Mass.: P. Smith, 1974), 19. Morgan's arguments about the "enlargement of the sources of subsistence" have been recently elaborated upon by Jared Diamond, who in *Guns, Germs and Steel* identifies the availability of plants and animals for domestication as the significant determinant in the developmental differences between the Old and New Worlds. Diamond, however, also makes an important contribution to Morgan's theory by discussing the impact of the alignment of the different continents on "enlarging the sources of subsistence" (New York: W.W. Norton and Co., 1999), 176–214.

13  Eleanor Leacock, introduction to Frederick Engels's *The Origin of the Family, Private Property and the State* (New York: International Publishers, 1972), 11, and Eleanor Burke Leacock, introduction to Lewis Henry Morgan's *Ancient Society,* iv–v.

14  Morgan, *Ancient Society,* 3–4.

15  The international aboriginal rights organization Survival International, for example, has recently embarked upon a media campaign called Stamp It Out, encouraging supporters to challenge what it calls the "racist descriptions" of tribal peoples as "stone age" and "primitive." See "Isolated Tribe Not Primitive, Says Leading Minister," www.surival-international.org/news/2301 (accessed 31 July 2007).

16  Richard Dawkins, for example, states in *Climbing Mount Improbable* that "stoneflies are rather primitive flying insects." Dawkins makes this categorization because "primitive means that, although [stoneflies] are modern living insects, they are thought to resemble ancestors more than other modern insects resemble ancestors" (New York: Norton, 1996), 136.

17  Morgan, *Ancient Society,* 9–10, 13, 21.

18  Morton Fried, *The Evolution of Political Society* (New York: Random House, 1967), 51–107.

19  Morgan, *Ancient Society,* 13–14.

20  Brian M. Fagan, *In the Beginning: An Introduction to Archaeology,* 4th ed. (Boston: Little, Brown, 1981), 297.

21  Morgan, *Ancient Society,* 11–12.

22  Ibid., 5–7.

23  Ibid., 43.

24  See Leslie A. White, *The Concept of Culture* (Minneapolis: Burgess Publishing Company, 1973), 52, for discussion of this point.

25  George Novack, "Uneven and Combined Development in World History," in *Understanding History* (New York: Pathfinder Press, 1972), 99.

26  For a discussion of Houston's influence see James Houston, *Confessions of an Igloo Dweller: Memories of the Old Arctic* (New York: Houghton Mifflin, 1996).

27  John H. Bodley, *Cultural Anthropology: Tribes, States, and the Global System* (Mountain View, Calif.: Mayfield, 1997), 456–7.

28  White, *The Concept of Culture*, 49–56.

29  Bodley, *Cultural Anthropology*, 457. This agenda of Boas also led him to misinterpret data. See, for example, "Truth above All," *Globe and Mail*, 9 October 2002.

30  Morgan, *Ancient Society*, 8.

31  Ibid., 16–22.

32  One particularly disturbing body of work in this regard is the writing of Charles C. Mann, a contributing editor to *Atlantic* and a science correspondent. Mann recently wrote *1491: New Revelations of the Americas before Columbus* (New York: Knopf, 2005). In "Native Ingenuity," an article he wrote for the *Boston Globe,* Mann states that "scholars have known for decades that Native American societies were in many ways more technologically sophisticated then their European counterparts" (*Boston Globe*, 4 September 2005).

33  David Henige, "Their Numbers Become Thick," in *The Invented Indian*, ed. Clifton, 169–92.

34  Marion Lloyd, "Earth Movers," *Chronicle of Higher Education*, 3 December 2004. This view is criticized in the same article by Betty J. Meggers, the director of the Latin American Archaeology Program at the Smithsonian Institution's Museum of Natural History, who has studied the area for four decades. She maintains that the archaeologists making claims about dense populations in this area "have not done enough work to establish whether it was a single large settlement or a result of intermittent occupation over longer periods of time." She also notes that they have ignored the Smithsonian Institution's surveys conducted over four decades. According to Meggers, "the idea that the indigenous population has secrets that we don't know about is not supported by anything except wishful thinking and the myth of El Dorado."

35  See, for example, George Basalla, *The Evolution of Technology* (New York: Cambridge University Press, 1988), 8.

36 Such scepticism, in fact, was expressed in the early twentieth century. William H. Holmes claimed that "the possibility that these toys are of post-Discovery manufacture must be taken into account," and George C. Valliant doubted the pre-contact nature of these artifacts as late as 1944. See George C. Valliant, *Handbook of Aboriginal American Antiquities,* Smithsonian Institution, Bureau of American Ethnology, Bulletin 60 (New York: Smithsonian Institution, Bureau of American Ethnology), Bulletin 60, 152; and George C. Valliant, *Aztecs of Mexico* (Garden City: Doubleday Doran, 1941), 152.

37 Robert Kaplan, *The Nothing That Is: A Natural History of Zero* (Oxford: Oxford University Press), 80–9.

38 See, for example, Michael D. Coe, *Breaking the Maya Code* (Thames & Hudson, 1992), 209–11.

39 Margaret Mead, *Applied Anthropology* (1955), cited in B.G. Sivertz, "Cultural Change: Fast or Slow?," *North* 10, no. 5 (September–October 1963): 5.

40 Ibid.

41 Stuart Sim, ed., *The Icon Dictionary of Postmodern Thought* (Cambridge: Icon Books, 1998).

42 For two of the more substantial critiques of postmodernism, see Paul R. Gross and Norman Levitt, *Higher Superstition: The Academic Left and Its Quarrels with Science* (Baltimore: Johns Hopkins University Press, 1994), and Alan Sokal and Jean Bricmont, *Fashionable Nonsense: Postmodern Intellectuals' Abuse of Science* (New York: Picador, 1998).

43 Gross and Levitt, for example, point out a number of these tactics, including "a reliance on special pleading and appeals to political solidarity," copious name-dropping and self-congratulation, and the dressing up of illogical and irrational ideas with impenetrable pretentious language (*Higher Superstition,* 240).

44 See Frances Widdowson and Albert Howard, "Duplicity in the North: A Reply to Graham White," *Policy Options* (September 1999): 66.

45 See, for example, Howard Adams, *A Tortured People: The Politics of Colonization* (Penticton: Theytus Books, 1999), 29.

46 Vine Deloria, Jr., *Custer Died for Your Sins* (New York: Macmillan, 1969), 94.

47 Ibid., 95.

48 Alan Sokal, "A Plea for Reason, Evidence and Logic," *New Politics* 6, no. 2 (winter 1997): 126–9.

49 Ian Hodder, cited in Lawrence A. Kuznar's *Reclaiming a Scientific Anthropology* (Walnut Creek, Calif.: AltaMira Press, 1997), 165.

50 Brian Kooyman and Jane Kelley, introduction to *Archaeology on the Edge,* ed. Kooyman and Kelley, 2.

51 Trigger, "A Present of Their Past?," *Culture* 8, no. 1 (1988).

52 Anne McIlroy, "Who Were the First North Americans?," *Globe and Mail*, 6 September 2003.

53 McGhee, "Between Racism and Romanticism," 16–17.

54 Andrew L. Slayman, "A Battle over Bones," *Archaeology* (January–February 1997): 16–23.

55 Val Ross, "A Prairie Home Companion for Canadians and Russians," *Globe and Mail*, 2 January 2007.

56 Robert McGhee, "Archaeology, Anthropology, and the Myth of the Aboriginal," paper prepared for presentation to curators at the Canadian Museum of Civilization, March 2007, 1 (in authors' possession).

57 Keith Windschuttle, *The Killing of History: How Literary Critics and Social Theorists Are Murdering Our Past* (San Francisco: Encounter Books, 1996), 19.

58 Ibid., 227 and 231.

59 Ibid., 30–2.

60 See http://mqup.mcgill.ca/book.php?bookid=537 (accessed 3 February 2008).

61 This problem is discussed in detail in Widdowson's paper, "The Killing of Political Economy," presented at the First Nations, First Thoughts Conference, University of Edinburgh, May 2005.

62 Georges Sioui, *For an Amerindian Autohistory: An Essay on the Foundations of a Social Ethic* (Montreal: McGill-Queen's University Press, 1995), xxii.

63 Ibid., 10.

64 Trigger, foreword, in ibid., xi.

65 Trigger, *Sociocultural Evolution: Calculation and Contingency* (Oxford: Blackwell Press, 1998), 99.

66 Ibid., 231.

67 www.chairs.gc.ca/web/chairholders (accessed 15 November 2006).

68 Kiera L. Ladner, "Governing within an Ecological Context: Creating an AlterNative Understanding of Blackfoot Governance," *Studies in Political Economy* 70 (Spring 2003): 125–52.

69 Ladner, "Up the Creek: Fishing for a New Constitutional Order," *Canadian Journal of Political Science* 38, no. 4 (December 2005): 936–7.

70 See Frances Widdowson, "Prayers, Religious Imposition and the CPSA," www.listes.ulaval.ca/cgi-bin/wa?A1=ind0406&L=polcan, 18 June 2004 (accessed 17 January 2007).

71 Elizabeth Cook-Lynn, *Anti-Indianism in Modern America* (Chicago: University of Illinois Press, 2001).

72 Peggy Brizinski, *Knots in a String: An Introduction to Native Studies in Canada*, 2nd ed. (Saskatoon: University Extension Press, University of Saskatchewan, 1993), 1.

73 www.oncampus.richmond.edu/faculty/ASAIL/guide/Canada.html (accessed 15 November 2006).

74 Peter Kulchyski, Don McCaskill, and David Newhouse, *In the Words of the Elders: Aboriginal Cultures in Transition* (Toronto: University of Toronto Press, 2000), xi.

75 Ibid., xii–xiii.

76 He has written three books since 1999, including *Wasáse: Indigenous Pathways of Action and Freedom*; *Peace, Power and Righteousness: An Indigenous Manifesto*; and *Heeding the Voices of Our Ancestors: Kahnawake Mohawk Politics and the Rise of Native Nationalism.*

77 Margaret Wente, "The New Warrior Class," *Globe and Mail*, 15 July 2006.

78 www.taiaiake.com (accessed 17 January 2007).

79 www.firstnationsuniversity.ca (accessed 17 January 2007).

80 Stanley Fish, "Conspiracy Theories 101," *New York Times*, 23 July 2006.

81 Manning Marable, *Race, Reform and Rebellion* (Jackson: University Press of Mississippi, 1991), 249–56.

82 Du Bois, cited in ibid., 3.

83 E.O. Wright, *Class Counts: Comparative Studies in Class Analysis* (Cambridge: Cambridge University Press, 1997): 9–13.

84 Robert Reasoner, "The True Meaning of Self-Esteem," www.self-esteem-nase.org/whatisselfesteem.shtml (accessed 10 March 2008).

85 Maggie Fox, "Too Much Self-Esteem Could Be Bad for Kids, Psychologists Warn," *Toronto Star*, 6 August 1998.

## CHAPTER THREE

1 Heather Scofield, "Ottawa Prices Native Demands at $200 Billion," *Globe and Mail*, 26 October 1999. Although $200 billion has been estimated as the "worst case scenario," this figure does not include the fifty-seven comprehensive claims being negotiated in British Columbia, or the two thousand claims being researched.

2 After leaving the department, Swain went on to become a director of Hambros Bank "to use expertise and contacts he developed while deputy minister in the Indian and Northern Affairs Department to tap into a potential market for aboriginal capital markets" (John Partridge, "Ex-Mandarin Hired to Help Hambros," *Globe and Mail*, 26 November 1996).

3 Cited in Dan Smith, *The Seventh Fire: The Struggle for Aboriginal Government.* (Toronto: Key Porter, 1993), 74.

4 Department of Indian Affairs and Northern Development, "Statement on Claims of Indian and Inuit People," press release, August 1973, cited in

Melvin Smith, *Our Home or Native Land* (Victoria: Crown Western, 1995), 7.

5  James S. Frideres and René Gadacz, *Aboriginal Peoples in Canada: Contemporary Conflicts*, 6th ed. (Toronto: Prentice Hall, 2001), 192, 208.

6  Comprehensive Claims Branch, Claims and Indian Government Sector, Indian Affairs and Northern Development, *General Briefing Note on the Comprehensive Land Claims Policy of Canada and the Status of Claims*, March 2007, http://www.ainc-inac.gc.ca/ps/clm/gbn/gbn_e.pdf (accessed 13 November 2007), 1.

7  Department of Indian and Northern Affairs, *Comprehensive Claims Policy and Status of Claims*, www.ainc-inac.gc.ca/ps/clm/brieff_e.pdf, 1 (accessed 1 June 2004).

8  For a description of specific claims, see Frideres and Gadacz, *Aboriginal Peoples in Canada*, 201–2.

9  There are more than eight hundred outstanding specific claims in Canada. See "New Law Expected to Speed up Land Claims," CBC *News Online*, http://www.cbc.ca/canada/story/2007/06/11/land-claims.html?ref=rss, 11 June 2007 (accessed 13 November 2007).

10  Carolyn Swayze, *Hard Choices: A Life of Tom Berger* (Vancouver: Douglas & McIntyre, 1987), 79.

11  Department of Indian and Northern Affairs, *Comprehensive Claims Policy*, 1–2.

12  Tim Harper, "Court Ruling Ushers in New Era in Land Claims," *Toronto Star*, 12 December 1997.

13  Tom Flanagan, *First Nations? Second Thoughts* (Montreal: McGill-Queen's University Press, 2000), 128.

14  *Delgamuukw v. The Queen* [1997], 153 D.L.R. (4th), 243, cited in Flanagan, *First Nations*, 128.

15  Comprehensive Claims Branch, *General Briefing Note*, 4–13.

16  "Specific Claims Branch," Indian and Northern Affairs Canada, www.ainc-inac.gc.ca/ps/clm/scb_html (accessed 22 November 2006).

17  Indian and Northern Affairs Canada, "National Mini Summary – Specific Claims Branch," Reporting Period: 1970/04/01–2006/09/30, www.ainc-inac.gc.ca/ps/clm/nms_e.pdf (accessed 22 November 2006).

18  Indian and Northern Affairs Canada, "National Mini Summary – Specific Claims Branch," Reporting Period 1970/04/01 – 2002/03/31.

19  "Specific Claims Branch," Indian and Northern Affairs Canada, www.ainc-inac.gc.ca/ps/clm/scb_html (accessed 22 November 2006).

20  Calvin Helin, *Dances with Dependency: Indigenous Success through Self-Reliance* (Vancouver: Orca, 2006), 160–1.

21 Flanagan, *First Nations*, 128.
22 Ibid., 128–9.
23 *Delgamuukw v. The Queen* [1997], 153 D.L.R. (4th), 265–6, cited in
   Flanagan, *First Nations*, 130.
24 Ibid., 132–3.
25 This process, however, excluded the Nisga'a agreement, which was negotiated
   under a separate process. This process had cost the Nisga'a $25 million and
   federal negotiators $5.3 million as of 1995 ("Negotiations Costly in Nisga'a
   Land Claim Bill," CP *Newswire*, 18 February 1995).
26 Comprehensive Claims Branch, *General Briefing Note*, 32.
27 It is not clear from the literature developed by the federal government, the B.C.
   Treaty Commission, and the B.C. government how many agreements have
   actually been finalized, as groups sign an "Agreement in Principle," which is
   evidently not the final stage in the process. The federal government has noted,
   for example, that in the fall of 2006 three final agreements were "initialled"
   (Comprehensive Claims Branch, *General Briefing Note*, 32). More recently, the
   B.C. Treaty Commission has stated that seven groups are in "stage 5" and have
   "signed agreements in principle (AIPs) – the blueprint for a final treaty"
   (www.bctreaty.net/files/updates.php [accessed 13 November 2007]).
28 Bernard Schulmann, "Getting Treaty Talks off Square One," *Policy Options*
   (October 2000), 59.
29 "B.C. Treaty Process Questionable," *Globe and Mail*, 2 December 2006.
30 http://www.bctreaty.net/files/funding.php (accessed 13 November 2007).
31 B.C. Treaty Commission, *Treaty Commission Annual Report 2006*,
   http://www.bctreaty.net/files/pdf_documents/BCTC06AR-FINAL.pdf, 5.
32 Indian Claims Commission, Annual Report, 2005–06, 13,
   www.indianclaims.ca/pdf/AR_05–06_eng.pdf, 82 (accessed November 2006).
33 Sue Bailey, "Phil Fontaine, Once Head of Canada's Largest Native Advocacy
   Group, Has Been Picked to Lead the Much Maligned Indian Claims Commission That He Once Criticized Too," *Canadian Press Newswire*, 29 August
   2001
34 www.indianclaims.ca/menu-en.asp (accessed November 22, 2006).
35 Indian Claims Commission, *Annual Report, 2005/2006*, www.indianclaims.ca/
   pdf/AR_05–06_eng.pdf, 11–13 (accessed November 2006).
36 Royal Commission on Aboriginal Peoples [RCAP], *Report of the Royal Commission on Aboriginal Peoples [Final Report]*, vol. 1, 40–1n4.
37 RCAP, *Final Report*, vol. 2: 1, 41–2.
38 Schulmann, "Getting Treaty Talks off Square One," 61.
39 Ibid., 61–2.
40 Ibid., 62.

41 Harry B. Hawthorn, ed., *A Survey of the Contemporary Indians in Canada*, vol. 1 (Ottawa: Indian Affairs Branch, 1966), 21.

42 For a discussion of aboriginal peoples' economic circumstances, see Terry Wotherspoon and Vic Satzewich, *First Nations: Race, Class, and Gender Relations* (Saskatoon: Canadian Plains Research Centre, 2000), 50–72.

43 Comeau and Santin, *The First Canadians*, 91.

44 Wotherspoon and Satzewich, *First Nations*, 6–11.

45 Gabrielle Slowey, "Globalization and Self-Government: Impacts and Implications for First Nations in Canada," *American Review of Canadian Studies* 31, nos. 1/2 (spring/summer 2001).

46 RCAP, *Final Report*, vol. 2: 1, 5.

47 Janet Somerville, "The Innu, the Inuit and Inco: Can Their Cultures Coexist?," *Catholic New Times*, 29 June 1997, 21.

48 Harold Cardinal, *The Unjust Society* (Edmonton: Hurtig, 1969), 62–3.

49 Ibid., 94.

50 Cited in Comeau and Santin, *The First Canadians*, 92.

51 The most extensive of these arguments has been made recently by the Royal Commission on Aboriginal Peoples. For this analysis, see RCAP, *Final Report*, vol. 5, 55–79.

52 Helin, *Dances with Dependency*, 30.

53 "Devise Better Plan for Nunavut before Increasing Grants," *Canadian Press Newswire*, 28 February 2001.

54 Del Anaquod, "Education, Training, Employment and Economic Development," in RCAP, *Sharing the Harvest* (Ottawa: Minister of Supply and Services, 1993), 177.

55 Mark Nagler, "Minority Values and Economic Achievement: The Case of the North American Indian, in *Perspectives on the North American Indians*, ed. Nagler (Toronto: McClelland & Stewart, 1972), 141.

56 Cited in Comeau and Santin, *The First Canadians*, 91–2.

57 Flanagan, *First Nations*, 184.

58 "Musqueam Band Endorses Massive Rent Increases," *Canadian Press Newswire*, 8 January 1999.

59 "Musqueam Land Worth Only Half of Non-Native Land, Highest Court Rules," *Canadian Press Newswire*, 9 November 2000.

60 Flanagan, *First Nations*, 131–2.

61 "Musqueam Band Endorses Massive Rent Increases," *Canadian Press Newswire*, 8 January 1999.

62 "Outgoing Chief Takes Stand for Musqueam Renters," *Canadian Press Newswire*, 29 December 1998.

63 See, for example, Helin, *Dances with Dependency*, 177.

64 For an in-depth discussion of the unviability of land claims, see Frances
   Widdowson, "The Political Economy of Aboriginal Dependency: A Critique
   of the Royal Commission on Aboriginal Peoples," ph.d. dissertation, York
   University, April 2006, 503–62.
65 Smith, *Our Home or Native Land*, 36.
66 See, for example, Kim Lunman, "New Bill Calls for Native Institutes," *Globe
   and Mail*, 3 December 2002.
67 Carol Howes, "The New Native Tycoons," *Financial Post (National Post)*,
   27 January 2001. Calvin Helin also maintains that the number of self-
   employed aboriginal people has increased by 30.7 per cent since 1996, which
   amounts to a rate nine times higher than for the Canadian population as a
   whole (*Dances with Dependency*, 177).
68 Howes, "The New Native Tycoons."
69 "Aboriginal Financial Institutions," http://strategis.ic.gc.ca/epic/site/
   abc-eac.nsf/en/h_ab00155e.html (accessed 12 November 2007).
70 Comeau and Santin, *The First Canadians*, 95.
71 See, for example, Helin, *Dances with Dependency*, 177–90.
72 Comeau and Santin, *The First Canadians*, 104.
73 Ibid., 96.
74 See, for example, Frideres and Gadacz, *Aboriginal Peoples in Canada*,
   362.
75 Ibid., 362, 365–6.
76 Ibid., 366.
77 Comeau and Santin, *The First Canadians*, 102–3.
78 Jonathan Fowlie and Carly Weeks, "Mohawks Put Police under Siege,"
   *Globe and Mail*, 13 January 2004.
79 "Gambling Is a Part of Culture," *Windspeaker* 14, no. 6 (October 1996).
80 "Crime Ring Broken," *Montreal Gazette*, 13 September 1997.
81 Tom Fennell, "The Human Smugglers," *Media* 7, no. 2 (summer 2000):
   24–5.
82 "Aboriginals Running Guns, rcmp Report Says," *Montreal Gazette*, 3
   November 1997.
83 This even holds for critics of aboriginal policy such as Tom Flanagan and
   Calvin Helin.
84 Frideres and Gagacz, *Aboriginal Peoples in Canada*, 95–7.
85 Allan Moscovitch and Andrew Webster, "Aboriginal Social Assistance Expenditures," in *How Ottawa Spends, 1995–96: Mid-Life Crises*, ed. Susan D.
   Phillips (Ottawa: Carleton University Press), 1995.
86 rcap, *Final Report*, vol. 2: 2, 773.
87 See, for example, Wotherspoon and Satzewich, *First Nations*, 49–52.

88 For a discussion of labour and its relationship to human evolution see Charles Woolfson, *The Labour Theory of Culture* (London: Routledge & Kegan Paul, 1982).

89 See Leo Huberman, *Man's Worldly Goods: The Story of the Wealth of Nations* (New York: Monthly Review Press, 1968), 112–21.

90 Paul Phillips, introduction to H. Clare Pentland, *Labour and Capital in Canada* (Toronto: Lorimer, 1981), xv–xi. For an in-depth discussion of this transformation, see Widdowson, "The Political Economy of Aboriginal Dependency," 411–37.

91 Brody, *The Other Side of Eden* (Vancouver: Douglas & McIntyre, 2001), 133.

92 The expression "Indian time" is another euphemism for this. See, for example, "'Indian Time Doesn't Cut It' for Innovative Chief with on-the-Edge Humor," *Globe and Mail*, 21 September 2006.

93 Brody, *The Other Side of Eden*, 295.

94 See Rolf Knight, *Indians at Work* (Vancouver: New Star Books, 1978), 73; Jean Allard, "Big Bear's Treaty," *Inroads* 11 (June 2002): 143; and Helin, *Dances with Dependency*, 244, for a discussion of this circumstance.

95 Daniel Ashini, cited in Somerville, "The Innu, the Inuit and Inco."

96 W.E. Moore, cited in E.P. Thompson, "Time, Work-Discipline, and Industrial Capitalism," *Past & Present* 38 (1967): 94.

97 Edward W. Van Dyke, "Families in Other Cultures," unpublished paper for Bear-Spike Holdings Ltd., Calgary, May 1998, 2.

98 Pentland, *Labour and Capital in Canada*, 179.

99 Paul Guillet, "Labour and Aboriginal Relations: Strategies for the New Millennium," *Briarpatch* 26, no. 8 (October 1997): 25–8.

100 Calvin Helin addresses this to some extent in his discussion of the "culture of expectancy," which he maintains has been created by the "welfare trap" (*Dances with Dependency*, 115–26).

101 Wotherspoon and Satzewich, *First Nations*, 62. See also Helin, *Dances with Dependency*, 134–5.

102 Reneé Depuis, "Aboriginal Peoples and Employment Equity," in RCAP, *Sharing the Harvest*, 167.

103 For a discussion of the dominance of government employment in northern economies see Ed Weick, "Can Canada Afford the North?, *Policy Options* (March 1994): 16–18.

104 Helin, *Dances with Dependency*, 165–76.

105 Howard Adams, *Prison of Grass: Canada from a Native Point of View* (Toronto: New Press, 1975), 126–7.

106 Take, for example, the case of Jamesie Kopalik in Jill Mahoney's "Nunavut Creating Two Classes of Inuit," *Globe and Mail*, 5 April 1999.

107 Pentland, *Labour and Capital in Canada*, 198.

108 Ibid., 198–9.

109 Ibid., 197.

110 For a further discussion of this circumstance see Frances Widdowson, "The Killing of Political Economy," paper presented at the First Nations, First Thoughts Conference, Edinburgh, 2005.

111 See Simon Brascoupé, "Strengthening Traditional Economies and Perspectives," in RCAP, *Sharing the Harvest*, 103–7, for the application of these ideas.

112 Brody, *The Other Side of Eden*, 118.

113 Ibid., 325.

114 RCAP, *Final Report*, vol. 1, 94n52; vol. 2: 2, 462–3; and Brody, *The Other Side of Eden*, 7, 86.

115 Thomas Berger, *A Long and Terrible Shadow* (Vancouver: Douglas & McIntyre, 1991), 126–39, cited in RCAP, *Final Report*, vol. 2: 2, 462.

116 Ian Keay and Cherie Metcalf, "Aboriginal Rights, Customary Law and the Economics of Renewable Resource Exploitation," *Canadian Public Policy* 30, no. 1 (2004): 18n21.

117 By 1792, one year *before* Mackenzie's journal entry, there were already twenty-one European vessels engaged in trade on the northwest coast of North America. See Eric Wolf, *Europe and the People without History* (Berkeley: University of California Press, 1997), 182–3.

118 *R. v. Gladstone*, [1996] 2 S.C.R., 723.

119 Sheila Robinson, quoted in Paula Pryce, "The Manipulation of Culture and History: A Critique of Two Expert Witnesses," *Native Studies Review* 8, no. 1 (1992): 43.

120 See, for example, Erin Sherry and Heather Myers, "Traditional Environmental Knowledge in Practice," *Society of Natural Resources* 15 (2002): 354, and Lea Bill, Jean Crozier, and Dennis Surrendi, "Synthesis Report No. 12: A Report of Wisdom Synthesized from the Traditional Knowledge Component Studies," *Northern River Basins Study* (Edmonton: NRBS, 1996), 94.

121 For two other examples of this tactic, see Brascoupé, "Strengthening Traditional Economies and Perspectives," 103–9, and Paul Barnsley, "Assimilation Argument in Article Infuriates Natives," *Windspeaker* 19, no. 9 (January 2002): 9–10.

122 Brascoupé, "Strengthening Traditional Economies and Perspectives," 101, 107.

123 James Tully, "Aboriginal Peoples: Negotiating Reconciliation," in *Canadian Politics*, ed. James Bickerton and Alain G. Gagnon (Toronto: Broadview Press, 1999), 429.

124 See, for example, Michael Asch, "The Economics of Dene Self-Determination," in *Challenging Anthropology*, ed. David H. Turner and Gavin A. Smith (Toronto: McGraw-Hill Ryerson, 1979).

125 Peter Usher, "Environment, Race and Nation Reconsidered," *Canadian Geographer* 47, no. 4 (2003): 372.

126 Peter Usher and Martin Weinstein, "Towards Assessing the Effects of Lake Winnipeg Regulation and Churchill River Diversion on Reserve Harvesting in Native Communities in Northern Manitoba," *Canadian Technical Report of Fisheries and Aquatic Sciences* no. 1794 (Winnipeg: Department of Fisheries and Oceans, 1991).

127 Usher, "Environment, Race and Nation Reconsidered," 372–4.

128 Ibid., 385.

129 For a detailed discussion of this, see Frances Widdowson, "The Political Economy of Nunavut: Internal Colony or Rentier Territory," paper presented at the Annual Meeting of the Canadian Political Science Association, University of Western Ontario, June 2005.

130 David R. Newhouse, "Modern Aboriginal Economies: Capitalism with an Aboriginal Face," in RCAP, *Sharing the Harvest*, 92–3.

131 See Widdowson, "The Political Economy of Nunavut."

132 This circumstance applies to all aboriginal communities, even those that are singled out as examples of functionality and prosperity. See, for example, John Gray, "From a Scattered Community, a Model Village," *Globe and Mail*, 7 November 1998.

133 See John Ibbitson, "A Bleak Choice for Young Indians," *Globe and Mail*, 8 August 2006, and Roger Sandall, "In Bluebeard's Castles," www.culturecult.com/spiked.htm#bluebeard (accessed November 2006).

134 Karen Howlett and Bill Curry, "Ottawa's Solution: Move Town to Timmins," *Globe and Mail*, 10 November 2006.

### CHAPTER FOUR

1 Saul Dubow, *Scientific Racism in Modern South Africa* (New York: Cambridge University Press, 1995).

2 Judy Scales-Trent, "Racial Purity Laws in the United States and Nazi Germany: The Targeting Process," *Human Rights Quarterly* 23 (May 2001): 260–307.

3 *Loving v. Virginia*, cited in http://www.eugenics-watch.com/roots/chap07.html#footnote (accessed 27 October 2007).

4 See also Roger Sandall, "In Bluebeard's Castles," for a discussion of this point in the Australian context.

5 Jack Danylchuk, "Judge Sees Racism in Indian Rules," *Edmonton Journal*, November 1993.

6 Ibid.

7 Letter from Jeannie Thomas for Richard J. Scott, chairman of the panel, to the Honourable Mr Justice F.C. Muldoon, 11 March 1998 (in the possession of the authors).

8 See, for example, Peter Usher, "The North: One Land, Two Ways of Life," in *Heartland and Hinterland*, ed. Larry McCann and Angus Gunn (Scarborough: Prentice-Hall, 1998), 365.

9 Elizabeth Rata refers to this as "culturalism" – the approach where "culture and ethnicity are merged and the ethnic group's interests are politicized" ("Rethinking Biculturalism," *Anthropological Theory* 5, no. 3 (2005): 270.

10 Royal Commission on Aboriginal Peoples [RCAP], *Report of the Royal Commission on Aboriginal Peoples [Final Report]*, vol. 2: 1, 107, 112, 115.

11 Taylor maintains that self-government is not racist because the word applies to groups like the Nazis or the Klu Klux Klan, which "operate out of a doctrine that a certain group is biologically inferior and so adopting policies that reflect that inferiority, including depriving the target group of certain rights and capacities that others enjoy" ("On the Nisga'a Treaty," *BC Studies* 120 [winter 1998/99]: 37). This, however, does describe those claims to self-government in which aboriginal peoples claim to have a spirituality that makes them better suited to looking after lands in North America than "whites."

12 John A. Price, "Ethical Advocacy versus Propaganda: Canada's Indian Support Groups," in *The Invented Indian*, ed. Clifton, 258–9.

13 For a similar argument see Flanagan, *First Nations? Second Thoughts* (Montreal: McGill-Queen's University Press, 2000), 11–26.

14 Ovide Mercredi and Mary Ellen Turpel, *In the Rapids: Navigating the Future of First Nations* (Toronto: Viking, 1993), 95.

15 David Crombie, the minister of Indian and Northern Affairs in the 1980s, developed a negotiating branch for "second track" self-government negotiations. However, five years and $50 million later, Crombie's department had failed to reach a single deal. See Dan Smith, *The Seventh Fire: The Struggle for Aboriginal Government* (Toronto: Key Porter, 1993), 83.

16 This is also the view of the Royal Commission on Aboriginal Peoples. See RCAP, *Final Report*, vol. 2: 1, 202–12, for the Royal Commission's reasoning.

17 www.ainc-inac.gc.ca/pr/agr/index-e.html#backgrounderandhighlights1 (accessed December 2006).

18 "Indian Affairs Spending Poorly Tracked, Audit Finds," *Globe and Mail*, 5 June 2002.

19 Brennan Clarke, "Self-Government Deal for Westbank First Nation," *Kelowna Daily Courier*, 9 July 1998.

20 For an in-depth overview of the development of the Indian Act and its functions, see John F. Leslie, "The Indian Act: An Historical Perspective," *Canadian Parliamentary Review* 25, no. 2 (summer 2002): 23–7.

21 For a discussion of the Trudeau government's reasons for proposing the White Paper, see Pauline Comeau and Aldo Santin, *The First Canadians: A Profile of Canada's Native People Today* (Toronto: Lorimer, 1995), 10–13.

22 Paul Barnsley, "Two Hundred Organizations Buck AFN Boycott," *Windspeaker* 19, no. 3 (July 2001): 6–7.

23 "Aboriginals Protest as Ottawa Introduces New Indian Act," *Canadian Press Newswire*, 12 December 1996.

24 Paul Barnsley, "New Plan Reminiscent of Irwin," *Windspeaker* 18, no. 10 (February, 2001); and Bill Curry, "Ottawa Shelves Reform Plans on Native Governance," *Globe and Mail*, 16 December 2006.

25 See, for example, "Indian Act Paternalistic but Aboriginals Suspicious of Change," *Canadian Press Newswire*, 23 September 1996, and "Saskatchewan Aboriginal Group Proceeding with Court Challenge to Indian Act Changes," *Canadian Press Newswire*, 1 September 2003.

26 This has also occurred with respect to attempts to repeal Section 67 of the Canadian Human Rights Act, which exempted the Indian Act. For a discussion of this, see Karen Selick, "There Are Some 'Rights' We Can All Do Without," *Globe and Mail*, 24 August 2007.

27 Fred R. Fenwick, "First Nations Governance Act: The Inherent Right to Self-Government. What's in a Name?" *Law Now* 28, no. 3 (December 2003/January 2004).

28 Stephanie Boisard, "Why First Nations People Cannot Accept Robert Nault's Initiative," *Canadian Dimension* 36, no. 4 (July/August 2002): 33.

29 Cited in Menno Boldt and J. Anthony Long, eds., *The Quest for Justice: Aboriginal Peoples and Aboriginal Rights* (Toronto: University of Toronto Press, 1985), appendix B, 359.

30 For an extensive discussion of this point, see Flanagan, *First Nations*, 67–88.

31 Cited in Will Kymlicka, *Multicultural Citizenship: A Liberal Theory of Minority Rights* (Oxford: Oxford University Press, 1995), 27.

32 Ibid., 18.

33 Patrick Macklem, *Indigenous Difference and the Constitution of Canada* (Toronto: University of Toronto Press, 2001), 4.

34 Ibid., 4–5.

35 Ibid., 5–6.

36 A more detailed version of this argument appears in Frances Widdowson, "Inventing Nationhood: The Political Economy of Aboriginal Self-Government in the Context of Quebec Sovereignty," paper presented at the Annual Meeting of the Canadian Political Science Association, June 2004.

37 This type of authority was identified with Max Weber along with two other types – traditional and charismatic. Charismatic authority is also vested in individuals, but in "the personal qualities of the charismatic leader, rather than in tradition or in birth." For a further elaboration upon this type of authority, see Janine Brodie, "Power and Politics," *Critical Concepts: An Introduction to Politics*, in Janine Brodie and Sandra Rein, eds. (Toronto: Prentice Hall, 2005), 9.

38 Peter M. Blau and Marshall W. Meyer, *Bureaucracy in Modern Society*, 3rd ed. (New York: Random House, 1987), 64–5. For discussions of how traditional, not legal-rational, forms of authority exist in aboriginal communities, see Boldt and Long, *The Quest for Justice*, 337–8; and Paul Nadasdy, *Hunters and Bureaucrats: Power, Knowledge and Aboriginal-State Relations in the Southwest Yukon* (Vancouver: UBC Press, 2004), 6–8.

39 Blau and Meyer, *Bureaucracy in Modern Society*, 64.

40 Ibid., 65.

41 Nadasdy, *Hunters and Bureaucrats*, 67–8.

42 RCAP, *Final Report*, vol. 2: 1, 134–6.

43 Jean Allard, "Big Bear's Treaty," *Inroads* 11 (June 2002), 144–53, and Calvin Helin, *Dances with Dependency: Indigenous Success through Self-Reliance* (Vancouver: Orca, 2006), 141–57.

44 See, for example, Noah Black, "Conflict on Reserve: How to Stop It before It Happens," *Windspeaker* 14, no. 4 (August 1996), 18–19.

45 Sue Bailey, "First Nations Strive for Open Government, Job Creation and Reports of Mismanagement," *Canadian Press Newswire*, 2 March 2000.

46 Helin, *Dances with Dependency*, 147.

47 Allard, "Big Bear's Treaty," 134. The most significant example of this problem can be seen in the case of the Mohawks of Kahnawake. See E.J. Dickson-Gilmore, "History, Factionalist Competition, and the Assumption of Imposition in the Kahnawake Mohawk Nation," *Ethnohistory* 46, no. 3 (1999).

48 See, for example, Erin Anderssen, "Reform, Fontaine Square off over Racism," *Globe and Mail*, 9 April 1998, A3; Jeff Colbourne, "Problems at Pauktuutit," *News/North*, 4 May 1998; Tibbetts, "Fontaine Gets Raise after First Year as Grand Chief," *Canadian Press Newswire*, 1 July 1998; Peter Moon, "Reserve Headed toward Trusteeship," *Globe and Mail*, 1 September 1998; Peter Cheney, "The Money Pit: An Indian Band's Story," *Globe and*

*Mail*, 24 October 1998; Gordon Laird, "The Outlaw," *Saturday Night* 114, no. 5 (June 1999): 64; and *Globe and Mail*, 10 March 2000.

49  Gordon Laird, "The Outlaw," *Saturday Night* 114, no. 5, June 1999; and Erin Anderssen, "Reform, Fontaine Square off over Racism," *Globe and Mail*, 9 April 1998.

50  *Globe and Mail*, 10 March 2000.

51  "Watt Ousted," *Windspeaker* 12, no. 3 (April 1994).

52  Allard, "Big Bear's Treaty," 148–9.

53  Laird, "The Outlaw," 66.

54  For some critical observations of the native leadership, see James Burke, *Paper Tomahawks* (Winnipeg: Queenston House, 1975): 111, 164; Doug Daniels, "Dreams and Realities of Dene Government," *Canadian Journal of Native Studies* 7, no. 1 (1987): 95–110; and Jeremy Hull, *Aboriginal People and Social Classes in Manitoba* (Winnipeg: Canadian Centre for Policy Alternatives, 2001).

55  Howard Adams, *Prison of Grass*, 185–6.

56  Howard Adams, *A Tortured People: The Politics of Colonization* (Penticton: Theytus Books, 1995), 79.

57  Menno Boldt, *Surviving as Indians: The Challenge of Self-Government* (Toronto: University of Toronto Press, 1993), 120.

58  This is even the case in the arguments of Calvin Helin and Jean Allard, who are very critical of the political systems currently in place in aboriginal communities. See, for example, Helin, *Dances with Dependency*, 152–3, and Allard, "Big Bear's Treaty," 118–21. In his foreword to Allard's piece, Gordon Gibson also asserts that the "Indian Act authority has displaced traditional Indian checks and balances on their leaders" (Gibson, foreword, *Inroads* 11).

59  For a discussion of the economic factors behind increasing stratification, see Morton Fried, *The Evolution of Political Society* (New York: Random House, 1967), 182–4, 192–6.

60  Elizabeth Rata, "Late Capitalism and Ethnic Revivalism," *Anthropological Theory* 3, no. 1 (2003): 45.

61  David Ahenakew, "Aboriginal Title and Aboriginal Rights," in *The Quest for Justice*, ed. Boldt and Long, 28–9.

62  Kiera Ladner, "Rethinking Aboriginal Governance," in *Reinventing Canada*, ed. Janine Brodie and Linda Trimble (Toronto: Prentice Hall, 2003), 45.

63  See also Dan Russell, *A People's Dream: Aboriginal Self-Government in Canada* (Vancouver: UBC Press, 2001), 99–100, and Calvin Helin, *Dances with Dependency*, 70–3.

64  Elisabeth Tooker, "The United States Constitution and the Iroquois League," in *The Imaginary Indian*, ed. Clifton, 108–12.

65 Leonard W. Labaree, ed., *The Papers of Benjamin Franklin*, vol. 4 (New Haven: Yale University Press, 1961), 118–19; ibid., 110.

66 Francis Jennings, *Benjamin Franklin: Politician* (New York: W.W. Norton, 1996), 86, cited in Bruce E. Johansen, "Native American Political Systems and the Evolution of Democracy: An Annotated Bibliography," http://www.ratical.org/many_worlds/6Nations/NAPSnEOD.html (accessed 12 November 2007), 3.

67 Ibid.

68 The Royal Commission, for example, criticizes Locke's views as being insulting to aboriginals on this basis (RCAP, *Final Report*, vol. 1, 44–5.

69 Barbara Mann and Jerry Fields, cited in Bruce E. Johansen, "Dating the Iroquois Confederacy," *Akwasasne Notes New Series*, 3–4 (fall 1995): 62–3.

70 Ibid.

71 RCAP, *Final Report*, vol. 1, 54.

72 Ibid., 61.

73 Ibid., 656.

74 Johansen, "Dating the Iroquois Confederacy," 62–3.

75 See also RCAP, *Final Report*, vol. 1, 55, for a similar conflation of myth with history in the case of the Iroquois Confederacy.

76 Cited in Johansen, "Dating the Iroquois Confederacy," 62–3.

77 Vine Deloria Jr., "Comfortable Fictions and the Struggle for Turf: An Essay Review of The Invented Indian: Cultural Fictions and Government Policies," *American Indian Quarterly* (summer 1992): 398.

78 Ibid., 403–5.

79 See Tooker, "The United States Constitution," 114–15, for a description of the Iroquois League and how it had little in common with what was being proposed in the Constitutional Convention meeting in 1787.

80 Tim Schõuls, J. Olthuis, and Diane Engelstad, "The Basic Dilemma: Sovereignty or Assimilation," in *Nation to Nation,* ed. Diane Engelstead and John Bird (Concord: Anansi, 2002), 17.

81 Elizabeth Rata, "Rethinking Biculturalism," *Anthropological Theory* 5, no. 3 (2005), 272–3.

82 See, for example, John Stackhouse, "Norma Rae of the Okanagan," *Globe and Mail*, 8 November 2001.

83 Janet Mary Nicol, "'Unions Aren't Native': The Muckamuck Restaurant Labour Dispute, Vancouver, B.C. (1978–1983)," *Labour* 40 (fall 1997): 235–51.

84 There even has been an attempt to discourage the use of the word "tribalism" as "offensively paternalistic." See, for example, Graham White, "The

Tundra's Always Greener: A Response to Widdowson and Howard," *Policy Options* (March 2000).

## CHAPTER FIVE

1  Jane Gadd, "Homeless Alcoholic Pleads Guilty to Bashing Lover to Death," *Globe and Mail*, 19 February 2000.
2  Brian Laghi, "Fear of Bearwalkers Still Haunts Some Ojibway," *Globe and Mail*, 31 May 1997.
3  Ibid.
4  For a discussion of this problem, see Edward W. Van Dyke, "Community Perspectives of the Police," unpublished paper, Bear-Spike Holdings Ltd., Calgary, 1982, 6.
5  Wendy McCann, "Drunkenness Defence Incenses Victims' Groups," CP *Newswire*, 26 September 1999.
6  See, for example, "It's Alarming How Many Aboriginals Are in Prison," *Globe and Mail*, 19 October 2006.
7  C.M. Sinclair, foreword to Anne McGillivray and Brenda Comasky, *Black Eyes All of the Time: Intimate Violence, Aboriginal Women, and the Justice System* (Toronto: University of Toronto Press, 1999), x.
8  Laura E. Klein and Lillian A. Ackerman, eds., *Women and Power in Native North America* (Norman: University of Oklahoma Press, 2000).
9  See, for example, E. Friedl, *Women and Men* (New York: Holt, Rinehart and Winston, 1975).
10  Steven Pinker, *The Blank Slate: The Modern Denial of Human Nature* (New York: Viking, 2002), 330–2.
11  Marianne O. Nielsen, "Criminal Justice and Native Self-Government," in *Aboriginal Peoples and Canadian Criminal Justice*, ed. Marianne O. Nielsen and Robert Silverman (Toronto: Butterworths, 1992), 244. See Morton Fried, *The Evolution of Political Society* (New York: Random House, 1967), 90–4, for a criticism of assertions of law in egalitarian societies.
12  Pauline Comeau and Aldo Santin, *The First Canadians: A Profile of Canada's Native People Today* (Toronto: Lorimer, 1995), 160–80.
13  For an example of the federal government's response, see "Prisons Expect More Aboriginal Inmates," *Globe and Mail*, 19 February 1998.
14  This approach is promoted by Royal Commission on Aboriginal Peoples [RCAP], *Report of the Royal Commission on Aboriginal Peoples [Final Report]*, vol. 3, 83–6.
15  Julian V. Roberts and Carol LaPrairie "Sentencing Circles: Some Unanswered Questions," *Criminal Law Quarterly* 39 (1996): 73–4.

16 See, for example, P.J. Hartson, "Equal Justice," *News/North*, 14 October 1996.

17 Carol LaPrairie, in *Aboriginal Peoples and Canadian Criminal Justice*, ed. Silverman and Nielsen, 137–9.

18 Ibid.

19 Tracey Tyler, "Special Toronto Court Planned for Aboriginals," *Toronto Star*, 3 October 2001.

20 For a number of cases that reflect this trend, see C.T. Griffiths and A.L. Patenaude, "Aboriginal Peoples and the Criminal Law," in *Aboriginal Peoples and Canadian Criminal Justice*, ed. Silverman and Nielsen, 1992.

21 L. Sarkadi, "Sex Assaults in North Are Often Less Violent, Judge Says," *Edmonton Journal*, 20 December 1989.

22 Margo L. Nightingale, "Judicial Attitudes and Differential Treatment: Native Women in Sexual Assault Cases," *Ottawa Law Review* 23, no. 1 (1991): 83.

23 Justice de Weerdt, cited in ibid., 87.

24 Bourassa, cited in Northwest Territories, *In the Matter of an Inquiry into the Conduct of Judge R.M. Bourassa*, 28 September 1990, cited in ibid., 90.

25 Justice de Weerdt, cited in Nightingale, "Judicial Attitudes," 91.

26 Jane George, "Accused in Child Sexual Assaults Aquitted [*sic*] in Kuujjuaq," *Nunatsiaq News*, 17 December 1999.

27 *Breaking Free: A Proposal for Change to Aboriginal Family Violence* (Thunder Bay: Ontario Native Women's Association, 1989), 19, cited in Nightingale, "Judicial Attitudes and Differential Treatment," 94.

28 In the most extreme cases, violent resistance occurs. See, for example, "Northern Showdown: The Innu of Davis Inlet Claim a Victory in Their Fight for a New Justice System," *Maclean's* 107, no. 38 (September 19, 1994): 14–15.

29 Emma LaRocque, "Re-Examining Culturally Appropriate Models of Criminal Justice Applications," in *Aboriginal and Treaty Rights in Canada: Essays on Law, Equality, and Respect for Difference*, ed. Michael Asch (Vancouver: University of British Columbia Press, 1997).

30 James [Sakéj] Youngblood Henderson, "First Nations' Legal Inheritances in Canada: The Mikmaq Model," *Manitoba Law Journal* 23 (January 1996); John Burrows, *Indigenous Legal Traditions*, report prepared for the Law Commission of Canada (January 2006), 60.

31 See, for example, Comeau and Santin, *The First Canadians*, 132.

32 Griffiths and Patenaude, "Aboriginal Peoples and the Criminal Law," 72.

33 Franz Boas, *The Central Eskimo* (Lincoln: University of Nebraska Press, 1964), 174; Philip Drucker, *Cultures of the North Pacific Coast* (San Francisco: Chandler, 1965), 73; Elizabeth Dickson-Gilmore, "Resurrecting the

Peace: Traditionalist Approaches to Separate Justice in the Kahnawake Mohawk Nation," in *Aboriginal Peoples and Canadian Criminal Justice*, ed. Silverman and Nielsen, 267–9.

34 Leslie A. White, *The Evolution of Culture* (New York: McGraw-Hill, 1959), 316–17.

35 Mandamin et al., *Justice on Trial Task Force*, 9.

36 "Traditional justice" in the case of the Mohawks, for example, includes the different weighting of crimes depending upon the status of the victim. See Dickson-Gilmore, "Resurrecting the Peace," 259–77.

37 Roberts and LaPrairie, "Sentencing Circles," 81–2.

38 In political economy, this circumstance is referred to as the "relative autonomy" of the law. See Amy Bartholomew and Susan Boyd, "Toward a Political Economy of Law," in *The New Canadian Political Economy*, ed. Wallace Clement and Glen Williams (Montreal: McGill-Queen's University Press, 1989), 218–19.

39 See, for example, Gloria Galloway, "Native-White Justice Drawing Mixed Reviews," CP *Newswire*, 1 February 1995, and John Ibbitson, "The Double Standard on Canada's Reserves," *Globe and Mail*, 21 November 2006.

40 Larry Chartrand and Celeste McKay, "A Review of Research on Criminal Victimization and First Nations, Métis and Inuit Peoples, 1990 to 2001," report prepared for the Policy Centre for Victim Issues, January 2006, 25, 50–2; and Michael Bopp, Judie Bopp, and Phil Lane, Jr., "Aboriginal Domestic Violence in Canada," Aboriginal Healing Foundation Research Series, 2003, 3, 56, 63.

41 Joyce Green, "Constitutionalising the Patriarchy," *Constitutional Forum* 4, no. 4 (summer 1993): 118.

42 See for example "Sentenced to Hunt for Victim," *News/North*, 9 March 1998; "DARE Training Done," *News/North*, 14 December 1998.

43 "Sask. Appeals," *Edmonton Journal*, 24 June 1995.

44 This sentiment was also expressed by Ernie Louttit, a Cree policeman in Saskatchewan (John Stackhouse, "Welcome to Harlem on the Prairies," *Globe and Mail*, 3 November 2001.

45 Nielsen, "Criminal Justice and Native Self-Government," 54.

46 LaRocque, "Re-examining Culturally Appropriate Models," 90. See also Green, "Constitutionalising the Patriarchy," 118, for a discussion of this circumstance.

47 LaRocque, "Re-examining Culturally Appropriate Models," 93.

48 Holly Nathan, "Native Justice System Abused, Critics Charge," *Eye Opener* (1993): 79–80; Galloway, "Native-White Justice Drawing Mixed Reviews"; "Sentencing Circles Need Credibility," *Yellowknifer*, 26 July 1996.

49 Rupert Ross, *Dancing with a Ghost: Exploring Indian Reality* (New York: Butterworth-Heinemann, 1992), 58–9.

50 Ibid., 62.

51 "Three Theories Merge on Alcohol-Violence Link," *The Journal* (Addiction Research Foundation) 25, no. 2 (March/April 1996): 8.

52 Ibid.

53 See, for example, Michael Friscolanti, "Doctor Charged with Abandoning Daughter in Car," *National Post*, 9 May 2001.

54 See, for example, "Chief of Mba's Largest Reserve Pleads Guilty to Pointing Gun at Friend's Head," *Canadian Press Newswire*, 8 June 2001.

55 "Colville Re-Elects Jailed Chief," *News/North*, 19 August 1996.

56 Sean McKibbon, "Former Nunavut Speaker Guilty of Sexual Assault," *Nunatsiaq News*, 18 August 2000.

57 Jane George, "Arrested on Assault Charges, Nunavut's Education Minister Resigns," *Nunatsiaq News*, 1 September 2000.

58 "Open Letter to Paul Okalik," *Nunatsiaq News*, 1 September 2000.

59 Aaron Spitzer, "Arvaluk Acquitted," *Nunatsiaq News*, 22 June 2001.

60 Maria Canton, "Back on Top," *Northern News Services*, 20 December 1999.

61 Jim Bell, "Paul Quassa's 10-Month Credit Card Orgy Revealed," *Nunatsiaq News*, 15 December 2000.

62 Jim Bell, "Paul Quassa to Nunatsiaq News: 'You Hate My Guts, I Know. Sticks and Stones Will Hurt My Bones but Names Will Never Hurt Me,'" *Nunatsiaq News*, 22 December 2000.

63 This, however, concerned relations within the group. In the case of the Cree shortly after contact "it was considered praiseworthy to steal horses, objects or even people from another tribe ... but internally ... there was little or no theft" (Nielsen, "Criminal Justice and Native Self-Government," 250).

64 Michael Robinson, "Joan Ryan (1932–2005)," *Arctic* 59, no. 4 (December 2006): 447–8.

65 Joan Ryan, *Doing Things the Right Way* (Calgary: Arctic Institute of North America, 1995), 87.

66 Ibid., 88.

67 Ibid., 78.

68 Ibid., 79.

69 Ibid., 80

70 Ibid., 79n2, 3.

71 See also Griffiths and Patenaude, "Aboriginal Peoples and the Criminal Law," 72.

72 See also Ryan, *Doing Things the Right Way*, 75n1.

73  Len Kruzenga, "Justice Denied Continues to Haunt," *Windspeaker* 16, no. 11 (March 1999).

74  "New Killer Named in 25-Year-Old Osborne Murder," CP *Newswire*, 27 November 1996.

75  "Sexual Assault – A Brutal Reality," *News/North*, 15 February 1999.

76  Glen Korstrom, "In Mourning: Death Attributed to Alcohol, Not Assault," *News/North*, 30 August 1999.

77  Korstrom, "An Unsettling Death: Initial Finding Supported by RCMP," *News/North*, 6 September 1999.

78  Korstrom, "Stopping Violence: Alcohol Can Be a Mask," *News/North*, 6 September 1999.

79  All interviews except for the meeting with Inspector Popovic took place in September–October 1999.

80  This conversation took place on 29 September 1999.

81  Robert A. Silverman and Marianne O. Nielsen, "Incarceration," in *Aboriginal Peoples and Canadian Criminal Justice*, ed. Nielson and Silverman, 172.

82  McGillivray and Comasky, *Black Eyes All of the Time*, 29. See also John Richards, "Reserves Are Only Good for Some People," *Journal of Canadian Studies*, 35, no. 1 (spring 2000): 190–202.

## CHAPTER SIX

1  Brad Evenson, "The Native Son," *Montreal Gazette*, 18 April 1998.

2  Evenson's account of the Cashore adoption is also very selective. An interview with Cashore's daughter in another article paints a much more positive picture of her adoption. For a more detailed examination of her case, see Deborah Jones, "Canada's Real Adoption Crisis," *Chatelaine* 71, no. 5 (May 1998): 44–5.

3  The argument becomes even more unconvincing when we look at the consequences of Michel Chrétien discovering "who he was." He was back in court in 1996 for assaulting his girlfriend and her son.

4  See, for example, Nancy J. White, "Families by Choice," *Toronto Star*, 22 July 2006.

5  See, for example, Margaret Philp, "The Battle over Native Adoption," *Globe and Mail*, 23 February 1999.

6  More recent coverage of Michel Chrétien generally has continued to perpetuate the "identity crisis" explanation. See, for example, Lawrence Martin, "'We Will Continue to Stand by Him,'" *Globe and Mail*, 30 July 2002. The one journalist who has identified the problem is Margaret Wente, a columnist

who is described as a "contrarian" (Wente, "Searching for a Tragic Link," *Globe and Mail*, 30 July 2002.

7 RCAP, *Report of the Royal Commission on Aboriginal Peoples [Final Report]*, vol. 3, 132–4.

8 "Epidemic of Fetal Alcohol Syndrome Found," *Canadian Press Newswire*, 27 February 1997; David Square, "Fetal Alcohol Syndrome Epidemic on Manitoba Reserve," *Canadian Medical Association Journal* 157, no. 1 (1 July 1997): 59–60; Ian Elliot, "A Dangerous Combination," *News/North*, 17 November 1997.

9 Although finding statistics on the number of aboriginal births in Canada is difficult, it was noted recently that the aboriginal population (not including the Métis) has increased by 19,000 per year, and that there are approximately 330,000 births per year in Canada. Assuming that the aboriginal population increase was due to births, this would make the number of aboriginal births approximately 6 per cent of the national total (Bill Curry, "Rising Number of Natives Creates 'Policy Time Bomb,'" *Globe and Mail*, 16 January 2008).

10 Lutra Associates Ltd., "Damaged and Needing Help," in RCAP, *For Seven Generations* (Ottawa: Libraxis, 1997).

11 Jane Ashley, "Alcohol-Related Birth Defects," in *Aboriginal Substance Use: Research Issues*, ed. Diane McKenzie (Ottawa: Canadian Centre on Substance Abuse, 1992); House of Commons, Report of the Standing Committee on Health and Welfare, Social Affairs, Seniors and the Status of Women, *Foetal Alcohol Syndrome: A Preventable Tragedy* (Ottawa: Supply and Services, 1992); Marilyn Bibber, "FAS among Aboriginal Communities in Canada: A Review of Existing Epidemiological Research and Current Preventative and Intervention Approaches," unpublished research study prepared for the RCAP, 1993. FAS/FAE is also only mentioned briefly in the context of funding arrangements in the Royal Commission's roundtable report on aboriginal health, *The Path to Healing* (Ottawa: Minister of Supply and Services, 1993). It is not mentioned in *Aboriginal Health in Canada: Historical, Cultural, and Epidemiological Perspectives*, by J.B. Waldram, D.A. Herring, and T.K. Young (Toronto: University of Toronto Press, 1995).

12 Standing Committee on Health and Welfare, "Foetal Alcohol Syndrome," 27–8, cited in RCAP, *Final Report*, vol. 3, 134.

13 Van Bibber, "FAS among Aboriginal Communities in Canada," cited in ibid.

14 Standing Committee on Health and Welfare, *Foetal Alcohol Syndrome*, 27–8, cited in ibid. This approach seemed to be undergoing a change in 2001, when $60 million was proposed to address the problem by the Liberal government (Luiza Chwialkowska, "PM Set to Overhaul Native Policy," *National Post*, 8 December 2001).

15 A similar argument is made in Margaret Philp, "Middle Class FAS: A Silent Epidemic?," *Globe and Mail,* 1 February 2003.

16 Square, "Fetal Alcohol Syndrome Epidemic on Manitoba Reserve," 59–60.

17 Suzanne Fournier and Ernie Crey, *Stolen from Our Embrace* (Toronto: Douglas & McIntyre, 1997), 178–9.

18 Ibid., 195.

19 Ibid., 178.

20 Paul Jay, "Program Nurtures a Native Identity, Helping to Prevent Addictions," *Journal of Addiction & Mental Health* 3, no. 5 (September/October 2000): 13.

21 Ian Elliot, "A Dangerous Combination," *News/North,* 17 November 1997.

22 Patrick Johnston, *Native Children and the Child Welfare System* (Toronto: Canadian Council on Social Development, 1983).

23 Fournier and Crey, *Stolen from Our Embrace,* 88.

24 The words "overzealous" are constantly used with respect to social workers in this context. See, for example, Erin Anderssen, "Manitoba Metis Take Foster-Care Protest to the UN," *Globe and Mail,* 5 April 1999 and Philp, "The Battle over Native Adoption."

25 Brad McKenzie and Peter Hudson, "Native Children, Child Welfare and the Colonization of Native People," in *The Challenge of Child Welfare,* ed. Kenneth L. Levitt and Brian Wharf (Vancouver: UBC Press, 1985), 126.

26 Ibid., 129.

27 Ibid., 131–2.

28 See Terry Glavin, *Canadian Geographic* 118, no. 2 (March/April 1998): 18; and Suzanne Methot, *Quill and Quire* 64, no. 1 (January 1998): 28.

29 Fournier and Crey, *Stolen from Our Embrace,* 84–9.

30 See Canadian Welfare Council and Canadian Association of Social Workers, *Joint Submission to the Special Joint Committee of the Senate and the House of Commons Appointed to Examine and Consider the Indian Act* (Ottawa: The Committee, 1947). When this circumstance is mentioned in the literature, however, it is minimized. See, for example, Arthur Milner, "The Sixties Scoop Thirty Years Later," *Inroads* 10 (2001).

31 Fournier and Crey, *Stolen from Our Embrace,* 122–3.

32 Ibid.

33 Ibid., 85. See also Viola Thomas's comments in Paul Barnsley's "Two-Year-Old Could Be Taken."

34 McKenzie and Hudson, "Native Children," 130–1. Fournier and Crey impart this idea with a quote from Wayne Christian who maintains "his mother had almost been destroyed by the removal of her children; although she had not

been alcoholic before, she had turned to drinking as a release" (Fournier and Crey, *Stolen from Our Embrace,* 89).

35 See, for example, Faith Richardson's testimony in ibid., 102. Joyce Timpson, a social worker who undertook research for the Royal Commission, also indicates that "the colonialist and assimilationist explanation of the 'Sixties Scoop' may underplay the reality that Aboriginal families were dealing with the severe disruption caused by social, economic and cultural changes" (RCAP, *Final Report,* vol. 3, 26.

36 Cited in Fournier and Crey, *Stolen from Our Embrace,* 148.

37 RCAP, *Final Report,* vol. 3, 39.

38 McKenzie and Hudson, "Native Children," 137; RCAP, *Final Report,* vol. 3, 30; Fournier and Crey, *Stolen from Our Embrace,* 231.

39 RCAP, *Final Report,* vol. 3, 32.

40 McKenzie and Hudson, "Native Children," 137–8; Margaret Philp, "The Land of Lost Children," *Globe and Mail,* 21 December 2002.

41 Margaret Wente, "Who Cares for Baby Andy?," *Globe and Mail,* 28 September 2002.

42 RCAP, *Final Report,* vol. 3, 165.

43 Fournier and Crey, *Stolen from Our Embrace,* 236.

44 See, for example, Ruth Teichroeb, *Flowers on My Grave: How an Ojibwa Boy's Death Helped Break the Silence on Child Abuse* (Toronto: HarperCollins, 1998), 4.

45 This circumstance is obliquely mentioned by McKenzie and Hudson, who state that "permissiveness in a native family or the independence and autonomy afforded as a young child in self-care or school attendance may create certain problems" ("Native Children," 132). In other words, school attendance in aboriginal communities is sporadic because parents do not provide a structured environment for their children. Margaret Wente also mentions this problem in a column on social dysfunction in the community of Pikangikum. For her analysis, see "Who Will Save Kitty Turtle," *Globe and Mail,* 23 June 2001.

46 Philp, "The Land of Lost Children"; Barbara Jo Fidler, cited in Margaret Wente, "Who Will Save Kitty Turtle?," *Globe and Mail,* 23 June 2001.

47 Rupert Ross, "Leaving Our White Eyes Behind," 148.

48 Ruth Teichroeb, *Flowers on My Grave,* 37–8.

49 Pete Hudson and Brad McKenzie, *Evaluation of Dakota Ojibway Child and Family Services,* prepared for Dakota Ojibway Child and Family Services and Evaluation Branch, Department of Indian Affairs and Northern Development, June 1984.

50 McKenzie and Hudson, "Native Children," 136–7.

51 Ibid., 139.

52 Cited in Teichroeb, *Flowers on my Grave*, 39.

53 Department of Justice, Manitoba, *Report by Provincial Judge Brian Dale Giesbrecht on the Inquest Respecting the Death of Lester Norman Desjarlais*, 31 August 1992.

54 Giesbrecht, cited in Teichroeb, *Flowers on My Grave*, 155.

55 Cook, cited in ibid., 124.

56 Ibid., 139–40.

57 Ibid., 122.

58 Ibid., 101–2.

59 Manitoba, *Report of the First Nations' Child and Family Task Force: Children First – Our Responsibility*, November 1993.

60 Teichroeb, *Flowers on My Grave*, 199.

61 Ibid., 197.

62 Ibid., 198.

63 Pauline Comeau and Aldo Santin, *The First Canadians: A Profile of Canada's Native People Today* (Toronto: Lorimer, 1995), 156.

64 Teichroeb, *Flowers on My Grave*, 173.

65 Ibid., 168.

66 Comeau and Santin, *The First Canadians*, 155, 158.

67 Ibid., 158.

68 Cited in ibid., 151.

69 Ibid., 156.

70 Fournier and Crey, *Stolen from Our Embrace*, 142, 108–9.

71 See, for example, Philp, "The Land of Lost Children"; Wente, "Who Cares for Baby Andy"; and Mary Jo LaForest, "Father Jailed in Death of Son Left Unsupervised," *Toronto Star*, 3 May 2001.

### CHAPTER SEVEN

1 Angus Graham, *The Golden Grindstone: The Adventures of George Mitchell* (Toronto: Oxford University Press, 1935), 191–2.

2 Ibid., 192–3.

3 Jennifer Pritchett, "Surgery Performed on the Land," *News/North*, 16 November 1998.

4 John D. O'Neil and Brian D. Postl, "Community Healing and Aboriginal Self-Government: Is the Circle Closing?" in *Aboriginal Self-Government in Canada*, ed. John H. Hylton (Saskatoon: Purich Publishing, 1994), 67–8; Pauline Comeau and Also Santin, *The First Canadians: A Profile of Canada's Native People Today* (Toronto: Lorimer, 1995); James B. Waldram et al.,

*Aboriginal Health in Canada* (Toronto: University of Toronto Press, 1995), ix, 3; RCAP, *Report of the Royal Commission on Aboriginal Peoples [Final Report]*, vol. 3, 107–11; Erin Anderssen, "Aboriginal Health Far Below Standard," *Globe and Mail*, 25 September 2003.

5  Comeau and Santin, *The First Canadians*, 105.

6  Elizabeth Roberts, "Health Care Providers: The Solution or the Problem?," in *Health Care Issues in the Canadian North*, ed. David E. Young (Edmonton: Boreal Institute for Native Studies, 1988), 128; Louis T. Montour, introduction, RCAP, *The Path to Healing* (Ottawa: Ministry of Supplies and Services, 1993), 9–12.

7  See, for example, the arguments of Matthew Coon Come in "Brave Words from a Native Leader," *Toronto Star*, 2 March 2001.

8  O'Neil and Postl, "Community Healing and Aboriginal Self-Government, 82.

9  Ibid., 68–9.

10  See, for example, RCAP, *Final Report*, vol. 3, 111–13.

11  Diamond, *Guns, Germs and Steel* (New York: W.W. Norton, 1999), 195–238; and Waldram et al., *Aboriginal Health in Canada*, 24–5.

12  Pekka Kuusi, *This World of Man* (London: A. Wheaton and Co., 1985), 76–7.

13  Leslie A. White, *The Evolution of Culture* (New York: McGraw-Hill, 1959), 277.

14  David E. Young et al., "The Psoriasis Research Project: An Overview," in *Health Care Issues in the Canadian North*, ed. D. Young, 76–80; Rachael Jalan, "Integrating Science and Traditional Culture," in RCAP, *The Path to Healing*, 215; and RCAP, *Final Report*, vol. 1, 628–31.

15  Waldram et al., *Aboriginal Health in Canada*, 102.

16  White, *The Evolution of Culture*, 277; for an in-depth discussion of such practices, see W.H.R. Rivers, *Medicine, Magic and Religion* (London: Kegan Paul, Trench, Trubner & Co., 1924).

17  Keith Thomas, *Religion and the Decline of Magic* (New York: Oxford University Press, 1997).

18  Wee-Chong Tan, *Emotions in Yin-Yang and Five Elements System*, 1997, unpublished pamphlet (in authors' possession).

19  Roy Conlogue, "Sure It's Art, but Is It Medicine?," *Globe and Mail*, 7 March 2003.

20  RCAP, *Final Report*, vol. 3, 348; Waldram et al., *Aboriginal Health in Canada*, 99–100.

21  O'Neil and Postl, "Community Healing and Aboriginal Self-Government," 79.

22  Ibid., 68.

23  Waldram et al., *Aboriginal Health in Canada*, 216.

24 See, for example, Jane Gadd, "'Faith Healer' Jailed for Sexual Assault of Girl," *Globe and Mail,* 17 October 2002.

25 See "Referrals to Traditional Healers," in *Health Care Issues in the Canadian North*, ed. Young, 32–3.

26 See, for example, ibid., 35.

27 Waldram et al., *Aboriginal Health in Canada,* 86.

28 RCAP, *Final Report,* vol. 3, chapter 3.

29 RCAP, *Final Report,* vol. 1, 648; Young et al., "The Psoriasis Research Project," 79.

30 Celia Haig-Brown, Kathy Hodgson-Smith, Robert Regnier, and Jo-ann Archibald, eds., *Making the Spirit Dance Within* (Toronto: Lorimer, 1997), 39.

31 Comeau and Santin, *The First Canadians,* 106; Waldram et al., *Aboriginal Health in Canada,* 84.

32 Comeau and Santin, *The First Canadians,* 111.

33 O'Neil and Postl, "Community Healing and Aboriginal Self-Government," 73.

34 RCAP, *Final Report,* vol. 3, 110–11.

35 Comeau and Santin, *The First Canadians,* 120.

36 RCAP, *Final Report,* vol. 3, 110.

37 Ibid., 229.

38 RCAP, *Final Report,* vol. 3, 348, 361.

39 Ibid., 357.

40 O'Neil and Postl, "Community Healing and Aboriginal Self-Government, 81.

41 O'Neil, "Referrals to Traditional Healers," 35.

42 Rebecca Caldwell, "Ancient Homegrown Secrets," *Globe and Mail,* 2 July 2002.

43 Young et al., "The Psoriasis Research Project," 83–4n2.

44 See Haig-Brown et al., *Making the Spirit Dance Within,* 47; Young et al., "The Psoriasis Research Project," 79; RCAP, *Final Report,* vol. 3, 226; and Waldram et al., *Aboriginal Health in Canada,* 101.

45 Robert Dale Rogers, "The Case for Alternative Medicine," in *Health Care Issues in the Canadian North*, ed. D. Young, 15.

46 David E. Young, "Part I: Orthodox vs. Alternative Medicine: An Evolving Relationship," in *Health Care Issues in the Canadian North*, ed. D. Young, 7.

47 Theodore Mala, "Traditional versus Non-Traditional Medicine," in *Health Care Issues in the Canadian North*, ed. D. Young, 45.

48 RCAP, *Final Report,* vol. 3, 357.

49 John Ruscio, "The Emptiness of Holism," *Skeptical Inquirer* 26, no. 2 (March/April 2002): 49–50.

50 K.A. Scott, "Funding Policy for Indigenous Human Services," in RCAP, *The Path to Healing*, 91; Waldram et al., *Aboriginal Health in Canada*, 86, 121; and RCAP, *Final Report*, vol. 3, 226–7.

51 See, for example, Caldwell, "Ancient Homegrown Secrets."

52 James S. McCormack, "To Wear the White Coat: Options for Traditional Healers in a Canadian Medical Future," in *Health Care Issues in the Canadian North*, ed. D. Young, 8–10.

53 Kimball C. Atwood, "Bioterrorism and the NCCAM," *Skeptical Inquirer* 26, no. 2 (March/April 2002): 18.

54 Ibid., 75–6.

55 Ibid., 83.

56 Richard Schultes and Siri Von Reis, introduction to *Ethnobotany: Evolution of a Discipline*, ed. Schultes and Von Reis (New York: Timber Press, 1995), 11–12.

57 Ethnobotany also consists of the more legitimate study of the *uses* of plants by aboriginal tribes. It is not this aspect of ethnobotany that we are taking issue with here but claims about aboriginal peoples' pharmacological knowledge of the properties of plants, and that this knowledge has been useful to modern medicine.

58 E. Wade Davis, "An Old Practice, A New Discipline," in *Ethnobotany*, ed. Schultes and Von Reis, 40.

59 Ibid., 47.

60 RCAP, *Final Report*, vol. 3, 112n9.

61 Dickason, *Canada's First Nations, A History of Founding Peoples from Earliest Times* (Toronto: McClelland & Stewart, 1994), 43–4, cited in RCAP, *Final Report*, vol. 3, chapter 3, s.1.2.

62 Virgil J. Vogel, *American Indian Medicine* (Norman: University of Oklahoma Press, 1970), 9; Daniel E. Moermon, *Medicinal Plants of Native America*, 2 vols. (Ann Arbor, University of Michigan Museum of Anthropology Technical Report No. 19, 1986); Charles H. Talbot, "America and the European Drug Trade," *First Images* 2: 813–32; Alfred Goldsworthy Bailey, *The Conflict of European and Eastern Algonkian Cultures, 1504–1700*, 2nd ed. (Toronto: University of Toronto Press, 1969), 120–1.

63 Waldram et al., *Aboriginal Health in Canada*, 104.

64 Ibid., 105.

65 This list was compiled from an analysis of Virgil J. Vogel's "American Indian Contributions to Pharmacology," in *American Indian Medicine*, 267–414.

66 V. Gordon Childe, *Man Makes Himself* (London: Watts & Co., 1936), 175.

67 Richard Schultes, *Where the Gods Reign* (Arizona: Synergetic Press, 1988).

68 "Drug," *Encyclopaedia Britannica Online,* 28 March 2007, http://www.search.eb.com/eb/article-9106187.

69 Atwood, for example, maintains that one of the dubious claims of complementary and alternative medicine is that "long-used botanical products, ignored by the pharmaceutical industry, are likely to yield powerful new therapies" (Atwood, "Bioterrorism and NCCAM," 18).

70 Schultes and Von Reis, introduction, *Ethnobotany,* 12.

71 Ibid., 21.

72 Ibid., 73.

73 RCAP, *Final Report,* vol. 3, 352.

74 Priscilla George and Barbra Nahwegahbow, "Anishnawbe Health," in RCAP, *The Path to Healing,* 242.

75 See, for example, "Matthew Coon Come, "Brave Words from a Native Leader," *The Toronto Star,* 2 March 2001.

## CHAPTER EIGHT

1 Carl Sagan, *The Dragons of Eden* (New York: Ballantyne Books, 1977), 202.

2 Ibid., 201–2.

3 The words "cognitive imperialism" were used by Marrie Battiste and cited in RCAP, *Report of the Royal Commission on Aboriginal Peoples [Final Report],* vol. 3, 464.

4 See ibid., chapter 3, for an overview of some of the problems.

5 John Richards and Aidan Vining, "Aboriginal Off-Reserve Education: A Time for Action," C.D. Howe Institute Commentary 198 (April 2004), 5–7.

6 Ibid.

7 Michael Mendelson, "Aboriginal Peoples and Postsecondary Education in Canada," Caledon Institute of Social Policy, July 2006, 16, http://www.caledoninst.org/Publications/.

8 For a discussion of special "aboriginal" programs, see RCAP, *Final Report,* vol. 3, 490–8.

9 For extensive examples of this position see K.P. Binda and Sharilyn Calliou, eds., *Aboriginal Education in Canada: A Study in Decolonization* (Mississauga: Canadian Educators' Press, 2001).

10 See Lenore A. Stiffarm, ed., *As We See It: Aboriginal Pedagogy* (Saskatoon: University of Saskatchewan Press, 1998) for various proponents of this view.

11 National Indian Brotherhood, *Indian Control over Indian Education* (Ottawa: National Indian Brotherhood, 1972), 3.

12 Eber Hampton and Steven Wolfson, "Education for Self-Determination," in *Aboriginal Self-Government in Canada*, ed. John Hylton (Saskatoon: Purich Publishing, 1994), 92–3.

13 See, for example, Celia Haig-Brown, Kathy Hodgson-Smith, Robert Regnier, and Jo-ann Archibald, eds., *Making the Spirit Dance Within*, 33–43; and Brenda Tsioniaon LaFrance, "Culturally Negotiated Education in First Nation Communities, Empowering Ourselves for Future Generations," in *For Seven Generations* (Ottawa: Libraxis, 1997).

14 Sharilyn Calliou, "Activism and Self-Determination in Education," in *Aboriginal Self-Government in Canada,* ed. J. Hylton, 179–80.

15 See, for example, Lillian E. Dyck, "An Analysis of Western, Feminist and Aboriginal Science Using the Medicine Wheel of the Plains Indians," *Native Studies Review* 11, no. 2 (1996).

16 Dyck, "Analysis of Western, Feminist and Aboriginal Science," 97.

17 Jane Harp, "Traditional Parenting," in *As We See It*, ed. L. Stiffarm, 67–9.

18 Ida Swan, "Modelling: An Aboriginal Approach," in Stiffarm, ed., *As We See It,* 49–58.

19 Robert Leavitt, "Language and Cultural Content in Native Education," in *First Nations Education in Canada: The Circle Unfolds*, ed. Marie Battiste and Jean Barman (Vancouver: UBC Press, 1995), 130.

20 Ibid., 132. See also Madeleine McIvor, "Redefining Science Education for Aboriginal Students," in *First Nations Education in Canada*, ed. Battiste and Barman, 77.

21 Paul Nadasdy, *Hunters and Bureaucrats* (Vancouver: UBC Press, 2003, 97–101.

22 Leavitt, "Language and Cultural Content," 128.

23 Ibid., 130–1.

24 John Taylor, "Non-Native Teachers Teaching in Native Communities," in *First Nations Education in Canada,* ed. Battiste and Barman, 101–12.

25 McIvor, "Redefining Science Education for Aboriginal Students," 80.

26 Robert Leavitt, "Language and Cultural Content in Native Education, in *Aboriginal Languages and Education*," ed. S. Morris et al., 125.

27 Mike McNeney, "Making Minds Strong," *UVic Torch Alumni Magazine* (autumn 2002), 4.

28 Eber Hampton, "Towards a Redefinition of Indian Education," in *First Nations Education in Canada*, ed. Battiste and Barman, 6–7.

29 Margaret Mead, *Continuities in Cultural Evolution* (New Haven: Yale University Press, 1964). See also J.R. Miller, *Shingwauk's Vision: A History of Native Residential Schools* (Toronto: University of Toronto Press, 1996).

30 The problems of "lack of supervision" and neglect were also identified by government authorities in the late 1960s and early 1970s. See RCAP, *Final Report*, vol. 1, 349n99–102.

31 "Time Is a Culture Thing," editorial, *Northern News Services Online,* Monday, 4 September 2000, http://www.nnsl.com/frames/newspapers/2000-09/sep4_00edit.html (accessed March 2002).

32 Editorial, *Northern News Services Online,* 22 October 1999, http://www.nnsl.com/frames/newspapers/1999-10/oct25_99edit.html (accessed March 2002).

33 Maryanne Wolf, *Proust and the Squid* (New York: HarperCollins, 2007), 65–6.

34 This aspect of the evolution of knowledge is obscured by criticisms that scientific research is "compartmentalized." See, for example, Nadasdy, *Hunters and Bureaucrats,* 123–6.

35 *Toronto Star,* 20 March 2001.

36 See, for example, "At Nunavut U, It's Come As You Are," *Globe and Mail,* 2 March 2001.

37 John Geddes, "Northern Son," *Maclean's,* 23 April 2001, 18.

38 The best example of such an "evaluation" is Haig-Brown et al., *Making the Spirit Dance Within.*

39 For a discussion of the importance of testing, see Norman Henchey, "Aboriginal Education," *Society for the Advancement of Excellence in Education,* www.saee.ca/policy/d_073_HHH_LON.php (accessed March 2007).

40 See, for example, RCAP, *Final Report*, vol. 3, 462.

41 National Indian Brotherhood, *Indian Control over Indian Education,* 10.

42 Deborah L. Begoray, "Reading Tests Flawed," *Times-Colonist,* 17 November 2001.

43 Band-operated schools on reserves that are governed under the Indian Act do not participate in standardized testing or publish student results (Janet Steffenhagen, *Vancouver Sun,* 9 February 2006), and currently only the province of British Columbia tracks aboriginal educational performance in the mainstream educational system ("Literacy among Aboriginal Children," *Globe and Mail,* 14 January 2008).

44 Low educational levels, in fact, are obscured by the promotion of "storytelling" as a form of "aboriginal pedagogy." MaryAnne Lanigan, for example, maintains that students were able to answer more questions correctly after listening to a story than when reading one silently to themselves. Although Lanigan concludes that this shows "the importance of storytelling for all students, but especially for students who are having difficulties," what it actually

indicates is the low literacy level in her class (Lanigan, "Aboriginal Pedagogy: Storytelling," in *As We See It,* ed. L. Stiffarm, 112–13).

45 Morris, McLeod, and Danesi, eds., *Aboriginal Languages and Education,* i.

46 Sagan, *The Dragons of Eden,* 4, 26.

47 V. Gordon Childe, *Man Makes Himself* (London: Watts and Co, 1936), 144–5.

48 Alexander von Gernet, *Oral Narratives and Aboriginal Pasts: An Interdisciplinary Review of the Literature on Oral Traditions and Oral Histories* (Ottawa: Department of Indian and Northern Affairs, 1996), 11.

49 Wolf, Proust and the Squid, 7.

50 Indigenous Knowledge Systems Research Colloqium, January 20–22, 2005, Alaska Native Science Association, www.nativescience.org/pubs, 12 (accessed March 2007).

51 See Lanigan, "Aboriginal Pedagogy," 108; RCAP, *Final Report,* vol. 3, 464; Earl Shorris, "The Last Word: Can the World's Small Languages Be Saved?," *Harper's* (August 2000): 35–43.

52 Walter J. Ong, *Orality and Literacy* (New York: Methuen, 1988), 15, 52, 57, 174.

53 I.J. Gelb, *A Study of Writing* (University of Chicago Press, 1963).

54 The rebus principle occurs when a picture that refers to a concept is used to represent the same sound that is present in another word (for example, a picture of an eye being used to represent the word "I"). See Andrew Robinson, *The Story of Writing* (London: Thames and Hudson, 1995), 42.

55 For Gelb's views on the evolution of writing, see his *A Study of Writing,* 190–8.

56 Robinson, *The Story of Writing,* 185.

57 The largest vocabulary among the alphabetic languages is English, which has between 500,000 and 1,000,000 words. This is in contrast to 185,000 words in German and about 100,000 for French. For a discussion of this point, see Robert McCrum, Robert MacNeil, and William Cran, *The Story of English* (New York: Penguin, 1992), 1–2.

58 Edmund Peck, *Eskimo-English Dictionary* (Hamilton: Anglican Church of Canada, 1925).

59 Dickason, *Canada's First Nations, A History of Founding Peoples from Earliest Times* (Toronto: McClelland & Stewart, 1994), 241–2; Keith J. Crowe, *The History of the Original Peoples of Northern Canada* (Montreal: McGill-Queen's University Press, 1986), 146–7.

60 See John Price, *Indians of Canada: Cultural Dynamics* (Englewood Cliffs: Prentice-Hall, 1979), 33, and Arthur Thibert, introduction to *English-Eskimo, Eskimo-English Dictionary* (Ottawa: Canadian Research Centre for Anthropology, 1970), for a discussion of this point.

61 Ann Meekitjuk Hanson, with contributions from Joe Otokiak, "Language," www.nunavut.com (accessed March 2002).

62 Allice Legat, ed., *Report of the Traditional Knowledge Working Group* (Northwest Territories: Culture and Communications, 1991), 1.

63 There is also the problem in the translation of aboriginal languages that different translators will come up with very different interpretations of the same text. See, for example, "Matter of Interpretation," *News/North*, 10 November 1997.

64 Doug Ashbury, "Legal Languages a World Apart," *News/North*, 24 November 1997.

65 Personal communication with Betty Harnum, language commissioner of the Northwest Territory, August 1994.

66 See, for example, David Crystal, *Language Death* (Cambridge: Cambridge University Press, 2001).

67 Diamond Jenness, *The Indians of Canada* (Toronto: University of Toronto Press, 1977), 22.

68 The evolution of mathematics is a major difference between pre-literate and modern languages. Price notes that in Inuktitut, for example, amounts are clumped together in a way that makes simple arithmetic impossible (Price, *Indians of Canada*, 31–2). Hunter-gatherers only having numbers for "one," "two," and "many" also has been noted by Napoleon Chagnon in the case of the Yanomamö, a primitive tribe in the Amazon rainforest. According to Chagnon, "linguistically, and this is not unusual, their ways of evaluating and enumerating things in the external world are more based on the specific properties of things; like the arrow that has a slight bend in it, or the arrow that has a scorch mark on it. If you show a Yanomamö ten arrows, and you decide to steal one from him, he will notice immediately that it has gone because he recognizes the arrow by its individual properties. But they have no way of saying: 'I have ten arrows.' They will say. 'More than two arrows.' In their language the words they have for enumerating objects are 'one,' 'two,' and then 'bruka,' and bruka can mean anything from three to three-million" (Napoleon Chagnon, "Then You Are in Bad Luck," http://www.froes.dds.nl/CHAGNON.htm, accessed 16 February 2008).

69 It has been discovered, in fact, that pre-literate languages, in general, tend to have only two to four words for different colours. See Philip E. Ross, "Draining the Language out of Colour," *Scientific American* (April 2004).

70 Jenness, *The Indians of Canada*, 24–5.

71 Ibid., 25.

72 Steven Pinker, *The Language Instinct* (New York: Harper Perennial, 1995).

73 Anthony C. Woodbury, University of Texas at Austin, "Counting Eskimo Words for Snow"; Lexemes refers to snow and snow-related notions in Steven

A. Jacobson's (1984) *Yup'ik Eskimo Dictionary*, July 1991,
www.linguistlist.org/issues/5/5-1239.html (accessed March 2002).

74 Childe, *Man Makes Himself*, 32; John R. Baker, *Race* (Oxford: Oxford University Press, 1975, 500–2); and Price, *Indians of Canada*, 30.

75 Scott Heron, "Snow Job," www.herodios.com/snowjob.html (accessed March 2002).

76 W. Wayt Gibbs, "Saving Languages," *Scientific American* (August 2002): 79–83.

77 Canadian Linguistic Association, Committee on Endangered Languages, www.ucs.mun.ca/~cdyck/ab.lang.html/aboutcommittee.html (accessed March 2002).

78 Megan Crowhurst, "The LSA Committee on Endangered Languages and Their Preservation," paper presented at the workshop on Web-Based Language Documentation and Description, 12–15 December 2000, Philadelphia, www.ldc.upenn.edu/exploration/expl2000/papers/crowhurst/crowhurst.htm (accessed March 2002).

79 See, for example, Earl Shorris, "Can the World's Small Languages Be Saved?," *Harper's* (August 2000), 35–43; Thomas Homer-Dixon, "We Need a Forest of Tongues," *Globe and Mail*, 7 July 2001.

## CHAPTER NINE

1 George Manuel and Michael Posluns, *The Fourth World* (Toronto: Collier-Macmillan, 1974).

2 Peter McFarlane, *From Brotherhood to Nationhood* (Toronto: Between the Lines, 1993).

3 Frances Widdowson and Albert Howard, "Natural Stewards or Profit Makers," *Globe and Mail*, 2 May 1998.

4 All e-mail correspondence in this section is in the authors' possession.

5 *Salt Lake City Tribune*, 1 January 1999.

6 David Orton, "My Path to Left Biocentrism: Part 4 – Aboriginal Issues and Left Biocentrism," *Green Web Bulletin* 71, http://fox.nstn.ca/~greenweb/GW71-Path.html (accessed November 1998), 6.

7 For a detailed criticism of the existence of an aboriginal "conservation ethic," see Frances Widdowson, "Aboriginal Rights and Canadian Environmental Policy: Enhancing Sustainability or a Justification of Deregulation?," unpublished paper presented at the Annual Meeting of the Canadian Political Science Association, University of Saskatchewan, May 2007.

8 Fred Plain, "A Treatise on the Rights of Aboriginal Peoples of the Continent of North America," in *The Quest for Justice: Aboriginal Peoples and Aborigi-*

*nal Rights*, ed. Menno Boldt and J. Anthony Long (Toronto: University of Toronto Press, 1985), 34; Winona LaDuke, "Social Justice, Racism and the Environmental Movement," 28 September 1993, www.zmag.org/zmag/articles/barladuke.htm (accessed November 2006); and Jace Weaver, ed., *Defending Mother Earth: Native American Perspectives on Environmental Justice* (New York: Orbis Books, 1996).

9 Royal Commission on Aboriginal Peoples [RCAP], *Report of the Royal Commission on Aboriginal Peoples [Final Report]*, vol. 2: 2, chapter 4, section 3.2; E.E. Sherry and H.M. Myers, "Traditional Knowledge in Practice," *Society and Natural Resources* 15, no. 4 (2002): 354; Sherrie Blakney, "Aboriginal Forestry in New Brunswick," *Environments* 31, no. 1 (2003); Ian Keay and Cherie Metcalf, "Aboriginal Rights, Customary Law and the Economics of Renewable Resource Exploitation," *Canadian Public Policy* 30, no. 1 (March 2004): 3–5.

10 LaDuke, "Social Justice, Racism, and the Environmental Movement."

11 J.R. Miller, *Skyscrapers Hide the Heavens* (Toronto: University of Toronto Press, 1989), 17; Oren Lyons, "Traditional Native Philosophies Relating to Aboriginal Rights," in *The Quest for Justice*, ed. Boldt and Long, 20.

12 See, for example, H.A. Feit, "James Bay Cree Indian Management and Moral Considerations of Fur-Bearers," in *Native People and Renewable Resource Management* (Edmonton: Alberta Native Affairs, 1986), 49–65; Fikret Berkes, "Fishery Resource Use in a Subarctic Indian Community," *Human Ecology* 5, no. 4 (1977).

13 "Deep ecology" is essentially a philosophy that maintains that environmental destruction is due to a decline of spiritual values in the world today that prevents us from valuing nature for its own sake. For a discussion of this philosophy, see George Sessions, ed., *Deep Ecology for the 21st Century* (Boston: Shambhala, 1995).

14 See, for example, Bruce G. Trigger, "Ontario Native People and the Epidemics of 1634–1640," in Shepard Krech III, ed., *Indians, Animals and the Fur Trade* (Athens: University of Georgia Press, 1981), 27–8. The Jesuit Father Paul Le Jeune, for example, suggested designating particular territories to Montagnais families so that each would have "its own territory for hunting, without following in the tracks of its neighbours." As the Montagnais killed all beavers present in a lodge, he also attempted to instruct them "not to kill any but the males and of those only such as are large." In the case of caribou herds, there are cases of massive overkill and waste, including the killing of pregnant cows, and references to the fact that traders "reproved" Cree hunters when they "uselessly destroy'd" the herds (Krech, *The Ecological Indian*, 182, 185–6). Government officials also suggested imparting ideas of

conservation to the aboriginal population. With respect to the Inuit in the early 1920s, dominion government entomologist and conservationist C. Gordon Hewitt noted that "some of the Eskimo tribes entertain a belief that the caribou are sent to them by the spirit world to kill, and that unless they kill every caribou they meet, whether they require it or not for food or clothing, the spirit world will not send them any more." This belief, in Hewitt's view, "naturally leads to wasteful slaughter on the part of the Eskimos, and it is to be hoped that missionaries and others will endeavor to dispel such a pernicious idea" (C. Gordon Hewitt, *The Conservation of Wild Life in Canada* (New York: Charles Scribner's Sons, 1921), 12, 66, 286).

15 Stevenson, "The Possibility of Difference: Rethinking Co-Management," *Human Organization* (summer 2006).

16 This point was made succinctly by the frontier historian W.H. Hutchinson in his "The Remaking of the Amerind: A Dissenting Voice Raised against the Resurrection of the Myth of the Noble Savage," *Westways* (October 1972). For an elaboration of his views see Calvin Martin, "The War between Indians and Animals," in Shepard Krech III, ed., *Indians, Animals and the Fur Trade*, 13–14.

17 Shepard Krech, ed., *The Ecological Indian: Myth and History* (New York: W.W. Norton, 1999), 201–3.

18 Ibid., 203.

19 V. Gordon Childe, *Man Makes Himself* (London: Watts and Co., 1936), 61.

20 For a discussion of this point, see *The Ecological Indian*, ed. S. Krech, 203–4.

21 Krech, "'Throwing Bad Medicine': Sorcery, Disease, and the Fur Trade among the Kutchin and Other Northern Athapaskans," in *Indians, Animals and the Fur Trade*, ed. S. Krech, 87.

22 Stella Spak, "The Position of Indigenous Knowledge in Canadian Co-Management Organizations," *Anthropologica* 47, no. 2 (2005): 238.

23 Krech, *The Ecological Indian*, 33–4.

24 For a discussion, see Tom Flanagan, *First Nations? Second Thoughts* (Montreal: McGill-Queen's University Press, 2000), 12–13; Jared Diamond, *Guns, Germs and Steel* (New York: Norton, 1999), 46–7; and Bishop, "Northeastern Concepts of Conservation and the Fur Trade," in *Indians, Animals and the Fur Trade*, ed. Krech, 54.

25 For a series of essays on this subject, see *Indians, Animals and the Fur Trade* ed. S. Krech.

26 A government biologist, for example, noted decades ago that "there is no major instance on record where Treaty Indians have shown restraint in caribou hunting unless it has been imposed on them ... by authorities concerned with the welfare of caribou." See Kelsall, *The Migratory Barren-Ground*

*Caribou,* 286, cited in John Sandlos, "From the Outside Looking In: Aesthetics, Politics and Wildlife Conservation in the Canadian North," *Environmental History* 6, no. 1 (January 2001).

27 Cited in Rudoph Kaiser, "'A Fifth Gospel, Almost,'" in *Indians and Europe,* ed. Christian Feest (Omaha: University of Nebraska Press, 1989), 522.

28 Ibid., 505.

29 Donald A. Grinde and Bruce E. Johansen, *Ecocide of North America* (Santa Fe: Clear Light, 1995), 25.

30 Peter Knudtson and David Suzuki, *Wisdom of the Elders* (Toronto: Greystone, 1992), xvi.

31 Daniel Francis, *The Imaginary Indian: The Image of the Indian in Canadian Culture* (Vancouver: Arsenal Pulp Press, 1992), 141.

32 Henry A. Smith, "Scraps from a Diary: Chief Seattle – A Gentleman by Instinct, *Seattle Sunday Star,* 29 October 1887.

33 See also Grinde and Johansen, *Ecocide,* 38.

34 Knudtson and Suzuki, *Wisdom of the Elders,* xiii.

35 Sam Gill, "Mother Earth: An American Myth," in *The Invented Indian: Cultural Fictions and Government Policies,* ed. James Clifton (New Brunswick, N.J.): Transaction Publishers, 1996, 129–43.

36 J.W. MacMurray, "The Dreamers of the Columbia River Valley, in Washington Territory," *Transactions of the Albany Institute, 1887,* 247–8, cited in Gill, "Mother Earth," 129, 131.

37 See, for example, James Tully, *Strange Multiplicity: Constitutionalism in an Age of Diversity* (Cambridge: Cambridge University Press), 1995, 209.

38 Knudtson and Suzuki, *Wisdom of the Elders,* xxxii–xxxiv.

39 Cited in Jonathan Kay, "The Case for Assimiliation," *National Post,* 8 December 2001.

40 Knudtson and Suzuki, *Wisdom of the Elders,* xxxi–xxxii.

41 Benoit Aubin, "Dancing with the Enemy: After Three Decades of Strife, Quebec and the Cree Sign a Historic Agreement," *Maclean's* 115, no. 7 (18 February 2002): 20.

42 Rhéal Séguin, "Troubled Waters," *Globe and Mail,* 19 December 2006.

43 For example, after Dogrib Grand Chief Joe Rabsesca signed an Impact and Benefit Agreement, he noted that "We have always been open for business" ("BHP, Inuit Sign IBA," *News/North,* 14 December 1998.

44 Even if land claims have been settled, there can be aboriginal opposition if additional government funds are not forthcoming. See, for example, Steven Chase, "NWT Premier Requests Aid for Region," *Globe and Mail,* 5 February 2002.

45 Greg Poelzer, "Aboriginal Peoples and Canadian Environmental Policy: No Longer at the Margins," in *Canadian Environmental Policy: Context and*

*Cases*, ed. Debora L. VanNijnatten and Robert Boardman, 2nd ed. (Toronto: Oxford University Press, 2002), 88.

46 This is also the case with respect to commercial fishing on the West Coast. When the Fraser River was closed to commercial sockeye salmon fishing due to dwindling stocks, natives were allowed to continue to fish for food. This led a retailer to buy fish from native fishermen (Steven Chase, "DFO Seizes Salmon from B.C. Warehouse," *Globe and Mail,* 4 December 1999).

47 "When a Whale Is a Culture," *Globe and Mail,* 2 October 1998.

48 This is the conclusion of the Sea Shepherd Society, which claims to have obtained documentation through the Freedom of Information Act (U.S.) in October 1998, revealing the Makah Tribal Council's plans to start a whaling industry with Norway and Japan as clients (Sea Shepherd Conservation Society, "Makah Grey Whale Hunt to Be First Step in Commercial Enterprise," 23 October 1998). This document is in the authors' possession.

49 RCAP, *Final Report,* vol. 3, 188; Christian Huot, "Of Mines and Indians," *Canadian Dimension* 31, no. 2 (March/April, 1997): 21–3.

## CHAPTER TEN

1 Heather Busch and Burton Silver, *Why Cats Paint: A Theory of Feline Aesthetics* (California: Ten Speed Press, 1994).

2 Ibid., 8.

3 Ibid., 9.

4 Stephen C. Ellis, "Meaningful Consideration? A Review of Traditional Knowledge in Environmental Decision Making," *Arctic* 58, no. 1 (2005): 66–77; Henry P. Huntington, "Using Traditional Ecological Knowledge in Science: Methods and Applications," *Ecological Adaptations* 10, no. 5 (October 2005): 1270–4; Brenda Parlee et al., "Using Traditional Knowledge to Adapt to Ecological Change: Denesoline Monitoring of Caribou Movements," *Arctic* 58, no. 1 (2005): 26; Royal Commission on Aboriginal Peoples [RCAP], *Report of the Royal Commission on Aboriginal Peoples [Final Report]* (Ottawa: Supply and Services, 1996), vol. 1, 640.

5 Paul Sillitoe, "The Development of Indigenous Knowledge: A New Applied Anthropology," *Current Anthropology* 39, no. 2 (1998): 226; Fikret Berkes et al., introduction to *Navigating Social Ecological Systems* edited by Fikret Berkes et al. (Cambridge: Cambridge University Press, 2003); and P. O'B. Lyver and Lutsel K'e Dene First Nation, "Monitoring Barren-Ground Caribou Body Condition with Denesoline Traditional Knowledge," *Arctic* 58, no. 1 (2004): 44–5.

6 RCAP, *Final Report,* 4, 128.

7 Gregory Cajete, *Native Science: Natural Laws of Independence* (Santa Fe: Clear Light Publishers, 2000).

8 Winona LaDuke, "Social Justice, Racism and the Environmental Movement," 28 September 1993, www.zmag.org/zmag/articles/barladuke.htm (accessed November 2006); Deborah McGregor, "Traditional Ecological Knowledge," *Atlantis* 29, no. 2 (2005): 2–3.

9 Alan Reid et al., "Traditional Ecological Knowledge for Learning with Sustainability in Mind," *The Trumpeter* 18, no. 1 (2002): 2–8.

10 Fikret Berkes et al., "Rediscovery of Traditional Ecological Knowledge as Adaptive Management," *Ecological Adaptations* 10, no. 5 (2000): 1252; Ellis, "Meaningful Consideration?" 72.

11 Peggy Brizinski, *Knots in a String* (Saskatoon: University Extension Press, 1993).

12 Paul Nadasdy, *Hunters and Bureaucrats* (Vancouver: UBC Press, 2003), 84; and Gary P. Kofinas, "Caribou Hunters and Researchers at the Co-Management Interface: Emergent Dilemmas and the Dynamics of Legitimacy in Power Sharing," *Anthropologica* 47, no. 2 (2005): 184.

13 Peter Usher, "Traditional Knowledge in Environmental Assessment and Management," *Arctic* 53, no. 2 (2000): 191–2; Russel Lawrence Barsh, "Taking Indigenous Science Seriously," in *Biodiversity in Canada: Ecology, Ideas, Action*, ed. Stephen Bocking (Toronto: Broadview Press, 2000), 155–6. Marie Battiste and James Youngblood Henderson even oppose determining a definition in the first place since this is a "eurocentric" impulse that must be "decolonized." See Marie Battiste and James Youngblood Henderson, *Protecting Indigenous Knowledge and Heritage* (Saskatoon: Purich Publishing, 2000), 36–8.

14 E. Bielawski, "Inuit Indigenous Knowledge and Science in the Arctic," in *Climate Change: People and Resources in the Far North*, edited by D.L. Peterson and D.R. Johnson (Washington: Taylor and Francis, 1995), 221.

15 Fikret Berkes and Thomas Henley. "The Usefulness of Traditional Knowledge: Myth or Reality?," *Policy Options* (May 1997).

16 John Sallenave, "Giving Traditional Knowledge Its Rightful Place in Environmental Impact Assessment," *Northern Perspectives* 22, no. 1 (spring 1994).

17 Peter J. Usher, "Traditional Knowledge in Environmental Assessment and Management," Arctic 53, no. 2 (2000): 187.

18 For a discussion of these cases, see Boyce Rensberger, *How the World Works* (New York: William Morrow, 1986), 154–7, 222–5, 325.

19 Ibid., 14.

20 MacDonald Environmental Sciences Ltd., *Acquisition of Traditional Environmental Knowledge in the Lower Liard River Basin* (Ottawa: Indian and Northern Affairs Canada, 1995).

21  P. O'B. Lyver and Lutsel K'e Dene First Nation, "Monitoring Barren-Ground Caribou," 46–52.

22  Both of these studies note that they have obtained contradictory data which is difficult to summarize.

23  Theresa Nichols et al., "Climate Change and Sea Ice: Local Observations from the Canadian Western Arctic," *Arctic* 57, no. 1 (2004): 68–80.

24  M. Johnson and R.A. Ruttan, *Traditional Dene Environmental Knowledge* (Hay River, NWT: Dene Cultural Institute, 1993), 169.

25  Battiste and Henderson, *Protecting Indigenous Knowledge and Heritage*, 44.

26  Barsh, "Taking Indigenous Science Seriously," 157.

27  Jared Diamond, *Guns, Germs and Steel* (New York: Norton, 1999), 143.

28  Usher, "Traditional Knowledge in Environmental Assessment and Management," 187.

29  Fikret Berkes, *Sacred Ecology: Traditional Ecological Knowledge and Resource Management* (New York: Routledge, 1999), 10, 97–8, 100.

30  Ibid., 113.

31  See, for example, R.A. Caulfield, "Political Economy of Renewable Resources in the North," in *The Arctic: Environment, People, Policy*, ed. M. Nuttal and T.V. Callaghan (Toronto: Taylor & Francis, 2000), 506, and Barsh, "Taking Indigenous Science Seriously," 156.

32  Frances Abele, "Traditional Knowledge in Practice," *Arctic* 50, no. 4 (1997): iii.

33  See, for example, Graham White, "Culture Clash: Traditional Knowledge and EuroCanadian Governance Processes in Northern Claims Boards," paper presented at the First Nations, First Thoughts Conference, Centre of Canadian Studies, University of Edinburgh, May 13–20, 2005.

34  This occurred, for example, in a presentation made by Allice Legat at a public meeting held on 12 February 1997, which invited "All concerned Northerners" to attend "an evening of information about research being done in Slave Geological Province."

35  This is admitted by George Wenzel when he notes, following Bielawski, that traditional ecological knowledge "does [not] develop explanation for its own sake." See George Wenzel, "Traditional Ecological Knowledge and Inuit," *Arctic* 52, no. 2 (1999): 116.

36  Martha Johnson, "Indigenous Knowledge and Participatory Action Research," paper prepared for the Inuit Circumpolar Conference on Traditional Ecological Project/Arctic Monitoring Program, 11–2, 1993 (paper in authors' possession).

37  Nadasdy, *Hunters and Bureaucrats*, 62.

38  Cecil King, "The State of Aboriginal Education in Southern Canada," *For Seven Generations [CD-ROM]* (Ottawa: Libraxis, 1997).

39 See, for example, Stephen J. Augustine, "A Culturally Relevant Education for Aboriginal Youth: Is There Room for a Middle Ground, Accommodating Traditional Knowledge in Mainstream Education?," Master's thesis, Carleton University, 1998, 63.

40 Philip H. Duran, "On the Cosmic Order of Modern Physics and the Conceptual World of the American Indian," *World Futures* 63, no. 1 (January 2007): 2.

41 See, for example, Gregory Cajete, *Native Science*, and Leroy Little Bear, "What's Einstein Got to Do with It?," in *Continuing Poundmaker and Riel's Quest* edited by Richard Goose et al. (Saskatoon: Purich Publishing, 1994).

42 Little Bear, "What's Einstein Got to Do with It?," 70; Duran, "On the Cosmic Order," 5; Leroy Little Bear, foreword to Gregory Cajete, *Native Science*. For a similar discussion see David Peat, *Blackfoot Physics: A Journey into a Native American Universe* (London: Fourth Estate, 1996).

43 Dogrib Treaty 11 Council (Allice Legat, principle investigator [*sic*]), *Caribou Migration and the State of Their Habitat: Annual Report*, April 1999, 20.

44 Ellis, "Meaningful Consideration?" 72–3.

45 Nakashima, quoted in RCAP, *Final Report*, vol. 4, 139–40. See also Douglas J. Nakashima, *Application of Native Knowledge in EIA: Inuit, Eiders, and Hudson Bay Oil* (Hull, Quebec: Canadian Environmental Assessment Research Council, 1990), 5.

46 Rensberger, *How the World Works*, 234–5.

47 "Classication," *Encarta Online Encyclopedia*, 2006, http://encarta.msn.com (accessed 1 February 2007).

48 Dodes, "Junk Science and the Law," *Skeptical Inquirer* 31 (July/August 2001).

49 See, for example, TVOntario's "The First Scientists," which aired 19 September 2006.

50 Dene Cultural Institute, "Traditional Ecological Knowledge and Environmental Impact Assessment," in *Traditional Ecological Knowledge and Modern Environmental Assessment*, ed. B. Sadler and P. Boothroyd (Vancouver: University of British Columbia, Centre for Human Settlements, 1994, 5–19; Richard G. Kuhn and Frank Duerden, "A Review of Traditional Environmental Knowledge: An Interdisciplinary Canadian Perspective," *Culture* 15, no. 1 (1996): 72.

51 Stephen Bocking, "Scientists and Evolving Perceptions of Indigenous Knowledge in Northern Canada," in *Walking a Tightrope*, ed. U. Lischke and D.T. NcNab (Waterloo: Wilfrid Laurier Press, 2005), 225–6, 231.

52 Marc G. Stevenson, "Hunters and Bureaucrats: Power, Knowledge and Aboriginal-State Relations in the Southwest Yukon – Review," *Arctic* 57, no. 1 (2004): 104.

53 Martha Johnson, *Lore: Capturing Traditional Environmental Knowledge* (Hay River: Dene Cultural Institute, 1992), 5.

54 Judith McKenzie, *Environmental Politics in Canada* (Toronto: Oxford University Press, 2002), 38–42.

55 Spak, "The Position of Indigenous Knowledge," 234.

56 Berkes, *Sacred Ecology*, 17.

57 Quoted in Allice Legat, *Report of the Traditional Knowledge Working Group* (Yellowknife: Department of Culture and Communications, 1991), 1.

58 Usher, "Traditional Knowledge in Environmental Assessment and Management," 184.

59 Ellis, "Meaningful Consideration?"; Spak, "The Position of Indigenous Knowledge"; White, "Culture Clash"; Nadasdy, *Hunters and Bureaucrats*, 114–15.

60 RCAP, *Final Report*, vol. 3, 526; vol. 4, 457; Bocking, "Scientists and Evolving Perceptions of Indigenous Knowledge in Northern Canada," 237.

61 Nadasdy, *Hunters and Bureaucrats*, 118.

62 Bocking, "Scientists and Evolving Perceptions of Indigenous Knowledge in Northern Canada," 234–5; Nadasdy, *Hunters and Bureaucrats*, 132–43; RCAP, *Final Report*, vol. 3, 526; Spak, "The Position of Indigenous Knowledge," 243.

63 Nadasdy, *Hunters and Bureaucrats*, 118; Bocking, "Scientists and Evolving Perceptions of Indigenous Knowledge," 242.

64 Brian Laghi, "Tempest in a Teepee: Getting into the Spirit of Things," *Globe and Mail*, 9 August 1997, and Abele, "Traditional Knowledge in Practice."

65 Bocking, "Scientists and Evolving Perceptions of Indigenous Knowledge," 232.

66 Battiste and Henderson, *Protecting Indigenous Knowledge and Heritage*, 5, 277–8; Stevenson, "The Possibility of Difference."

67 Most of the material in this chapter, for example, was submitted to two peer-reviewed journals and rejected by both, despite receiving a number of favourable reviews. In the case of the second journal, *Arctic*, the paper went through a second round of review, where it did not go back to one of the original (and enthusiastic) commentators. Instead it was sent out to another reviewer who maintained that the arguments were "false" and were being put forward because they served our "political views." Another reviewer for this journal put the word science in ironic quotes, asserting that we were putting it "on a pedestal where it does not belong."

68 Frank Duerden, "Relationship between Traditional Knowledge and Western Science: A Northern Forum," *Arctic* 58, no. 3 (2005): 309–10; Stevenson, "The Possibility of Difference."

69  Aggie Brockman et al., "'When All Peoples Have the Same Story, Humans Will Cease to Exist': Protecting and Conserving Traditional Knowledge," report for the Biodiversity Convention Office, September 1997, 7.

70  This is perhaps the case with recent research pertaining to polar bears and bowhead whales, where elders who want hunting quotas increased are disputing the scientific population estimates for these animals.

71  See, for example, International Union for Conservation of Nature, *Indigenous Peoples and Sustainability* (Utrecht: IUCN and International Books, 1997), 42–3.

72  Frank Wilmer, *The Indigenous Voice* (Newbury Park: Sage, 1993), 141.

73  Albert Howard and Frances Widdowson, "Traditional Knowledge Threatens Environmental Assessment," *Policy Options* (November 1996). For the debate that ensued with respect to this article, see Fikret Berkes and Thomas Henley, "Co-management and Traditional Knowledge: Threat or Opportunity?" *Policy Options* (March 1997); Marc G. Stevenson, "Ignorance and Prejudice Threaten Environmental Assessment," *Policy Options* (March 1997); Albert Howard and Frances Widdowson, "Traditional Knowledge Advocates Weave a Tangled Web," *Policy Options* (April 1997); and Berkes and Henley, "The Usefulness of Traditional Knowledge." For the coverage of this debate in the national media, see Laghi, "Tempest in a Teepee."

74  Bocking, "Scientists and Evolving Perceptions," 235; and Dudgeon and Berkes, "Local Understandings of the Land," 80–1.

75  Augustine, "A Culturally Relevant Education for Aboriginal Youth," 61, and Nadasdy, *Hunters and Bureaucrats*, 279.

76  Usher, "Traditional Ecological Knowledge in Environmental Assessment and Management."

77  Mary Simon, "New Directions for Inuit Knowledge and Western Science," www.itk.ca/environment/tek-inuit-science-msimon.php (accessed August 2006).

78  This is not surprising when one considers that traditional knowledge advocates often make such misguided accusations when their research is challenged. Leanne R. Simpson, for example, notes that "if you want your knowledge to be legitimate in this society, you have to prove it is legitimate on western terms." According to Simpson, this "is not only epistemologically unsound, it is also racist" ("The Construction of Traditional Environmental Knowledge: Issues, Implications and Insights," PH.D. dissertation, University of Manitoba, 1999, 2).

### CONCLUSION

1  Clifton, "Introduction: Memoir, Exegesis," in *The Invented Indian*, ed. Clifton (New Brunswick, NJ: Transaction Publishers, 1990), 22.

2 Vine Deloria, Jr., "Comfortable Fictions and the Struggle for Turf: An Essay Review of *The Invented Indian: Cultural Fictions and Government Policies*," *American Indian Quarterly* 16, no. 3 (summer 1992): 398–9.

3 Ibid., 398.

4 Ward Churchill, *Fantasies of the Master Race: Literature, Cinema and the Colonization of American Indians* (San Francisco: City Lights Books, 1998), 122. Churchill recently has been involved in a number of controversies, including a questioning of his aboriginal ancestry and assertions that he fabricated, falsified, and plagiarized some of his research. See *Report of the Investigative Committee of the Standing Committee on Research Misconduct at the University of Colorado at Boulder concerning Allegations of Academic Misconduct against Professor Ward Churchill*, 9 May 2006.

5 "Native Leader Dismisses Calgary Professor's Call for Assimilation," *National Post*, 18 April 2000.

6 Suzanne Methot, "First Nations? Second Thoughts," *Quill & Quire* 66, no. 4 (April 2000): 44.

7 See, for example, Michael Murphy, "Citizens Plus: Aboriginal Peoples and the Canadian State," *Canadian Journal of Sociology* 25, no. 4 (fall 2000): 517; J.R. Miller, "Citizens Plus: Aboriginal Peoples and the Canadian State," *Canadian Historical Review* 82, no. 3 (September 2001): 558. Interestingly, Suzanne Methot states in this case in *Quill & Quire* 66, no. 3 (March 2000), 56, that "Cairns makes a cogent and compelling argument for integration as the middle road between assimilation and parallelism. The aboriginal political elite may deride his views as imperialistic. But in this case, they shouldn't be believed."

8 Patricia Monture-Angus, "Citizens Plus: Sensitivities versus Solutions," *The* CRIC *Papers: Bridging the Divide between Aboriginal Peoples and the Canadian State* (Centre for Research and Information on Canada, June 2001), 9–10.

9 Taiaiake Alfred, "Of White Heroes and Old Men Talking," *Windspeaker* 18, no. 2 (June 2000): 4.

10 Taiaiake Alfred and Adam Barker, "Book Review," *New Socialist* 58 (September–October 2006): 41.

11 Tom Flanagan, *First Nations? Second Thoughts* (Montreal: McGill-Queen's University Press, 2000), 197–8.

12 Ibid.

13 Calvin Helin, *Dances with Dependency: Indigenous Success through Self-Reliance* (Vancouver: Orca, 2006), 127–40.

14 Ibid., 15.

15 Alan Cairns and Tom Flanagan, "An Exchange," *Inroads* 10 (2001): 109.

16 Ibid., 113, 116.

17 See Bourgeault, "The Indian, the Métis and the Fur Trade," *Studies in Political Economy* 12 (fall 1983): 46–7.

18 Ron Bourgeault, "The Struggle for Class and Nation: The Origin of the Métis in Canada and the National Question," in Ron Bourgeault, Dave Broad, Lorne Brown, and Lori Foster, eds., *1492–1992: Five Centuries of Imperialism and Resistance* (Winnipeg/Halifax: Society for Socialist Studies, 1992), 175.

19 Bourgeault, "The Tragedy of Progress: Marxism, Modernity and the Aboriginal Question," *Labour* 52 (fall 2003): 267.

20 See Alan C. Cairns, *Citizens Plus: Aboriginal Peoples and the Canadian State* (Vancouver: UBC Press, 2000), 74, for discussion.

21 For an overview of this reactionary agenda, see Royal Commission on Aboriginal Peoples [RCAP], *Report of the Royal Commission on Aboriginal Peoples [Final Report]* (Ottawa: Supply and Services, 1996) vol. 4, 199–386.

22 Ibid., 245–7.

23 These comments were made on the program "Studio One," TVOntario, 22 May 2001.

24 Caroline Krause, quoted in Helin, *Dances with Dependency*, 213–14. Helin's analysis of this case is based on Margaret Wente's column "It's Pronounced Suc-cess-ful," *Vancouver Sun,* 20 November 2004.

25 Rondi Adamson, "Once Bitten: You'll Never Shy Away Again – History Bites Makes Historical Lessons Hysterical," *Globe Television* (March 2001): 9.

26 This also, unbelievably, was the view of Jared Diamond in 1987 in an article entitled "The Worst Mistake in the History of the Human Race" in *Discover Magazine (*May 1987).

27 For example, two books on aboriginal peoples – *Marxism and the Tragedy of Progress* and *Victims of Progress* – imply in their titles that progress is a disaster.

28 This is also the point of Elizabeth Rata in "Rethinking Biculturalism," *Anthropological Theory* 5, no. 3 (2005): 272.

29 Leslie White, *The Evolution of Culture* (New York: McGraw Hill, 1959), 278.

30 Radcliffe-Brown, cited in ibid., 121.

31 This was known as the "massacre at Bloody Falls," which occurred on the Coppermine River in the 1700s. See Samuel Hearne, *A Journey from Prince of Wales' Fort in Hudson's Bay, to the Northern Ocean ... in the Years 1769, 1770, 1771 and 1772* (London: Strahan and Cadell, 1795) www.uwo.ca/english/canadianpoetry/eng%20274e/hearne.htm, particularly July 1771 (accessed 25 December 2006).

32 Napoleon Chagnon, "Then You Are in Bad Luck," http://www.froes.dds.nl/CHAGNON.htm (accessed 19 February 2008)

33 Lawrence H. Keeley, *War before Civilization: The Myth of the Peaceful Savage* (New York: Oxford University Press, 1996).
34 Steven A. LeBlanc, *Constant Battles: The Myth of the Peaceful, Noble Savage* (New York: St Martin's Press, 2003).

# Index